A Bibliography of Modern British Novelists

A Bibliography of Modern British Novelists

by

Robert J. Stanton

Volume II

Iris Murdoch

V.S. Naipaul

Anthony Powell

Jean Rhys

Alan Sillitoe

C.P. Snow

Muriel Spark

Angus Wilson

The Whitston Publishing Company

Troy, New York

1978

Copyright 1978
Robert J. Stanton

Library of Congress Catalog Card Number 76-21471

ISBN 0-87875-115-7

Printed in the United States of America

[JEAN] IRIS MURDOCH
(Born in Dublin, 1919)

I. PRIMARY WORKS: NOVELS

1. *Under the Net.* London: Chatto and Windus, 1954, 1956, 1963; Toronto: Clarke, Irwin, 1954; New York: Viking, 1954, 1964; London: Reprint Society, 1955; Harmondsworth: Penguin, 1960, 1971; with an introduction and notes by Dorothy Jones. London: Longmans, 1966; New York: Avon Books, 1967; as *Gatti Ci Guardano.* Trans. Gaby Goering. Milan: Garzanti, 1956; as *Es Kapad.* Trans. Olov Jonason. Stockholm: Norstedt, 1956; as *Dans le fillet.* Trans. Clara Malraux. Paris: Plon, 1957; as *Unter Dem Netz.* Trans. Ilse Krämer. Zürich: Rascher, 1957; also Frankfurt and Hamburg: Fischer Bücherei, 1962; as *Bajo la red.* Trans. Consuelo Gironés. Barcelona: Plaza and Janés, 1962; also Barcelona: Círculo de Lectores, 1971; as *Sota la Xarxa.* Trans. Montserrat Abelló. Barcelona: Proa, 1965; as *Ami No Naka.* Trans. Suzuki Yasushi. Tokyo: Hakusuisha, 1965; as *Sotto la Rete.* Trans. Argia Micchettoni. Milan: Garzanti, 1966; as *Pod Set'ju.* Trans. M. Lorie. Moscow: Progress, 1966; as *Pod Mrežata.* Trans. Katja Gončarova. Sofija (Bulgaria): Nar. Mladež, 1968; as *Pod Síti.* Trans. Eliška Hornátová. Prague: Odeon, 1968; as *Under Nettet.* Trans. Vibeke Willumsen. Copenhagen: Nyt Nordisk Forlag, 1971; as *Prins In Mreje.* Trans. Ioana Maria Nicolau. Bucurest: Univers, 1971; as *Võrgu All.* Trans. Helga Kross. Tallin: Eésti raamat, 1971; as *A Háló Alatt.* Trans. Lászlo Báti. Budapest: Magvetö, 1971; also Bratislava: Madách Könyvkiadó, 1971; as *Onder het Net.* Trans. Clara Eggink. Amster-

dam: Contact, 1972.

2. *The Flight from the Enchanter.* London: Chatto and Windus, 1956; Toronto: Clarke, Irwin, 1956; New York: Viking, 1956, 1965; Harmondsworth: Penguin, 1962, 1969; New York: Warner Paperback Library, 1973; as *Flykten från Förtrollaren.* Trans. Lov Jonason. Stockholm: Norstedt, 1958; as *Huyendo del Encantador.* Trans. J. Ferrer Aleu. Barcelona: Plaza and Janés, 1964; as *Le Séducteur Quitte.* Trans. A. Der Neressian. Paris: Gallimard, 1964; as *Flucht vor dem Zauberer.* Trans. Werner Peterich. München: Piper, 1964; as *Majutsushi Kara Nogarette.* Trans. Inouchi Yûshiro. Tokyo: Taiyôsha, 1969; as *Bekstvo od Carobnika.* Trans. Dušanka Todorović. Novi Sad (Yugoslavia): Bratstvo-jedinstvo, 1970.

3. *The Sandcastle.* London: Chatto and Windus, 1957, 1969; Toronto: Clarke, Irwin, 1957; New York: Viking, 1957; London: Reprint Society, 1959; Harmondsworth: Penguin, 1960, 1968, 1971; New York: Warner Paperback Library, 1973; as *Die Sandburg.* Trans. Maria Wolff. München: Piper, 1958; also Berlin and Darmstadt: Buch-Gemeinschaft, 1964; as *Sandslottet.* Trans. Olov Jonason. Stockholm: Norstedt, 1958, 1964; as *Kula od Peska.* Trans. Jelena Stojanović. Subotica and Beograd (Yugoslavia): Minera, 1959; as *Sandslottet.* Trans. Michael Tejn. Copenhagen: Nyt Nordisk Forlag, 1961; also Copenhagen: Schønberg, 1968, 1972; as *Sandslottet.* Trans. Inger-Sophie Manthey. Oslo: Gyldendal, 1961; also Oslo: Bokklubben, 1964; as *Op Zand Gebouwd.* Trans. E. Veegens-Latorf. Amsterdam: Contact, 1963, 1965, 1966, 1969; as *El Castillo de Arena.* Trans. J. Ferrer Aleu. Barcelona: Plaza and Janés, 1964; as *Grad iz Peska.* Trans. Majda Stanovnik. Ljubljana (Yugoslavia): Državna založba slovenije, 1964; as *Hiekkalinna.* Trans. Mikko Kilpi. Porvoo and Helsinki: Werner Söderström, 1965; as *Suna No Shiro.* Trans. Kurihara Yukio. Tokyo: Taiyôsha, 1968; as *Hrad z Písku.* Trans. Helena Prokopová. Prague: Mladá fronta,

1972.

4. *The Bell.* London: Chatto and Windus, 1958, 1959; Toronto: Clarke, Irwin, 1958; New York: Viking, 1958; Harmondsworth: Penguin, 1962, 1969; New York: Avon, 1966; as *Klockan.* Trans. Olov Jonason. Stockholm: Norstedt, 1960; as *La Campana.* Trans. José Manuel Vergara. Buenos Aires: Ed. del nuevo extremo, 1960; as *Kello.* Trans. Mikko Kilpi. Porvoo and Helsinki: Werner Söderström, 1961; as *Les Eaux du Peché.* Trans. Jérôme Desseine. Paris: Plon, 1961; as *Die Wasser der Sünde.* Trans. Maria Wolff. München: Piper, 1962; as *De Klok.* Trans. Hella Haase. Amsterdam and Antwerp: Contact, 1962, 1965, 1968, 1970, 1971; as *Klokken.* Trans. Michael Tejn. Copenhagen: Nyt Nordisk Forlag, 1962; also Copenhagen: Schønberg, 1966, 1972; as *O Sino.* Trans. A. Neves Pedro. Lisbon: Portugália, 1965; as *Klokken.* Trans. Inger-Sophie Manthey. Oslo: Gyldendal, 1966; as *Kane.* Trans. Maruya Saiichi. Tokyo: Shûeisha, 1969; as *Die Wasser der Sünde.* Trans. Maria Wolff. Zurich: Neue Schweizer Bibliothek, 1970; as *Dzwon.* Trans. Krystyna Tarnowska. Warsaw: Pánst. Inst. Wydawn, 1972.

5. *A Severed Head.* London: Chatto and Windus, 1961; New York: Viking, 1961, 1963, 1965; Harmondsworth: Penguin, 1963, 1967, 1969; New York: Avon, 1966; as *Et Avhugget Hode.* Trans. Inger-Sophie Manthey. Oslo: Gyldendal, 1962; as *Et Afhugget Hoved.* Trans. Michael Tejn. Copenhagen: Nyt Nordisk Forlag, 1963; also Copenhagen: Schønberg, 1971; as *Kirareta Kubi.* Trans. Teruo Kudô. Tokyo: Shinchô-sha, 1963; as *Maskenspiel.* Trans. Karin Reese. München: Piper, 1963; as *Cabeza Cercenada.* Trans. Jorge Ferrel-Vidal. Barcelona: Plaza y Janés, 1964; as *Een Afgehouwen Hoofd.* Trans. H.W.J. Schaap. Antwerp: Contact, 1964, 1965; also Amsterdam: Contact, 1966, 1968, 1971; as *Une Tête Coupée.* Trans. Yvonne Davet. Paris: Gallimard, 1966; as *Meng Ching.* Trans. Ho Hsin. Taipei: Student's Book Company, 1968.

6. *An Unofficial Rose.* London: Chatto and Windus, 1962; Toronto: Clarke, Irwin, 1962; New York: Viking, 1962; Harmondsworth: Penguin, 1964, 1967, 1971; London: Reprint Society, 1964; New York: Warner Paperback Library, 1973; as *Epavirallinen Ruusu.* Trans. Eila Pennanen. Porvoo and Helsinki: Werner Söderström, 1963; as *En Uoffisiell Rose.* Trans. Inger-Sophie Manthey. Oslo: Gyldendal, 1963; as *En Hemlig Ros.* Trans. Maj Lorents. Stockholm: Norstedt, 1963; as *Warde Ahava.* Trans. M. Wieseltier. Tel-Aviv: Amichai, 1963; as *En Uofficiel Rose.* Trans. Michael Tejn. Copenhagen: Nyt Nordisk Forlag, 1964; as *Een Wilde Roos.* Trans. Katja Vrancken. Amsterdam: Contact, 1964, 1967; as *Une Rose Anonyme.* Trans. Anne-Marie Soulac. Paris: Gallimard, 1966; as *Dikaja Roza.* Trans. M. Lorie. Moscow: Progress, 1971.

7. *The Unicorn.* London: Chatto and Windus, 1963; Toronto: Clarke, Irwin, 1963; New York: Viking, 1963; Harmondsworth: Penguin, 1966, 1971; New York: Avon, 1964, 1970; as *Enhjørningen.* Trans. Karen Meldsted. Copenhagen: Nyt Nordisk Forlag, 1964; also Copenhagen: Schønberg, 1972; as *Yksisarvinen.* Trans. Eila Pennanen. Porvoo and Helsinki: Werner Söderström, 1964; as *Enhörningen.* Trans. Maj Lorents. Stockholm: Norstedt, 1964, 1967; as *Le Château de la Licorne.* Trans. Anne M. Soulac. Paris: Mercure de France, 1965; as *De Eenhoorn.* Trans. N. Funke-Bordewijk. Antwerp and Amsterdam: Contact, 1965, 1968, 1969, 1972.

8. *The Italian Girl.* London: Chatto and Windus, 1964; Toronto: Clarke, Irwin, 1964; New York: Viking, 1964; New York: Avon, 1965; Harmondsworth: Penguin, 1967, 1971; as *Het Italiaanse Meisje.* Trans. Jean A. Schalekamp. Antwerp: Contact, 1964, 1967; also Amsterdam: Contact, 1965, 1968, 1972; as *Den Italienske Pige.* Trans. Karen Meldsted. Copenhagen: Nyt Nordisk Forlag, 1965; as *La Ragazza Italiana.* Trans. Gabriella Fiori Andreini. Milan: Feltrinelli, 1965; as *Den Italien-*

ske Piken. Trans. Inger-Sophie Manthey. Oslo: Gyldendal, 1965; as *Den Italienska Flickan.* Trans. Magda Lagerman. Stockholm: Norstedt, 1965; as *Italialaistyttö.* Trans. Eila Pennanen. Porvoo and Helsinki: Werner Söderström, 1966; as *Italia No Onna.* Trans. Nakagawa Satoshi. Tokyo: Tôjusha, 1966; as *La Gouvernante Italienne.* Trans. Leo Lack. Paris: Gallimard, 1967; as *Den Italienske Pige.* Trans. Karen Meldsted. Copenhagen: Gyldendal, 1968; as *La Muchacha Italiana.* Trans. Rafael Vázquez Zamora. Barcelona: Destino, 1968; as *Devojka Italijanka.* Trans. Voja Colanović. Beograd: Rad, 1968; as *Italyan Kizi.* Trans. Celâl Üster. Istanbul: Senoğlu Matbaasi, 1970.

9. *The Red and the Green.* London: Chatto and Windus, 1965; Toronto: Clarke, Irwin, 1965; New York: Viking, 1965; London: Reprint Society, 1967; Harmondsworth: Penguin, 1967, 1971; New York: Avon, 1971; as *Rødt og Grønt.* Trans. Karen Tamara Meldsted. Copenhagen: Nyt Nordisk Forlag, 1966; as *Rött och Grönt.* Trans. Magda Lagerman. Stockholm: Norstedt, 1966, 1969; as *Rood en Groen.* Trans. N. Funke-Bordewijk. Amsterdam: Contact, 1966, 1969; as *Il Rosso e il Verde.* Trans. Gabriella Fiori Andreini. Milan: Feltrinelli, 1967; as *Aloe i Zelenoe.* Trans. M. Lorie. Moscow: Progress, 1968; as *Páques Sanglantes.* Trans. Anne-Marie Soulac. Paris: Mercure de France, 1968; as *Rød Påske.* Trans. Inger-Sophie Manthey. Oslo: Gyldendal, 1969; as *Aka to Midori.* Trans. Onodera Ken. Tokyo: Kawade shobô shinsha, 1970.

10. *The Time of the Angels.* London: Chatto and Windus, 1966; Toronto: Clarke, Irwin, 1966; New York: Viking, 1966; New York: Avon, 1967, 1971; Harmondsworth: Penguin, 1968, 1971; as *Praest uden gud.* Trans. Karina Windfeld-Hansen. Copenhagen: Nyt Nordisk Forlag, 1967; as *Englenes Tid.* Trans. Inger-Sophie Manthey. Oslo: Gyldendal, 1967; as *Änglarnas Tid.* Trans. Maj Lorents. Stockholm: Norstedt, 1967; as *Tenshi Tachi No Toki.* Trans. Ishida Kôtarô. Tokyo: Chikuma shobô,

1968; as *De Tijd van de Engelen.* Trans. Clara Eggink. Amsterdam: Contact, 1968; as *Enkelten Aika.* Trans. Eila Pennanen. Helsinki: Werner Söderström, 1969; as *Les angéliques.* Trans. Anne-Marie Soulac. Paris: Mercure de France, 1969; as *Czas Aniołów.* Trans. Agnieszka Glinczanka. Warsaw: Państw. Instytut Wydawn, 1970.

11. *The Nice and the Good.* London: Chatto and Windus, 1968; Toronto: Clarke, Irwin, 1968; New York: Viking, 1968; Harmondsworth: Penguin, 1969; New York: New American Library, 1969; as *Kaerlighedens Kabale.* Trans. Karina Windfeld-Hansen. Copenhagen: Nyt Nordisk Forlag, 1968; as *I Belli e i Buoni.* Trans. Gabriella Fiori Andreini. Milan: Feltrinelli, 1968; as *Hver Tar Sin.* Trans. Inger-Sophie Manthey. Oslo: Gyldendal, 1968; as *När Var Tar Sin.* Trans. Maj Lorents. Stockholm: Norstedt, 1968; as *Lauter Feine Leute.* Trans. Margitta de Hervás. Bern: Scherz, 1968, 1974; also München: Scherz, 1968; also Vienna: Scherz, 1968; as *Het Aardige en het Goede.* Trans. Clara Eggink. Amsterdam: Contact, 1968, 1971; as *Milé A Pekné Lásky.* Trans. Tat'jana Ruppeldtová. Bratislava: Tatran, 1970; as *Amigos y Amantes.* Trans. Andrés Bosch. Barcelona: Lumen, 1970; as *Les Demijustes.* Trans. Lola Tranec. Paris: Gallimard, 1970; as *Ai No Kiseki.* Trans. Ishida Kôtarô. Asaka (Japan): Sôgensha, 1972.

12. *Bruno's Dream.* London: Chatto and Windus, 1969; Toronto: Clarke, Irwin, 1969; New York: Viking, 1969; New York: Dell, 1969; Harmondsworth: Penguin, 1970; as *Bruno's Drøm.* Trans. Vibeke Willumsen. Copenhagen: Nyt Nordisk Forlag, 1969; also Copenhagen: Danske Bogsamleres Klub, 1971; as *Bruno No Yume.* Trans. Nakagawa Bin. Tokyo: Chikuma shobô, 1970; as *Bruno's Drøm.* Trans. Inger-Sophie Manthey. Oslo: Gyldendal, 1970; as *Bruno's Droom.* Trans. Clara Eggink. Amsterdam: Contact, 1970, 1972; as *Le Rêve de Bruno.* Trans. Jean Queval. Paris: Gallimard, 1971.

13. *A Fairly Honourable Defeat.* London: Chatto and Windus,

1970; Toronto: Clarke, Irwin, 1970; New York: Viking, 1970; Harmondsworth: Penguin, 1972; Greenwich, Connecticut: Fawcett, 1973; as *Nederlag Med Aere.* Trans. Inger-Sophie Manthey. Oslo: Gyldendal, 1972; as *Een Nogal Eervolle Aftocht.* Trans. Clara Eggink. Amsterdam: Contact, 1972; as *Hök och Duvor.* Trans. Marianne Gerland-Ekeroth. Stockholm: Norstedt, 1972; as *Une de faite assez honorable.* Trans. Yvonne Davet. Paris: Gallimard, 1972.

14. *An Accidental Man.* London: Chatto and Windus, 1971; New York: Viking, 1971; New York: Warner Paperback Library, 1973; Harmondsworth: Penguin, 1973; as *Tilfaeldighedens Spil.* Trans. Karina Windfeld-Hansen. Copenhagen: Nyt Nordisk Forlag, 1972; as *Un homme á catastrophes.* Trans. Yvonne Davet. Paris: Gallimard, 1974.

15. *The Black Prince.* London: Chatto and Windus, 1973; New York: Viking, 1973; New York: Warner Paperback Library, 1974; Harmondsworth: Penguin, 1975; as *Der Schwarze Prinz.* Trans. Herbert Schlüter. Düsseldorf: Claassen, 1975.

16. *The Sacred and Profane Love Machine.* London: Chatto and Windus, 1974; New York: Viking, 1974; New York: Warner Paperback Library, 1975.

17. *A Word Child.* London: Chatto and Windus, 1975; New York: Viking, 1975.

18. *Henry and Cato.* London: Chatto and Windus; and New York: Viking. Expected publication date is Winter 1976-77.

PRIMARY WORKS: SHORT STORIES

19. "Something Special." *Winter's Tales 3.* London: Macmillan, 1957; New York: St. Martin's Press, 1957;

Nendeln, Liechtenstein: Kraus Reprint, 1969, pp. 175-204.

PRIMARY WORKS: PLAYS

20. With J. B. Priestley. *A Severed Head* (produced in Bristol and London, 1963; in New York, 1964). London: Chatto and Windus, 1964; London: Samuel French, 1964; Toronto: Clarke, Irwin, 1964.

21. With James Saunders. *The Italian Girl* (produced in Bristol, 1967; in London, 1968). London and New York: Samuel French, 1968. A description of the London production is given in *The* (London) *Times* (11 January 1968), p. 6, col. 2.

22. "The Servants and the Snow" (produced in London, 1970).

23. *The Three Arrows, And, The Servants and the Snow.* London: Chatto and Windus, 1973; New York: Viking, 1974.

PRIMARY WORKS: POEMS

24. "Too Late." *Boston University Journal*, 23, No. 2 (1975), 29-31.

25. "John Sees a Stork at Zamorra." *Boston University Journal*, 23, No. 2 (1975), 31.

PRIMARY WORKS: OTHER

26. "Thinking and Language." *Proceedings of the Aristotelian Society*, 25 (1951), 25.

27. "Nostalgia for the Particular." *Proceedings of the Aristotelian Society*, 25 (1951-1952), 243.

28. "The Existential Political Myth." *Socratic*, 5 (1952), 52.

29. *Sartre: Romantic Rationalist.* London: Bowes and Bowes, 1953, 1962, 1965; Toronto: British Book Service, 1953; New Haven, Connecticut: Yale University Press, 1953, 1959, 1967; London: Fontana, 1967; as *Sarte Yazarliği ve Felsefesi.* Trans. Selâhattin Hilav. Istanbul: De Yayinevi, 1964; as *Sarte: romantic gôri shugisha.* Trans. Tanaka Seitarô and Nakaoka Hiroshi. Tokyo: Kokubunsha, 1968.

30. With Anthony Quinton, Stuart Hampshire, and Isaiah Berlin. "Philosophy and Beliefs." *Twentieth Century*, 157 (June 1955), 495-521. A discussion of the meaning of *Weltanschauung*.

31. "Knowing the Void." *Spectator*, 197 (2 November 1956), 613-614. Review of *The Notebooks of Simone Weil.* Trans. and ed. by Arthur Wills.

32. "Let Them Philosophise." *Spectator*, 197 (14 December 1956), 873. Review of *S. T. Coleridge*, ed. by H. St. J. Hart; *David Hume*, ed. by H. E. Root; and *Lessing's Theological Writings*, ed. by Henry Chadwick.

33. "Vision and Choice in Morality." *Proceedings of the Aristotelian Society*, 30 (1956), 32.

34. "Hegel in Modern Dress." *New Statesman and Nation*, 53 (25 May 1957), 675-676. Review of Jean-Paul Sartre's *Being and Nothingness*.

35. "Existentialist Bite." *Spectator*, 199 (12 July 1957), 68-69. Review of Everett W. Knight's *Literature Considered as Philosophy: The French Example*.

36. "Metaphysics and Ethics." *The Nature of Metaphysics*. Ed. D. F. Pears. London: Macmillan, 1957.

37. With Rosamond Lehmann, Angus Wilson, and others.

" 'Lolita.' " *The* (London) *Times* (23 January 1959), p. 11. A letter to the Editor. A plea against the possible banning of Nabokov's novel.

* 38. "The Sublime and the Good." *Chicago Review,* 13 (Autumn 1959), 42-55.

39. "The Sublime and the Beautiful Revisited." *Yale Review,* n.s. 49 (December 1959), 247-271. A philosophical introduction is followed by a discussion of the novel.

40. "A House of Theory." *Partisan Review,* 26 (Winter 1959), 17-31. On the socialist theory in England. She discusses Hume, Kant, and Marx.

41. With Margaret Hubbard. "Education of Girls." *The* (London) *Times* (16 January 1960), p. 9. A letter to the Editor. Murdoch and Hubbard ask that educational standards for girls be not lowered. They call for "a tough, straightforward education with some backbone to it..."

42. "Against Dryness: A Polemical Sketch." *Encounter,* 16 (January 1961), 16-20. Attack on Anglo-Saxon Liberal, and French existential philosophy as too narrow for modern man. "Through literature we can re-discover a sense of the density of our lives. Literature can arm us against consolation and fantasy and can help us to recover from the ailments of Romanticism."

43. With Doris Lessing, Angus Wilson and others. "Dr. Agostinho Neto." *The* (London) *Times* (2 October 1961), p. 13. A letter to the Editor. A plea that the Portuguese government release the distinguished Angolan writer from prison.

44. "Mass, Might and Myth." *Spectator,* 209 (7 September 1962), 337-338. Review of Elias Canetti's *Crowds and Power.* Trans. by Carol Stewart.

45. " 'Going into Europe.' " *Encounter,* 19 (December 1962),

64. Belief that England should not join the Common Market.

46. "The Idea of Perfection." *Yale Review,* n.s. 53 (Spring 1964), 342-380. A philosophical discussion.

47. With Kingsley Amis, Angus Wilson and others. "Rights Denied to Soviet Jews." *The* (London) *Times* (27 June 1966), p. 11. A letter to the Editor.

48. "The Darkness of Practical Reason." *Encounter,* 27 (July 1966), 46-50. Review of Stuart Hampshire's *Freedom of the Individual.*

49. "On 'God' and 'Good'." Study Group on Foundations of Cultural Unity, Meeting at Bowdoin College, Maine, August 1966.

50. "Political Morality." *Listener,* 78 (21 September 1967), 353-354. Murdoch attacks the American position on the Vietnam War.

51. *The Sovereignty of Good Over Other Concepts.* London: Cambridge University Press, 1967; London: Routledge and K. Paul, 1970; New York: Schocken Books, 1971. The Leslie Stephen Lecture of 1967.

52. "Loss of dignity." *The* (London) *Times* (18 June 1968), p. 9. A letter to the Editor. A defence of Danny Cohn-Bendit's right to come to England.

53. With Frederic Samson. "Forcing action." *The* (London) *Times* (31 August 1968), p. 7. A letter to the Editor. On the need for immediate relief aid for Biafra.

54. "Involvement: Writer's Reply." *London Magazine,* n.s. 8 (August 1968), 16. Murdoch answers a question put to her by the editor of *London Magazine.*

55. "Existentialists and Mystics: A Note on the Novel in the

New Utilitarian Age." *Essays and Poems Presented to Lord David Cecil.* Ed. W. W. Robson. London: Constable, 1970, pp. 169-183.

56. "Salvation by Words." *New York Review of Books,* 18 (15 June 1972), 3-4, 6. Excerpt from the Blashfield Address delivered to the American Academy of Arts and Letters, on May 17, 1972. On the condition of contemporary arts and philosophy. A defense of the arts, especially literature.

57. "Education policy." *The* (London) *Times* (2 July 1973), p. 15. A letter to the Editor. Murdoch mainly argues "that education should be...selective."

58. "Selection principle in education." *The* (London) *Times* (19 April 1974), p. 17. A letter to the Editor.

59. " 'I remember, I remember.' " *TLS* (6 December 1974), p. 1370. On her childhood reading.

II. GENERAL SECONDARY STUDIES, INTERVIEWS, BIOGRAPHICAL SKETCHES, AND MISCELLAENOUS ITEMS

General references to Murdoch's work also appear in the First Part of this bibliography. See the following numbers there: 5, 6, 7, 8, 11, 12, 14, 16, 17, 18, 19, 23, 26, 27, 29, 31, 32, 35, 36, 37, 38, 39, 40, 42, 44, 45, 47, 49, 53, 55, 56, 58, 60, 62, 66, 69, 70, 71, 72, 75, 76, 77, 78, 79, 80, 82, 89, 90, 91, 94, 96, 98, 100, 101, 102, 103, 104, 107, 108, 110, 111, 112, 113, 114, 115, 120, 122, 123, 124, 125, 126, 127, 128, 129, 132, 137, 143, 145, 165, 167, 171, 188, 206, 213, 214, 217, 236, 238, 241, 266, 276, 285, 293, 299, 305, 306, 318.

60. Ahlin, Lars, Lars Gustafsson, and Walter Ljungquist. "Den moderna romanen." *Bonniers Litterära Magasin,* 30 (1961), 280-289.

61. Anderson, Thayle Kermit. "Concepts of Love in the Novels of Iris Murdoch." Diss. Purdue, 1970. *Dissertation Abstracts,* 31A (1971), 5385-5386.

* 62. Anon. "Four named for Booker prize." *The* (London) *Times* (1 November 1973), p. 6. Announcement of nomination of Murdoch and three others for the annual Booker prize for fiction.

63. —. "Iris Murdoch." *The* (London) *Times* (13 February 1964), p. 15. An interview.

64. —. "Murdoch, (Jean) Iris." *World Authors 1950-1970.* Ed. John Wakeman and Stanley J. Kunitz. New York: H. W. Wilson, 1975, pp. 1046-1049.

GENERAL SECONDARY STUDIES

65. —. "Murdoch's Net." *TLS* (29 July 1965), p. 630. A discussion of Murdoch's aims.

66. —. *Observer* Profile: Iris Murdoch." *Observer* (17 June 1962), p. 23.

67. Baldanza, Frank. "Iris Murdoch and the Theory of Personality." *Criticism*, 7 (1965), 176-189.

68. —. *Iris Murdoch.* New York: Twayne, 1974.

69. —. "Iris Murdoch." *Wisconsin Studies in Contemporary Literature*, 8 (Summer 1967), 454-458.

70. —. "The Murdoch Manuscripts at the University of Iowa: An Addendum." *Modern Fiction Studies*, 16 (1970), 201-202.

71. Barrows, John. "Living Writers—7, Iris Murdoch." *John O'London's*, 4 (4 May 1961), 498.

* 72. Bellamy, Michael O'Neil. "The Artist and the Saint: An Approach to the Aesthetics and the Ethics of Iris Murdoch." Diss. Wisconsin at Madison, 1975. *Dissertation Abstracts*, 36A (1976), 6110.

73. Borklund, Elmer. Untitled comments. *Contemporary Novelists.* Ed. James Vinson. London and Chicago: St. James Press, 1972, pp. 912-915. A critical summary of Murdoch's intellectual position in relation to her novels.

74. Bradbury, Malcolm. "On from Murdoch." *Encounter*, 31 (July 1968), 72-74. On the influence of Murdoch's writings upon A. S. Byatt.

75. —. "The Romantic Miss Murdoch." *Spectator*, 215 (3 September 1965), 293. A discussion of Murdoch's concerns in her novels.

76. Bredella, Lothar. "Wirklichkeitserfahrung und Erzählstruktur in den Romanen von Iris Murdoch." *Miscellanea Anglo-Americana: Festschrift für Helmut Viebrock.* Ed. Kuno Schuhmann, et al. Munchen: Pressler, 1974, pp. 4-25.

77. Brugière, Bernard. "L'univers romanesque d'Iris Murdoch." *Mercure de France,* 352 (1964), 699-711.

78. Bryden, Ronald. "Talking to Iris Murdoch." *Listener,* 79 (4 April 1968), 433-434.

79. Byatt, Antonia S. *Degrees of Freedom: The Novels of Iris Murdoch.* London: Chatto and Windus, 1965; New York: Barnes and Noble, 1965.

80. Clayre, Alasdair. "Common Cause: A Garden in the Clearing." *TLS* (7 August 1959), pp. 30-31.

81. Culley, Ann, and John Feaster. "Criticism of Iris Murdoch: A Selected Checklist." *Modern Fiction Studies,* 15, No. 3 (1969), 449-457.

82. —. "Theory and Practice: Characterization in the Novels of Iris Murdoch." *Modern Fiction Studies,* 15, No. 3 (1969), 335-345.

83. Dick, Bernard F. "The Novels of Iris Murdoch: A Formula for Enchantment." *Bucknell Review,* 14, No. 2 (1966), 66-81.

84. Emerson, Donald. "Violence and Survival in the Novels of Iris Murdoch." *Transactions of the Wisconsin Academy of Sciences, Arts, and Letters,* 57 (1969), 21-28.

85. Fast, Lawrence Edgar. "Self-Discovery in the Novels of Iris Murdoch." Diss. Oregon, 1970. *Dissertation Abstracts,* 31A (1971), 5397.

86. Felheim, Marvin. "Symbolic Characterization in the Novels

of Iris Murdoch." *Texas Studies in Literature and Language*, 2 (Summer 1960), 189-197.

87. Fraser, G. S. "Iris Murdoch: The Solidity of the Normal." *International Literary Annual*, 2 (1959), 37-54.

88. Gérard, Albert. "Iris Murdoch." *Revue Nouvelle*, 39 (1964), 633-640.

89. German, Howard. "Allusions in the Early Novels of Iris Murdoch." *Modern Fiction Studies*, 15, No. 3 (1969), 361-377.

90. —. "The Range of Allusions in the Novels of Iris Murdoch." *Journal of Modern Literature*, 2 (September 1971), 58-85.

91. Gerstenberger, Donna Lorine. *Iris Murdoch*. The Irish Writers Series. Lewisburg, Pennsylvania: Bucknell University Press, 1975.

92. Gilligan, John T. "The Fiction and Philosophy of Iris Murdoch." Diss. Wisconsin, 1973. *Dissertation Abstracts*, 35A (August 1974), 1099-1100.

93. Gindin, James. "Images of Illusion in the Work of Iris Murdoch." *Texas Studies in Literature and Language*, 2 (Summer 1960), 180-188.

94. Goshgarian, Gary. "Feminist Values in the Novels of Iris Murdoch." *Revue des Langues Vivantes*, 40 (1974), 519-527.

95. —. "From Fable to Flesh: A Study of the Female Characters in the Novels of Iris Murdoch." Diss. Wisconsin, 1972. *Dissertation Abstracts*, 33A (1973), 3583.

96. Hall, James. "Blurring the Will: The Growth of Iris Murdoch." *Journal of English Literary History*, 32 (1965), 256-273.

97. Hall, William. " 'The Third Way': The Novels of Iris Murdoch." *Dalhousie Review,* 46 (1966), 306-318.

98. Hauerwas, Stanley. "The Significance of Vision: Toward an Aesthetic Ethic." *Studies in Religion,* 2 (1972), 36-49. On Murdoch's philosophical position.

99. Henderson, Gloria Ann Mason. "Dionysus and Apollo: Iris Murdoch and Love." Diss. Georgia State, 1974. *Dissertation Abstracts,* 36A (1975), 902-903.

100. Hermes, Liesel. *Formen und Funktionen des Symbolgebrauchs in den Werken Iris Murdochs.* Frankfurt and Wiesbaden: Humanitas-Verlag, 1972.

101. Heyd, Ruth. "An Interview with Iris Murdoch." *University of Windsor Review,* 1 (1965), 138-143.

102. Hirukawa, Hisayasu. "Futatsu no Sukoron." *Eigo Seinen,* 116 (1970), 576-577.

103. Hobson, Harold. "Lunch with Iris Murdoch." (London) *Sunday Times* (11 March 1962), p. 28. An interview.

104. Hoffman, Frederick J. "Iris Murdoch: The Reality of Persons." *Critique,* 7, No. 1 (Spring 1964), 48-57.

105. —. "The Miracle of Contingency: The Novels of Iris Murdoch." *Shenandoah,* 17, No. 1 (1965), 49-56.

106. Hope, Francis. "The Novels of Iris Murdoch." *London Magazine,* n.s. 1 (August 1961), 84-87.

107. Ivaševa, V. "Ot Džordž Eliot k Anglijskomu romanu 60-x godov." *Voprosy Literatury,* 15 (1971), 98-119.

108. —. "Ot Sartra k Platonu." *Voprosy Literatury,* 13, No. 11 (1969), 134-155.

109. Kaplan, Morton Neil. "Iris Murdoch and the Gothic Tradi-

tion." Diss. Columbia, 1969. *Dissertation Abstracts,* 31A (1970), 1231-1232.

110. Kaufmann, R. J. "The Progress of Iris Murdoch." *Nation,* 188 (21 March 1959), 255-256.

111. Keates, Lois Silver. "Varieties of the Quest-Myth in the Early Novels of Iris Murdoch." Diss. Pennsylvania, 1972. *Dissertation Abstracts,* 33A (1972), 1730.

112. Kellman, Steven G. "Raising the Net: Iris Murdoch and the Tradition of the Self-Begetting Novel." *English Studies,* 57 (February 1976), 43-50.

113. Kmetz, Gail. "People Don't Do Such Things! Business-As-Usual with Iris Murdoch." *Ms,* 5 (July 1976), 70, 72, 85-87. On all of her novels.

114. Kogan, Pauline. "Beyond Solipsism to Irrationalism: A Study of Iris Murdoch's Novels." *Literature and Ideology,* 2 (1969), 47-69.

115. Kuehl, Linda. "Iris Murdoch: The Novelist as Magician/the Magician as Artist." *Modern Fiction Studies,* 15, No. 3 (1969), 347-360.

116. Kuin, J. "Gabrek aan morele verantwoordelijkheid." *Raam,* 54 (1969), 58-62.

117. Lindman-Strafford, Kerstin. "Fortrollning och fangen-skap." *Finsk-Tidskrift,* 175-176 (1964), 402-410.

118. Maes-Jelinek, Hena. "A House for Free Characters: The Novels of Iris Murdoch." *Revue des Langues Vivantes,* 39 (1963), 45-69.

119. Majdiak, Daniel. "Romanticism in the Aesthetics of Iris Murdoch." *Texas Studies in Literature and Language,* 14 (Spring 1972), 359-375.

120. Martin, Graham. "Iris Murdoch and the Symbolist Novel." *British Journal of Aesthetics,* 5 (1965), 296-300.

121. Martz, Louis L. "Iris Murdoch: The London Novels." *Twentieth-Century Literature in Retrospect.* Harvard English Studies 2. Ed. Reuben A. Brower. Cambridge: Harvard University Press, 1971, pp. 65-86.

122. Meidner, Olga McDonald. "The Progress of Iris Murdoch." *English Studies in Africa,* 4 (1961), 17-38.

123. Micha, René. "Les Romans à Machines d'Iris Murdoch." *Critique,* No. 155 (April 1960), pp. 291-301.

124. Morrell, Roy. "Iris Murdoch: The Early Novels." *Critical Quarterly,* 9 (1967), 272-282.

125. Murrya, William M. "A Note on the Iris Murdoch Manuscripts in the University of Iowa Libraries." *Modern Fiction Studies,* 15, No. 3 (1969), 445-448.

126. Narita, Seiju. "Tokyo no Iris Murdoch." *Eigo Seinen,* 115 (1969), 218-219.

127. O'Connor, William Van. "Iris Murdoch: The Formal and the Contingent." *Critique,* 3, No. 2 (1959), 34-46.

128. O'Sullivan, Kevin. "Iris Murdoch and the Image of Liberal Man." *Yale Literary Magazine,* 131, No. 2 (1962), 27-36.

129. P.H.S. "Prize." *The* (London) *Times* (14 November 1974), p. 16. On Murdoch's Winning the £1,000 Whitbread Literary Award for her *The Sacred and Profane Love Machine.*

130. Pérez-Minik, Domingo. "Amigos y amantes, la comedia y la metafísica de Iris Murdoch." *Insula,* 26 (February 1971), 6.

GENERAL SECONDARY STUDIES

131. Petersen, Jes. "Iris Murdoch." *Dansk Udsyn,* 45 (1965), 196-203.

132. Pondrom, Cyrena N. "Iris Murdoch: An Existentialist?" *Comparative Literature Studies,* 5 (1968), 403-419.

133. Rabinovitz, Rubin. *Iris Murdoch.* Essays on Modern Writers. New York: Columbia University Press, 1968.

134. Rockefeller, Larry Jean. "Comedy and the Early Novels of Iris Murdoch." Diss. Bowling Green, 1968. *Dissertation Abstracts,* 29A (1969), 4018.

135. Rose, W. K. "An Interview with Iris Murdoch." *Shenandoah,* 19, No. 2 (1968), 3-22.

136. —. "Iris Murdoch, informally." *London Magazine,* n.s. 8 (June 1968), 59-73. An interview.

137. Schrickx, W. "Recente Engelse romankunst: Iris Murdoch." *De Vlaamse Gids,* 46 (1962), 516-532.

138. Schneidermeyer, Wilma Faye. "The Religious Dimension in the Works of Iris Murdoch." Diss. Southern California, 1974. *Dissertation Abstracts,* 35A (1974), 3113.

139. Souvage, J. "The Novels of Iris Murdoch." *Studia Germanica Gandensia,* 4 (1962), 225-252.

140. Stettler-Imfeld, B. *The Adolescent in the Novels of Iris Murdoch.* Zurich, Switzerland: Jurisverlag, 1970.

141. Stimpson, Catharine Roslyn. "The Early Novels of Iris Murdoch." Diss. Columbia, 1967. *Dissertation Abstracts,* 28A (1968), 5073-5074.

142. Sullivan, Zohreh Tawakuli. "Enchantment and the Demonic in the Novels of Iris Murdoch." Diss. Illinois at Urbana, 1970. *Dissertation Abstracts,* 32A (1971), 458.

143. Trotzig, Birgitta. "Den moderna romanen." *Bonniers Litterära Magasin,* 30 (1961), 369-370.

144. Vizioli, Paulo. "O romance de Iris Murdoch." *O Estado de São Paulo, Suplemento Literário,* 28 (January 1967), 3.

145. Weatherhead, A. K. "Backgrounds with Figures in Iris Murdoch." *Texas Studies in Literature and Language,* 10 (Winter 1969), 635-648.

146. Whitehorn, Katharine. "The Clanger by Iris Murdoch." *Observer* (11 February 1968), p. 30. A witty satirical piece on what a publisher's catalogue might say of a Murdoch novel.

147. Whiteside, George. "The Novels of Iris Murdoch." *Critique,* 7, No. 1 (Spring 1964), 27-47.

148. Widmann, R. L. "An Iris Murdoch Checklist." *Critique,* 10, No. 1 (1967), 17-29.

149. Wilson, George Robert, Jr. "The Quest Romance in Contemporary Fiction." Diss. Florida, 1968. *Dissertation Abstracts,* 30A (1969), 741. Includes comments on Murdoch's *The Unicorn,* and *A Severed Head.*

150. Wolf, Nancy Connors. "Philosophical Ambivalence in the Novels of Iris Murdoch." Diss. Connecticut, 1972. *Dissertation Abstracts,* 33A (1972), 2959.

151. Wolfe, Peter. "Philosophical Themes in the Novels of Iris Murdoch." Diss. Wisconsin, 1965. *Dissertation Abstracts,* 26 (1965), 3357-3358.

152. —. *The Disciplined Heart: Iris Murdoch and Her Novels.* Columbia, Missouri: University of Missouri Press, 1966.

III. STUDIES AND REVIEWS OF INDIVIDUAL WORKS

References to individual books by Murdoch also appear in the First Part of this bibliography. See the following numbers there: 3, 13, 33, 83, 94, 134, 139, 146, 149, 150, 151, 153, 155, 162, 163, 168, 169, 172, 174, 177, 184, 186, 187, 189, 195, 203, 209, 215, 220, 232, 237, 239, 243, 247, 248, 249, 251, 256, 261, 273, 279, 280, 282, 286, 287, 289, 290, 292, 294, 295, 301, 303, 312, 323, 324, 325, 326, 329, 331, 332, 333, 336, 339, 344, 346.

Under the Net

153. Amis, Kingsley. "New Novels." *Spectator,* 192 (11 June 1954), 722.

154. Anon. "Acceptance and Rebellion." *The* (London) *Times* (5 June 1954), 8.

155. —. "Town and Country." *TLS* (9 July 1954), p. 437.

156. —. *"Under the Net." Publishers' Weekly,* 191 (30 January 1967), 113.

157. Batchelor, Billie. "Revision in Iris Murdoch's *Under the Net." Books at Iowa,* 8 (1968), 30-36.

158. Bradbury, Malcolm. "Iris Murdoch's *Under the Net." Critical Quarterly,* 4 (Spring 1962), 47-54.

159. Corke, Hilary. "Crime Story." *Encounter,* 3 (November

1954), 66-72. P. 70.

160. Fries, Udo. "Iris Murdoch. *Under the Net:* Ein Beitrag zur Erzähltechnik im Ich-Roman." *Die Neueren Sprachen,* 18 (1969), 449-459.

161. Lane, Margaret. Untitled book review. *London Magazine,* 1 (September 1954), 101, 103-104, 106. Pp. 104, 106.

162. Paulding, Gouverneur. "Are Women Necessary? A Witty and Intelligent Novel." *New York Herald Tribune Book Review,* 30 (6 June 1954), 4.

163. Porter, Raymond J. *"Leitmotiv* in Iris Murdoch's *Under the Net." Modern Fiction Studies,* 15, No. 3 (1969), 379-385.

164. Raymond, John. "New Novels." *New Statesman and Nation,* 47 (5 June 1954), 737-738.

165. Souvage, Jacques. "The Unresolved Tension: An Interpretation of Iris Murdoch's *Under the Net." Revue des Langues Vivantes,* 26 (1960), 420-430.

166. Symons, Julian. "Aimless Hero." *Punch,* 227 (21 July 1954), 128-129.

167. Vickery, John B. "The Dilemmas of Language: Sartre's *La Nausee* and Iris Murdoch's *Under the Net." Journal of Narrative Technique,* 1 (May 1971), 69-76.

168. Viebrock, Helmut. "Iris Murdoch: *Under the Net." Der Moderne Englische Roman: Interpretationen.* Ed. Horst Oppel. Berlin: E. Schmidt, 1965, pp. 344-358.

* 169. Widmann, R. L. "Murdoch's *Under the Net:* Theory and Practice of Fiction." *Critique,* 10, No. 1 (1967), 5-16.

The Flight from the Enchanter

170. Anon. "Bad Spell in London." *Time,* 67 (14 May 1956), 133-134.

171. —. "Fiction." *Saturday Review,* 48 (26 June 1965), 42.

172. —. "Perpetual Motion." *TLS* (6 April 1956), p. 205.

173. Archer, Thomas. "New Novels." *Spectator,* 196 (30 March 1956), 418-419.

* 174. Corke, Hilary. "Conscientious Violence." *Encounter,* 6 (June 1956), 88-91. Pp. 88-89.

175. Fiedler, Leslie A. "The Novel in the Post-Political World." *Partisan Review,* 23 (Summer 1956), 358-365. Pp. 363-365.

176. Mackworth, Cecily. Untitled book review. *Twentieth Century,* 159 (June 1956), 616, 618. P. 618.

177. Meidner, Olga McDonald. "Reviewer's Bane: A Study of Iris Murdoch's *The Flight from the Enchanter.*" *Essays in Criticism,* 11 (October 1961), 435-447.

178. Mutis, C. Guido. "El mundo arquetípico de Iris Murdoch: El viaje y el descenso al infierno en *Flight from the Enchanter.*" *Estudios Filológicos,* No. 6 (1970), 229-289.

179. Paulding, Gouverneur. "Laughter, Horror Together in This Dream-Like Novel." *New York Herald Tribune Book Review,* 32 (29 April 1956), 6.

180. Price, R. G. G. "Over-Planned." *Punch,* 230 (6 June 1956), 690-691.

181. Richardson, Maurice. "New Novels." *New Statesman and Nation,* 51 (31 March 1956), 315-316. P. 315.

182. Woodcock, George. "Fiction Chronicle." *Tamarack Review*, 1 (Autumn 1956), 71-77. Pp. 76-77.

The Sandcastle

183. Anon. "Learning the Hard Way in a Difficult World." *The* (London) *Times* (9 May 1957), p. 15.

184. —. "Out of School." *TLS* (10 May 1957), p. 285.

185. —. *"The Sandcastle."* *Reporter,* 16 (30 May 1957), 48.

* 186. George, Daniel. "New Novels." *Spectator,* 198 (17 May 1957), 657.

187. Maclaren-Ross, J. "Character Work." *Punch,* 232 (29 May 1957), 684-685.

188. Mizener, Arthur. "Spring Fiction." *Kenyon Review,* 19 (Summer 1957), 484-493. Pp. 489-490.

189. Paulding, Gouverneur. "A Wealth of Life in Iris Murdoch's Latest Novel." *New York Herald Tribune Book Review,* 33 (12 May 1957), 5.

190. Richardson, Maurice. "New Novels." *New Statesman and Nation,* 53 (11 May 1957), 616.

191. Wyndham, Francis. Untitled book review. *London Magazine,* 4 (August 1957), 64-67. Pp. 64-65.

The Bell

192. Anon. "Fiction." *Saturday Review,* 49 (24 September 1966), 40.

193. —. "In the Heart or in the Head?" *TLS* (7 November 1958), p. 640.

194. —. "New Fiction." *The* (London) *Times* (6 November 1958), p. 13.

195. Bannon, Barbara A. *"The Bell."* Publishers' *Weekly,* 189 (13 June 1966), 129.

* 196. Clayre, Alasdair. "Common: Cause: A Garden in the Clearing." *TLS* (7 August 1959), xxx-xxxi. P. xxxi.

197. Fraser, Eileen. Untitled book review. *Twentieth Century,* 164 (December 1958), 607-609. Pp. 607-608.

198. Gannett, Lewis. "At the Bottom of a Lake was a Bell." *New York Herald Tribune Book Review,* 35 (16 November 1958), 8.

199. Graham, A. R. "All Our Failures are Failures in Love." *New York Times Book Review* (26 October 1958), pp. 5-6.

200. Howe, Irving. "Realities and Fictions." *Partisan Review,* 26 (Winter 1959), 130-136. Pp. 132-133.

201. Jones, Dorothy. "Love and Morality in Iris Murdoch's *The Bell."* *Meanjin Quarterly,* 26 (1967), 85-90.

202. Kermode, Frank. "Novels of Iris Murdoch." *Spectator,* 201 (7 November 1958), 618.

203. Kimber, John. *"The Bell:* Iris Murdoch." *Delta,* No. 18 (Summer 1959), pp. 31-34.

204. McGinnis, Robert M. "Murdoch's *The Bell."* *Explicator,* 28 (1969), Item 1.

205. Paul, David. "A Fictional Novel." *Punch,* 235 (19 November 1958), 674-675.

206. Raymond, John. "The Unclassifiable Image." *New Statesman,* 56 (15 November 1958), 697-698.

207. Rees, Goronwy. "New Novels." *Listener,* 60 (18 December 1958), 1046.

208. Souvage, Jacques. "Symbol as Narrative Device: An Interpretation of Iris Murdoch's *The Bell." English Studies,* 43, No. 2 (1962), 81-96.

209. Toye, William. *"The Bell." Tamarack Review,* 10 (Winter 1959), 106-107.

210. Wall, Stephen. "The Bell in *The Bell." Essays in Criticism,* 13 (July 1963), 265-273.

211. Wyndham, Francis. Untitled book review. *London Magazine,* 6 (January 1959), 70-73. Pp. 71-73.

A Severed Head

212. Anon. "Every Laugh Well Placed. Woman's View of Entangled World. Theatre Royal, Bristol: *A Severed Head." The* (London) *Times* (8 May 1963), p. 5.

213. —. "Iris Murdoch Dramatized—A Dazzling Play. Criterion Theatre: *A Severed Head." The* (London) *Times* (28 June 1963), p. 18.

214. —. "Leisured Philanderings." *TLS* (16 June 1961), p. 369.

215. —. "New Fiction." *The* (London) *Times* (15 June 1961), p. 17.

216. —. "Through Spangled Hoops. Criterion: *A Severed Head." The* (London) *Times* (24 June 1964), p. 6.

217. Baldanza, Frank. "The Manuscript of Iris Murdoch's *A Severed Head." Journal of Modern Literature,* 3 (February 1973), 75-90.

218. Bradbury, Malcolm. "New Novels." *Punch,* 241 (12 July

1961), 67-68.

219. Bryden, Ronald. "Phenomenon." *Spectator*, 206 (16 June 1961), 885.

220. Dent, Alan. "At the Play." *Punch*, 244 (22 May 1963), 751. Review of the stage production.

221. Duchene, Anne. "High, pathetic social comedy." *Manchester Guardian Weekly*, 84 (22 June 1964), 11.

222. Gregor, Ian. "Towards a Christian Literary Criticism." *Month*, 33 (1965), 239-249.

223. Hoskins, Robert Vernon. "The Symbol of the Severed Head in Twentieth-Century British and American Fiction." Diss. Kentucky, 1971. *Dissertation Abstracts*, 33A (1972), 756.

224. Jacobson, Dan. "Farce, Totem and Taboo." *New Statesman*, 61 (16 June 1961), 956-957.

225. Kane, Patricia. "The Furnishings of a Marriage: An Aspect of Characterization in Iris Murdoch's *A Severed Head.*" *Notes on Contemporary Literature*, 2, No. 5 (1972), 4-5.

226. Kenney, Alice P. "The Mythic History of *A Severed Head.*" *Modern Fiction Studies*, 15, No. 3 (1969), 387-401.

227. Mallett, Richard. "Cinema." *Punch*, 260 (27 January 1971), 132. Review of the movie version of the book.

228. O'Connor, William Van. "Iris Murdoch: *A Severed Head.*" *Critique*, 5, No. 1 (Spring-Summer 1962), 74-77.

229. Rolo, Charles. "Liaisons Dangereuses." *Atlantic*, 207 (May 1961), 98-100.

* 230. Saxton, Mark. "Ingenious and Bizarre Novel of Emotional

Ambushes in London." *New York Herald Tribune Book Review,* 37 (16 April 1961), 27.

231. Singer, Burns. "New Novels." *Listener,* 65 (15 June 1961), 1061.

* 232. Taylor, John Russell. "Merry-go-round to nowhere." *The* (London) *Times* (22 January 1971), p. 11. Review of the film version of the book.

An Unofficial Rose

233. Anon. "New Fiction." *The* (London) *Times* (7 June 1962), p. 16.

234. —. "Stretching the Net." *TLS* (8 June 1962), p. 425.

235. Bradbury, Malcolm. "Other New Novels." *Punch,* 242 (27 June 1962), 989-990. P. 990.

236. Bryden, Ronald. "Living Dolls." *Spectator,* 208 (8 June 1962), 755-756.

237. Eimerl, Sarel. "Thorns Without a Rose." *Reporter,* 26 (7 June 1962), 45-46.

238. Hobson, Harold. "London Comment: Miss Murdoch's 'Unofficial Rose'." *Christian Science Monitor,* 54 (19 July 1962), 11.

239. Paulding, Gouverneur. *"An Unofficial Rose."* New York *Herald Tribune Books,* 38 (17 June 1962), 4-5.

240. Reynolds, Stanley. *"An Unofficial Rose."* *The* (London) *Times* (30 December 1974), p. 5. On the BBC's serialization of the novel.

241. Ryan, Marjorie. "Iris Murdoch: *An Unofficial Rose."* *Critique,* 5, No. 3 (Winter 1962-1963), 117-121.

242. Scannell, Vernon. "New Novels." *Listener,* 67 (14 June 1962), 1043.

243. Taubman, Robert. "L'Année Dernière at Dungeness." *New Statesman,* 63 (8 June 1962), 836.

244. Wilson, Angus. "Love among the old roses." *Manchester Guardian Weekly,* 86 (14 June 1962), 11.

245. —. "Who Cares?" *Guardian* (8 June 1962), p. 6.

The Unicorn

246. Anon. "Fable Mates." *TLS* (6 September 1963), p. 669.

247. —. "New Fiction." *The* (London) *Times* (5 September 1963), p. 15.

248. Auchincloss, Eve. "Oxford Gothic." *New York Review of Books,* 1, No. 2 (1963), 38-39.

249. Bradbury, Malcolm. "Under the Symbol." *Spectator,* 211 (6 September 1963), 295.

* 250. Brooke, Jocelyn. "New Fiction." *Listener,* 70 (12 September 1963), 397.

251. Duchene, Anne. "Laying on the Gothick." *Manchester Guardian Weekly,* 89 (19 September 1963), 10.

252. Grigson, Geoffrey. "Entre les Tombes." *New Statesman,* 66 (13 September 1963), 321-322.

253. Jackson, Robert B. *"The Unicorn." Library Journal,* 88 (15 April 1963), 1688.

254. Mckay, A. G. *"The Unicorn." Tamarack Review,* 28 (Summer 1963), 91.

255. Paulding, Gouverneur. "Even the Landscape Has Homicidal Properties." *New York Herald Tribune Books,* 39 (19 May 1963), 3.

256. Pickrel, Paul. "Some Women Novelists." *Harper's,* 226 (June 1963), 106-108. Pp. 107-108.

257. Pondrom, Cyrena Norman. "Iris Murdoch: *The Unicorn.*" *Critique,* 6, No. 3 (Winter 1963), 177-180.

258. Price, R. G. G. "New Fiction." *Punch,* 245 (4 September 1963), 357-358.

259. Scholes, Robert. *The Fabulators.* New York: Oxford University Press, 1967. Contains a chapter on *The Unicorn.*

The Italian Girl

260. Anon. "Briefing: *The Italian Girl.*" *Observer* (22 January 1967), p. 22.

261. —. "Enter Someone." *TLS* (10 September 1964), p. 837.

262. —. "New Fiction." *The* (London) *Times* (10 September 1964), p. 15.

263. —. *"The Italian Girl."* *Virginia Quarterly Review,* 41 (Winter 1965), x.

264. Bronzwaer, W. J. M. *"The Italian Girl:* An Explication." *Tense in the Novel: An Investigation of Some Potentialities of Linguistic Criticism.* Groningen: Wolters-Noordhoff, 1970.

265. Burgess, Anthony. "Iridectomy." *Manchester Guardian Weekly,* 91 (17 September 1964), 10.

266. Dick, Kay. "Murdoch's Eighth." *Spectator,* 213 (11 Sep-

tember 1964), 346.

267. Furbank, P. N. "Gowned Mortality." *Encounter,* 23 (November 1964), 88, 90.

268. Janeway, Elizabeth. "But Nobody Understands." *New York Times Book Review* (14 September 1964), p. 5.

269. Kingston, Jeremy. "Theatre." *Punch,* 254 (14 February 1968), 244. Review of the stage production of the novel.

270. Lerner, Arthur. *"The Italian Girl." Books Abroad,* 39 (Summer 1965), 351.

271. Pickrel, Paul. "Heading Toward Postcivilization: Bewitched or Bewitching." *Harper's,* 229 (October 1964), 128.

272. Popkin, Henry. "Surprise and a little fun." *The* (London) *Times* (7 February 1968), p. 6. Review of the play version of the book.

273. Raven, Simon. "Ordinary families?" *Observer* (13 September 1964), p. 25.

274. Salvesen, Christopher. "A Hieroglyph." *New Statesman,* 68 (11 September 1964), 365-366. P. 365.

275. Sheed, Wilfrid. "Making a meal of antipasto." *Book Week,* 2 (13 September 1964), 5, 12.

276. Wall, Stephen. "New Novels." *Listener,* 72 (10 September 1964), 401.

277. Young, B. A. "New Novels." *Punch,* 247 (23 September 1964), 472.

The Red and the Green

278. Anon. "Irish Stew." *Newsweek,* 66 (22 November 1965), 113A & B-114.

279. —. "Paperbacks: *The Red and the Green." The* (London) *Times* (9 December 1967), p. 18.

280. —. "Republic and Private." *TLS* (14 October 1965), p. 912.

281. —. *"The Red and the Green." Choice,* 3 (June 1966), 310.

282. —. *"The Red and the Green." Kirkus,* 33 (1 August 1965), 789.

283. —. "Unbelievable Don." *Time,* 86 (19 November 1965), 139.

284. Bowen, John. "One Must Also Say Something." *New York Times Book Review* (7 November 1965), pp. 4-5.

285. Clarke, John J. *"The Red and the Green." Best Sellers,* 25 (15 November 1965), 324-325.

286. Cook, Roderick. *"The Red and the Green." Harper's,* 231 (November 1965), 129.

287. Fytton, Francis. Untitled book review. *London Magazine,* n.s. 5 (November 1965), 99-102. Pp. 99-100.

288. Galloway, David D. "The Iris Problem." *Spectator,* 215 (22 October 1965), 520.

289. Griffin, Lloyd W. *"The Red and the Green." Library Journal,* 90 (1 November 1965), 4807.

290. Hicks, Granville. "Easter Monday Insights." *Saturday Review,* 48 (30 October 1965), 41-42.

291. Kemp, Peter. "The Fight Against Fantasy: Iris Murdoch's *The Red and the Green.*" *Modern Fiction Studies*, 15, No. 3 (1969), 403-415.

292. Ostermann, R. Review of *The Red and the Green,* in the *National Observer*, 4 (8 November 1965), 22.

293. Poirier, Richard. "Biting the hand that reads you." *Book Week*, 3 (14 November 1965), 5, 21-24.

294. Pryce-Jones, Alan. Review of *The Red and the Green,* in the *Herald Tribune*, 125 (4 November 1965), 23.

295. Ricks, Christopher. "A Sort of Mystery Novel." *New Statesman*, 70 (22 October 1965), 604-605.

296. Rome, Joy. "A Respect for the Contingent: A Study of Iris Murdoch's Novel *The Red and the Green.*" *English Studies in Africa*, 14 (1971), 87-98.

297. Sheed, W. "An Irish Clue to What Iris Has Been Saying." *Life*, 59 (5 November 1965), 15, 21.

298. Trachtenberg, Stanley. "Accommodation and Protest." *Yale Review*, n.s. 55 (Spring 1966), 444-450. Pp. 448-449.

299. Webb, W. L. "Irish Murdoch." *Manchester Guardian Weekly*, 93 (21 October 1965), 11.

300. Weeks, Edward. "Easter 1916." *Atlantic Monthly*, 216 (December 1965), 138.

301. Whittington-Egan, R. Review of *The Red and the Green,* in *Books and Bookmen*, 11 (December 1965), 40.

The Time of the Angels

302. Allen, Walter. "Anything Goes." *New York Times Book*

Review (25 September 1966), pp. 5, 62.

303. Anon. "Paperbacks: *The Time of Angels.*" *The* (London) *Times* (24 August 1968), p. 20.

304. —. "Picking up the Pieces." *TLS* (8 September 1966), p. 798.

305. —. *"The Time of the Angels."* *Booklist*, 63 (1 September 1966), 34.

306. —. *"The Time of the Angels."* *Choice*, 4 (May 1967), 290.

307. —. *"The Time of the Angels."* *Kirkus*, 34 (15 July 1966), 706.

308. —. *"The Time of the Angels."* *Publishers' Weekly*, 192 (23 October 1967), 53.

309. Berthoff, Warner. "The Enemy of Freedom is Fantasy." *Massachusetts Review*, 8 (Summer 1967), 580-584.

310. Byrom, Bill. "Symbol Clash." *Spectator*, 217 (9 September 1966), 326.

311. Coleman, John. "Sexual Permutations." *Observer* (11 September 1966), p. 27.

312. Cook, Roderick. *"The Time of the Angels."* *Harper's*, 233 (November 1966), 141.

313. Cooper, William. "New Novels." *Listener*, 76 (8 September 1966), 361.

314. Cruttwell, Patrick. "Fiction Chronicle." *Hudson Review*, 20 (Spring 1967), 163-176. P. 176.

315. Davenport, Guy. "History with its Eyes Wide Open." *National Review*, 18 (29 November 1966), 1227, 1228. P. 1227.

316. Donoghue, Denis. "Magic Defeated." *New York Review of Books,* 7 (17 November 1966), 22-25. Pp. 22-23.

317. Eimerl, Sarel. "Choreography of Despair." *Reporter,* 35 (3 November 1966), 45-46.

318. Garis, Robert. "Playing Games." *Commentary,* 43 (March 1967), 97-100.

319. Griffin, Lloyd W. *"The Time of the Angels."* Library Journal, 91 (1 September 1966), 3973.

320. Hicks, Granville. "Rector for a Dead God." *Saturday Review,* 49 (29 October 1966), 25-26.

321. Hill, William B. *"The Time of Angels."* America, 115 (26 November 1966), 707.

322. Kitching, Jessie. *"The Time of the Angles."* Publishers' Weekly, 190 (25 July 1966), 70-71.

323. Lipnack, Linda Victoria. *"The Time of the Angels."* Commonweal, 85 (13 January 1967), 408.

324. Moore, H. T. Review of *The Time of Angels,* in *Books Today,* 3 (9 October 1966), 5.

325. Muggeridge, Malcolm. "Books." *Esquire,* 67 (February 1967), 44, 50. P. 44.

326. Ostermann, R. Review of *The Time of Angels,* in the *National Observer,* 5 (17 October 1966), 23.

327. Phillipson, John S. *"The Time of the Angels."* Best Sellers, 26 (1 October 1966), 236.

328. Toynbee, Philip. "Miss Murdoch's Monster Rally." *New Republic,* 155 (22 October 1966), 24.

329. Weeks, Edward. "Satan in a Fog." *Atlantic Monthly,* 218

(October 1966), 138.

330. West, Paul. "O tempora, O mores." *Book Week,* 4 (25 September 1966), 18.

The Nice and the Good

331. Anon. "By Love Possessed." *Time,* 91 (5 January 1968), 76, 80.

332. —. "Characters in Love." *TLS* (25 January 1968), p. 77.

333. —. *"The Nice and the Good."* *Choice,* 5 (April 1968), 196.

334. —. *"The Nice and the Good."* *Kirkus,* 35 (1 November 1967), 1338.

335. —. *"The Nice and the Good."* *Publishers' Weekly,* 192 (23 October 1967), 48.

336. Baldanza, Frank. *"The Nice and the Good."* *Modern Fiction Studies,* 15, No. 3 (1969), 417-428.

337. Bartek, Zenka. "Dramatized Games." *The* (London) *Times* (27 January 1968), p. 20.

338. Bergonzi, Bernard. "Nice But Not Good." *New York Review of Books,* 10 (11 April 1968), 36-38.

339. Byatt, A. S. "Kiss and Make Up." *New Statesman,* 75 (26 January 1968), 113-114.

340. Cassill, R. V. "Hell fires banked for home use." *Book World,* 2 (7 January 1968), 5.

341. Fremantle, Anne. "The Probable and the Possible." *Reporter,* 38 (25 January 1968), 47-49.

342. Gathorne-Hardy, Jonathan. Untitled book review. *London*

Magazine, n.s. 7 (February 1968), 97-99.

343. Griffin, Lloyd W. *"The Nice and [the] Good."* *Library Journal,* 92 (15 December 1967), 4524.

344. Hicks, Granville. "Love Runs Rampant." *Saturday Review,* 51 (6 January 1968), 27-28.

345. Hill, William B. *"The Nice and the Good."* *America,* 118 (4 May 1968), 622.

346. Jackson, Katherine Gauss. "Books in Brief." *Harper's,* 236 (February 1968), 100.

347. Janeway, Elizabeth. "Everyone is Involved." *New York Times Book Review* (14 January 1968), p. 4.

348. Palmer, Tony. "Artistic Privilege." *London Magazine,* n.s. 8 (May 1968), 47-52. Pp. 48-50.

349. Raven, Simon. "Good news from Hades." *Observer* (21 January 1968), p. 31.

350. Seymour-Smith, Martin. "Virtue its own reward." *Spectator,* 220 (26 January 1968), 103-104.

351. Siggins, Clara M. *"The Nice and the Good."* *Best Sellers,* 27 (15 January 1968), 402.

352. Simon, M. Review of *The Nice and the Good,* in the *National Observer,* 7 (12 February 1968), 21.

353. Sokolov, Raymond A. "Fleshy Rococo." *Newsweek,* 71 (15 January 1968), 73.

354. Taubman, Robert. "Not Caring." *Listener,* 79 (1 February 1968), 148.

355. Weeks, Edward. "Nice is not always safe." *Atlantic,* 221 (February 1968), 135-136.

356. Williams, David. "New Novels." *Punch*, 254 (31 January 1968), 174.

Bruno's Dream

357. Allen, Walter. *"Bruno's Dream."* *New York Times Book Review* (19 January 1969), pp. 5, 34.

358. Anon. *"Bruno's Dream."* *Choice*, 6 (February 1970), 1754-1755.

359. —. *"Bruno's Dream."* *Publishers' Weekly*, 194 (4 December 1968), 48.

360. —. "Spiders and Flies." *TLS* (16 January 1969), p. 53; response by Mary Ellmann in *TLS* (13 February 1969), p. 159.

361. Baker, Roger. "Personal crises." *Books and Bookmen*, 14 (March 1969), 24.

362. Blackburn, Sara. "Book Marks." *Nation*, 208 (27 January 1969), 124.

363. Byatt, A. S. "The Spider's Web." *New Statesman*, 77 (17 January 1969), 86.

364. Dawson, Helen. "Briefing: *Bruno's Dream.*" *Observer* (20 December 1970), p. 19.

365. Freedman, Richard. "Dialogue as trenchant as a 5-to-1 Martini." *Book World*, 3 (12 January 1969), 3.

366. Hall, William F. *"Bruno's Dream:* Technique and Meaning in the Novels of Iris Murdoch." *Modern Fiction Studies*, 15, No. 3 (1969), 429-443.

367. Hill, William B. *"Bruno's Dream."* *America*, 120 (3 May 1969), 538.

368. —. *"Bruno's Dream."* Best Sellers, 28 (15 January 1969), 426-427.

369. Jackson, Katherine Gauss. *"Bruno's Dream."* Harper's, 238 (February 1969), 102-103.

370. Kavanagh, P. J. "Masterly but marred." *Guardian Weekly,* 100 (23 January 1969), 15.

371. Kermode, Frank. "Necessary Persons." *Listener,* 81 (16 January 1969), 84-85.

372. Thomson, P. W. "Iris Murdoch's Honest Puppetry—The Characters of *Bruno's Dream." Critical Quarterly,* 11 (1969), 277-283.

373. Tube, Henry. "Women's rites." *Spectator,* 222 (17 January 1969), 79-80.

374. Wain, John. "Women's Work." *New York Review of Books,* 12 (24 April 1969), 38-40.

375. Wall, Stephan. "The Murdoch manner." *Observer* (19 January 1969), p. 29.

376. Williams, David. "New Novels." *Punch,* 256 (15 January 1969), 106.

377. Wood, Michael. "Take your partners: or, what's going on?" *The* (London) *Times* (18 January 1969), p. 20.

A Fairly Honourable Defeat

378. Anon. *"A Fairly Honourable Defeat."* British Book News (April 1970), p. 338.

379. —. *"A Fairly Honourable Defeat."* Choice, 7 (June 1970), 545.

380. —. *"A Fairly Honourable Defeat."* Kirkus, 37 (15 November 1969), 1224.

381. —. *"A Fairly Honourable Defeat."* Publishers' Weekly, 196 (8 December 1969), 41.

382. —. "Re-run for the enchanter." TLS (29 January 1970), p. 101.

383. Avant, John Alfred. *"A Fairly Honourable Defeat."* Library Journal, 94 (15 December 1969), 4539.

384. Culligan, Glendy. *"A Fairly Honourable Defeat."* Saturday Review, 53 (7 February 1970), 37-38.

385. Dawson, Helen. "Briefing: *A Fairly Honourable Defeat.*" Observer (30 April 1972), p. 30.

386. Foss, John. "Near parody." Books and Bookmen, 15 (March 1970), 22-23.

387. Gray, Paul Edward. "New Fiction in Review." Yale Review, n.s. 60 (Autumn 1970), 101-108. Pp. 102-103.

388. Hill, William B. *"A Fairly Honourable Defeat."* America, 122 (2 May 1970), 478.

389. Hoskins, Robert. "Iris Murdoch's Midsummer Nightmare." Twentieth Century Literature, 18 (July 1972), 191-198.

390. Mahon, Derek. "Oh God." Listener, 83 (29 January 1970), 154-155.

391. Nott, Kathleen. "Pale blue." Guardian Weekly, 102 (7 February 1970), 18.

392. Oates, Joyce Carol. "Diversions of a literary puppet-mistress." Book World, 4 (1 February 1970), 4.

393. O'Faolain, Nuala. "Sitting ducks in SW 10." The (London)

Times (31 January 1970), p. IV.

394. Paul, Anthony. "Eternal polygon." *Financial Times* (5 February 1970), p. 24.

395. Rabinovitz, Rubin. "Iris Murdoch's thirteenth novel, about evil." *New York Times Book Review* (8 February 1970), pp. 1, 28.

396. Reynolds, Stanley. "Artful Anarchy." *New Statesman*, 79 (30 January 1970), 157.

397. Ricks, Christopher. "Man Hunt." *New York Review of Books*, 14 (23 April 1970), 37-41. Pp. 37-39.

398. Thomas, Edward. "Veteran Propellors." *London Magazine*, n.s. 10 (April 1970), 100-103. Pp. 101-103.

399. Tomalin, Claire. "A symbolist pantomime." *Observer* (1 February 1970), p. 30.

400. Tube, Henry. "Tu quoque." *Spectator*, 224 (24 January 1970), 111-112.

401. Vince, Thomas L. *"A Fairly Honourable Defeat."* *Best Sellers*, 30 (1 April 1970), 12-13.

402. Watrin, J. "Iris Murdoch's *A Fairly Honourable Defeat.*" *Revue Des Langues Vivantes*, 38, No. 1 (1972), 46-64.

An Accidental Man

403. Anon. *"An Accidental Man."* *Booklist*, 68 (1 March 1972), 550.

404. —. *"An Accidental Man."* *British Book News* (January 1972), pp. 83-84.

405. —. *"An Accidental Man."* *Choice*, 9 (April 1972), 215.

406. —. *"An Accidental Man."* Kirkus, 39 (15 November 1971), 1230.

407. —. *"An Accidental Man."* Publishers' Weekly, 200 (29 November 1971), 29.

408. —. "Change of life." *Economist*, 241 (6 November 1971), Autumn Survey, vi-vii.

409. —. "I'll move mine if you move yours." *TLS* (22 October 1971), p. 1305.

410. —. "Paperbacks." *Observer* (29 April 1973), p. 35.

411. Avant, John Alfred. *"An Accidental Man."* Library Journal, 97 (15 January 1972), 215.

412. Harcourt, Joan. Untitled book review. *Queen's Quarterly*, 79 (Autumn 1972), 420-421.

413. Hill, William B. *"An Accidental Man."* America, 126 (20 May 1972), 549.

414. Hirsch, Foster. "Ruled by Some Power, Not Benign." *Nation*, 215 (24 July 1972), 59-60.

415. Hope, Francis. "Really Necessary?" *New Statesman*, 82 (22 October 1971), 561.

416. Kennedy, Eileen. *"An Accidental Man."* Best Sellers, 31 (1 March 1972), 530.

417. Kermode, Frank. "Dark Folds." *Listener*, 86 (28 October 1971), 578-579.

418. Oates, Joyce Carol. "So many people!" *Book World*, 6 (23 January 1972), 3.

419. Paul, Anthony. "Accident and essence." *Financial Times* (21 October 1971), p. 34.

420. Sayre, Nora. *"An Accidental Man."* *New York Times Book Review* (23 January 1972), 7, 10.

421. Waugh, Auberon. "Auberon Waugh on Murdoch and Raven." *Spectator,* 227 (23 October 1971), 590. Response is made by Margot Walmsley in *Spectator,* 227 (6 November 1971), 662.

422. Williams, David. "Locke under the dryer." *The* (London) *Times* (21 October 1971), p. 12.

The Black Prince

423. Amis, Martin. "Alas, Poor Bradley." *New Statesman,* 85 (23 February 1973), 278-279.

424. Annan, Gabriele. "Hamlet on the Central Line." *Listener,* 89 (22 February 1973), 249-251.

425. Anon. "Letting others be." *TLS* (23 February 1973), p. 197.

426. —. *"The Black Prince."* *Booklist* , 69 (15 July 1973), 1050.

427. —. *"The Black Prince."* *British Book News* (June 1973), p. 413.

428. —. *"The Black Prince."* *Choice,* 10 (September 1973), 981.

429. —. *"The Black Prince."* *Kirkus,* 41 (15 March 1973), 339.

430. —. *"The Black Prince."* *New York Times Book Review* (11 August 1974), p. 20.

431. —. *"The Black Prince."* *Publishers' Weekly,* 203 (16 April 1973), 48.

432. —. *"The Black Prince."* *Virginia Quarterly Review,* 49 (Fall

1973), cxxxvi.

433. Avant, John Alfred. *"The Black Prince."* *Library Journal*, 98 (1 June 1973), 1844.

434. Dick, Kay. "Critics' Choice." *The* (London) *Times* (29 November 1973), p. iv.

435. Graver, Lawrence. "A new novel by Bradley Pearson (his last) in a new novel by Iris Murdoch (one of her best)." *New York Times Book Review* (3 June 1973), pp. 1, 12, 14.

436. Hill, William B. *"The Black Prince."* *America*, 129 (17 November 1973), 382.

437. Hope, Francis. "Strange and unnatural." *Observer* (25 February 1973), p. 36.

438. Hillier, Bevis. "Critics' Choice." *The* (London) *Times* (29 November 1973), p. IV.

439. Keating, H. R. F. "Critics' Choice." *The* (London) *Times* (29 November 1973), p. IV.

440. Lindroth, James R. *"The Black Prince."* *America*, 129 (1 September 1973), 130.

441. Pearson, Gabriel. "Murdoch's mystifications." *Guardian*, 108 (3 March 1973), 22.

442. Phillipson, John S. *"The Black Prince."* *Best Sellers*, 33 (15 June 1973), 140-141.

443. Potter, Dennis. "Critics' Choice." *The* (London) *Times* (29 November 1973), p. V.

444. Ratcliffe, Michael. "Critics' Choice." *The* (London) *Times* (29 November 1973), p. V.

445. Raynor, Vivien. "Something Keeps One Reading." *Book World,* 7 (17 June 1973), 4-5.

446. Snow, C. P. "Women and gurus." *Financial Times* (1 March 1973), p. 29.

447. Trewin, Ion. "The Booker Prize's place in the autumn publishing traffic jam." *The* (London) *Times* (2 November 1973), p. 16.

448. Waugh, Auberon. "A source of wonder and delight." *Spectator,* 230 (24 February 1973), 235-236.

The Sacred and Profane Love Machine

449. Ackroyd, Peter. "Iris is no pupil." *Spectator,* 232 (23 March 1974), 363-364.

450. Amis, Martin. "Queasy Rider." *New Statesman,* 87 (22 March 1974), 414.

451. Anon. "In a recognizable world." *TLS* (22 March 1974), p. 281.

452. —. *"The Sacred and Profane Love Machine."* *Booklist,* 71 (1 December 1974), 367.

453. —. *"The Sacred and Profane Love Machine."* *British Book News* (July 1974), p. 493.

454. —. *"The Sacred and Profane Love Machine."* *Choice,* 12 (March 1975), 76-77.

455. —. *"The Sacred and Profane Love Machine."* *Kirkus,* 42 (15 July 1974), 761.

456. —. *"The Sacred and Profane Love Machine."* *Publishers' Weekly,* 206 (5 August 1974), 51.

457. Avant, John Alfred. *"The Sacred and Profane Love Machine."* *Library Journal,* 99 (August 1974), 1985.

458. Bailey, Paul. "Naming love." *Guardian,* 110 (6 April 1974), 22.

459. Birstein, Ann. "Intimate Enemies and Stranger Lovers." *Book World* (15 September 1974), p. 1.

460. Cooper, Susan. "Fiction: Vintage, intricate Murdoch." *Christian Science Monitor,* 66 (23 October 1974), 13.

461. Fallowell, Duncan. "Plotting the emotional course." *Books and Bookmen,* 19 (June 1974), 85-86.

462. O'Hara, T. *"The Sacred and Profane Love Machine."* *Best Sellers,* 34 (1 October 1974), 297-298.

463. Sage, Lorna. "Civil engineer." *New Review,* 1 (April 1974), 92-93.

464. Sale, Roger. "Winter's Tales." *New York Review of Books,* 21 (12 December 1974), 18-22. P. 18.

465. Spender, Stephen. "Books of the Year." *Observer* (15 December 1974), p. 19.

466. Thwaite, Anthony. "Chapters of accidents." *Observer* (24 March 1974), p. 39.

467. Vaizey, John. "A Sense of Doom." *Listener,* 91 (21 March 1974), 379-380.

468. Wain, John. "Books of the Year." *Observer* (15 December 1974), p. 19.

469. —. "Iris Murdoch's novel about one man and two women." *New York Times Book Review* (22 September 1974), pp. 1-2.

470. Weeks, Edward. *"The Sacred and Profane Love Machine."* *Atlantic*, 234 (November 1974), 120-122.

A Word Child

471. Adams, Phoebe. *"A Word Child."* *Atlantic*, 236 (September 1975), 85.

472. Anon. *"A Word Child."* *Booklist*, 72 (15 September 1975), 114.

473. —. *"A Word Child."* *Kirkus*, 43 (15 June 1975), 677.

474. —. *"A Word Child."* *Publishers' Weekly*, 207 (16 June 1975), 73.

475. Kermode, Frank. "Ladder to a Vacuum." *Listener*, 93 (17 April 1975), 516.

476. Pendleton, Dennis. *"A Word Child."* *Library Journal*, 100 (1 October 1975), 1845-1846.

477. Quigly, Isabel. "Inner circles." *Financial Times* (17 April 1975), p. 34.

478. Warnock, Mary. "Inner circles." *New Statesman*, 89 (18 April 1975), 519-520.

* 479. Weeks, Brigitte. "First Degree Murdoch." *Book World* (7 September 1975), p. 4.

The Three Arrows, And, The Servants and the Snow

480. Anon. "Hitlerian parallels." *TLS* (23 November 1973), p. 1418.

481. —. *"The Three Arrows and The Servants and the Snow."* *British Book News* (January 1974), p. 58.

482. —. *"The Three Arrows and The Servants and the Snow; plays."* *Choice,* 11 (July-August 1974), 762.

483. —. *"The Three Arrows and The Servants and the Snow."* *Publishers' Weekly,* 205 (25 February 1974), 106.

484. Curtis, Anthony. *"The Servants and the Snow."* *Financial Times* (2 October 1970), p. 3. Review of play performed at the Greenwich Theatre.

485. Drabble, Margaret. "Gothic Hollywood." *Listener,* 91 (17 January 1974), 89.

486. Harding, William James. *"The Three Arrows and The Servants and the Snow."* *Library Journal,* 99 (15 April 1974), 1148.

487. Hayman, Ronald. "Out of the tutorial." *The* (London) *Times* (30 September 1970), p. 13. An interview with Murdoch about the play, *The Servants and the Snow.*

488. Jebb, Julian. "Deep conviction." *The* (London) *Times* (2 October 1970), p. 13.

489. Lewsen, Charles. *"The Three Arrows."* *The* (London) *Times* (25 October 1972), p. 15.

490. Review of *Three Arrows, and, The Servants and the Snow,* in the *National Observer,* 13 (13 July 1974), 19.

Sarte: Romantic Rationalist

491. Anon. "Romantic Rationalist." *TLS* (15 January 1954), p. 45.

492. Arnold, G. L. *"Sartre: Romantic Rationalist."* *Twentieth Century,* 155 (January 1954), 89-91.

493. Cranston, Maurice. Untitled book review. *London Maga-*

zine, 1 (February 1954), 99-100, 102. P. 102.

494. Frank, Joseph. "Sartre and Junger." *Partisan Review,* 21 (March-April 1954), 204-208. Pp. 206-207.

495. Hampshire, Stuart. "The Latest Hegelian." *New Statesman and Nation,* 47 (2 January 1954), 19.

496. Scholes, Robert. *Structuralism in Literature: An Introduction.* New Haven and London: Yale University Press, 1974, pp. 195-198.

497. Williams, Raymond. "Novels, politics, and ideas." *Manchester Guardian Weekly,* 96 (18 May 1967), 11.

The Sovereignty of Good Over Other Concepts

498. Anon. "Paying attention." *TLS* (26 February 1971), p. 241.

499. —. *"The Soverignty of Good."* British Book News (February 1971), p. 99.

500. Baelz, Peter. "Politely Odd." *Cambridge Review,* 89A (19 April 1968), 387-389.

501. Bambrough, Renford. "Diabolical liberty." *Spectator,* 225 (5 December 1970), 731.

502. Cummings, Philip W. *"The Sovereignty of Good."* Library Journal, 96 (15 April 1971), 1372.

503. Downey, Berchmans. *"The Soverignty of the Good."* Best Sellers, 31 (1 April 1971), 8-9.

504. Griffin, James. "The Fat Ego." *Essays in Criticism,* 22 (1972), 74-83.

505. Kenny, Anthony. "Luciferian moralists." *Listener,* 85 (7

January 1971), 23.

506. Potter, Dennis. "Books of the year: *Times* critics choose their favourite new reading of 1970." *The* (London) *Times* (31 December 1970), 8.

507. Toynbee, Philip. "For Goodness' sake." *Observer* (10 January 1971), p. 27.

V[IDIADHAR] S[URAJPRASAD] NAIPAUL
(Born in Trinidad 1932)

I. PRIMARY WORKS: NOVELS

1. *The Mystic Masseur.* London: Deutsch, 1957, 1969; New York: Vanguard Press, 1959; Harmondsworth: Penguin, 1964, 1969; with introduction by Paul Edwards and Kenneth Ramchand. London: Heinemann, 1971; Atlantic Highlands, New Jersey: Humanities Press, 1975; as *El curandero místico.* Trans. Sara Piña. Buenos Aires: Compañía General Fabril Editoria, 1965; as *Le masseur mystique.* Trans. Marie-Lise Marliére. Paris: Gallimard, 1965; as *Il Massaggio Mistico.* Trans. Giorgio Monicelli. Milano: Mondadori, 1966; as *Ha-Ish mi-Trinidad.* Trans. A. Agmon. Tel-Aviv: Amichai, 1966.

2. *The Suffrage of Elvira.* London: Deutsch, 1958, 1968, 1969; Harmondsworth: Penguin, 1969, 1975.

3. *Miguel Street.* London: Deutsch, 1959, 1964; New York: Vanguard Press, 1960; London: World Distributors, 1960; London: Four Square, 1966; Harmondsworth: Penguin, 1971; London: Heinemann, 1975; as *Miguel Street.* Trans. Pauline Verdun. Paris: Gallimard, 1967; as *Calypso.* Trans. Olav Hr. Rue. Oslo: Samlaget, 1966; as *Blaue Karren im Calypsoland.* Trans. Janheinz Jahn. Herrenalb/Schwarzw: Erdmann, 1966; also Stuttgart: Europäischer Buch—u. Phonoklub, 1970; also Stuttgart: Europäische Bildungsgemeinschaft, 1970.

4. *A House for Mr. Biswas.* London: Deutsch, 1961; New York: McGraw Hill, 1962; London: Collins, 1963,

1966; Harmondsworth: Penguin, 1969, 1976; as *Una casa para el señor Biswas.* Trans. Floreal Mazía. Buenos Aires: Companía General Fabril Editora, 1965; as *Une Maison pour Monsieur Biswas.* Trans. Louise Servicen. Paris: Gallimard, 1964; as *Una Casa per il Signor Biswas.* Trans. Vincenzo Mantovani. Milano: Mondadori, 1964.

5. *Mr. Stone and the Knights Companion.* London: Deutsch, 1963; New York: Macmillan, 1964; London: Four Square, 1966.

6. *The Mimic Men.* London: Deutsch, 1967; New York: Macmillan, 1967; Harmondsworth: Penguin, 1969; as *Marionetki.* Trans. Maria Zborowska. Warsaw: Ksiazka i Wiedza, 1971; as *Herr und Sklave.* Trans. Ursula von Zedlitz zu Hohenlohe. Zug, Switzerland: Edition Bergh im Ingse-Verlag, 1974.

7. *In a Free State.* London: Deutsch, 1971; New York: Knopf, 1971; Harmondsworth: Penguin, 1973.

8. *Guerrilas.* London: Deutsch, 1975; New York: Knopf, 1975.

PRIMARY WORKS: SHORT STORIES

9. "Boots in the Corridor." *Punch,* 234 (9 April 1958), 486-487.

10. "A Letter to Maria." *New Statesman,* 56 (5 July 1958), 14.

11. "Caribbean Medley." *Vogue,* 134 (15 November 1959), 90.

12. "A Christmas Story." *Encounter,* 22 (March 1964), 41-52.

13. *A Flag on the Island.* London: Deutsch, 1967; New York: Macmillan, 1968; Harmondsworth: Penguin, 1969; as *Un drapeau sur l'ile.* Trans. Pauline Verdun. Paris: Gallimard, 1971.

Contents: "My Aunt's Gold Teeth"—"The Raffle"—"A Christmas Story"—"The Mourners"—"The Night Watchman's Occurrence Book"—"The Enemy"—"Greenie and Yellow"—"The Perfect Tenants"—"The Heart"—"The Baker's Story"—"A Flag on the Island".

14. "One out of many." *Atlantic*, 227 (April 1971), 71-78, 81-82.

PRIMARY WORKS: OTHER

15. " 'Wonne with a Nut.' " *New Statesman*, 54 (23 November 1957), 703-704. Review of *The Descent of Euphues*, edited by James Winny.

16. "Insider Out." *New Statesman*, 54 (21 December 1957), 859. Review of Harold Nicolson's *Journey to Java*.

17. "Where the Rum Comes From." *New Statesman*, 55 (4 January 1958), 20-21. Review of four books on Jamaica: F. Heriques's *Jamaica*, Edith Clarke's *My Mother Who Fathered Me*, Peter Abrahams's *Jamaica*, and Mona Macmillan's *The Land of Look Behind*.

18. "Letter from Little Rock." *New Statesman*, 55 (25 January 1958), 112. Review of Ved Mehta's autobiography, *Face to Face*.

19. "New Fiction." *New Statesman*, 55 (5 April 1958), 444-445. Review of Amos Tutuola's *The Brave African Huntress*, Anna Kavan's *A Bright Green Field*, May Sarton's *The Birth of a Grandfather*, and Weldon Hill's *Onionhead*.

20. "Autobiographies." *New Statesman*, 55 (19 April 1958), 507. Review of Richard Rumbold's *My Father's Son*, Geoffrey Household's *Against the Wind*, and John Lodwick's *Bid the Soldiers Shoot*.

21. "New Novels." *New Statesman,* 55 (3 May 1958), 572-573. Review of J. Tanizaki's *The Makioka Sisters,* Jean Gamo's *Héresmédan,* Leslie Blight's *Love and Idleness,* and Colin Murry's *The Golden Valley.*

22. "Flowers for the Frau." *New Statesman,* 55 (17 May 1958), 645. Review of Gustie L. Herrigel's *Zen in the Art of Flower Arrangement.*

23. "New Novels." *New Statesman,* 55 (31 May 1958), 705. Review of Hermann Hesse's *Demian,* Veronica Hull's *The Monkey Puzzle,* and Anthony Bloomfield's *The Delinquents.*

24. "Seven Ages of Humour: Young Men Forget." *Punch,* 234 (4 June 1958), 734-736. An account of his difficulties in being a writer from Trinidad.

25. "New Novels." *New Statesman,* 55 (28 June 1958), 844-845. Review of Jack Schaefer's *Company of Cowards,* P. G. Wodehouse's *Cocktail Time,* James Hanley's *An End and a Beginning,* Francois-Regis Bastide's *The Aliens,* and Michael Wharton's *Sheldrake.*

26. "New Novels." *New Statesman,* 56 (12 July 1958), 54-55. Review of Mary McMinnies's *The Visitors,* Paul-André Lesort's *The Branding Iron,* H. E. Bates's *The Darling Buds of May,* and Henri Troyat's *Amélie and Pierre.*

27. "Three Boyhoods." *New Statesman,* 56 (26 July 1958), 123-124. Review of James Kenward's *Prep School,* Jack Lindsay's *Life Rarely Tells,* John Giscard's *A Place of Stones.*

28. "New Novels." *New Statesman,* 56 (9 August 1958), 174-175. Review of Roger Vailland's *The Law,* Michael McLaverty's *The Choice,* and Kenneth Allsop's *Rare Bird.*

29. "The Regional Barrier." *TLS* (15 August 1958), pp. xxxvii-xxxviii; reprinted as "London," in his *The Overcrowded*

Barracoon (see main entry), pp. 9-16. On being a foreign writer in England.

30. "New Novels." *New Statesman,* 56 (30 August 1958), 252-253. Review of James Agee's *A Death in the Family,* Warren Miller's *The Way We Live Now,* Rachel Cecil's *Theresa's Choice,* Herbert Steinhouse's *Ten Years After,* and H. Russcol and M. Banai's *Kilometer 95.*

31. "New Novels." *New Statesman,* 56 (4 October 1958), 471. Review of Penelope Mortimer's *Daddy's Gone A-Hunting,* and Christopher Davis's *Lost Summer.*

32. "New Novels." *New Statesman,* 56 (1 November 1958), 608, 610. Review of H. L. Humes's *The Underground City,* Michel Butor's *Second Thoughts,* William Sansom's *The Cautious Heart,* and Isak Dinesen's *Anecdotes of Destiny.*

33. "New Novels." *New Statesman,* 56 (6 December 1958), 826-827. Review of Samuel Selvon's *Turn Again Tiger,* George Lamming's *Of Age and Innocence,* and Jan Carew's *The Wild Coast.*

34. "New Novels." *New Statesman,* 57 (17 January 1959), 79. Review of Alexander Cordell's *Rape of the Fair Country,* James Courage's *A Way of Love,* and Compton Mackenzie's *The Lunatic Republic.*

35. "Other New Novels." *New Statesman,* 57 (14 February 1959), 229-230. Review of Hermann Hesse's *Goldmund,* David Caute's *At Fever Pitch,* Loys Masson's *The Tortoises,* Alfred Maund's *The Big Boxcar,* and Dennis Murphy's *The Sergeant.*

36. "New Novels." *New Statesman,* 57 (14 March 1959), 376. Review of Joyce Cary's *The Captive and the Free,* Marilyn Duckworth's *A Gap in the Spectrum,* John Wain's *A Travelling Woman,* and Hans Koningsberger's *The Affair.*

37. "Death on the Telephone." *New Statesman*, 57 (28 March 1959), 452. Review of Muriel Spark's *Momento Mori*.

38. "Other New Novels." *New Statesman*, 57 (18 April 1959), 551-552. Review of D. A. Rayner's *The Small Spark of Courage*, Mark Oliver's *As Though They Had Never Been*, José André Lacour's *Death in that Garden*, Albert J. Guerard's *The Bystander*, and Nancy Pearson's *Mademoiselle B—*.

39. "New Fiction." *New Statesman*, 57 (16 May 1959), 700. Review of Peter Towry's *Trial by Battle*, Philip Callow's *Native Ground*, Paul Bowles's *The Hours After Noon*, Livia De Stefani's *The Vine of Dark Grapes*, and Roger Longrigg's *Wrong Number*.

40. "New Novels." *New Statesman*, 57 (20 June 1959), 871. Review of P. N. Newby's *A Guest and His Going*, John Masters's *Fandango Rock*, and Edith De Born's *The House in Vienna*.

41. "New Novels." *New Statesman*, 58 (18 July 1959), 89-90. Review of Robert Kee's *Broadstrop in Season*, Yael Dayan's *New Face in the Mirror*, Oswell Blakeston's *Hop Thief*, and Michel-Droit's *Pueblo*.

42. "New Fiction." *New Statesman*, 58 (15 August 1959), 200-201. Review of John Prebble's *The Buffalo Soldiers*, Francis Irby Gwaltney's *The Numbers of Our Days*, Walter Clemons's *The Poison Tree*, and Oriel Malet's *The Horses of the Sun*.

43. "New Novels." *New Statesman*, 58 (26 September 1959), 401-402. Review of Pamela Hansford Johnson's *The Humbler Creation*, Yukio Mishima's *The Temple of the Golden Pavilion*, and Kathleen Sully's *A Man Talking to Seagulls*.

44. "New Novels." *New Statesman*, 58 (17 October 1959), 516-517. Review of Peter De Vries's *Tents of Wicked-*

ness, Raymond Postgate's *Every Man is God*, Mordecai Roshwald's *Level Seven*, Robert Shaw's *The Hiding Place*, and Morris West's *The Devil's Advocate*.

45. "New Novels—II." *New Statesman*, 58 (7 November 1959), 637-638. Review of six novels.

46. "New Novels." *New Statesman*, 58 (28 November 1959), 770-771. Review of Susan Tweedsmuir's *Dashbury Park*, Michael Redgrave's *The Mountebank's Tale*, E. J. Howard's *The Sea Change*, and Robert Hardy's *A Winter's Tale*.

47. "New Novels." *New Statesman*, 59 (9 January 1960), 49-50. Review of Alberto Moravia's *The Wayward Wife*, G. O. Jones's *The Catalyst*, Stephen Birmingham's *Barbara Greer*, John W. Wadleigh's *The Bitter Passion*, and Julian Mayfield's *The Long Night*.

48. "New Novels." *New Statesman*, 59 (6 February 1960), 195-196. Review of six novels, including Irwin Shaw's *Two Weeks in Another Town*.

49. "New Novels." *New Statesman*, 59 (27 February 1960), 306-307. Review of Martin Walser's *The Gadarene Club*, Alfred Duggan's *The Cunning of the Dove*, John Harvey's *Within and Without*, Ben Barzman's *Out of this World*, and Francoise Sagan's *Aimez-vous Brahms*.

50. "New Novels." *New Statesman*, 59 (26 March 1960), 461-452. Review of Vladimir Nabokov's *Bend Sinister*, Elizabeth Avery's *The Marigold Summer*, and Alan Clark's *Bargains at Special Prices*.

51. "New Novels." *New Statesman*, 59 (23 April 1960), 602. Review of Agnar Mykle's *Lasso Round the Moon*, and Gil Buhet's *Mamizelle Bon Voyage*.

52. "New Novels." *New Statesman*, 59 (21 May 1960), 764-765. Review of six novels, including L. P. Hartley's

Facial Justice.

53. "New Novels." *New Statesman*, 59 (18 June 1960), 914-915. Review of Jeremy Brooks's *Jampot Smith*, Hamilton Johnston's *Dying Nicely*, Nancy Hale's *Dear Beast*, C. Hodder-Williams's *Final Approach*, and Raymond Queneau's *Zazie.*

54. "New Novels." *New Statesman*, 60 (16 July 1960), 97-98. Review of Edna O'Brien's *The Country Girls*, Neville Dawes's *The Last Enchantment*, and Jack Kerouac's *The Subterraneans.*

55. "New Novels." *New Statesman*, 60 (20 August 1960), 251-252. Review of Colette's *Claudine Married*, Alexander Lernet-Holenia's *Count Luna and Baron Bagge*, Peter Vansittart's *A Sort of Forgetting*, and Roger Manvell's *The Passion.*

56. "On St. George's Hill." *New Statesman*, 61 (12 May 1961), 758. Review of five novels: David Caute's *Comrade Jacob*, Godfrey Smith's *The Business of Loving*, Dola De Jong's *The Tree and the Vine*, David Pryce-Jones's *Owls and Satyrs*, and Ronald Duncan's *Saint Spiv.*

57. "Reliques." *New Statesman*, 61 (9 June 1961), 924. Review of four novels: Samuel Yellen's *The Wedding Band*, Hilde Speil's *The Darkened Room*, John Thirkell's *The End Product*, and Daphne Rooke's *A Lover for Estelle.*

58. "Taluqdars." *New Statesman*, 62 (7 July 1961), 22-23. Review of seven novels.

59. "The Little More." *The* (London) *Times* (13 July 1961), p. 13. On what he has read.

60. "Tricks and Secrets." *New Statesman*, 62 (28 July 1961), 126-127. Review of Jean Forton's *The Harm is Done*, Ignazio Silone's *The Fox and the Camellias*, and Mario Pomilio's *The New Line.*

61. "Dark Places." *New Statesman,* 62 (18 August 1961), 221-222. Review of Hamilton Basso's book of travel articles, *A Quota of Seaweed.*

62. "Red Rat-Traps." *New Statesman,* 62 (25 August 1961), 248-249. Review of four novels: Robin Jenkins's *Dust on the Paw,* Terry Taylor's *Baron's Court, All Change,* Richard Condon's *Some Angry Angel,* and Romain Rolland's *John Christopher in Paris.*

63. Untitled book review. *Listener,* 66 (7 September 1961), 358. Review of Colin MacInnes's collected essays, *England, Half English.*

64. "Vacancies." *New Statesman,* 62 (22 September 1961), 394-395. Review of three novels: Ivy Compton-Burnett's *The Mighty and Their Fall,* Francis King's *The Custom House,* and Pamela Hansford Johnson's *This Bed Thy Centre.*

65. " 'Living like a millionaire.' " *Vogue,* 138 (15 October 1961), 92-93, 144, 147. Personal narrative.

66. "When I was a Kid." *New Statesman,* 62 (22 December 1961), 963-964. Review of Paul Gallico's *Confessions of a Story-Teller; Pick of Today's Short Stories 12,* edited by John Pudney; and *Stories from the New Yorker: 1950-1960.*

67. "The Immigrants: Lo! The Poor West Indian." *Punch,* 242 (17 January 1962), 124-126. On the importance of England to the West Indian. Naipaul argues against the passage of an Immigration Bill that would keep West Indians from entering England.

68. "Trollope in the West Indies." *Listener,* 67 (15 March 1962), 461. On Trollope's *The West Indies and the Spanish Main.*

69. "In the Middle of the Journey." *Illustrated Weekly of India*

(28 October 1962); reprinted in his *The Overcrowded Barracoon* (see main entry), pp. 41-46. A view of India after an experience of it for six months.

70. *The Middle Passage: Impressions of Five Societies—British, French and Dutch—in the West Indies and South America.* London: Deutsch, 1962; New York: Macmillan, 1963; Harmondsworth: Penguin, 1969.

71. "Jamshed into Jimmy." *New Statesman,* 65 (25 January 1963), 129-130; reprinted in his *The Overcrowded Barracoon* (see main entry), pp. 47-54. On his experience of Calcutta.

72. "Castles of Fear." *Spectator,* 211 (5 July 1963), 16. Review of J. P. Donleavy's *The Ginger Man.*

73. "Sporting Life." *Encounter,* 21 (September 1963), 73-75; reprinted as "Cricket," in his *The Overcrowded Barracoon* (see main entry), pp. 17-22. Review of C. L. R. James's *Beyond a Boundary.*

74. "Black Man's Burden." *New York Review of Books,* 1 (31 October 1963), 19-20. Review of Bernard Semmel's *Jamaican Blood and Victorian Conscience.*

75. "Sebastian Rides Again." *Spectator,* 212 (24 April 1964), 559, 561. Review of J. P. Donleavy's *A Singular Man.*

76. "Trinidad." *Mademoiselle,* 59 (May 1964), 187-188.

77. "Words on their Own." *TLS* (4 June 1964), pp. 472-473; reprinted as "Jasmine," in his *The Overcrowded Barracoon* (see main entry), pp. 23-29. On his reading and reaction to English literature.

78. "Australia Deserta." *Spectator,* 213 (16 October 1964), 513. Review of Patrick White's *The Burnt Ones.*

79. "The documentary heresy." *Twentieth Century,* 173

(Winter 1964/65), 107-108. On "intellectual" violence.

80. "Indian Autobiographies." *New Statesman,* 69 (29 January 1965), 156-158; reprinted in his *The Overcrowded Barracoon* (see main entry), pp. 55-60. A review of five autobiographies.

81. *An Area of Darkness: An Experience of India.* London: Deutsch, 1964; New York: Macmillan, 1965; Harmondsworth: Penguin, 1968, 1970; as *L'Inde sans espoir.* Trans. Janine Michel. Paris: Gallimard, 1968.

82. "East Indian, West Indian." *Reporter,* 32 (17 June 1965), 35-37; reprinted as "East Indian," in his *The Overcrowded Barracoon* (see main entry), pp. 30-38. On being an Indian from the West Indies.

83. "Images." *New Statesman,* 70 (24 September 1965), 452-453. Review of *Commonwealth Literature,* edited by John Press.

84. "Roman life after Hannibal." *Manchester Guardian Weekly,* 93 (30 December 1965), 10. Review of Arnold J. Toynbee's *Hannibal's Legacy: The Hannibalic War's Effects on Roman Life.*

85. "The Last of the Aryans." *Encounter,* 26 (January 1966), 61-64, 66; reprinted in his *The Overcrowded Barracoon* (see main entry), pp. 61-70. Review of N. C. Chaudhuri's *The Continent of Circe.*

86. "The Writer." *New Statesman,* 71 (18 March 1966), 381-382. Review of Christopher Isherwood's *Exhumations.*

87. "Theatrical Natives." *New Statesman,* 72 (2 December 1966), 844; reprinted in his *The Overcrowded Barracoon* (see main entry), pp. 71-75. Review of two books on Kipling.

88. "Speaking Out: What's Wrong with Being a Snob?" *Satur-*

day Evening Post, 240 (3 June 1967), 12, 18. A new definition of the word *Snob,* and its relation to democracy.

89. "Mr. Matsuda's Million-Dollar Gamble." *Daily Telegraph Magazine* (14 July 1967); reprinted in his *The Overcrowded Barracoon* (see main entry), pp. 141-154. A report of Naipaul's interviewing Mr. Morihiro Matsuda, author of *Bible of Wisdom.*

90. "Tragedy: The Missing Sense." *Daily Telegraph Magazine* (11 August 1967); reprinted under main title "A Second Visit," in his *The Overcrowded Barracoon* (see main entry), pp. 76-86. On the absurdity of life in India. Naipaul reports on his discussions with various officials in India.

91. "Magic and Dependence." *Daily Telegraph Magazine* (18 August 1967); reprinted in his *The Overcrowded Barracoon* (see main entry), pp. 86-97. On India's need to reform itself; and to begin this by a thorough self-examination and by a giving up of its beliefs in magic.

92. "Columbus and Crusoe." *Listener,* 78 (28 December 1967), 845-846; reprinted in his *The Overcrowded Barracoon* (see main entry), pp. 203-207. Review of Björn Landström's *Columbus.*

93. "Jacques Soustelle and the Decline of the West." *Daily Telegraph Magazine* (26 January 1968); reprinted in his *The Overcrowded Barracoon* (see main entry), pp. 190-200. A biographical account of a French political exile.

94. "Out of the Air: In black ink." *Listener,* 79 (23 May 1968), 666. Naipaul comments on how, where, and when he writes.

95. With Graham Greene, Muriel Spark, and Auberon Waugh. "Biafra's Rights." *The* (London) *Times* (13 November 1968), p. 11. A letter to the Editor.

96. "Anguilla: The Shipwrecked 6000." *New York Review of Books,* 12 (24 April 1969), 9-10, 12, 14, 16; reprinted in his *The Overcrowded Barracoon* (see main entry), pp. 232-245. A short history of the Caribbean islands of Anguilla.

97. "St. Kitts: Papa and the Power Set." *New York Review of Books,* 12 (8 May 1969), 23-27; reprinted in his *The Overcrowded Barracoon* (see main entry), pp. 220-231. On the Caribbean island of St. Kitts, and its leader Robert Bradshaw.

98. "The Ultimate Colony." *Daily Telegraph Magazine* (4 July 1969); reprinted in his *The Overcrowded Barracoon* (see main entry), pp. 208-219. On the Governor, and the Premier of British Honduras.

99. "Et in America ego—the American poet Robert Lowell talks to the novelist V. S. Naipaul about art, power, and the dramatisation of the self." *Listener,* 82 (4 September 1969), 302-304.

100. "New York with Norman Mailer." *Daily Telegraph Magazine* (10 October 1969); reprinted in his *The Overcrowded Barracoon* (see main entry), 169-189. A report on Mailer's running for the office of New York City's Mayor.

101. "Books of the Year." *Observer* (21 December 1969), p. 17. Naipaul chooses his three top selections.

102. *The Loss of El Dorado: A History.* London: Deutsch, 1969; New York: Knopf, 1970; revised ed. Harmondsworth: Penguin, 1973; as *La perdida de El Dorado.* Trans. Julia J. de Natino. Caracas: Monte Avila, 1971; as *Utrata El Dorado.* Trans. Maria Zborowska. Warsaw: Ksiazka i Wiedza, 1972.

103. "New Year Predictions." *Listener,* 83 (1 January 1970), 17. Naipaul comments on the differences between the

rich nations and the poor ones.

104. "Cannery Row revisited." *Daily Telegraph* (3 April 1970), p. 24; reprinted as "Steinbeck in Monterey," in his *The Overcrowded Barracoon* (see main entry), pp. 155-168. On the people and their lives in Cannery Row, 1970.

105. "Power to the Caribbean People." *New York Review of Books*, 15 (3 September 1970), 32-34; reprinted as "Power?" in his *The Overcrowded Barracoon* (see main entry), pp. 246-254. Response ("No Joke") is made by A. D. H. Jones in *New York Review of Books*, 15 (19 November 1970), 53-54. On the Black Power Movement in the Caribbean Islands.

106. "The Election in Ajmer." (London) *Sunday Times Magazine* (15 and 22 August 1971), pp. 8 and 18 respectively; reprinted in his *The Overcrowded Barracoon* (see main entry), pp. 98-138.

107. "Escape from the puritan ethic." *Daily Telegraph Magazine* (10 December 1971), p. 38.

108. "The Corpse at the Iron Gate." *New York Review of Books*, 19 (10 April 1972), 3-4, 6-8. On Juan and Eva Perón, and the people of Argentina.

109. "Without a Dog's Chance." *New York Review of Books*, 18 (8 May 1972), 29-31. Review of Rhys' *After Leaving Mr. Mackenzie.*

110. "Mauritius: The overcrowded barracoon." (London) *Sunday Times Magazine* (16 July 1972), p. 4; reprinted as "The Overcrowded Barracoon," in his *The Overcrowded Barracoon* (see main entry), pp. 255-286. On people and events on the Ocean island of Mauritius.

111. "The King over the water: Juan Peron." (London) *Sunday Times* (6 August 1972), pp. 29-30.

112. "Comprehending Borges." *New York Review of Books,* 19 (19 October 1972), 3-4, 6. Comments on Borges as man and writer. Includes discussion of several works by Borges.

113. "It is not easy to be famous in a small town." *Daily Telegraph* (17 November 1972), p. 37.

114. *The Overcrowded Barracoon and Other Articles.* London: Deutsch, 1972; New York: Knopf, 1973.

> Contents: "London"—"Cricket"—"Jasmine" —"East Indian"—"In the Middle of the Journey"—"Jamshed into Jimmy"—"Indian Autobiographies"—"The Last of the Aryans"—"Theatrical Natives"—"A Second Visit: i Tragedy: the Missing Sense ii Magic and Dependence"— "The Election in Ajmer"—"Mr. Matsuda's Million-Dollar Gamble"—"Steinbeck in Monterey"—"New York with Norman Mailer"—"Jacques Soustelle and the Decline of the West"—"Columbus and Crusoe"—"The Ultimate Colony"—"St. Kitts: Papa and the Power Set"—"Anguilla: the Shipwrecked Six Thousand"—"Power?"—"The Overcrowded Barracoon."

115. "V. S. Naipaul Tells How Writing Changes a Writer." *Tapia,* 3, No. 48 (1973), 11.

116. "A Country Dying on Its Feet: V. S. Naipaul on Uruguay, where the polarisation between Left and Right is fraticidal and inflation soars to calamitous proportions." *Observer* (10 February 1974), p. 25; reprinted without subtitle in *New York Review of Books,* 21 (4 April 1974), 21-23.

117. "Argentina: The Brothels Behind the Graveyard." *New York Review of Books,* 21 (19 September 1974), 12-16. On Perón, and on several aspects of life and institutions in Argentina.

118. "Conrad's Darkness." *New York Review of Books,* 21 (17

October 1974), 16-21. On Conrad's obsession to fidelity and its negative effect on his style. On his reading "experience" of Conrad (there is more concentration on short stories than novels, and several passages from Conrad's letters are discussed). On Conrad's interests, abilities, inabilities, and myths. Reply to essay by Charles O. McDonald. *New York Review of Books,* 21 (28 November 1974), 46.

119. "India: A Wounded Civilization." *New York Review of Books,* 23 (29 April 1976), 18-22, 27-29. On modern India.

120. "The Wounds of India." *New York Review of Books,* 23 (13 May 1976), 8, 10, 12, 14. On R. K. Narayan's *Mr. Sampath,* and *The Vendor of Sweets.*

121. "Bombay: The Skyscrapers and the Chawls." *New York Review of Books,* 23 (10 June 1976), 26-29. On his personal experience of the city.

122. "India: New Claim on the Land." *New York Review of Books,* 23 (24 June 1976), 11-12, 14-16, 18. On his personal experience of India.

* 123. "India: A Defect of Vision." *New York Review of Books,* 23 (5 August 1976), 9-10, 12-14. On Mahatma Gandhi's *The Story of My Experiments with Truth,* and U. R. Anantamurti's novel *Samskara.*

124. "Foreword" to *The Adventures of Gurudeva, and Other Stories* by Seepersad Naipaul. London: Deutsch, 1976.

II. GENERAL SECONDARY STUDIES, INTERVIEWS, BIOGRAPHICAL SKETCHES, AND MISCELLANEOUS ITEMS

General references to Naipaul's work also appear in the First Part of this bibliography. See the following numbers there: 18, 58, 61, 63, 79, 85, 97, 115, 132, 226.

125. Amis, Kingsley. "Fresh Winds from the West." *Spectator*, 200 (2 May 1958), 565-566. Discusses the first two novels by Naipaul.

126. Anon. "An Area of Brilliance." *Observer* (28 November 1971), p. 8. A profile on Naipaul.

127. —. "Awards to Writers by Phoenix Trust." *The* (London) *Times* (7 January 1963), p. 10. A notice of Naipaul's receiving £500 "to enable him to write a book on India."

128. —. "Briefing." *Observer* (30 March 1969), p. 34. Short review of five of Naipaul's books: *The Mystic Masseur, The Suffrage of Elvira, The Mimic Men, The Middle Passage,* and *A Flag on the Island.*

129. —. "Commentary." *TLS* (26 November 1971), p. 1478. On Naipaul's winning the Booker Prize for his *In a Free State.*

130. —. "Hawthornden Prize Winner." *The* (London) *Times* (8 April 1964), p. 10. A notice of Naipaul's winning the prize for his *Mr. Stone and the Knights Companion.*

131. —. "John Llewelyn Rhys Prize Winner." *The* (London)

Times (25 April 1958), p. 7. A notice of Naipaul's receiving the prize for his *The Mystic Masseur.*

132. —. "The Caribbean Mixture: Variations and Fusions in Race and Style." *TLS* (10 August 1962), p. 578. Much of the article consists of a discussion of Naipaul. Reply by C. L. R. James, followed by response by reviewer, in *TLS* (28 September 1962), p. 766.

133. —. "Two Deserving Literary Prize winners." *Guardian* (26 November 1971), p. 12. On Naipaul's winning the £5,000 Booker Prize for his *In a Free State.*

134. Bingham, Nigel. "The Novelist V. S. Naipaul talks to Nigel Bingham about his childhood in Trinidad." *Listener,* 88 (7 September 1972), 306-307.

135. Blodgett, Harriet. "Beyond Trinidad: Five Novels by V. S. Naipaul." *South Atlantic Quarterly,* 73 (Summer 1974), 388-403.

* 136. Boxill, Anthony. "V. S. Naipaul's Starting Point." *Journal of Commonwealth Literature,* 10 (August 1975), 1-9.

137. Bryden, Ronald. "The Novelist V. S. Naipaul Talks About His Work." *Listener,* 89 (22 March 1973), 367-368, 370. An interview.

138. Carr, W. I. "Reflections on the Novel in the British Caribbean." *Queen's Quarterly,* 70 (Winter 1964), 585-597. Pp. 588, 589, 594, 596.

139. Clare, John. "V. S. Naipaul Stories win £5,000 prize." *The* (London) *Times* (26 November 1971), p. 5. On his winning the Booker prize for his *In a Free State.*

140. Collymore, Frank A. "Writing in the West Indies: A Survey." *Tamarack Review,* 14 (Winter 1960), 111-124. P. 122. On Naipaul's sophistication.

141. Dathorne, O. R., ed. "Introduction," to his *Caribbean Narrative: An Anthology of West Indian Writing.* London: Heinemann, 1966, pp. 1-16. Naipaul is discussed, among others, almost throughout.

142. Davies, M. Bryn. "Criticism from India." *Journal of Commonwealth Literature,* No. 3 (July 1967), pp. 123-124. P. 123. On Naipaul's view of Trinidad and India.

143. Derrick, A. C. "Naipaul's Technique as a Novelist." *Journal of Commonwealth Literature,* 7 (July 1969), 32-44.

144. Drayton, Arthur D. "West Indian Fiction and West Indian Society." *Kenyon Review,* 25 (Winter 1963), 129-141. P. 131. A paragraph on Naipaul's West Indian characters.

145. Garebian, Keith. "V. S. Naipaul's Negative Sense of Place." *Journal of Commonwealth Literature,* 10 (August 1975), 23-35.

146. Gurr, A. J. "Third-World Novels: Naipaul and After." *Journal of Commonwealth Literature,* 7 (June 1972), 6-13.

147. Hamilton, Alex. "Living a Life on Approval." *Guardian* (4 October 1971), p. 8. An interview.

148. Hamilton, Ian. "Without a Place." *TLS* (30 July 1971), pp. 897-898. An interview.

149. Hamner, Robert Daniel. "An Island Voice: The Novels of V. S. Naipaul." Diss. Texas, 1971. *Dissertation Abstracts,* 32A (1972), 6427-6428.

150. —. *Critical Perspectives on V. S. Naipaul.* Washington, D. C.: Three Continents Press, 1976.

151. —. "V. S. Naipaul: A Selected Bibliography." *Journal of Commonwealth Literature,* 10 (August 1975), 36-44.

152. —. *V. S. Naipaul.* New York: Twayne, 1973.

153. Hancock, Kathleen M., and Kenneth R. Richardson. "Naipaul." *Twentieth-Century Writing: A Reader's Guide to Contemporary Literature.* Ed. Kenneth Richardson. London: Newnes Books, 1969, p. 447.

154. Harrison, Deborah. "V. S. Naipaul and Colonial Mentality." *Canadian Forum,* 55 (December-January 1975/1976), 44-47.

155. Henry, Jim Douglas. "Unfurnished Entrails—the novelist V. S. Naipaul in conversation with Jim Douglas Henry." *Listener,* 86 (25 November 1971), 721.

156. James, Louis. Untitled comments. *Contemporary Novelists.* Ed. James Vinson. London and Chicago: St. James Press, 1972, pp. 921-923.

157. Jones, Joseph, and Johanna Jones. *Authors and Areas of the West Indies: People and Places in World English Literature, No. 2.* Austin, Texas: Steck-Vaughn, 1970, pp. 48-49.

158. Kemoli, Arthur. "The Theme of 'The Past' in Caribbean Literature." *World Literature Written in English,* 12 (November 1973), 304-325. Pp. 309-311. On Naipaul's negative attitude toward West Indian society.

159. Lee, R. H. "The Novels of V. S. Naipaul." *Theoria,* 27 (1966), 31-46.

160. Maes-Jelinek, H. "V. S. Naipaul: A Commonwealth Writer?" *Revue des Langues Vivantes,* 33 (1967), 499-513.

161. Mellors, John. "Mimics into Puppets: the fiction of V. S. Naipaul." *London Magazine,* 15 (February/March 1976), 117-121.

162. Mitchell, Julian. "Novel of a Somebody." *New Statesman,* 82 (17 December 1971), 868. Refers to the importance of Naipaul in the contemporary world of literature.

163. Moore, Gerald. "East Indians and West: The Novels of V. S. Naipaul." *Black Orpheus,* 7 (June 1960), 11-15.

164. Morris, Robert K. *Paradoxes of Order: Some Perspectives on the Fiction of V. S. Naipaul.* Columbia, Missouri: University of Missouri Press, 1975.

165. Naipaul, Shiva. "The writer without a society." *Commonwealth.* Papers delivered at the conference of Commonwealth literature, Aarhus University, 26-30 April 1971. Ed. Anna Rutherford. Aarhus, Denmark: Akademisk Boghandel Universitetsparken, 1971, pp. 114-123.

166. Nandkumar, Prema. "V. S. Naipaul." *The Glory and the Good.* New Delhi: Asia Publishing House, 1965.

167. Ormerod, David. "In a Derelict Land: The Novels of V. S. Naipaul." *Contemporary Literature,* 9 (Winter 1968), 74-90.

168. Page, Malcolm. "West Indian Writers." *Novel: A Forum on Fiction,* 3, No. 2 (Winter 1970), 167-172. Pp. 170-171.

169. Pooter. Untitled comments. *The* (London) *Times* (9 November 1968), p. 23. On Naipaul's winning the W. H. Smith Award for his *The Mimic Men.* Naipaul is interviewed.

170. Pritchett, V. S. "Crack-Up." *New York Review of Books,* 10 (11 April 1968), 10, 12-14. Review of *The Mimic Men* and *A Flag on the Island.*

171. Ramchand, Kenneth. *The West Indian Novel and Its Background.* London: Faber and Faber, 1970, pp. 5-9, 25, 27-28, 41, 90, 91, 102, 114, 123-125, 135, 136, 176,

189-204, 212, 223, 240, 261, 273.

172. —. *West Indian Narrative: An Introductory Anthology.* Ed. Kenneth Ramchand. London: Nelson, 1966, pp. 2, 147.

173. Rohlehr, Gordon. "The Ironic Approach: The Novels of V. S. Naipaul." *The Islands in Between: Essays in West Indian Literature.* Ed. Louis James. London: Oxford University Press, 1968, pp. 121-139.

174. Rowe-Evans, Adrian. "V. S. Naipaul." *Transition,* 40 (1971), 56-62. An interview.

175. Sertima, Ivan Van. "V. S. Naipaul," in his *Caribbean Writers: Critical Essays.* London and Port of Spain: New Beacon Books, 1968, pp. 39-41.

176. Shenker, Israel. "V. S. Naipaul, Man Without a Society." *New York Times Book Review* (October 1971), pp. 4, 22-24.

177. Theroux, Paul. *V. S. Naipaul: An Introduction to His Work.* London: Deutsch, 1972.

178. Thieme, John. "V. S. Naipaul's Third World: A Not So Free State." *Journal of Commonwealth Literature,* 10 (August 1975), 10-22.

179. Wakeman, John, and Stanley J. Kunitz, eds. "V(idiadhar) S(urajprasad) Naipaul," in their *World Authors 1950-1970.* New York: H. W. Wilson Company, 1975, pp. 1055-1056.

180. Walsh, William. "Necessary and Accommodated: The Work of V. S. Naipaul." *Lugano Review,* 1 (1965), 169-181.

181. —. "V. S. Naipaul." *A Manifold Voice: Studies in Commonwealth Literature.* London: Chatto and Windus, 1970; New York: Barnes and Noble, 1970, pp. 62-85.

182. —. "V. S. Naipaul: Mr. Biswas." *The Literary Criterion,* 10 (Summer 1972), 27-37.

183. —. *V. S. Naipaul.* Modern Writers Series. Edinburgh: Oliver and Boyd, 1973; reprinted in New York: Barnes and Noble, 1973.

III. STUDIES AND REVIEWS OF INDIVIDUAL WORKS

References to individual books by Naipaul also appear in the First Part of this bibliography. See the following numbers there: 147, 151, 175, 180, 182, 200, 251, 257, 263, 307, 327, 344.

The Mystic Masseur

184. Anon. "Briefing: *The Mystic Masseur.*" *Observer* (18 October 1964), p. 22.

185. —. "Huckster Hindu." *Time,* 73 (6 April 1959), 99.

186. —. "New Fiction." *The* (London) *Times* (23 May 1957), p. 15.

187. —. "Out of Joint." *TLS* (31 May 1957), p. 333.

188. Balliett, Whitney. "Made in the U.S.A." *New Yorker,* 35 (30 May 1959), 105-108. Pp. 107-108.

189. Baro, Gene. "Ganesh's Beguiling Exploits." *New York Herald Tribune Book Review,* 35 (7 June 1959), 6.

190. Bayley, John. "New Novels." *Spectator,* 198 (24 May 1957), 687-688. P. 688.

191. Levin, Martin. "How the Ball Bounces Down Trinidad Way." *New York Times Book Review* (12 April 1959), p. 5.

192. Nyren, Karl. *"The Mystic Masseur."* *Library Journal*, 84 (1 May 1959), 1533.

193. Quinton, Anthony. "New Novels." *New Statesman and Nation*, 53 (18 May 1957), 648-649. P. 649.

194. R. G. *"The Mystic Masseur."* *Punch*, 232 (26 June 1957), 807.

195. Wood, Percy. Review of *The Mystic Masseur*, in the *Chicago Sunday Tribune* (12 July 1959), p. 5.

The Suffrage of Elvira

196. Anon. "New Fiction." *The* (London) *Times* (24 April 1958), p. 13.

* 197. —. "Tropical Heat." *TLS* (2 May 1958), p. 237.

198. Newby, P. H. Untitled book review. *London Magazine*, 5 (November 1958), 82-84. Pp. 83-84.

199. Powell, Anthony. "Electoral Roll." *Punch*, 234 (30 April 1958), 587-588.

200. Richardson, Maurice. "New Novels." *New Statesman*, 55 (19 April 1958), 510-511.

Miguel Street

201. Anon. *"Miguel Street."* *Booklist*, 56 (1 July 1960), 654.

202. —. *"Miguel Street."* *Time*, 75 (30 May 1960), 79.

203. —. "New Fiction." *The* (London) *Times* (23 April 1959), p. 15.

204. —. "Street Scene." *TLS* (24 April 1959), p. 237.

205. Balliett, Whitney. "Soft Coal, Hard Coal." *New Yorker,* 36 (27 August 1960), 97-98, 100-101. Pp. 98, 100.

* 206. Coleman, John. "Last Words." *Spectator,* 202 (24 April 1959), 595.

207. Dawson, Helen. "Briefing: *Miguel Street." Observer* (15 August 1971), p. 18.

208. McMichael, George. Review of *Miguel Street,* in the *San Francisco Chronicle* (22 May 1960), p. 26.

209. Malone, Robert M. *"Miguel Street." Library Journal,* 85 (15 May 1960), 1938.

210. Payne, Robert. "Caribbean Carnival." *Saturday Review,* 43 (2 July 1960), 18.

211. Poore, Charles. "Books of the Times." *New York Times,* 109 (5 May 1960), 33.

212. R. S. Review of *Miguel Street,* in *Mexican Life,* 36 (June 1960), p. 35.

213. Richardson, Maurice. "New Novels." *New Statesman,* 57 (2 May 1959), 618-619. P. 618.

214. Rodman, Selden. "Catfish Row, Trinidad." *New York Times Book Review* (15 May 1960), p. 43.

215. Shrapnel, Norman. "This Mr. Cambridge Go Bawl." *Manchester Guardian* (24 April 1959), p. 4.

216. Wickenden, Dan. "Stories Told Under the Sun of Trinidad." *New York Herald Tribune Book Review,* 36 (22 May 1960), 10.

217. Wood, Percy. Review of *Miguel Street,* in the *Chicago Sunday Tribune* (15 May 1960), p. 6.

218. Wyndham, Francis.   Untitled book review.   *London Maga-zine*, 6 (September 1959), 78-81, 83-84.   Pp. 80-81.

A House for Mr. Biswas

219. Anon.   *"A House for Mr. Biswas."*   *Kirkus*, 30 (1 March 1962), 249.

220. —.   "Also Current."   *Time*, 79 (22 June 1962), 96.

221. —.   "High Jinks in Trinidad."   *TLS* (29 September 1961), p. 641.

222. Archer, Rosanne K.   *"A House for Mr. Biswas."*   *New York Herald Tribune Books*, 38 (24 June 1962), 6-7.

223. Bagai, Leona Bell.   *"A House for Mr. Biswas."*   *Books Abroad*, 36 (Autumn 1962), 453.

224. Balliett, Whitney.   "Wrong Pulpit."   *New Yorker*, 38 (4 August 1962), 69-71.   Pp. 70-71.

225. Braithwaite, Edward.   "West Indian Prose Fiction in the Sixties: A Survey."   *Critical Survey*, 3 (Winter 1967), 169-174; reprinted in *Caribbean Quarterly*, 16 (September 1970), 5-17.   Includes comments on *A House for Mr. Biswas*.

226. Chapin, Louis.   "Fiction of South India and the West Indies: *A House for Mr. Biswas.*"   *Christian Science Monitor*, 54 (19 July 1962), 11.

227. Dawson, Helen.   "Briefing: *A House for Mr. Biswas.*"   *Observer* (2 November 1969), p. 31.

228. Eimerl, Sarel.   "A Trinidadian Dickens."   *Reporter*, 27 (19 July 1962), 56-57.

229. Fido, Martin.   "Mr. Biswas and Mr. Polly."   *Ariel*, 5 (Octo-

ber 1974), 30-37.

230. Figueroa, John J. M. "Some Provisional Comments on West Indian Novels." *Commonwealth Literature.* Ed. John Press. London: Heinemann, 1965.

231. Gilbert, Morris. "Hapless Defiance." *New York Times Book Review* (24 June 1962), p. 30.

232. Harris, Wilson. "Comedy of Pathos," in his *Tradition and the West Indian Novel.* London: Telmow Press, 1965; London: Beacon, 1967, pp. 39-40.

233. —. *Modern Black Novelists: A Collection of Critical Essays.* Ed. Michael G. Cooke. Englewood Cliffs, New Jersey: Prentice-Hall, 1971, p. 38.

234. Jacobson, Dan. "Self-Help in Hot Places." *New Statesman,* 62 (29 September 1961), 440-441.

235. James, Louis. "Islands of Man: Reflections on the Emergence of a West Indian Literature." *Southern Review,* 2, No. 2 (1966), 150-163. Includes comments on *A House for Mr. Biswas.*

236. Keown, Eric. "New Fiction." *Punch,* 241 (25 October 1961), 624.

237. Krikler, Bernard. "V. S. Naipaul's *A House for Mr. Biswas.*" *Listener,* 71 (13 February 1964), 270-271.

* 238. Lamming, George. Review of *A House for Mr. Biswas,* in *Time and Tide* (5 October 1961), p. 1657.

239. Mann, Charles W., Jr. *"A House for Mr. Biswas." Library Journal,* 87 (15 May 1962), 1917.

240. Mehta, D. N. "Naipaul's Ambivalence: *A House for Mr. Biswas." Vidya,* 14, No. 1 (1971), 11-26.

241. Ormerod, David. "Theme and Image in V. S. Naipaul's *A House for Mr. Biswas.*" *Texas Studies in Literature and Language,* 8 (Winter 1967), 589-602.

242. Ramchand, Kenneth. "The West Indies." *Literature of the World in English.* Ed. Bruce King. London and Boston: Routledge and Kegan Paul, 1974, pp. 192-211. Pp. 206-208.

243. Rogers, W. G. "Be It Ever So Humble." *Saturday Review,* 45 (9 June 1962), 37.

244. Rohlehr, Gordon. "Character and Rebellion in *A House for Mr. Biswas.*" *New World Quarterly,* 4, No. 4 (1968), 66-72.

245. Shenfield, Margaret. "Mr. Biswas and Mr. Polly." *English,* 23 (Autumn 1974), 95-100.

246. Wyndham, Francis. *"A House for Mr. Biswas."* *London Magazine,* n.s. 1 (October 1961), 90-93.

Mr. Stone and the Knights Companion

247. Allen, Walter. "London Again." *New York Review of Books,* 2 (19 March 1964), 21.

248. Anon. "A Short, Painful Life." *Time,* 83 (28 February 1964), 110, 112.

249. —. "Briefly Noted." *New Yorker,* 40 (7 March 1964), 181.

250. —. "New Fiction." *The* (London) *Times* (30 May 1963), p. 16.

251. —. "Sunk in Suburbia." *TLS* (31 May 1963), p. 385.

252. Boxill, A. "Concept of Spring in V. S. Naipaul's *Mr. Stone and the Knights Companion.*" *Ariel,* 5 (October 1974),

21-28.

253. Brooke, Jocelyn. "Two Comedies." *Listener,* 69 (30 May 1963), 934.

254. Cruttwell, Patrick. "Fiction Chronicle." *Hudson Review,* 17 (Summer 1964), 303-311. P. 311.

255. Dathorne, O. R. Review of *Mr. Stone and the Knights Companion,* in *Black Orpheus,* 14 (February 1964), 59-60.

256. Duchene, Anne. "A martyr of the suburbs." *Manchester Guardian Weekly,* 88 (6 June 1963), 11.

257. Frakes, James. "10K Golden Years." *Book Week,* 1 (22 March 1964), 16.

258. Gleason, J. Review of *Mr. Stone and the Knights Companion,* in the *San Francisco Chronicle* (15 March 1964), p. 41.

259. Mann, Charles W., Jr. *"Mr. Stone and the Knights Companion." Library Journal,* 88 (15 December 1963), 4789.

260. Mitchell, Adrian. "Styles and Dreams." *Spectator,* 210 (21 June 1963), 815.

261. Price, R. G. G. "New Novels." *Punch,* 244 (12 June 1963), 865-866. P. 865.

262. Pritchett, V. S. "Climacteric." *New Statesman,* 65 (31 May 1963), 831-832.

263. Pryce-Jones, Alan. Review of *Mr. Stone and the Knights Companion,* in the *New York Herald Tribune* (7 March 1964), p. 13.

264. Ross, Alan. Review of *Mr. Stone and the Knights Companion,* in *London Magazine,* 3 (August 1963), 87-88.

265. Wood, Percy. Review of *Mr. Stone and the Knights Companion*, in the *Chicago Sunday Tribune Magazine* (9 February 1964), p. 4.

The Mimic Men

266. Anon. "Suburbia in the Sun." *TLS* (27 April 1967), p. 349.

267. —. *"The Mimic Men."* *Kirkus*, 35 (15 July 1967), 831.

268. —. *"The Mimic Men."* *Publishers' Weekly*, 192 (10 July 1967), 176.

269. Beloff, Max. "Verandahs of Impotence." *Encounter*, 29 (October 1967), 87-88, 90.

270. Blackburn, Sara. "Book Marks." *Nation*, 205 (9 October 1967), 347-348.

271. Boston, Richard. "Caribbean and Aegean." *The* (London) *Times* (27 April 1967), p. 16.

272. Corke, Hilary. "New Fiction." *Listener*, 77 (25 May 1967), 693.

273. Curley, Arthur. *"The Mimic Men."* *Library Journal*, 92 (15 September 1967), 3057.

274. Gray, Simon. "A Man of Style." *New Statesman*, 73 (5 May 1967), 622-623.

275. Lask, Thomas. "Shadow and Substance." *New York Times*, 117 (16 December 1967), 39.

276. Maloff, Saul. "Yesterday in Isabella." *New York Times Book Review* (15 October 1967), p. 55.

277. Miller, Karl. "V. S. Naipaul and the New Order." *Kenyon*

Review, 29 (November 1967), 685-698.

278. Plant, Richard. "Caribbean Seesaw." *Saturday Review,* 50 (23 December 1967), 32-33.

279. Price, R. G. G. "New Novels." *Punch,* 252 (10 May 1967), 696.

280. Pryce-Jones, David. Untitled book review. *London Magazine,* n.s. 7 (May 1967), 82-84.

281. Ramraj, Victor. "The All-Embracing Christlike Vision: Tone and Attitude in *The Mimic Men." Commonwealth.* Papers delivered at the conference of Commonwealth Literature, Aarhus University, 26-30 April 1971. Ed. Anna Rutherford. Aarhus, Denmark: Akademisk Boghandel Universitetsparken, 1971, pp. 125-134.

282. Rickards, C. Review of *The Mimic Men,* in *Books and Bookmen,* 13 (October 1967), 47.

283. Seymour-Smith, Martin. "Exile's story." *Spectator,* 218 (5 May 1967), 528-529. P. 528.

284. Thorpe, Marjorie. *"The Mimic Men:* A Study in Isolation." *New World Quarterly,* 4, No. 4 (1968), 55-59.

285. Wain, John. "Trouble in the Family." *New York Review of Books,* 9 (26 October 1967), 32-35. Pp. 33-35.

286. Wilson, Angus. "Between two islands." *Observer* (30 April 1967), p. 27.

In A Free State

287. Adams, Phoebe. *"In a Free State." Atlantic,* 228 (December 1971), 135.

288. Anon. *"In a Free State."* British Book News (January

1972), p. 84.

289. —. *"In a Free State."* Kirkus, 39 (15 July 1971), 768.

290. —. *"In a Free State."* Publishers' Weekly, 200 (12 July 1971), 65.

291. —. "Nowhere to go." *TLS* (8 October 1971), p. 1199.

* 292. —. "Unstable sequence." *Economist*, 241 (6 November 1971), Autumn Survey, iii-iv.

293. Calder, Angus. "Darkest Naipaulia." *New Statesman*, 82 (8 October 1971), 482-483.

294. Cheuse, Alan. "This Was the Famous View." *Nation*, 214 (17 January 1972), 87-88.

295. Enright, D. J. *"In a Free State."* BBC Arts Commentary, 1971; reprinted in *Readings in Commonwealth Literature.* Ed. William Walsh. Oxford: Clarendon Press, 1973, pp. 337-339.

296. Gordimer, Nadine. "White expatriates and black mimics." *New York Times Book Review* (17 October 1971), pp. 5, 20.

297. Gross, John. "Books of the Year." *Observer* (19 December 1971), p. 17.

298. Hope, Francis. "Displaced persons." *Observer* (3 October 1971), p. 37.

299. Kazin, Alfred. "Displaced Person." *New York Review of Books*, 17 (30 December 1971), 3-4.

300. Lane, M. Travis. "The Casualties of Freedom: V. S. Naipaul's *In a Free State." World Literature Written in English*, 12 (April 1973), 106-110.

301. Larson, Charles R. *"In a Free State."* *Saturday Review*, 54 (23 October 1971), 91-92.

302. Lask, Thomas. "Where Is the Enemy?" *New York Times*, 121 (25 December 1971), 15.

303. McGuinness, Frank. "A Rough Game." *London Magazine*, n.s. 11 (October/November 1971), 156-158.

304. Maloff, Saul. *"In a Free State."* *Commonweal*, 95 (3 December 1971), 232.

305. Mann, Charles W., Jr. *"In a Free State."* *Library Journal*, 96 (1 September 1971), 2671-2672.

306. Murray, Isobel. "Questions of freedom." *Financial Times* (7 October 1971), p. 28.

307. Parker, Dorothy L. "All very far from home." *Christian Science Monitor*, 63 (26 November 1971), B4.

308. Potter, Dennis. "A long way from Home." *The* (London) *Times* (4 October 1971), p. 15.

309. Theroux, Paul. "To be without roots." *Book World*, 5 (5 December 1971), 22.

310. Waugh, Auberon. "Auberon Waugh on V. S. Naipaul." *Spectator*, 227 (9 October 1971), 511. Response by Alison Clode in *Spectator*, 227 (16 October 1971), 560.

311. Webb, W. L. "Exiles." *Guardian*, 105 (16 October 1971), 23.

312. Wyndham, Francis. "V. S. Naipaul." *Listener*, 86 (7 October 1971), 461-462.

Guerrillas

313. Ackroyd, Peter. "On heat." *Spectator,* 235 (13 September 1975), 350.

314. Anon. *"Guerrillas."* *British Book News* (December 1975), p. 926.

315. —. *"Guerrillas."* *Kirkus,* 43 (1 September 1975), 1016.

316. —. *"Guerrillas."* *Publishers' Weekly,* 208 (22 September 1975), 130.

317. —. *"Guerrillas."* *Virginia Quarterly Review,* 52 (Spring 1976), 56.

318. Coombs, Orde. "Madness Among the Made-Up People." *National Observer* (31 January 1976), p. 21.

319. DeMott, Benjamin. "Lost Worlds, Lost Heroes." *Saturday Review,* 3 (15 November 1975), 23-24.

320. Hamner, Robert D. *"Guerrillas."* *Library Journal,* 100 (1 October 1975), 1846.

321. Jones, D. A. N. "Little warriors in search of a war." *TLS* (12 September 1975), p. 1013.

322. Kramer, Hilton. "Naipaul's Guerrillas and Oates's Assassins." *Commentary,* 61 (March 1976), 54-57.

323. Miller, Karl. "In Scorn and Pity." *New York Review of Books,* 22 (11 December 1975), 3-4.

324. Reedy, Gerard C. "The Best Springtime Reading: *Guerrillas."* *America,* 134 (1 May 1976), 385.

325. Review of *Guerrillas,* in *Guardian Weekly,* 113 (20 September 1975), p. 23.

326. Review of *Guerrillas*, in the *Listener*, 94 (25 September 1975), 410.

327. Thwaite, Anthony. "The heart of darkness." *Observer* (14 September 1975), p. 25.

328. Walsh, William. "Unhealing powers." *New Review*, 2 (October 1975), 64-65.

329. Wyndham, Francis. "Services Rendered." *New Statesman*, 90 (19 September 1975), 339-340.

A Flag on the Island

330. Anon. *"A Flag on the Island."* *Kirkus*, 36 (1 January 1968), 25.

331. —. *"A Flag on the Island."* *Publishers' Weekly*, 193 (15 January 1968), 83.

332. —. "Movietone." *TLS* (14 September 1967), p. 813.

333. Barker, Paul. "Fiction of the week." *The* (London) *Times* (14 September 1967), p. 11.

334. Buchan, William. "Out of school." *Spectator*, 219 (22 September 1967), 328-329.

335. Hartman, John W. *"A Flag on the Island."* *Best Sellers*, 28 (15 April 1968), 29.

336. McInnis, Raymond G. *"A Flag on the Island."* *Library Journal*, 93 (1 March 1968), 1021.

337. MacNamara, Desmond. "Flayed Skin." *New Statesman*, 74 (15 September 1967), 325.

338. Marsh, Pamela. " 'Fiction-concentrate.' " *Christian Science Monitor*, 60 (29 March 1968), 13.

339. Miller, Karl. "Naipaul's Emergent Country." *Listener,* 78 (28 September 1967), 402-403.

340. Plant, Richard. "Potpourri of the Antilles." *New York Times Book Review* (8 June 1968), p. 52.

341. Price, R. G. G. "New Novels." *Punch,* 253 (27 September 1967), 484.

342. Wain, John. "Characters in the Sun." *New York Times Book Review* (7 April 1968), p. 4.

The Middle Passage

342. Allen, Walter. "Fear of Trinidad." *New Statesman,* 64 (3 August 1962), 149-150.

343. Anon. "Credit Balance." *Punch,* 243 (8 August 1962), 213.

344. —. "General." *New Yorker,* 39 (12 October 1963), 213-214.

345. —. "On and Off Miguel Street." *The* (London) *Times* (2 August 1962), p. 13.

346. —. *"The Middle Passage."* *Encounter,* 19 (September 1962), 84.

347. —. "The Re-Engagement of Mr. Naipaul." *TLS* (10 August 1962), p. 578.

348. Bedford, Sybille. "Stoic Traveler." *New York Review of Books,* 1 (14 November 1963), 4-5.

349. Bryden, Ronald. "New Map of Hell." *Spectator,* 209 (3 August 1962), 161.

350. Davies, Barrie. "The Sense of Abroad: Aspects of the West

Indian Novel in England." *World Literature Written in English*, 11 (November 1972), 67-80. P. 68.

351. Di Giovanni, Norman T. "Return of a West Indian." *Nation*, 197 (26 October 1963), 262-263.

352. Dolbier, Maurice. Review of *The Middle Passage*, in the *New York Herald Tribune* (3 September 1963), p. 19.

353. J. N. Review of *The Middle Passage*, in *Mexican Life*, 39 (October 1963), 36-37.

354. Jabavu, Noni. "Return of an Insider." *New York Times Book Review* (22 September 1963), p. 14.

355. Johansson, Bertram B. "Caribbean Counterpoint." *Christian Science Monitor*, 55 (30 October 1963), 9.

356. Lucie-Smith, Edward. Review of *The Middle Passage*, in the *Listener*, 68 (16 August 1962), 254-255.

357. Malan, Harrison B. *"The Middle Passage..."* *Library Journal*, 88 (15 October 1963), 3842-3843.

* 358. Poore, Charles. "A Native's Return to the Caribbean World." *New York Times*, 112 (7 September 1963), 17.

An Area of Darkness

359. Anon. *"An Area of Darkness."* *Booklist*, 61 (15 May 1965), 897-898.

360. —. *"An Area of Darkness."* *Time*, 85 (23 April 1965), 109-110.

361. —. "Areas of Promise." *TLS* (24 September 1964), p. 879.

362. —. "Mr. Naipaul's Passage to India." *TLS* (24 September 1964), p. 881.

363. —. "Paperbacks: *An Area of Darkness.*" *The* (London) *Times* (16 November 1968), p. 23.

364. —. "Too Great a Burden." *Economist,* 213 (12 December 1964), 1257.

365. —. "West Indian Writer Visits Home of His Ancestors." *The* (London) *Times* (17 September 1964), p. 17.

366. Benda, Harry J. "India and Indonesia." *Yale Review,* n.s. 55 (Autumn 1965), 121-126. Pp. 121-123.

367. Biswas, Robin. "Exhaustion and Persistence." *Tamarack Review,* 35 (Spring 1965), 75-80.

368. Bram, Joseph. *"An Area of Darkness."* *Library Journal,* 90 (15 April 1965), 1904.

369. Casson, Sir Hugh. "Books of the Year." *Observer* (20 December 1964), p. 7.

370. Dathorne, O. R. Review of *An Area of Darkness,* in *Black Orpheus,* 18 (October 1965), 60-61.

371. Delany, Austin. "Mother India as Bitch." *Transition,* 5, No. 26 (1966), 50-51.

372. Enright, D. J. "Who is India? On V. S. Naipaul's Journey into 'Darkness'." *Encounter,* 23 (December 1964), 59-62, 64.

373. Gupta, K. *"An Area of Darkness: An Experience of India."* *Canadian Forum,* 45 (June 1965), 70.

374. Hitrec, Joseph. "A Disenchanted Journey." *Saturday Review,* 48 (1 May 1965), 42.

375. Kapoor, S. D. "A Study in Contrasts." *Calcutta Review,* 178 (March 1966), 165-170. P. 170.

376. Mander, John. "The Anglo-Indian Theme." *Commentary,* 39 (June 1965), 94-97.

377. Muggeridge, Malcolm. "Books." *Esquire,* 64 (October 1965), 26, 28, 32. P. 28.

378. Narasimhaiah, C. D. " 'Somewhere Something Has Snapped': A Close Look at V. S. Naipaul's *An Area of Darkness." Literary Criterion, Mysore,* 6, No. 4 (1965), 83-96.

379. Natwar-Singh, K. "Unhappy Pilgrim." *New York Times Book Review* (11 July 1965), p. 35.

380. Oberbeck, Stephen. "Angry Young Indian." *Newsweek,* 65 (19 April 1965), 103-104. Includes Oberbeck's interview of Naipaul.

381. Prescott, Orville. "The Land of His Ancestors." *New York Times,* 114 (16 April 1965), 27.

382. Pritchett, V. S. "Back to India." *New Statesman,* 68 (11 September 1964), 361-362.

383. Pryce-Jones, Alan. Review of *An Area of Darkness,* in the *New York Herald Tribune,* 125 (20 April 1965), 25.

384. Rao, Raja. "Out of step with Shiva." *Book Week,* 2 (29 August 1965), 4, 14.

385. Rau, Santha Rama. "Two Descriptions of the Elephant." *Reporter,* 33 (9 September 1965), 40, 42-43. Pp. 40, 42.

386. Reed, Henry. "Passage to India." *Spectator,* 213 (2 October 1964), 452-453.

387. Sheehan, Edward R. F. "Cities of the Dreadful Night." *Nation,* 202 (14 March 1966), 300-302. P. 300.

388. Wain, John. "Mother India." *Observer* (13 September

1964), p. 24.

389. Walsh, William. "Meeting Extremes." *Journal of Commonwealth Literature,* No. 1 (September 1965), 169-172. Pp. 170-172.

390. Wordsworth, Christopher. "A pageant of apathy." *Manchester Guardian Weekly,* 91 (17 September 1964), 10.

The Loss of El Dorado

391. Adams, Phoebe. *"The Loss of El Dorado."* Atlantic, 225 (May 1970), 132.

392. Anon. "Slave Colony." *Economist,* 233 (8 November 1969), Autumn Survey, iv.

393. —. "The failings of an Empire." *TLS* (25 December 1969), p. 1471.

394. —. *"The Loss of El Dorado; a history."* Booklist, 67 (1 September 1970), 34.

395. —. *"The Loss of El Dorado: a History."* British Book News (February 1970), p. 166.

396. —. *"The Loss of El Dorado."* Kirkus, 38 (15 February 1970), 224.

397. —. *"The Loss of El Dorado."* Publishers' Weekly, 197 (2 February 1970), 86.

398. —. "The Year's Best Books." *Time,* 97 (4 January 1971), 76.

399. —. "To Dream No More." *Time,* 95 (25 May 1970), 105-106.

400. Bromé, Joseph A. *"The Loss of El Dorado."* Library

Journal, 95 (1 April 1970), 1367.

401. Bryden, Ronald. "Between the Epics." *New Statesman,* 78 (7 November 1969), 661-662.

402. Cheuse, Alan. "The Realms of Gold." *Nation,* 211 (5 October 1970), 311-312.

403. Dawson, Helen. "Briefing: *The Loss of El Dorado.*" *Observer* (23 September 1973), p. 33.

404. Elliott, J. H. "Triste Trinidad." *New York Review of Books,* 14 (21 May 1970), 25-27.

405. Gott, Richard. "Trinidad legacy." *Guardian Weekly,* 101 (29 November 1969), 18.

406. Greene, Graham. "Terror in Trinidad." *Observer* (26 October 1969), p. 34.

407. Innes, Hammond. "For God and Profit." *Spectator,* 223 (8 November 1969), 647-648.

408. Knappman, Edward W. "Colonial Vicitms." *Progressive,* 35 (April 1971), 49-51.

409. Lask, Thomas. "Brave New World." *New York Times,* 119 (20 June 1970), 27.

410. Maes-Jelinek, Hena. "The Myth of El Dorado in the Caribbean Novel." *Journal of Commonwealth Literature,* 6 (June 1971), 113-128. Pp. 113-116, 127.

411. May, Derwent. "A black tale." *The* (London) *Times* (1 November 1969), p. V.

412. Millar, Neil. "Slavery's high cost." *Christian Science Monitor,* 62 (28 May 1970), 13.

413. Miller, Karl. "Power, Glory and Imposture." *Listener,*

82 (13 November 1969), 673-674.

414. Plumb, J. H. "A Nightmare World of Fantasy and Murder." *Book World*, 4 (19 April 1970), 1, 3.

415. Rabassa, Gregory. "The Dark Obverse Side of the Shining Myth." *New York Times Book Review* (24 May 1970), pp. 7, 22.

416. Review of *The Loss of El Dorado*, in the *American Historical Review*, 76 (June 1971), 848.

417. Rodman, Selden. "Three on Latin America." *National Review*, 22 (6 October 1970), 1064-1065. P. 1065.

418. Updike, John. "Fool's Gold." *New Yorker*, 46 (8 August 1970), 72-76.

The Overcrowded Barracoon

419. Anon. "Briefing: Paperback choice." *Observer* (11 July 1976), p. 21.

420. —. "In search of another country." *TLS* (17 November 1972), p. 1391.

421. —. *"The Overcrowded Barracoon and Other Articles."* *British Book News* (March 1973), p. 212.

422. —. *"The Overcrowded Barracoon."* *Choice,* 10 (June 1973), 610.

423. —. *"The Overcrowded Barracoon."* *Kirkus,* 41 (1 February 1973), 171.

424. —. *"The Overcrowded Barracoon."* *New York Times Book Review* (16 September 1973), p. 18.

425. —. *"The Overcrowded Barracoon."* *Publishers' Weekly,*

203 (22 January 1973), 62.

426. Bryden, Ronald. "The Hurricane." *Listener,* 88 (9 November 1972), 641.

427. Green, Martin. "Naipaul's burden." *Guardian,* 107 (4 November 1972), 21.

428. Harrison, Tony. "Fantasia-Asia." *London Magazine,* n.s. 12 (December 1972/January 1973), 135-140.

429. Hope, Francis. "Areas of darkness." *Observer* (29 October 1972), p. 38.

430. Jebb, Julian. "Cogent prophet." *Financial Times* (15 December 1972), p. 34.

431. McSweeney, Kerry. "The Editor's Column." *Queen's Quarterly,* 80 (Autumn 1973), 494-497. Pp. 495-497.

432. Mukherjee, Bharati. "Colonies: Caste Adrift." *Book World,* 7 (18 March 1973), 4, 8.

433. Parker, Dorothy L. " 'To be a member of a minority always seemed to me attractive.' " *Christian Science Monitor,* 65 (14 March 1973), 13.

434. Potter, Dennis. "The writer and his myth." *The* (London) *Times* (4 December 1972), p. 6.

435. Theroux, Paul. "Perfection, punctuality and Gloucester cheese." *Daily Telegraph Magazine* (27 October 1972), pp. 37-38, 40.

ANTHONY [DYMOKE] POWELL
(Born in London 1905)

I. PRIMARY WORKS: EARLY NOVELS

1. *Afternoon Men.* London: Duckworth, 1931; New York: Holt, 1932; London: Heinemann, 1952, 1954, 1960, 1967; Harmondsworth: Penguin, 1963; Boston: Little, Brown, 1963; London: Fontana, 1973.

2. *Venusberg.* London: Duckworth, 1932; London: Heinemann, 1955, 1957, 1962; Harmondsworth: Penguin, 1961; as *Venusbjerget.* Trans. Ole Storm. Copenhagen: Aschehoug, 1948; as *Venusberg.* Trans. Bruno Fonzi. Turin: Einaudi, 1969.

3. *From a View to a Death.* London: Duckworth, 1933; London: John Lehmann, 1948, 1952; London: Heinemann, 1954, 1960; Harmondsworth: Penguin, 1961; Boston: Little, Brown, 1964, 1968; London: Fontana, 1968; as *Mr. Zouch: Superman: From a View to a Death.* New York: Vanguard, 1934; as *Paesaggio E Morte.* Trans. Giuliana Scudder. Milano: Garzanti, 1963.

4. *Agents and Patients.* London: Duckworth, 1936, 1938; London: Heinemann, 1955, 1957, 1962; Harmondsworth: Penguin, 1962; with *Venusberg,* as *Two Novels.* New York: Periscope-Holliday, 1952; Boston: Little, Brown, 1965.

5. *What's Become of Waring.* London: Cassell, 1939; London: Heinemann, 1953, 1961, 1964; Harmondsworth:

Penguin, 1962; Boston: Little, Brown, 1963; London: Fontana, 1969.

A Dance to the Music of Time Series

6. *A Question of Upbringing.* London: Heinemann, 1951, 1954, 1955, 1961, 1963; New York: Scribners, 1951; Harmondsworth: Penguin, 1962; New York: Berkley, 1965; London: Fontana, 1967; as *Question d'education.* Trans. Renée Villoteau. Paris: Julliard, 1954; as *En Fråga om Uppfostran.* Trans. Sonja Bergvall. Stockholm: A. Bonnier, 1964.

7. *A Buyer's Market.* London: Heinemann, 1952, 1954, 1964; New York: Scribners, 1953; Harmondsworth: Penguin, 1962; New York: Berkley, 1965; London: Fontana, 1967; as *Les mouvements du coeur.* Paris: Julliard, 1955; as *Köparens Marknad.* Trans. Sonja Bergvall. Stockholm: A. Bonnier, 1965.

8. *The Acceptance World.* London: Heinemann, 1955, 1956, 1968; New York: Farrar, Straus, 1956; New York: Meridian, 1960; Harmondsworth: Penguin, 1962; New York: Berkley, 1965; London: Fontana, 1967; with *A Question of Upbringing* and *A Buyer's Market,* as *A Dance to the Music of Time: First Movement.* London: Heinemann, 1962; Boston: Little, Brown, 1962; as *Tanz zur Zeitmusik.* Trans. Bernard Schlenzmann. Stuttgart: Verlags-Anstalt, 1966; as *L'acceptation.* Trans. Renée Villoteau. Paris: Julliard, 1956.

9. *At Lady Molly's.* London: Heinemann, 1957; Boston: Little, Brown, 1958; Harmondsworth: Penguin, 1963; London: Fontana, 1969; as *Lady Molly's Menagerie.* Trans. Katharina Focke. Stuttgart: Cotta, 1961.

10. *Casanova's Chinese Restaurant.* London: Heinemann, 1960; Boston: Little, Brown, 1960; Harmondsworth: Penguin, 1964; London: Fontana, 1970.

11. *The Kindly Ones.* London: Heinemann, 1962; Boston: Little, Brown, 1962; Harmondsworth: Penguin, 1965; London: Fontana, 1971; with *At Lady Molly's* and *Casanova's Chinese Restaurant,* as *A Dance to the Music of Time: Second Movement.* Boston: Little, Brown, 1964.

12. *The Valley of Bones.* London: Heinemann, 1964; Boston: Little, Brown, 1964; n.p., 1968; Harmondsworth: Penguin, 1968; London: Fontana, 1973.

13. *The Soldier's Art.* London: Heinemann, 1966; Boston: Little, Brown, 1966; London: Fontana, 1968.

14. *The Military Philosophers.* London: Heinemann, 1968; Boston: Little, Brown, 1969; London: Fontana, 1971; with *The Valley of Bones* and *The Soldier's Art,* as *A Dance to the Music of Time: Third Movement.* Boston: Little, Brown, 1971.

15. *Books Do Furnish A Room.* London: Heinemann, 1971; Boston: Little, Brown, 1971; London: Fontana, 1972.

16. *Temporary Kings.* London: Heinemann, 1973; Boston: Little, Brown, 1973; London: Fontana, 1974.

17. *Hearing Secret Harmonies.* London: Heinemann, 1975; Boston: Little, Brown, 1976; with *Books Do Furnish A Room* and *Temporary Kings,* as *A Dance to the Music of Time: Fourth Movement.* Boston: Little, Brown, 1976.

18. Four volumes of *A Dance to the Music of Time* are expected to be completed in the Winter 1976-1977 by Popular Library, in New York. Each volume contains three novels, beginning with *Spring* which contains the

first three of the sequence. The final volume, *Winter,* will contain the last three of the sequence. The middle volumes are *Summer* and *Autumn.*

PRIMARY WORKS: SHORT STORIES

19. "Greyfriars Nationalized." *Punch,* 224 (15 April 1953), 458-459. A short story farce.

20. "Hal o' the Ministry." *Punch,* 228 (9 February 1955), 196-197.

21. "Angus and the Rag." *Punch,* 234 (5 March 1958), 326.

22. "A Reference to Mellors." *Vogue,* 148 (December 1966), 126-127; reprinted in *Winter's Tales 12.* Ed. A. D. Maclean. London: Macmillan, 1966.

23. "Richard Walker." *Punch,* 261 (6 October 1971), 465. A delightful short story by Powell about a man who becomes obsessed in reading *A Dance to the Music of Time.*

PRIMARY WORKS: PLAYS

24. "Afternoon Men" (produced in London, 1963).

25. *Two Plays: The Garden God* and *The Rest I'll Whistle.* With four set designs by Osbert Lancaster. London: Heinemann, 1971; Boston: Little, Brown, 1972.

PRIMARY WORKS: POEMS

26. *Caledonia.* Privately printed, 1934.

27. "Lost Leaders or Strayed Revellers?" *New Statesman and Nation,* 19 (17 February 1940), 204.

PRIMARY WORKS: OTHER

28. Editor. *Barnard Letters, 1778-1824*. London: Duckworth, 1928.

29. "The Wat'ry Glade." *The Old School: Essays by Divers Hands*. Ed. Graham Greene. London: Cape, 1934, pp. 147-162. A memoir of Eton.

30. "The Derwentwater Claimant." *Spectator*, 159 (26 November 1937), 946-947. On Amelia Mary Tudor Radcliffe, Countess of Derwentwater.

31. "Marginal Comments." *Spectator*, 159 (3 December 1937), 991. On the *Left Review* pamphlet, *Authors Take Sides*.

32. "Marginal Comments." *Spectator*, 159 (10 December 1937), 1047. On the false image of the British people in the minds of Americans.

33. "Marginal Comments." *Spectator*, 159 (31 December 1937), 1175. On European cooking.

34. "The Starry Messengers." *Spectator*, 162 (21 April 1939), 664-665. On 17th-century astrologers.

35. "John Aubrey." *TLS* (1 July 1939), p. 390. A letter to the editor. Powell requests information from the public on Aubrey.

36. "Aspects of Uncertainty." *Spectator*, 163 (11 August 1939), 225. Review of four autobiographies: H. M. Taylor's *No One to Blame: An Autobiography*, Alyse Simpson's *The Convent*, Lady Sybil Lubbock's *The Child in the Crystal*, and B. L. Coombes's *These Poor Hands: a Miner's Autobiography*.

37. " 'There Lies a Vale in Ida.' " *Spectator*, 163 (22 September 1939), 415-416. Review of two travel books: Sidney

W. Hopper's *Greek Earth,* and Dorothy Una Ratcliffe's *News of Persephone.*

38. "The Headmaster's Benjamin." *Spectator,* 163 (6 October 1939), 480. Review of A. A. Milne's *It's Too Late Now: the Autobiography of a Writer.*

39. "A Studio with a View." *Spectator,* 163 (13 October 1939), 516, 518. Review of Jacques-Emile Blanche's *More Portraits of a Lifetime: 1918-1938.*

40. "Three Americans." *Spectator,* 163 (20 October 1939), 552, 554. Review of Ruth St. Denis's *An Unfinished Life,* Maurice Hindus's *Green Worlds: A Story of Two Villages,* and R. Smith and N. Beasley's *Carter Glass: A Biography.*

41. "Bat and Ball." *Spectator,* 163 (27 October 1939), 598. Review of C. B. Fry's autobiography, *Life Worth Living: Some Phases of an Englishman.*

42. "Der Grossbritannischermilitarattache." *Spectator,* 163 (17 November 1939), 706. Review of Colonel Sir Thomas Montgomery-Cuninghame's autobiography, *Dusty Measure: a Record of Troubled Times.*

43. "Enter a Child." *Spectator,* 163 (24 November 1939), 756. Review of Dormer Creston's *Enter a Child.*

44. "Lively Lives." *Spectator,* 163 (1 December 1939), 794. Review of three autobiographies: Owen Berkeley-Hill's *All Too Human: An Unconventional Autobiography,* William Holt's *I Haven't Unpacked: An Autobiography,* and Edward J. Bing's *Of the Meek and the Mighty.*

45. "War in the Snow." *Spectator,* 163 (8 December 1939), 826. Review of J. O. Hannula's *Finland's War of Independence.*

46. "Left Wings—They Never Grow Weary." *Spectator,* 163

(15 December 1939), 874, 876. Review of John Lehmann's *Down River: a Danubian Study*, and Leonard Mosley's *Down Stream.*

47. "The Other Amiel—I." *Cornhill*, 161 (December 1945), 481-488. On Henri-Fréderic Amiel's diary, *Journal Intime.*

48. "Brains Trusteeship." *Spectator*, 176 (1 February 1946), 122. Review of A. B. Campbell's *Come Alongside.*

49. "Brogan Meats." *Spectator*, 176 (22 February 1946), 202, 204. Review of Colm Brogan's *The Democrat at the Supper Table.*

50. "John Aubrey." *TLS* (2 March 1946), p. 103. A letter to the editor; Powell requests information on a lost manuscript of Aubrey's.

51. "Periodical Depressions." *Spectator*, 176 (5 April 1946), 358. Review of four periodicals: *Orion: A Miscellany* (2), *The Windmill*, *New Writing*, and *Writing To-day.*

52. "The Other Amiel—II." *Cornhill*, 162 (April 1946), 78-86. A continuation of I.

53. "The Writing of Dan McGrew." *Spectator*, 176 (3 May 1946), 460. Review of Robert W. Service's *Ploughman of the Moon: An Adventure into Memory.*

54. "Our Recent Writers." *Spectator*, 176 (21 June 1946), 642, 644. Review of H. V. Routh's *English History and Ideas in the Twentieth Century.*

55. "Passing Periodicals." *Spectator*, 177 (19 July 1946), 68, 70. Review of seven periodicals.

56. "American Angles." *Spectator*, 177 (26 July 1946), 94, 96. Review of Robert S. Arbib Jr's *Here We Are Together: The Notebook of an American Soldier in Bri-*

tain, and Damon Runyon's *Runyon à la Carte.*

57. "What is History For?" *Spectator,* 177 (16 August 1946), 172. Review of R. G. Collingwood's *The Idea of History.*

58. "The Critical Approach." *Spectator,* 177 (30 August 1946), 220, 222. Review of L. C. Knight's *Explorations: Essays in Criticism Mainly on the Literature of the Seventeenth Century.*

59. "The Cult of Sermonizing." *Spectator,* 177 (18 October 1946), 396, 398. Review of Rex Warner's *The Cult of Power: Essays.*

60. "The Fairies' Midwife." *Spectator,* 177 (1 November 1946), 460. Review of Roger Lancelyn Green's *Andrew Lang: A Critical Biography.*

61. "Periodical Prejudices." *Spectator,* 177 (8 November 1946), 488. Review of six periodicals.

62. "Mr. Douglas Looks Back." *Spectator,* 177 (20 December 1946), 684. Review of Norman Douglas's *Late Harvest.*

63. "An Immense Sensibility." *Spectator,* 178 (24 January 1947), 114. Review of F. O. Matthiessen's *Henry James: The Major Phase.*

64. "Heavy Weather." *Spectator,* 178 (7 March 1947), 244. Review of C. E. Vulliamy's *Man and the Atom.*

65. "Fellow-Traveller's Cheques." *Spectator,* 178 (16 May 1947), 564, 566. Review of Vincent Sheean's *This House Against This House.*

66. "Requiescat in Limbo." *Spectator,* 179 (25 July 1947), 118. Review of Edward Dahlberg's *Sing O Barren.*

67. Editor. *Novels of High Society from the Victorian Age.* London: Pilot Press, 1947.

68. *John Aubrey and His Friends.* London: Eyre and Spottis-woode, 1948; New York: Scribners, 1948; Philadelphia: Richard West, 1948; rev. ed. London: Heinemann, 1959, 1963; New York: Barnes and Noble, 1963.

69. Editor. *Brief Lives and Other Selected Writings of John Aubrey.* London: Cresset Press, 1949; New York: Scribners, 1949.

70. " 'Mr. Uniades.' " *TLS* (17 August 1951), p. 517. A letter to the editor, on the possible identity of an acquaintance to John Aubrey.

71. "Bottes, Bottes, Bottes." *Punch,* 224 (11 March 1953), 334-335. Review of *Kipling: Poèmes Choisis par T. S. Eliot,* trans. by Jules Castier.

72. *"The Military Necessity."* *Punch,* 224 (18 March 1953), 360-361. Review of Alfred de Vigny's book of stories.

73. "An Austrian Proust?" *Punch,* 224 (25 March 1953), 388-389. Review of Robert Musil's *The Man Without Qualities.*

74. "Gibson Girl Days." *Punch,* 224 (8 April 1953), 444. Review of Edith Wharton's *The Age of Innocence* and *The House of Mirth.*

75. *"The Weeping and the Laughter."* *Punch,* 224 (15 April 1953), 473. Review of J. Maclaren-Ross' autobiography.

76. "Words and Mujik." *Punch,* 224 (22 April 1953), 500-501. Review of *Autobiography of Maxim Gorky,* trans. by I. Schneider.

77. *"The Passing of a Hero."* *Punch,* 224 (22 April 1953), 501-502. Review of Jocelyn Brooke's novel.

78. "Claudine at 80." *Punch,* 224 (29 April 1953), 527-528. Review of Margaret Crosland's *Madame Colette: A*

Provincial in Paris.

79. "The Drying Room: or, The Termination of the Predica-
    ment, by Gr*h*m Gr**n*." *Punch,* 224 (6 May 1953),
    536-537. A short farce.

80. *"The Final Solution."* *Punch,* 224 (6 May 1953), 557-558.
    Review of Gerald Reitlinger's book on the attempts to
    exterminate the Jews during WWII.

81. "Maxism." *Punch,* 224 (13 May 1953), 584-585. Review
    of Max Beerbohm's *Around Theatres.*

82. *"Save Me the Waltz."* *Punch,* 224 (13 May 1953), 586.
    Review of Zelda Fitzgerald's book on her marriage to
    F. Scott.

83. "Sand Castle." *Punch,* 224 (20 May 1953), 612-613. Re-
    view of André Maurois's *Lélia: The Life of George Sand.*

84. "Autumn or Fall?" *Punch,* 224 (27 May 1953), 640-641.
    Review of G. F. Carey's *American into English.*

85. "Night-Thoughts from a Day-Bed, by Cyr*l C*nn*lly."
    Punch, 224 (10 June 1953), 676-677. A satire, in the
    style of Swift, on a magazine titled *Perimeter.*

86. "Speed's Mappes." *Punch,* 224 (17 June 1953), 724-725.
    Review of *John Speed's England.*

87. *"Lady Eleanor Smith: A Memoir."* *Punch,* 224 (17 June
    1953), 725. Review of Lord Birkenhead's book.

88. "Henry James, Jr." *Punch,* 224 (24 June 1953), 752-
    753. Review of Leon Edel's *Henry James: The Untried
    Years, 1843-1870.*

89. "Through French Windows." *Punch,* 224 (1 July 1953),
    778-779. Review of Roger Martin du Garde's *Notes on
    André Gide,* and *Day of Wrath: The Autobiography of*

Maurice Sachs.

90. *"Mr. Stimson and Mr. Gorse."* *Punch,* 224 (1 July 1953), 780. Review of Patrick Hamilton's book.

91. "Eating and Drinking." *Punch,* 224 (8 July 1953), 72-73. Review of Samuel Chamberlain's *Bouquet de France.*

92. "Orwell." *Punch,* 224 (15 July 1953), 100-101. Review of Tom Hopkinson's *George Orwell.*

93. "Steerforth on Copperfield." *Punch,* 224 (29 July 1953), 136-137. A witty monologue.

94. "Unpublished Edward Lear." *Punch,* 224 (29 July 1953), 144. A biographical sketch.

95. "Dr. Munthe." *Punch,* 224 (5 August 1953), 186-187. Review of *The Story of Axel Munthe,* a biography by Gustav Munthe and Gudrun Uexküll.

96. "Uncle Norman." *Punch,* 224 (12 August 1953), 214-215. Review of Constantine FitzGibbon's *Norman Douglas.*

97. "Americans in the '20s." *Punch,* 224 (19 August 1953), 242-243. Review of F. Scott Fitzgerald's *Tender is the Night.*

98. *"Painters of the Victorian Scene."* *Punch,* 224 (19 August 1953), 244. Review of a book by Graham Reynolds.

99. *"The Desire and Pursuit of the Whole."* *Punch,* 224 (26 August 1953), 271. Review of Frederick Rolfe's book.

100. "English Letters To-day." *Punch,* 224 (2 September 1953), 302-303. Review of G. S. Fraser's *The Modern Writer and His World.*

101. *"The Angry Admiral."* *Punch,* 224 (2 September 1953), 303. Review of Cyril H. Hartmann's biography of Ad-

miral Edward Vernon.

102. *"A Different Face."* Punch, 224 (9 September 1953), 331. Review of Olivia Manning's novel.

103. "Kafka à Trois." *Punch,* 224 (30 September 1953), 414. Review of Kafka's *Letters to Milena.*

104. "Ancient Lights." *Punch,* 225 (7 October 1953), 442-443. Review of Joan Wake's *The Brudenells of Deene.*

105. *"The Go-between."* Punch, 225 (14 October 1953), 471. Review of L. P. Hartley's novel.

106. *"The Time of Indifference."* Punch, 225 (21 October 1953), 503. Review of Albert Moravia's novel.

107. *"Gigi* and *The Cat."* Punch, 225 (28 October 1953), 531. Review of two novels by Colette.

108. "The Stocking: or Christmas with Kafka." *Punch,* 225 (2 November 1953), 12-13. A humorous pastiche of Kafka's style.

109. "Sherlock and After." *Punch,* 225 (4 November 1953), 558-559. Review of S. C. Roberts's *Holmes and Watson: a Miscellany.*

110. *"The Man in Control."* Punch, 225 (4 November 1953), 559. Review of Hugh McGraw's novel.

111. "Looking at Pictures." *Punch,* 225 (11 November 1953), 586-587. Review of Bernard Berenson's *Seeing and Knowing,* and *Caravaggio: His Incongruity and His Fame.*

112. "Window in Bloomsbury." *Punch,* 225 (18 November 1953), 614. Review of Virginia Woolf's *A Writer's Diary.*

113. *"Leopardi: A Study in Solitude."* Punch, 225 (18 Novem-

ber 1953), 615. Review of Iris Origo's biography.

114. *"Boswell on the Grand Tour: Germany and Switzerland, 1764."* Punch, 225 (25 November 1953), 647. Review of book edited by Frederick A. Pottle.

115. "Boy Into Author." *Punch,* 225 (9 December 1953), 710-711. Review of David Garnett's *The Golden Echo.*

116. *"The Ever-Interesting Topic."* Punch, 225 (9 December 1953), 711. Review of William Cooper's novel.

117. *"England Your England and Other Essays."* Punch, 225 (16 December 1953), 739. Review of George Orwell's book.

118. *"Teapots and Quails: and other new nonsense."* Punch, 225 (16 December 1953), 740. Review of Edward Lear's book of poems and drawings.

119. "Ruinenlust." *Punch,* 225 (23 December 1953), 768-769. Review of Rose Macaulay's *Pleasure of Ruins.*

120. "Lost Horizon." *Punch,* 225 (30 December 1953), 799-800. Review of *The Golden Horizon,* edited by Cyril Connolly.

121. "The Stinging Butterfly." *Punch,* 226 (13 January 1954), 102-103. Review of James McNeill Whistler's *The Gentle Art of Making Enemies.*

122. "Stroheim Redivivus." *Punch,* 226 (20 January 1954), 114-115. A biographical sketch of the film-maker, Erich Von Stroheim.

123. *"The Life of Joseph Addison."* Punch, 226 (27 January 1954), 160. Review of Peter Smithers's book.

124. "Marshal of Finland." *Punch,* 226 (3 February 1954), 187. Review of *The Memoirs of Marshal Mannerheim.*

125. *"Lucky Jim."* *Punch*, 226 (3 February 1954), 188. Review of Amis's book.

126. "Educating Aldous." *Punch*, 226 (17 February 1954), 243. Review of Aldous Huxley's essay, *The Doors of Perception.*

127. *"In Love."* *Punch*, 226 (17 February 1954), 244. Review of Alfred Hayes's novel.

128. *"Members of the Long Parliament."* *Punch*, 226 (24 February 1954), 274. Review of a book by D. Brunton and D. H. Pennington.

129. "The Pompadour's Fan." *Punch*, 226 (3 March 1954), 301. Review of Nancy Mitford's biography, *Madame de Pompadour.*

130. "Anchor or Banner Screen." *Punch*, 226 (10 March 1954), 318-319. Review of Ardern Holt's *Gentlemen's Fancy Dress: How to Choose It (1882).*

131. "mr e e cummings." *Punch*, 226 (10 March 1954), 330. Review of *i: six nonlectures by e e cummings.*

132. "Notes by W. Shakespeare?" *Punch*, 226 (17 March 1954), 359-360. Review of *The Annotator* by Alan Keen and Roger Lubbock.

133. "Take a Chair." *Punch*, 226 (24 March 1954), 387-388. Review of *The Dictionary of English Furniture* by Percy Macquoid and Ralph Edwards; rev. and enlarged by Ralph Edwards.

134. "Malraux on Art." *Punch*, 226 (31 March 1954), 418. Review of André Malraux's *The Voices of Silence.*

135. *"The Man Without Qualities."* *Punch*, 226 (7 April 1954), 451. Review of Robert Musil's novel.

136. "Letters from Flaubert." *Punch*, 226 (14 April 1954), 478. Review of *Selected Letters of Gustave Flaubert*, ed. by Francis Steegmuller.

137. *"Rough Island Story."* *Punch*, 226 (14 April 1954), 479. Review of Hugh McGraw's novel.

138. "Magarshack on Turgenev." *Punch*, 226 (21 April 1954), 506. Review of David Magarshack's *Turgenev*.

139. *"Bitter Honeymoon and Other Stories."* *Punch*, 226 (21 April 1954), 507. Review of Albert Moravia's book.

140. "Battles Long Ago." *Punch*, 226 (28 April 1954), 529. Review of Richard Aldington's *Pinorman*.

141. "Speak No Evil." *Punch*, 226 (5 May 1954), 561-562. Review of V. H. Collins's *One Word and Another*.

142. *"His Majesty Preserved."* *Punch*, 226 (12 May 1954), 590. Review of book reprinted from First Edition; introduced by William Rees-Mogg.

143. "Critic's Spain." *Punch*, 226 (19 May 1954), 620-621. Review of V. S. Pritchett's *The Spanish Temper*.

144. *"They Came with the Conqueror."* *Punch*, 226 (19 May 1954), 621. Review of L. G. Pine's book on Norman ancestry.

145. *"Petrus Borel: The Lycanthrope."* *Punch*, 226 (2 June 1954), 677. Review of Enid Starkie's book.

146. "Author and Critic." *Punch*, 226 (23 June 1954), 760. Review of Amanda M. Ros's *St. Scandalbags*, ed. by T. Stanler Mercer.

147. *"Matthew Arnold: Poetry and Prose."* *Punch*, 227 (7 July 1954), 73. Review of book edited by John Bryson.

148. "In Exile." *Punch*, 227 (14 July 1954), 100. Review of *The Journal of William Beckford in Portugal and Spain, 1787-1788*, ed. by Boyd Alexander.

149. "American Realism." *Punch*, 227 (21 July 1954), 128. Review of *Stephen Crane: An Omnibus*, ed. by R. Wooster Stallman.

150. *"A Few Late Chrysanthemums."* *Punch*, 227 (21 July 1954), 129. Review of John Betjman's book of poems.

151. "The Mode." *Punch*, 227 (4 August 1954), 184. Review of Cecil Beaton's *The Glass of Fashion*.

152. *"The Four Continents."* *Punch*, 227 (11 August 1954), 213. Review of Sir Osbert Sitwell's book.

153. "English Sculpture." *Punch*, 227 (18 August 1954), 240-241. Review of M. I. Webb's biography, *Michael Rysbrack: Sculptor*.

154. *"Patrick Campbell's Omnibus."* *Punch*, 227 (18 August 1954), 241.

155. "The Duke." *Punch*, 227 (25 August 1954), 268. Review of *My Dear Mrs. Jones: The Letters of the First Duke of Wellington to Mrs. Jones of Pantglas*.

156. *"A Biographical Dictionary of English Architects, 1660-1840."* *Punch*, 227 (25 August 1954), 269. Review of book by H. M. Colvin.

157. "The Times of Van Wyck Brooks." *Punch*, 227 (1 September 1954), 295. Review of Van Wyck Brooks's *Scenes and Portraits*.

158. "Diversities." *Punch*, 227 (8 September 1954), 324. Review of *People: Places*, ed. by Geoffrey Grigson and C. H. Gibbs-Smith.

159. *"Son of Oscar Wilde."* Punch, 227 (15 September 1954), 365. Review of Vyvyan Holland's autobiography.

160. " 'Half-way between a fiend and a tallow-chandler.' " *Punch*, 227 (22 September 1954), 392. Review of Joan Evans's biography, *John Ruskin.*

161. *"The White Wand: and Other Stories."* Punch, 227 (22 September 1954), 393. Review of L. P. Hartley's book.

162. "Love and Autumn." *Punch*, 227 (6 October 1954), 451-452. Review of Marcel Adéma's *Apollinaire.*

163. *"Collected Poems."* Punch, 227 (13 October 1954), 484. Review of Frances Cornford's book.

164. "In Lamb's Clothing." *Punch*, 227 (20 October 1954), 516. Review of David Cecil's biography of Melbourne, *Lord M.*

165. "Novels and Novelists." *Punch*, 227 (27 October 1954), 548. Review of W. Somerset Maugham's *Ten Novels and Their Authors.*

166. *"Leda and the Goose."* Punch, 227 (27 October 1954), 549. Review of Tristram Hillier's autobiography.

167. *"Conquest of Man: The Saga of Early Exploration and Discovery."* Punch. 227 (27 October 1954), 550. Review of Paul Herrman's book.

168. "By Way of the Chimney, or Christmas with Pirandello." *Punch*, 227 (1 November 1954), 3-4. A short, witty spoof in drama form.

169. "Change at Rugby?" *Punch*, 227 (10 November 1954), 608. Review of G. F. Bradby's novel, *The Lanchester Tradition.*

170. *"The English Novel."* Punch, 227 (10 November 1954),

609. Review of Walter Allen's book.

171. *"Sir Philip Sidney and the English Renaissance."* Punch, 227 (24 November 1954), 671. Review of John Buxton's book.

172. *"Wedding Preparations and Other Pieces."* Punch, 227 (24 November 1954), 671-672. Review of Kafka's book.

173. "Moby Dick Spouts Again." *Punch*, 227 (1 December 1954), 696. A spoof on the wealthy Onassis, in a pastiche of Melville.

174. "Russian Despot." *Punch*, 227 (1 December 1954), 704-705. Review of Constantin de Grunwald's *Tsar Nicholas I.*

175. "Sutherlands's 'Churchill'." *Punch*, 227 (8 December 1954), 710. On the painter's portrait of Churchill.

176. "Four Studies." *Punch*, 227 (8 December 1954), 736-737. Review of Jocelyn Brooke's *Private View.*

177. *"The Postman."* Punch, 227 (15 December 1954), 769. Review of Roger Martin du Gard's novel.

178. "The Ruthless Pencil." *Punch*, 227 (29 December 1954), 828. Review of M. Dorothy George's *Political and Personal Satires, 1828-1832.*

179. "Quennell's Symbolists." *Punch*, 228 (5 January 1955), 72. Review of Peter Quennell's *Baudelaire and the Symbolists.*

180. *"Early Conversation Pictures."* Punch, 228 (5 January 1955), 73. Review of Ralph Edwards's book.

181. "Fan-Mail." *Punch*, 228 (12 January 1955), 100. Review of *I Kiss Your Hand: The Letters of Guy de Maupassant and Marie Bashkirtseff.*

182. Untitled book review. *Punch*, 228 (12 January 1955), 101. Review of Jack Loudan's biography *O Rare Amanda!*, and Amanda Ros's *Donald Dudley: The Bastard Critic*, ed. by T. S. Mercer.

183. "Ex Africa." *Punch*, 228 (26 January 1955), 155-156. Review of *African Folktales and Sculptures*, ed. by Paul Radin, et. al.

184. "Songs of Araby." *Punch*, 228 (2 February 1955), 184. Review of Richard Aldington's *Lawrence of Arabia*.

185. *"A Victorian Boyhood."* *Punch*, 228 (9 February 1955), 215. Review of L. E. Jones's book.

186. "Unhappy Families." *Punch*, 228 (16 February 1955), 243. Review of Ivy Compton-Burnett's novel, *Mother and Son*.

187. *"The Mint."* *Punch*, 228 (16 February 1955), 243. Review of T. E. Lawrence's account of his life in the R.A.F.

188. "Impresario." *Punch*, 228 (23 February 1955), 270. Review of Arnold Haskell's biography, *Diaghileff*.

189. *"A Ghost at Noon."* *Punch*, 228 (23 February 1955), 271. Review of Alberto Moravia's novel.

190. *"Jean Cocteau."* *Punch*, 228 (2 March 1955), 299. Review of Margaret Crosland's biography.

191. "The Great Gregory." *Punch*, 228 (9 March 1955), 326. Review of Gerald Macmillan's biography of Maundy Gregory, *Honours for Sale*.

192. *"A World of Love."* *Punch*, 228 (9 March 1955), 327. Review of Elizabeth Bowen's novel.

193. *"William Balston: Paper-Maker."* *Punch*, 228 (16 March 1955), 355. Review of Thomas Balston's biography.

194. "Professional Gaiety." *Punch*, 228 (23 March 1955), 382-383. Review of Elsa Maxwell's autobiography, *I Married the World.*

195. "Gods and Goddesses." *Punch*, 228 (6 April 1953), 450. Review of Robert Graves's *The Greek Myths.*

196. "The Importance of Being Ernest." *Punch*, 228 (20 April 1955), 505. Review of Charles A. Fenton's biography, *The Apprenticeship of Ernest Hemingway.*

197. "Profession or Occupation?" *Punch*, 228 (27 April 1955), 521-522. On the employment of artists and writers in areas other than art or literature.

198. " 'L' Affaire.' " *Punch*, 228 (27 April 1955), 536. Review of Guy Chapman's *The Dreyfus Case: A Reassessment.*

199. *"Letters to Frau Gudi Nölke." Punch*, 228 (27 April 1955), 537. Review of Rainer Maria Rilke's letters.

200. "Dostoevsky *en Touriste." Punch*, 228 (11 May 1955), 592. Review of Dostoevsky's *Summer Impressions.*

201. "Celtic Mist." *Punch*, 228 (18 May 1955), 620. Review of. W. B. Yeats's *Autobiographies*, and *The Letters of W. B. Yeats*, ed. by Allan Wade.

202. "I Miss My Swiss." *Punch*, 228 (25 May 1955), 657. Review of *The Letters of Jacob Burckhardt*, selected, ed. and trans. by Alexander Dru.

203. *"Treasures of the Great National Galleries." Punch*, 228 (25 May 1955), 658. Review of Hans Tietze's book.

204. "Monsieur de Beyle." *Punch*, 228 (1 June 1955), 688. Review of *The Private Diaries of Stendhal*, ed. by Robert Sage.

205. "B-ll--l M-n." *Punch*, 228 (15 June 1955), 746. Review of

Balliol Rhymes, ed. by W. G. Hiscock.

206. "Delicate Mr. Gray." *Punch,* 228 (22 June 1955), 773. Review of R. W. Ketton-Cremer's *Thomas Gray.*

207. *"Young Törless." Punch,* 228 (22 June 1955), 774. Review of Rober Musil's novel.

208. "Là Bas." *Punch,* 229 (6 July 1955), 24. Review of Robert Baldick's *The Life of J.-K. Huysmans.*

209. *"Officers and Gentlemen." Punch,* 229 (13 July 1955), 53. Review of Evelyn Waugh's novel.

210. *"Sculpture in Britain in the Middle Ages." Punch,* 229 (20 July 1955), 81. Review of Lawrence Stone's book.

211. "A Day at Versailles." *Punch,* 229 (27 July 1955), 108. Review of *An Adventure* by C. A. E. Moberly and E. F. Jourdain. Ed. by Joan Evans.

212. *"Hogarth's Progress." Punch,* 229 (27 July 1955), 109. Review of Peter Quennell's biography.

213. *"The Paintings of Tiepolo." Punch,* 229 (3 August 1955), 139-140. Review of Antonio Morassi's book.

214. "Life on a Tiger-Skin." *Punch,* 229 (10 August 1955), 166-167. Review of Anthony Glyn's *Elinor Glyn: A Biography.*

215. "Whiskers and Claws." *Punch,* 229 (31 August 1955), 251. Review of *The Art of Beatrix Potter.*

216. "Through the Galleries with Baudelaire." *Punch,* 229 (7 September 1955), 280. Review of Baudelaire's *The Mirror of Art: Critical Studies.*

217. "Nice People With Nice Manners." *Punch,* 229 (21 September 1955), 336. Review of Harold Nicolson's *Good Be-*

havior.

218. "Proust in Bond Street." *Punch*, 229 (12 October 1955), 426-427.

219. "Man and Wife." *Punch*, 229 (12 October 1955), 436. Review of Marcel Jouhandeau's *Marcel and Elise.*

220. "A Lehmann's View." *Punch*, 229 (26 October 1955), 499. Review of John Lehmann's *The Whispering Gallery.*

221. *"The Flowers of the Forest." Punch*, 229 (2 November 1955), 529. Review of David Garnett's second volume of autobiography.

222. *"Boswell on the Grand Tour." Punch*, 229 (2 November 1955), 529. Review of the 1765-1766 period. Ed. by Frank Brady and Frederick A. Pottle.

223. "A Day at the Zoo: Submitted by P*t*r Fl*m*ng." *Punch*, 229 (7 November 1955), 31. A parody.

224. "Where Breaks the Blue Sicilian Sea." *Punch*, 229 (9 November 1955), 556. Review of Jocelyn Brooke's *The Dog at Clambercrown.*

225. *"Is She a Lady?" Punch*, 229 (16 November 1955), 585. . Review of Nina Hamnett's book.

226. *"Santeuil's Way." Punch*, 229 (23 November 1955), 611. Review of Marcel Proust's *Jean Santeuil.*

227. *"Hokusai." Punch*, 229 (23 November 1955), 612. Review of J. Hillier's book on the Japanese painter.

228. "When Kiplin' Smote 'is Bloomin' Lyre." *Punch*, 229 (14 December 1955), 715. Review of Charles Carrington's *Rudyard Kipling: His Life and Work.*

229. *"The Paintings of Bruegel." Punch*, 229 (21 December

1955), 743. Review of F. Grossmann's book.

230. *"English Drawing."* *Punch,* 229 (28 December 1955), 774. Review of Geoffrey Grigson's book.

231. Untitled autobiographical comments. *Twentieth Century Authors: First Supplement.* Ed. Stanley J. Kunitz. New York: H. W. Wilson, 1955, pp. 789-790.

232. "Catching the Post." *Punch,* 230 (11 January 1956), 100. Review of *Letters from Madame de Sévigné,* selected and trans. by Violet Hammersley.

233. "Michael Angelo Titmarsh." *Punch,* 230 (18 January 1956), 128. Review of Gordon N. Ray's *Thackeray: The Uses of Adversity.*

234. *"Old Calabria."* *Punch,* 230 (1 February 1956), 185. Review of Norman Douglas's book.

235. "Evelyn Revisited." *Punch,* 230 (8 February 1956), 212. Review of *The Diary of John Evelyn,* ed. by E. S. de Beer.

236. "Chesterfield Writes Again." *Punch,* 230 (15 February 1956), 220-221. A pastiche, in the form of a letter from Chesterfield to his great-great-great-great-great grandson.

237. "Kind Hearts Less than Coronets." *Punch,* 230 (15 February 1956), 239. Review of the French edition of *Saint-Simon: Mémoires.*

238. "Lorenzo the Critical." *Punch,* 230 (29 February 1956), 280-281. Review of *D. H. Lawrence: Selected Literary Criticism,* ed. by Anthony Beal.

239. *"Selected Letters of Henry James."* *Punch,* 230 (7 March 1956), 302. Review of book edited by Leon Edel.

240. *"My Friend Henry Miller."* *Punch,* 230 (14 March 1956),

323. Review of Alfred Perlès's book.

241. "The O. B." *Punch*, 230 (21 March 1956), 341. Review of H. E. Wortham's *Victorian Eton and Cambridge: Being the Life and Times of Oscar Browning.*

242. "A. E. Housman and W. B. Yeats." *Punch*, 230 (28 March 1956), 362. Review of Richard Aldington's book.

243. "Hugoism." *Punch*, 230 (4 April 1956), 389. Review of André Maurois's biography, *Victor Hugo.*

244. *"Stonehenge."* *Punch*, 230 (11 April 1956), 428. Review of R. J. C. Atkinson's book.

245. *"Heaven and Hell."* *Punch*, 230 (18 April 1956), 464. Review of Aldous Huxley's book.

246. "Biedermeier Books." *Punch*, 230 (25 April 1956), 502. Review of Mario Praz's *The Hero in Eclipse in Victorian Fiction.*

247. "Dylan Plain." *Punch*, 230 (2 May 1956), 532-533. Review of John Malcolm Brinnin's *Dylan Thomas in America.*

248. *"The Adults."* *Punch*, 230 (9 May 1956), 565. Review of Inez Holden's novel.

249. *"Noblesse Oblige."* *Punch*, 230 (30 May 1956), 662. Review of a book edited by Nancy Mitford.

250. "Rare Books." *Punch*, 230 (6 June 1956), 690. Review of Percy Muir's *Minding My Own Business: An Autobiography.*

251. "Scientist and Architect." *Punch*, 230 (27 June 1956), 775. Review of Margaret 'Espinasse's biography, *Robert Hooke.*

252. *"M. R. James: Letters to a Friend."* *Punch*, 230 (27 June 1956), 776-777. Review of book edited by Gwendolen McBryde.

253. "Criticus Americanus." *Punch*, 231 (4 July 1956), 24-25. Review of *The Shock of Recognition*, ed. by Edmund Wilson, and his *Red, Black, Blond and Olive.*

254. "The Wren Goes to It." *Punch*, 231 (11 July 1956), 52. Review of Michael Alexander's *The Reluctant Légionnaire.* This review contains comments on Amis.

255. *"A Young Girl's Touch."* *Punch*, 231 (11 July 1956), 53. Review of Barbara Skelton's novel.

256. "Firbank." *Punch*, 231 (15 August 1956), 194. Review of Ronald Firbank's novel, *Valmouth.*

257. "Hollis on Orwell." *Punch*, 231 (29 August 1956), 255. Review of Christopher Hollis's *A Study of George Orwell.*

258. "Army Mail." *Punch*, 231 (5 September 1956), 286. Review of *Last Letters from Stalingrad,* selected by Heinz Schröter.

259. "Tell Your Palm." *Punch*, 231 (12 September 1956), 315. Review of Noel Jaquin's *The Human Hand: the Living Symbol.*

260. "666." *Punch*, 231 (19 September 1956), 346. Review of W. Somerset Maugham's novel, *The Magician.*

261. "The Hermit of Ebury Street." *Punch*, 231 (26 September 1956), 384. Review of Nancy Cunard's memoir, *GM: Memories of George Moore.*

262. *"Roman Tales."* *Punch*, 231 (17 October 1956), 481. Review of Alberto Moravia's book of stories.

263. "Eros and Agape." *Punch*, 231 (24 October 1956), 510.

Review of Denis de Rougemont's study of Romantic love, *Passion and Society.*

264. *"Adonis and the Alphabet."* Punch, 231 (24 October 1956), 511. Review of Aldous Huxley's book.

265. *"Modern English Painters: Lewis to Moore."* Punch, 231 (24 October 1956), 511-512. Review of John Rothenstein's book.

266. "Leaves from Notable New Diaries: Kingsley Amis." *Punch,* 232 (5 November 1956), 7. A parody, in the form of a "diary" kept by Amis for the month of May, 1957.

267. "Adams to Ziegfield." *Punch,* 231 (7 November 1956), 571. Review of James D. Hart's *The Oxford Companion to American Literature.*

268. "Prince Perkin." *Punch,* 231 (14 November 1956), 599-600. Review of Bryan Little's *The Monmouth Episode.*

269. "The Booksters." *Punch,* 231 (21 November 1956), 629. Review of John Carter's *Books and Book Collecting.*

270. *"Old Friends: Personal Recollections."* Punch, 231 (21 November 1956), 631. Review of Clive Bell's book.

271. "Parthenopean Princes." *Punch,* 231 (12 December 1956), 730. Review of Harold Acton's *The Bourbons of Naples.*

272. "Brooke's Hrombo-Zombo." *Punch,* 231 (19 December 1956), 760-761. Review of Jocelyn Brooke's *The Crisis in Bulgaria, or Ibsen to the Rescue.*

273. *"The Last Days of Hitler."* Punch, 231 (19 December 1956), 761. Review of H. R. Trevor-Roper's book.

274. "On the Record." *Punch,* 231 (26 December 1956), 796. Review of *An Anthology of English Prose, 1400-1900,*

ed. by Eirian James.

275. *"The Curious Past."* *Punch*, 231 (26 December 1956), 797. Review of Robin Atthill's book.

276. Translator. *Eroica* by Carl Pidoll. London: Methuen, 1956.

277. " 'Andley Cross." *Punch*, 232 (2 January 1957), 77. Review of R. S. Surtees's *Hunting with Mr. Jorrocks.*

278. Untitled book review. *Punch*, 232 (2 January 1957), 78. Review of Germaine Brée's *Marcel Proust and Deliverance From Time,* and *Marcel Proust: Letters to his Mother,* trans. by George D. Painter.

279. "The Girls of St. Hugh's." *Punch*, 232 (16 January 1957), 140. Review of Lucille Iremonger's *The Ghosts of Versailles.*

280. "M. de Norpois's Secrets." *Punch*, 232 (6 February 1957), 228. Review of Maurice Paléologue's *My Secret Diary of the Dreyfus Case.*

281. *"Early Netherlandish Painting from Van Eyck to Bruegel."* *Punch*, 232 (13 February 1957), 257. Review of Max J. Friedländer's book.

282. "Gothick Approaches." *Punch*, 232 (20 February 1957), 284. Review of *Life at Fonthill: From the Correspondence of William Beckford,* trans. and ed. by Boyd Alexander.

283. "Red Rudyard." *Punch*, 232 (20 February 1957), 284-285. Review of *The Collected Stories of Isaac Babel.*

284. "The Mysterious Dwarf." *Punch*, 232 (27 February 1957), 312. Review of David Magarshack's biography, *Gogul.*

285. *"Lord Byron's Marriage."* *Punch*, 232 (27 February 1957), 313. Review of G. Wilson Knight's book.

286. "Montparnos and Others." *Punch,* 232 (20 March 1957), 394. Review of Michel Georges-Michel's *From Renoir to Picasso: Artists I Have Known.*

287. *"English Historical Research in the Sixteenth and Seventeenth centuries."* *Punch,* 232 (20 March 1957), 395. Review of book edited by Len Fox.

288. " 'a way a lone.' " *Punch,* 232 (27 March 1957), 424. Review of Patricia Hutchins's *James Joyce's World.*

289. "Putlitz Revisited." *Punch,* 232 (10 April 1957), 480. Review of Wolfgang zu Putlitz's memoirs, *The Putlitz Dossier.*

290. *"Brigitta."* *Punch,* 232 (10 April 1957), 481. Review of Adalbut Stifter's novel.

291. "National Faces." *Punch,* 232 (1 May 1957), 572. Review of *British Historical Portraits: A Selection from the National Portrait Gallery with Biographical Notes.*

292. *"Siren Land* and *Fountains in the Sand."* *Punch,* 232 (1 May 1957), 573. Review of Norman Douglas's first two travel books.

293. " 'Awake, My Little Ones, and Fill the Cup.' " *Punch,* 232 (8 May 1957), 600. Review of L. W. Marrison's *Wines and Spirits.*

294. *"Proust's Way."* *Punch,* 232 (15 May 1957), 629. Review of Georges Piroué's critical study.

295. "Harris, George and J." *Punch,* 232 (22 May 1957), 656. Review of Jerome K. Jerome's *Three Men in a Boat,* and *Three Men on the Bummel.*

296. "Dantan's Inferno." *Punch,* 232 (29 May 1957), 684. Review of Janet Seligman's *Figures of Fun: The Caricature-Statuettes of Jeanne-Pierre Dantan.*

297. *"Matthew Prior."* *Punch,* 232 (29 May 1957), 685. Review of R. W. Ketton-Cremer's Memorial to the poet.

298. *"The Gilded Fly."* *Punch,* 232 (29 May 1957), 685. Review of Hamilton Macallister's novel.

299. "Thus Spake Nietzsche." *Punch,* 232 (5 June 1957), 720. Review of F. A. Lea's *The Tragic Philosopher: A Study of Friedrich Nietzsche.*

300. *"An Introduction to Italian Renaissance Painting."* *Punch,* 232 (12 June 1957), 749. Review of Cecil Gould's book.

301. " 'The Unfrocked Romantic.' " *Punch,* 232 (19 June 1957), 775. Review of Harold Nicolson's biography, *Sainte-Beuve.*

302. *"The Sponger."* *Punch,* 232 (19 June 1957), 776. Review of Jules Renard's novel.

303. "Big Tich." *Punch,* 232 (26 June 1957), 806-807. Review of Douglas Woodruff's *The Tichborne Claimant.*

304. "Philosopher of Common Sense." *Punch,* 233 (3 July 1957), 24. Review of Maurice Cranston's *John Locke.*

305. *"The Letters of James Joyce."* *Punch,* 233 (3 July 1957), 25. Review of book edited by Stuart Gilbert.

306. "Lewisite." *Punch,* 233 (10 July 1957), 52. Review of Geoffrey Wagner's *Wyndham Lewis: A Portrait of the Artist as the Enemy.*

307. "For Highbrows Only." *Punch,* 233 (17 July 1957), 79. Review of André Malraux's *Saturn: An Essay on Goya,* and Wilhelm Worringer's *Form in Gothic.*

308. *"Close to Colette."* *Punch,* 233 (24 July 1957), 109. Review of Maurice Goudeket's book on his famous wife.

309. "Flowers, Good and Evil." *Punch*, 233 (31 July 1957), 138. Review of Enid Starkie's *Baudelaire.*

310. *"The Ordeal of Gilbert Pinfold." Punch*, 233 (31 July 1957), 139. Review of Evelyn Waugh's novel.

311. "A Man of Flavour." *Punch*, 233 (7 August 1957), 166-167. Review of *Boswell in Search of a Wife, 1766-1769*, ed. by Frank Brady and Frederick A. Pottle.

312. " 'The Count.' " *Punch*, 233 (14 August 1957), 194. Review of Gérard Jean-Aubry's *The Sea Dreamer: A Definitive Biography of Joseph Conrad.*

313. " 'Boeotian Savage Landor.' " *Punch*, 233 (21 August 1957), 222. Review of R. H. Super's biography, *Walter Savage Landor.*

314. *"To a Lady: The Songs and Sonnets of the Earl of Surrey." Punch*, 233 (21 August 1957), 223. Review of book edited by Douglas Geary.

315. Untitled book review. *Punch*, 233 (28 August 1957), 250. Review of Walter A. Strauss' *Proust and Literature*, and Milton L. Miller's *Nostalgia: A Psychoanalytic Study of Proust.*

316. "Honi Soit Qui Malaparte." *Punch*, 232 (4 September 1957), 277. Review of Curzio Malaparte's *The Volga Rises in Europe.*

317. "D-Day 1066." *Punch*, 233 (11 September 1957), 306. Review of *The Bayeux Tapestry: A Comprehensive Survey*, ed. by Sir Francis Stenton, et. al.

318. "Chimpism." *Punch*, 233 (2 October 1957), 396. A spoof on paintings done by apes and on view to the public.

319. "Hostess and Guest." *Punch*, 233 (9 October 1957), 428. Review of *George Moore: Letters to Lady Cunard, 1895-*

1933, ed. by Rupert Hart-Davis.

320. "Artist at Large." *Punch*, 233 (16 October 1957), 460. Review of Michael Ayrton's book of essays, *Golden Sections.*

321. *"The Selected Writing of Sydney Smith."* *Punch*, 233 (16 October 1957), 461. Review of book edited by W. H. Auden.

322. "The Jowler." *Punch*, 233 (30 October 1957), 518. Review of Geoffrey Faber's biography of a Master of Balliol, *Jowett.*

323. *"The English Face."* *Punch*, 233 (30 October 1957), 519. Review of David Piper's book about portraiture.

324. "The Isle of Glass." *Punch*, 233 (6 November 1957), 550. Review of Geoffrey Ashe's *King Arthur's Avalon: The Story of Glastonbury.*

325. "As I was Saying..." *Punch*, 233 (13 November 1957), 581. Review of *The Maxims of the Duc de la Rochefoucauld*, trans. by Constantine FitzGibbon.

326. *"Norfolk Assembly."* *Punch*, 233 (27 November 1957), 639. Review of R. W. Ketton-Cremer's book.

327. "The Great Leacock." *Punch*, 233 (4 December 1957), 670. Review of *The Bodley Head Leacock*, ed. by J. B. Priestley.

328. *"Edward Tennyson Reed."* *Punch*, 233 (4 December 1957), 671. Review of book edited by Shane Leslie.

329. "Post-Scrooge Christmas at Cratchit's." *Punch*, 233 (11 December 1957), 699-700. A humorous sequel to Charles Dickens's "A Christmas Carol."

330. "Where Venice Sate in State..." *Punch*, 233 (11 December

1957), 706. Review of Ippolito Nievo's novel, *The Castle of Fratta.*

331. "The Khivan Kove." *Punch*, 233 (18 December 1957), 734. Review of Michael Alexander's *The True Blue: The Life and Adventures of Colonel Fred Burnaby, 1842-1885.*

332. *"The Game of Hearts: Harriette Wilson and her Memoirs."* *Punch*, 233 (18 December 1957), 735. Review of book edited by Lesley Blanch.

333. "Confess Your Favourite Fancy." *Punch*, 233 (25 December 1957), 746. A spoof on quizz questions.

334. "Artists Under Virgo." *Punch*, 233 (25 December 1957), 762. Review of Max Beerbohm's *Mainly on the Air*, and Oscar Wilde's *Salome: A Tragedy in One Act*, trans. by R. A. Walker.

335. *"The Changing Face of Beauty."* *Punch*, 233 (25 December 1957), 763. Review of Madge Garland's book.

336. *"Thomas Chippendale: A New Edition of Thomas Chippendale's The Gentleman and Cabinet-maker's Director."* *Punch*, 233 (25 December 1957), 764. Review of book introduced by Ralph Edwards.

337. "Critics and Conrad." *Punch*, 234 (1 January 1958), 76. Review of Thomas Moser's *Joseph Conrad: Achievement and Decline*, and Richard Curle's *Joseph Conrad and his Characters.*

338. *"Dwarfs and Jesters in Art."* *Punch*, 234 (8 January 1958), 105. Review of book by E. Tietze-Conrat.

339. "The Tender Passion." *Punch*, 234 (15 January 1958), 132. Review of Stendhal's *Love.*

340. "The Lot Fell Upon Jonah." *Punch*, 234 (22 January

1958), 160.   Review of L. E. Jones's autobiography, *Georgian Afternoon.*

341. "On Fontarabian Echoes Borne." *Punch,* 234 (29 January 1958), 188.   Review of *The Song of Roland,* trans. by Dorothy L. Sayers.

342. "Oh, for a Night in Bohemia." *Punch,* 234 (5 February 1958), 216-217.   Review of Philip O'Connor's autobiography, *Memoirs of Public Baby.*

343. "Keeping Cool." *Punch,* 234 (12 February 1958), 244. Review of *The Complete Works of Montaigne,* trans. by Donald M. Frame.

344. "Broken Friendship." *Punch,* 234 (5 March 1958), 329. Review of *Henry James and H. G. Wells: A Record of their Friendship and their Quarrel,* ed. by Leon Edel and Gordon N. Ray.

345. "Plomer on Plomer." *Punch,* 234 (12 March 1958), 361. Review of William Plomer's *At Home: Memoirs.*

346. *"Greek Myths."* *Punch,* 234 (12 March 1958), 362. Review of book by Robert Graves.

347. "On Egdon Heath." *Punch,* 234 (19 March 1958), 393. Review of Thomas Hardy's *The Return of the Native.*

348. *"The Miscreant."* *Punch,* 234 (19 March 1958), 394. Review of Jean Cocteau's novel.

349. "Musical Correspondence." *Punch,* 234 (26 March 1958), 423. Review of Edward Lockspeiser's *The Literary Clef.*

350. *"The Trianon Adventure: A Symposium."* *Punch,* 234 (26 March 1958), 424. Review of book edited by A. O. Gibbons.

351. *"Selected Writing of Gérard de Nerval."* *Punch,* 234 (26

March 1958), 425. Review of book trans. by Geoffrey Wagner.

352. "Russian Relations." *Punch*, 234 (2 April 1958), 459. Review of Dostoevsky's *The Brothers Karamazov*, trans. by David Magarshack.

353. "Author as Critic." *Punch*, 234 (9 April 1958), 493-494. Review of Marcel Proust's *By Way of Sainte-Beuve*, trans. by Sylvia Townsend Warner.

354. *"The Magic of Aleister Crowley."* *Punch*, 234 (16 April 1958), 524. Review of book by John Symonds.

355. "Thackeray in Love." *Punch*, 234 (23 April 1958), 553. Review of Gordon N. Ray's *Thackeray: The Age of Wisdom. 1847-1863.*

356. " 'Don't be Dainty.' " *Punch*, 234 (30 April 1958), 587. Review of Diana Cooper's autobiography, *The Rainbow Comes and Goes.*

357. "Electoral Roll." *Punch*, 234 (30 April 1958), 587-588. Review of V. S. Naipaul's *The Suffrage of Elvira.*

358. "General Buona-Parté." *Punch*, 234 (7 May 1958), 619-620. Review of Jean Savant's *Napoleon in his Time.*

359. *"On Modern Art."* *Punch*, 234 (7 May 1958), 621. Review of Salvador Dali's book.

360. *"Eustace and Hilda: A Trilogy."* *Punch*, 234 (14 May 1958), 652. Review of Hartley's collection.

361. "Wiener Blut." *Punch*, 234 (21 May 1958), 687. Review of Richard Barkeley's *The Road to Mayerling: Life and Death of Crown Prince Rudolph of Austria.*

362. " 'Unable to Bear Arms.' " *Punch*, 234 (28 May 1958), 719. Review of Franz Jetzinger's *Hitler's Youth.*

363. " 'Anger's self I needs must Kiss.' " *Punch*, 234 (4 June 1958), 755-756. Review of Kenneth Allsop's *The Angry Decade: A Survey of the Cultural Trends of the Nineteen-fifties.*

364. "Swedish Punch." *Punch*, 234 (11 June 1958), 787. Review of *Three Plays by August Strindberg: The Father-Miss Julia—Easter*, trans. by Peter Watts.

365. "Romantic Realism." *Punch*, 234 (18 June 1958), 819. Review of Mikhail Yurevich Lermontov's *A Hero of Our Own Times.*

366. *"Essays in Appreciation." Punch*, 234 (18 June 1958), 820. Review of Bernard Berenson's book.

367. *"England's on the Anvil: Portraits and Essays." Punch*, 234 (25 June 1958), 850. Review of John Raymond's book.

368. "Memoirs of a Younger Son." *Punch*, 235 (2 July 1958), 22. Review of Stanislaus Joyce's *My Brother's Keeper.*

369. "French Without Tears." *Punch*, 235 (9 July 1958), 55-56. Review of *An Age of Fiction: The French Novel from Gide to Camus*, by Germaine Brée and Margaret Guiton.

370. "Gone to the Devil." *Punch*, 235 (16 July 1958), 87. Review of Stuart Atkins's *Goethe's Faust: A Literary Analysis.*

371. "Gissing Time." *Punch*, 235 (30 July 1958), 149. Review of George Gissing's *New Grub Street*, with an introduction by G. W. Stonier.

372. *"Two Women." Punch*, 235 (6 August 1958), 182. Review of Alberto Moravia's novel.

373. "That Old, Bold Cheater, Time." *Punch*, 235 (13 August

1958), 214. Review of J. W. Dunne's study, *An Experiment with Time.*

374. "Beakers and Barrows." *Punch,* 235 (20 August 1958), 248. Review of L. V. Grinsell's *The Archaeology of Wessex.*

375. "Through a Rose-Coloured Waistcoat." *Punch,* 235 (27 August 1958), 282. Review of Joanna Richardson's *Théophile Gautier: His Life and Times.*

376. *"Claybook for James Joyce." Punch,* 235 (3 September 1958), 315. Review of Louis Gillet's book.

377. "Land of King Minos." *Punch,* 235 (17 September 1958), 378. Review of John Chadwick's *The Decipherment of Linear B,* and T. B. L. Webster's *From Mycenae to Homer.*

378. *"The Intruder." Punch,* 235 (17 September 1958), 379. Review of Adriaan van der Veen's novel.

379. *"Doctor Zhivago." Punch,* 235 (24 September 1958), 415. Review of Boris Pasternak's novel.

380. "Arabian Days." *Punch,* 235 (1 October 1958), 446-447. Review of Hans Helfritz's *The Yemen: A Secret Journey.*

381. "Wolfe Whistles." *Punch,* 235 (8 October 1958), 479. Review of Thomas Wolfe's *Look Homeward, Angel,* and *Selected Letters of Thomas Wolfe,* selected and introduced by Elizabeth Nowell.

382. "Dear Lady." *Punch,* 235 (15 October 1958), 511. Review of *Letters of Rainer Maria Rilke and Princess Marie von Thurn und Taxis,* trans. and introduced by Norah Wydenbruck.

383. "Blue Periods and Red Periods." *Punch,* 235 (5 November 1958), 609. Review of Roland Penrose's *Picasso: His*

Life and Work.

384. "The Maugham and Sixpence." *Punch,* 235 (19 November 1958), 674. Review of W. Somerset Maugham's *Points of View.*

385. Untitled book review. *Punch,* 235 (19 November 1958), 675. Review of F. Scott Fitzgerald's *Afternoon of an Author,* and *The Bodley Head Scott Fitzgerald.*

386. " 'Elizabeth.' " *Punch,* 235 (26 November 1958), 705. Review of Leslie de Charms's *Elizabeth of the German Garden: A Biography.*

387. *"Valley on the March."* *Punch,* 235 (26 November 1958), 706. Review of Lord Rennel of Rodd's study of manors in Wales.

388. *"The Love Letters of Voltaire to his Niece."* *Punch,* 235 (26 November 1958), 706. Review of book edited and trans. by Theodore Besterman.

389. "Boyhood of Beyle." *Punch,* 235 (3 December 1958), 737. Review of Stendhal's autobiography, *The Life of Henry Brulard.*

390. *"Burke's Landed Gentry of Ireland, 1958."* *Punch,* 235 (3 December 1958), 738. Review of book edited by L. G. Pine.

391. *"Max's Nineties."* *Punch,* 235 (3 December 1958), 738. Review of book of Max Beerbohm's early caricatures, introduced by Osbert Lancaster.

392. "Sequel to *Middlemarch.*" *Punch,* 235 (10 December 1958), 774. Review of Roy Jenkins's *Sir Charles Dilke: A Victorian Tragedy.*

393. *"A Leaf from the Yellow Book: The Correspondence of George Egerton."* *Punch,* 235 (10 December 1958), 775.

Review of book edited by Terence de Vere White.

394. "The Swan of Wantage." *Punch*, 235 (17 December 1958), 806. Review of John Betjeman's *Collected Poems*.

395. *"The Last Medici."* *Punch*, 235 (17 December 1958), 807. Review of Harold Acton's book.

396. *"Eimi: The Journal of a Trip to Russia."* *Punch*, 235 (17 December 1958), 808. Review of E. E. Cummings's book.

397. "Johnsonian Gleanings." *Punch*, 235 (24 December 1958), 844. Review of *Diaries, Prayers, and Annals of Samuel Johnson*, ed. by E. L. McAdam, Jr., et. al.

398. *"A History of Book Illustration."* *Punch*, 235 (31 December 1958), 877-878. Review of David Bland's book.

399. *"Turgenev's Literary Reminiscences."* *Punch*, 236 (11 February 1959), 234. Review of book trans. by David Magarshack, with an Essay by Edmund Wilson.

400. "The Pleasures of Knowing Rose Macaulay." *Encounter*, 12 (March 1959), 29-30.

401. "Bourbon on the Rocks." *Spectator*, 202 (10 April 1959), 518. Review of V. Sackville-West's *Daughter of France: The Life of Anne Marie Louise d'Orleans...*

402. *"Modigliani: Man and Myth."* *Punch*, 236 (20 May 1959), 692. Review of Jeanne Modigliani's biography of her father.

403. "Carmen to Cottard." *Encounter*, 12 (May 1959), 71-73. Review of Mina Curtiss' *Bizet and His World*.

404. *"Vermeer."* *Punch*, 237 (2 September 1959), 119. Review of Ludwig Goldscheider's book.

405. Untitled book review. *Punch*, 237 (2 September 1959), 120. Review of *Edouard Manet: Paintings and Drawings*, introduced by John Richardson; and *Raoul Dufy: Paintings and Watercolours*, selected by René Ben Sussan with an introduction by Marcel Brion.

406. *"Model Soldiers: A Collector's Guide." Punch*, 237 (30 September 1959), 251. Review of John G. Garratt's book.

407. *"The Doge of Dover: Portraits and Essays." Punch*, 238 (30 March 1960), 463. Review of John Raymond's book.

408. "Speaking of Writing." *New York Times Book Review* (19 June 1960), p. 2. In defence of thesis writing and publication of same.

409. "Self-Made Connoisseur." *Punch*, 239 (3 August 1960), 176. Review of Peggy Guggenheim's *Confessions of an Art Addict*.

410. *"The Man Without Qualities." Punch*, 239 (5 October 1960), 504. Review of Robert Musil's novel.

411. *"Ferdydurke." Punch*, 240 (15 March 1961), 442. Review of Witold Gombrowicz's novel.

412. "The Neapolitan Kings." *Punch*, 241 (22 November 1961), 769. Review of Harold Acton's *The Last Bourbons of Naples*.

413. "Preface." *The Complete Ronald Firbank*. London: Duckworth, 1961; New York: New Directions, 1961, pp. 1-16.

414. "Military Glory." *Punch*, 244 (16 January 1963), 104. Review of Cecil C. P. Lawson's *A History of the Uniforms of the British Army: Vol. I: The Beginnings.*

415. "Right Dress." *Punch*, 245 (31 July 1963), 177. Review of Cecil C. P. Lawson's *A History of the Uniforms of the British Army: Vol. II, 1715-1760.*

416. "Kingsley's Heroes." *Spectator*, 211 (29 November 1963), 709-710. Review of Amis's *One Fat Englishman.*

417. "Holding out on his pen pals." *Book Week*, 1 (12 April 1964), 6, 16. Review of *The Letters of Wyndham Lewis*, ed. by W. K. Rose.

418. "Anthony Powell: Some Questions Answered." *Anglo-Welsh Review*, 14 (1964), 77-79.

419. *"Lautrec by Lautrec."* *Apollo*, 81 (February 1965), 157-158.

420. "Reflections on the Landed Gentry." *Burke's Genealogical and Heraldic History of the Landed Gentry.* London: Burke's Peerage, 1965, pp. xxv-xxviii.

421. "With Wittgenstein's Corps." *Punch*, 251 (3 August 1966), 199. Review of Cecil C. P. Lawson's *History of the Uniforms of the British Army: Vol. IV.*

422. "Three Evocations of Evelyn Waugh. I: A Memoir." *Adam International Review*, 301-303 (1966), pp. 7-9.

423. "George Orwell: a personal memoir." *The* (London) *Times* (14 October 1967), pp. 17, 24. Powell continues his discussion in a letter to the Editor of *The Times* (27 October 1967), p. 9.

424. "George Orwell: A Memoir." *Atlantic*, 220 (October 1967), 62-68.

425. "British Squares." *Punch*, 253 (22 November 1967), 798. Review of four books on the British army.

426. "Fading Away." *Punch*, 254 (22 May 1968), 759. Review

of four books on the military.

427. "Involvement: Writer's Reply." *London Magazine,* n.s. 8 (August 1968), 5. Powell answers a question put to him by the editor of *London Magazine.*

428. "Ivy Compton-Burnett." *Spectator,* 223 (6 September 1969), 304-305. On her attitudes toward life, and on her subject matter and themes in her novels.

429. "Hollywood canteen: A memoir of Scott Fitzgerald in 1937." *The* (London) *Times* (3 October 1970), p. 15; reprinted in *Fitzgerald/Hemingway Annual 1971.* Ed. Matthew J. Bruccoli and C. E. Frazer Clark Jr. Washington, D. C.: Microcard Editions, 1971.

430. "Marston and Jorrocks." *TLS* (2 April 1971), p. 396. A letter to the Editor. A "footnote" to the plays of John Marston.

431. "Proust the soldier." *The* (London) *Times* (3 July 1971), p. 5; reprinted and enlarged in *Marcel Proust, 1871-1922: A Centennial Volume.* Ed. Peter Quennell. London: Weidenfeld and Nicolson, 1971; New York: Simon and Schuster, 1971. On Marcel Proust's year in the French 76th Regiment of infantry.

432. "Constant Lambert: A Memoir." *The* (London) *Times* (30 December 1972), p. 9; reprinted as the introduction to Richard Shead's *Constant Lambert.* London: Simon Publications, 1973.

433. "The Flight from Romanticism: Picasso's Great Harlequinade." *Encounter,* 40 (February 1973), 53-55. Review of three books on Picasso.

434. With Kingsley Amis and others. "Tibor Szamuely." *The* (London) *Times* (3 April 1973), p. 15. A letter to the Editor. An announcement of their inauguration of a Tibor Szamuely Memorial Prize.

435. "Evelyn's Diary." *London Magazine,* n.s. 13 (August/September 1973), 67-72. On the diaries of Evelyn Waugh.

436. "Mrs. Massingberd." *TLS* (26 July 1974), p. 801. A letter to the Editor. On the identity of this woman so as to clear her name from ill repute.

437. "Conrad and Proust." *TLS* (27 September 1974), p. 1042. A letter to the Editor.

438. "The Bowra World and Bowra Lore." *The* (London) *Times* (19 October 1974), pp. 6-7; reprinted in *Maurice Bowra: a celebration.* London: Duckworth, 1974. On Powell's life at Oxford, with a concentration on the gatherings he and Henry Green attended at Professor Bowra's rooms at Wadham, and other meetings, without Green, elsewhere.

439. "Inez Holden: A Memoir." *London Magazine,* 14 (October/November 1974), 88-94.

* 440. Volume I of Anthony Powell's Memoirs. London: Heinemann. Expected date of publication is October, 1976.

II. GENERAL SECONDARY STUDIES, INTERVIEWS, BIOGRAPHICAL SKETCHES, AND MISCELLANEOUS ITEMS

General references to Powell's work also appear in the First Part of this bibliography. See the following numbers there: 4, 6, 7, 11, 12, 16, 20, 29, 31, 32, 34, 36, 37, 38, 39, 40, 41, 49, 50, 55, 56, 57, 60, 66, 71, 75, 78, 80, 81, 84, 85, 89, 90, 91, 92, 93, 94, 96, 98, 101, 104, 107, 110, 112, 116, 118, 122, 123, 125, 126, 127, 128, 129, 133, 137, 140, 141, 158, 159, 171, 185, 211, 213, 214, 226, 241, 249, 250, 293, 298, 299, 305, 306, 308, 340.

441. Allen, Walter. " 'The Music of Time.' " *Listener,* 59 (3 April 1958), 583-584. On all of the sequence novels up to and including *At Lady Molly's.*

442. Amory, Mark. "Powell's people." (London) *Sunday Times Magazine* (7 September 1975).

443. Anon. "A Who's Who of *The Music of Time.*" *Time and Tide,* 41 (2 and 9 July 1960), 764-765, 808-809 respectively.

444. —. "Anthony Powell." *The* (London) *Times* (5 December 1963), p. 16. An interview.

445. —. "Anthony Powell: A *Summary* Interview." *Summary,* 1 (Autumn 1970), 129-139.

446. —. "Gallery Trustee." *The* (London) *Times* (9 February 1962), p. 18. A notice of Powell's appointment to the National Portrait Gallery.

447. —. "James Tait Black Awards." *The* (London) *Times* (31 January 1958), p. 10. A notice of Powell's receiving the award for his *At Lady Molly's*.

448. —. "Music of Time." *New Yorker*, 41 (3 July 1965), 17-18. An informal interview with Powell in New York. He discusses his writing habits, methods, ideas, and literary likes and dislikes.

449. —. "Neglected Novelist." *Newsweek*, 40 (8 December 1952), 96, 98. A short history of Powell's publishing record, and comments on *Venusberg* and *Agents and Patients*.

450. —. "Novelist's Novelist." *Newsweek*, 41 (9 March 1953), 89-90. On the first two books of *A Dance to the Music of Time*.

451. —. "Powell, Anthony (Dymoke) 1905-." *Contemporary Authors: A Bio-Bibliographical Guide to Current Authors and Their Works*. Eds. James M. Ethridge and Barbara Kopala. Vol. 4. Detroit, Michigan: Gale Research, 1967, p. 770.

* 452. —. "Presentation of W. H. Smith £1,000 Award to Anthony Powell." *Bookseller* (30 November 1974), pp. 2770-2771.

453. —. "Work-in-Progress." *Newsweek*, 59 (22 January 1962), 81-82. On the first three volumes of *A Dance to the Music of Time*, and an interview under the title "Talk with the Author" (p. 82).

454. Antonini, Giacomo. "Anthony Powell and True Moderation." *Summary*, 1 (Autumn 1970), 106-110.

455. Arnold, Bruce. "Powell: *The Music of Time*." *European Patterns: Contemporary Patterns in European Writing; A Series of Essays by Bruce Arnold and Others*. Ed. Timothy Blake Harward. Chester Springs, Pennsylvania:

Dufour Editions, 1967, pp. 49-52.

456. Barrett, William. " 'Quintessentially English.' " *Atlantic,* 209 (March 1962), 146-148. Pp. 146-147. Comments on Powell's work in general.

457. —. "Reader's Choice." *Atlantic,* 213 (February 1964), 138, 140. Comments on the Second Movement of *A Dance to the Music of Time.*

458. Bergonzi, Bernard. *Anthony Powell.* Writers and Their Work Series, 144. London and New York: Longmans, Green, 1962; rev. and enlarged. Writers and Their Work series, 221. Harlow, Essex: Longmans, Green, 1971.

459. —. "Anthony Powell: 9/12." *Critical Quarterly,* 11 (1969), 76-86. On the first nine novels.

460. Bjornson, Barbara Ann. "An Examination of Narrative Strategy in *A La Recherche Du Temps Perdu* and *A Dance to the Music of Time.*" Diss. Washington, 1968. *Dissertation Abstracts,* 30A (1969), 679.

461. Bliven, Naomi. "The Credibility of Nicholas Jenkins." *Summary,* 1 (Autumn 1970), 84-86.

462. Blow, Simon. "Burton's *Anatomy of Melancholy* holds the key to Anthony Powell's 12-volume panoply of English life, now complete." *Guardian* (6 September 1975), p. 8.

463. Boston, Richard. "A Talk with Anthony Powell." *New York Times Book Review* (9 March 1969), pp. 2, 36.

464. Bowen, Elizabeth. "Three Novels by an English Writer with a Keen and Sardonic Eye." *New York Herald Tribune Book Review,* 29 (15 February 1953), 1, 8. Review of *Agents and Patients, Venusberg,* and *A Buyer's Market.*

* 465. Brennan, Neil. *Anthony Powell.* New York: Twayne,

1974.

466. Brooke, Jocelyn. "From Wauchope to Widmerpool." *London Magazine,* 7 (September 1960), 60-64. On Powell's style and "technique of rejection."

467. Brownjohn, Alan. "Anthony Powell." *New Review,* 1 (September 1974), 21-28. An interview.

468. —. "The Social Comedy of Anthony Powell." *Gemini,* 1, No. 2 (Summer 1957), 7-15. On the first three books of *A Dance to the Music of Time.*

469. Cloyne, George. "Three-fifths of a Set of Five." *New York Herald Tribune Books,* 38 (11 February 1962), 6. On the first three books of *A Dance to the Music of Time.*

470. Davis, Douglas M. "An Interview with Anthony Powell: Frome, England, June 1962." *College English,* 24 (April 1963), 533-536.

471. Duffy, Joseph M. "The Dancer and the Dance: Anthony Powell's *Music of Time.*" *Summary,* 1 (Autumn 1970), 74-81.

472. Egan, Michael. "Anthony Powell's Danse Macabre." *Cambridge Review,* 90 (29 November 1968), 189-191. Powell is seen as a Victorian novelist; comparisons are made to the techniques of Henry James.

473. Eimerl, Sarel. "Belgravia Lingers On." *Reporter,* 26 (1 February 1962), 54-56. On *A Dance to the Music of Time* sequence, especially regarding Powell's concern with the upper classes of England.

474. Ellis, G. U. *Twilight on Parnassus: A Survey of Post-War Fiction and Pre-War Criticism.* London: Michael Joseph, 1939. Includes extensive comments on Powell.

475. Fuller, Edmund. "A Satirical Chronicle." *Wall Street*

Journal, 163 (9 March 1964), 12. On the first six novels in *A Dance to the Music of Time.*

476. —. "The Dance Goes On." *Wall Street Journal,* 173 (16 May 1969), 18. On the war trilogy.

477. Fuller, Roy. "Comedy, Realism and Poetry in *The Music of Time.*" *Summary,* 1 (Autumn 1970), 47-53.

478. Gant, Roland. "A Marche Militaire in *The Music of Time.*" *Summary,* 1 (Autumn 1970), 87-90. On the subject of war in the novels.

479. Glazebrook, Mark. "The Art of Horace Isbister, E. Bosworth Deacon and Ralph Barnby." *London Magazine,* 7 (November 1967), 76-82.

480. Gutierrez, Donald K. "A Critical Study of Anthony Powell's *A Dance to the Music of Time.*" Diss. California (Los Angeles), 1969. *Dissertation Abstracts,* 30A (1969), 724.

* 481. —. "Power in *A Dance to the Music of Time.*" *Connecticut Review,* 6, No. 2 (1973), 50-60.

482. Gutwillig, Robert. "A Walk Around London with Anthony Powell." *New York Times Book Review* (30 September 1962), pp. 5, 36. An interview.

483. Hall, James. "The Uses of Polite Surprise: Anthony Powell." *Essays in Criticism,* 12 (April 1962), 167-183; reprinted and enlarged in his *The Tragic Comedians: Seven Modern British Novelists* (see First Part No. 50), pp. 129-150.

484. Hardwick, Elizabeth. "English Traits: Fiction and Autobiography." *Harper's,* 224 (March 1962), 106, 108. Review of first three books of *A Dance to the Music of Time.*

485. Herbert, Hugh. "A word in Jenkin's ear." *Guardian* (15

February 1971), p. 8. An interview.

486. Herring, H. D. "Anthony Powell: A Reaction Against Determinism." *Ball State University Forum,* 9 (Winter 1968), 17-21.

487. Hicks, Granville. "Life's Pirouettes and Pavanes." *Saturday Review,* 45 (27 January 1962), 13. On the first five books of *A Dance to the Music of Time,* and a comparison to Snow's sequence.

488. Hillman, Serrell. "Powell from the Other Side." *Summary,* 1 (Autumn 1970), 120-124. Includes an interview.

489. Howarth, Herbert. "Discords in the *Music of Time.*" *Commentary,* 53 (January 1972), 70-75.

490. Hyman, Stanley Edgar. "A Dance in Intricate Measure." *New Leader,* 45 (22 January 1962), 26-27. On the first three books of *A Dance to the Music of Time.*

491. Hynes, Sam. "Novelist of Society." *Commonweal,* 70 (31 July 1959), 396-397.

492. Janeway, Elizabeth. "Anthony Powell: The Serial Novel." *Summary,* 1 (Autumn 1970), 54-57.

493. Jones, Richard. "Anthony Powell's Music: Swansong of the Metropolitan Romance." *Virginia Quarterly Review,* 52 (Summer 1976), 353-369.

494. Kamera, Willy David. "A Descriptive Index of the Characters in Anthony Powell's *Music of Time.*" Diss. Cornell, 1973. *Dissertation Abstracts,* 34A (1974), 7235.

495. Karl, Frederick. "Sisyphus Descending: Mythical Patterns in the Novels of Anthony Powell." *Mosaic,* 4 (Spring 1971), 13-22.

496. Lambourne, David. "Understanding the Past: Anthony

Powell's Classicism." *Summary,* 1 (Autumn 1970), 111-116.

497. Leclaire, Lucien A. "Anthony Powell: Biographie Spirituelle d' une Génération." *Etudes Anglaises,* 9 (1956), 23-27.

498. Lee, James Ward. "The Novels of Anthony Powell." Diss. Auburn, 1964. *Dissertation Abstracts,* 25A (1965), 5281-5282.

499. Longford, Elizabeth. "A Talk with Anthony Powell." *New York Times Book Review* (11 April 1976), p. 47.

500. Lurie, Alison. "Up Jenkins." *Summary,* 1 (Autumn 1970), 82-83.

501. McCall, Raymond G. "Anthony Powell's Gallery." *College English,* 27 (December 1965), 227-232.

502. McCleon, Dan D. "The Art of Anthony Powell." Diss. Claremont, 1969. *Dissertation Abstracts,* 30A (1969), 1174.

503. McLaughlin, Richard. "Anthony Powell: *The Music of Time."* *Books and Bookmen,* 16 (April 1971), 4-8.

504. —. "In the Comic Tradition." *American Mercury,* 87 (November 1958), 154-155.

505. McLeod, Dan. "Anthony Powell: Some Notes on the Art of the Sequence Novel." *Studies in the Novel,* 3, No. 1 (Spring 1971), 44-63. On the first nine novels of *The Music of Time.*

506. Maddocks, Melvin. "Anthony Powell and 'The Music of Time'." *Christian Science Monitor,* 54 (8 February 1962), 5. On the first three novels of the sequence.

507. Maes-Jelinex, Hena. "Anthony Powell." *Criticism of*

Society in the English Novel Between the Wars. Paris: Société d'Editions, 1970, pp. 499-518.

508. Marsh, Pamela. "Powell at large." *Christian Science Monitor,* 59 (16 March 1967), 15. Remarks by Powell, based on an interview.

509. Martin, W. R. "Style as Achievement in Anthony Powell's *The Music of Time.*" *English Studies in Africa,* 14 (1971), 73-86.

510. Mizener, Arthur. *"A Dance to the Music of Time:* The Novels of Anthony Powell." *Kenyon Review,* 22 (Winter 1960), 79-92.

511. —. "The Novel and Nature in the Twentieth Century: Anthony Powell and James Gould Cozzens," in his *The Sense of Life in the Modern Novel.* Boston: Houghton Mifflin Company, 1964, pp. 79-103.

512. Moore, John Rees. "Anthony Powell's England: *A Dance to the Music of Time.*" *Hollins Critic,* 8, No. 4 (October 1971), 1-16.

513. Morris, Robert K. "Mars Mercurial: Anthony Powell's War Trilogy." *Summary,* 1 (Autumn 1970), 91-105.

514. —. Untitled comments. *Comtemporary Novelists.* Ed. James Vinson. London and Chicago: St. James Press, 1972.

515. —. "The Early Novels of Anthony Powell: A Thematic Study." Diss. Wisconsin, 1964. *Dissertation Abstracts,* 25A (1965), 4152-4153.

516. —. *The Novels of Anthony Powell.* Critical Essays in Modern Literature. Pittsburgh: University of Pittsburgh Press, 1968.

517. Mudrick, Marvin. "Fiction and Truth." *Hudson Review,* 25

(Spring 1972), 142-156. Pp. 144-146. On four books in *A Dance to the Music of Time.*

518. Mylett, Andrew. "The musician of time." *Daily Telegraph* (15 June 1973), pp. 37-38, 40-41.

519. Orwell, George. *The Collected Essays, Journalism and Letters: In Front of Your Nose, 1945-1950.* Vol. 4. Ed. Sonia Orwell and Ian Angus. London: Secker and Warburg, 1968. Includes comments on Powell.

520. P. H. S. "More Powell." *The* (London) *Times* (20 November 1974), p. 16. On Powell's winning the £ 1,000 W. H. Smith literary prize for his *Temporary Kings.*

521. Parkes, David L. "Powell, Anthony (1905-)." *Twentieth Century Writing: A Reader's Guide to Contemporary Literature.* Ed. Kenneth Richardson. London: Newnes Books, 1969, p. 501.

522. Phillipson, John S. *"A Dance to the Music of Time..."* *Best Sellers,* 21 (1 February 1962), 431. On the first three novels of the sequence.

523. Pooter. Untitled interview with Anthony Powell. *The* (London) *Times* (21 March 1970), p. I.

524. Pritchett, V. S. "London Letter." *New York Times Book Review* (12 January 1958), p. 22. On Powell as a comic novelist.

525. Quesenbery, W. D., Jr. "Anthony Powell." *Contemporary Literature,* 10 (Winter 1969), 124-126.

526. —. "Anthony Powell: The Anatomy of Decay." *Critique,* 7, No. 1 (Spring 1964), 5-26.

527. Radner, Sanford. "Powell, Anthony." *Encyclopedia of World Literature in the 20th Century.* Ed. Wolfgang Bernard Fleischmann. New York: Frederick Ungar,

1971, p. 105.

528. —. "Powell's Early Novels: A Study in Point of View." *Renascence,* 16 (Summer 1964), 194-200.

529. —. "The World of Anthony Powell." *Claremont Quarterly,* 10, No. 2 (Winter 1963), 41-57.

530. Raymond, John. "Isherwood and Powell." *Listener,* 52 (16 December 1954), p. 1067.

531. Riley, John James. "Gentlemen at Arms: A Comparison of the War Trilogies of Anthony Powell and Evelyn Waugh." Diss. Tufts, 1973. *Dissertation Abstracts,* 34A (1974), 5202.

532. Roudy, Pierre. "Anthony Powell et l'Angleterre proustienne." *Europe,* 49 (February-March 1971), 167-173.

533. Ruoff, Gene W. "Social Mobility and the Artist in *Manhattan Transfer* and *The Music of Time." Wisconsin Studies in Contemporary Literature,* 5, No. 1 (Winter-Spring 1964), 64-76.

534. Russell, John. *Anthony Powell: A Quintet, Sextet, and War.* Bloomington, Indiana: Indiana University Press, 1970.

535. —. "Humour and the Early Novels." *Summary,* 1 (Autumn 1970), 38-43; reprinted in his *Anthony Powell: A Quintet, Sextet, and War* (see main entry).

536. —. "Quintet from the '30s: Anthony Powell." *Kenyon Review,* 27 (Autumn 1965), 698-726. On Powell's first five novels.

537. —. "The War Trilogies of Anthony Powell and Evelyn Waugh." *Modern Age,* 16 (1972), 289-300.

538. Schlesinger, Arthur, Jr. "Anthony Powell: The Prosopo-

grapher as Novelist." *Summary,* 1 (Autumn 1970), 66-73.

539. Shapiro, Charles. "Looking Down from London Bridge." *Saturday Review,* 47 (25 January 1964), 38-39. Review of the Second Movement in *A Dance to the Music of Time.*

540. —. "Widmerpool and *The Music of Time,*" in his *Contemporary British Novelists* (see First Part No. 107), pp. 81-94.

541.Shor, Rachel. "WLB Biography: Anthony Powell." *Wilson Library Bulletin,* 38 (January 1964), 411, 424.

542. Sions, Harry. "The Relevance of Anthony Powell." *Summary,* 1 (Autumn 1970), 34-37.

543. Stanton, Lillian. "Art in the Dance: A Study of the Use of the Fine Arts in Anthony Powell's *A Dance to the Music of Time.*" Diss. Notre Dame, 1973. *Dissertation Abstracts,* 34A (1974), 4288.

543a. Stürzl, Erwin. "Anthony Powell." *Englische Literatur der Geganwart in Einzeldarstellungen.* Ed. Horst W. Drescher. Stuttgart: Kröner, 1970, pp. 65-85.

544. Taubman, Robert. "Da Capo." *New Statesman,* 64 (28 December 1962), 932. On the first three books of *A Dance to the Music of Time.*

* 545. Tucker, James. "A Guide to *A Dance to the Music of Time.*" *New Review,* 2 (August 1975), 25-37. A description of who's who and who's where in Powell's long sequence.

546. —. "Tribulations of a Powellite." *Daily Telegraph* (13 June 1974), p. 15.

547. Vaizey, John. "Notes on the Structure of *The Music of*

Time." Summary, 1 (Autumn 1970), 58-65.

548. Vinson, James. "Anthony Powell's *Music of Time." Perspective,* 10 (Summer-Autumn 1958), 146-152.

549. Voorhees, Richard J. "Anthony Powell: The First Phase." *Prairie Schooner,* 28 (Winter 1954), 337-344.

550. —. *"The Music of Time:* Themes and Variations." *Dalhousie Review,* 42 (Autumn 1962), 313-321.

551. Walcutt, Charles Child. "Modern Consequences," in his *Man's Changing Mask: Modes and Methods of Characterization in Fiction.* Minneapolis: Minnesota University Press, 1966, pp. 237-355. Pp. 336-339. On Powell's *A Dance to the Music of Time.*

552. Weatherby, W. J. "Taken from Life." *Twentieth Century,* 170 (July 1961), 50-53. An interview.

553. Weidman, Jerome. "A Note About Anthony Powell." *Summary,* 1 (Autumn 1970), 125-128. A personal "experience" in becoming aware of Powell, and then becoming addicted to reading his work.

554. White, Mary Ray. "Anthony Powell: Ten Volumes of *The Music of Time."* Diss. Cornell, 1973. *Dissertation Abstracts,* 34A (1973), 1300-1301.

555. Wilcox, Thomas W. "Anthony Powell and the Illusion of Possibility." *Contemporary Literature,* 17 (Spring 1976), 223-239.

556. Woodward, A. G. "The Novels of Anthony Powell." *English Studies in Africa,* 10 (September 1967), 117-128.

557. Zigerell, James J. "Anthony Powell's *Music of Time:* Chronicle of a Declining Establishment." *Twentieth Century Literature,* 12 (October 1966), 138-146.

558. Ziman, H. D. "The Private and the Public Powell." *Summary*, 1 (Autumn 1970), 117-119.

STUDIES AND REVIEWS OF
INDIVIDUAL WORKS

References to individual books by Powell also appear in the First Part of this bibliography. See the following numbers there: 138, 161, 162, 163, 164, 178, 184, 195, 197, 222, 230, 248, 251, 254, 264, 265, 267, 270, 273, 277, 284, 287, 288, 290, 300, 303, 323, 347.

Afternoon Men

559. Anon. *"Afternoon Men." TLS* (17 September 1931), p. 708.

560. —. "Briefly Noted." *New Yorker,* 39 (26 October 1963), 218.

561. —. "Cocktail Fiction." *New York Times Book Review* (14 February 1932), p. 7.

562. —. "Compromise in Stage Adaptation of Book. Arts Theatre: *Afternoon Men." The* (London) *Times* (23 August 1963), p. 11.

563. —. "New Novels." *Spectator,* 149 (22 August 1931), 252.

564. —. "Of No Import." *New York Herald Tribune Books,* 8 (14 February 1932), 12.

565. —. "Study in Emptiness." *Newsweek,* 62 (30 September 1963), 89.

566. Barrett, William. "Party going." *Atlantic,* 212 (October

1963), 155-156.

567. Boothroyd, Basil. "At the Play." *Punch,* 245 (4 September 1963), 354. Review of the stage production.

568. Bowen, John. "Everybody's Drifting." *New York Times Book Review* (20 October 1963), pp. 4, 44.

569. Cooper, Jilly. "Start of an Addiction." *Summary,* 1 (Autumn 1970), 44-46.

570. Hicks, Granville. "Guests of a Long-Playing Party." *Saturday Review,* 46 (28 September 1963), 49-50.

571. Igoe, W. J. Review of *Afternoon Men,* in the *Chicago Sunday Tribune Magazine of Books* (27 October 1963), p. 8.

572. Pryce-Jones, Alan. Review of *Afternoon Men,* in the *New York Herald Tribune* (1 October 1963), p. 25.

573. R. B. Review of *Afternoon Men,* in the *San Francisco Chronicle* (3 November 1963), p. 41.

574. Review of *Afternoon Men,* in the *Boston Evening Transcript* (25 June 1932), p. 3.

575. Spector, Donald. *"Afternoon Men." Book Week,* 1 (22 September 1963), 14.

576. Willis, Katherine Tappert. *"Afternoon Men." Library Journal,* 88 (1 September 1963), 3103.

Venusberg

577. Anon. *"Venusberg." New Statesman and Nation,* 4 (10 December 1932), 772.

578. —. *"Venusberg." TLS* (3 November 1932), p. 816.

579. Shuttleworth, Martin. "Drama: On the Road." *Listener,* 69 (14 February 1963), 309-310. P. 310. Review of radio broadcast of book.

From a View to a Death
or
Mr. Zouch: Superman

580. Anon. *"From a View to a Death."* *Booklist,* 64 (1 July 1968), 1220.

581. —. *"From a View to a Death."* *Choice,* 5 (June 1968), 486.

582. —. *"From a View to a Death."* *Kirkus,* 35 (15 November 1967), 1387.

583. —. *"From a View to a Death."* *Publishers' Weekly,* 192 (4 December 1967), 41.

584. —. *"From a View to a Death."* *TLS* (9 November 1933), p. 776.

585. Bell, Lisle. *"Mr. Zouch: Superman."* *New York Herald Tribune Books,* 10 (4 March 1934), 10.

586. Brickell, Herschel. "Long and Leisurely." *North American Review,* 237 (April 1934), 379.

587. Davis, D. M. Review of *From a View to a Death,* in the *National Observer,* 7 (8 January 1968), 23.

588. Freedman, Richard. "Amiable Britons quietly driving everyone bonkers." *Book World,* 2 (18 February 1968), 7.

589. G. S. *"Mr. Zouch: Superman."* *Saturday Review of Literature,* 10 (31 March 1934), 598.

590. Hartley, L. P. "The Literary Lounger." *Sketch,* 164 (25 October 1933), 174, X. P. X.

591. Maddocks, Melvin. "Anthony Powell's halfway house." *Christian Science Monitor,* 60 (25 January 1968), 13.

592. Poore, Charles. "When the Appalling Begins to Pall." *New York Times,* 117 (14 March 1968), 41.

593. Pritchard, William H. "Fiction Chronicle." *Hudson Review,* 21 (Summer 1968), 364-376. P. 373.

594. Sherman, Beatrice. *"Mr. Zouch: Superman."* New York *Times Book Review* (18 February 1934), p. 12.

595. Wolfe, Peter. "Eccentrics in a Closed Circle." *Saturday Review,* 51 (3 February 1968), 39.

Agents and Patients

596. Anon. "Orbis Modernis Notus." *TLS* (11 January 1936), p. 33.

597. Hartley, L. P. "The Literary Lounger." *Sketch,* 173 (15 January 1936), 122, 124. P. 122.

What's Become of Waring

598. Anon. "Briefly Noted." *New Yorker,* 39 (27 April 1963), 176.

599. —. "Disappearing Author." *TLS* (25 March 1939), p. xiii.

600. —. "Powell's Piano Exercise." *Time,* 81 (26 April 1963), 96, 98.

601. —. *"What's Become of Waring?"* TLS (28 January 1939), p. 59.

602. Cox, Thomas A. Review of *What's Become of Waring,* in the *San Francisco Chronicle* (14 July 1963), p. 28.

603. Fuller, Edmund. "Corpus but No Corpse." *New York Times Book Review* (28 April 1963), p. 4.

604. Hartley, L. P. "The Literary Lounger." *Sketch,* 185 (22 March 1939), 555, 556, IV. P. 555.

605. Igoe, W. J. Review of *What's Become of Waring,* in the *Chicago Sunday Tribune Magazine of Books* (28 April 1963), p. 3.

606. LaHaye, Judson. *"What's Become of Waring."* *Best Sellers,* 23 (1 May 1963), 60.

607. Lurie, Alison. "Early Powell." *New York Review of Books,* 1, No. 2 (1963), 27.

608. McLaughlin, Richard. "Anthony Powell's Microscopic Lens." *Commonweal,* 79 (27 September 1963), 20, 22.

609. Maddocks, Melvin. "Publishers A la Powell." *Christian Science Monitor,* 55 (2 May 1963), 11.

610. Manning, Olivia. *"What's Become of Waring?"* *Punch,* 224 (1 July 1953), 779.

611. O'Brien, Kate. "Fiction." *Spectator,* 162 (3 February 1939), 190.

612. Pickrel, Paul. "And Finally, Some Men." *Harper's,* 226 (June 1963), 108-109. P. 109.

613. Raymond, John. "Paperbacks." *Punch,* 255 (13 November 1968), 708.

614. Ready, William. *"What's Become of Waring."* *Critic,* 21 (June 1963), 73.

615. Shapiro, Charles K. "Death of a Traveler." *Saturday Review,* 46 (27 April 1963), 36.

616. Southern, Jane. "He Had it from the Start." *New York Herald Tribune Books*, 39 (28 April 1963), 4.

617. Willis, Katherine Tappert. *"What's Become of Waring?"* *Library Journal*, 88 (15 April 1963), 1688.

Two Novels: Venusberg and Agents and Patients

618. Anon. *"Two Novels: Venusberg; Agents and Patients."* *Choice*, 2 (June 1965), 228.

619. Barrett, William. "Knights and Knaves." *Atlantic*, 215 (May 1965), 151-152. Review of *Venusberg* and *Agents and Patients*.

620. Casey, Florence. "Powell party: Icy Lushington and others." *Christian Science Monitor*, 57 (18 March 1965), 11. Review of *Venusberg* and *Agents and Patients*.

621. Doyle, Paul A. *"Venusberg and Agents and Patients."* *Best Sellers*, 25 (1 April 1965), 10.

622. Lerman, Leo. "Foible-Tweaking Comedy." *New York Times Book Review* (14 December 1952), p. 4. Review of Anthony Powell's *Venusberg* and *Agents and Patients*.

623. Manning, Olivia. *"Venusberg: Agents and Patients."* *Punch*, 229 (17 August 1955), 195. A short review on both novels.

624. Moore, Harry T. "Death in a Droshky." *Saturday Review*, 48 (15 May 1965), 53-54. Review of *Venusberg* and *Agents and Patients*.

625. Poore, Charles. "The Worldly Bohemias of Anthony Powell." *New York Times*, 114 (6 March 1965), 23. Review of *Venusberg*, and *Agents and Patients*.

626. Rolo, Charles J. "England made them." *Atlantic Monthly*,

191 (February 1953), 81-82. P. 82. Review of *Venusberg* and *Agents and Patients.*

627. West, Anthony. "Wry Humor." *New Yorker,* 28 (13 December 1952), 170-171, 174, 177-178. Discussion includes comments on Powell's *Venusberg,* and *Agents and Patients.*

628. Willis, Katherine Tappert. *"Two Novels." Library Journal,* 77 (1 December 1952), 2072.

A Dance to the Music of Time Sequence:

A Question of Upbringing

629. Allen, Walter. Review of *A Question of Upbringing,* in the *Listener* (3 April 1958), p. 584.

630. Anon. *"A Question of Upbringing." Kirkus,* 19 (1 April 1951), 195.

631. —. "Briefly Noted." *New Yorker,* 27 (28 April 1951), 102-103.

632. —. "From a Chase to a View." *TLS* (16 February 1951), p. 100.

633. Fausset, Hugh I'A. "New Novels." *Manchester Guardian* (26 January 1951), p. 4.

634. Pippett, Roger. "Four Schoolboys." *New York Times Book Review* (8 July 1951), p. 11.

635. Raymond, John. "New Novels." *New Statesman and Nation,* 41 (27 January 1951), 104, 106. P. 104.

636. Stallings, Sylvia. "A Young Man's World." *New York Herald Tribune Book Review,* 27 (22 April 1951), 13.

637. Swados, Harvey. "Fiction Parade." *New Republic*, 125 (20 August 1951), 21.

638. Vogler, Lewis. Review of *A Question of Upbringing*, in the *San Francisco Chronicle* (6 May 1951), p. 22.

639. Worsley-Gough, Barbara. "Fiction." *Spectator*, 186 (9 February 1951), 188, 190. P. 190.

A Buyer's Market

640. Anon. "Men About Town." *TLS* (27 June 1952), p. 417.

641. Fitzgerald, Edward J. "Young Men About London-Town." *Saturday Review*, 36 (28 February 1953), 35.

642. Gill, Brendan. "Three Pasts." *New Yorker*, 28 (7 February 1953), 98, 101-102. Pp. 101-102.

643. Lean, Tangye. "Fiction." *Spectator*, 188 (27 June 1952), 866.

644. Pippett, Roger. "Luckless Widmerpool." *New York Times Book Review* (8 February 1953), p. 6.

645. Pritchett, V. S. "Books in General." *New Statesman and Nation*, 43 (28 June 1952), 774-775.

* 646. R. T. Review of *A Buyer's Market*, in the *San Francisco Chronicle* (22 March 1953), p. 16.

The Acceptance World

647. Amis, Kingsley. "Afternoon World." *Spectator*, 194 (13 May 1955), 619-620.

648. Anon. "Briefly Noted." *New Yorker*, 32 (17 March 1956), 179.

649. —. "Corpse in the Garden." *Time,* 67 (20 February 1956), 99.

650. —. "Learning How to Live." *The* (London) *Times* (12 May 1955), p. 13.

651. —. "Society Ritual." *TLS* (13 May 1955), p. 249.

652. —. *"The Acceptance World; a novel."* *Booklist,* 52 (1 March 1956), 276.

653. —. *"The Acceptance World."* *Kirkus,* 24 (1 February 1956), 91.

654. Arau, Anthony. "A Handful of Dust." *New Republic,* 134 (2 April 1956), 19-20.

655. Bailey, Anthony. "The Social Dance of Life." *Commonweal,* 63 (23 March 1956), 647-648.

* 656. Baro, Gene. "Light English Novel of a Dark Time." *New York Herald Tribune Book Review,* 32 (19 February 1956), 4.

657. Hawthorne, Hazel. "Remembrance of a Recent Past." *Nation,* 182 (31 March 1956), 263.

658. Hewitt, Douglas. "New Novels." *Manchester Guardian* (10 May 1955), p. 4.

659. Lister, Richard. "The Strange Case of Mr. Powell." *New Statesman and Nation,* 49 (28 May 1955), 754.

660. Pippett, Aileen. "If You Know the Trick." *New York Times Book Review* (19 February 1956), p. 4.

661. Powell, Dawn. "World Within London." *Saturday Review,* 39 (3 March 1956), 17.

662. Price, R. G. G. *"The Acceptance World."* *Punch,* 228 (8

June 1955), 718.

663. Rolo, Charles J. "Anthony Powell." *Atlantic,* 197 (April 1956), 86-87.

664. Stern, James, "A Variety of Satire." *Encounter,* 5 (July 1955), 86-88. Pp. 86-87.

665. Voiles, James. Review of *The Acceptance World,* in the *San Francisco Chronicle* (15 April 1956), p. 21.

666. Wagenknecht, Edward. Review of *The Acceptance World,* in the *Chicago Sunday Tribune* (26 February 1956), p. 2.

667. Wyndham, Francis. Untitled book review. *London Magazine,* 2 (September 1955), 77-79. Pp. 77-78.

At Lady Molly's

668. Anon. "Absolutely Anybody." *Time,* 72 (11 August 1958), 74.

669. —. *"At Lady Molly's." Booklist,* 55 (1 October 1958), 75.

670. —. *"At Lady Molly's." Bookmark,* 18 (October 1958), 14.

671. —. *"At Lady Molly's." Kirkus,* 26 (1 June 1958), 389.

672. —. "Briefly Noted." *New Yorker,* 34 (27 September 1958), 176.

673. —. "New Fiction." *The* (London) *Times* (31 October 1957), p. 13.

674. —. "Time Marches On." *TLS* (1 November 1957), p. 653.

675. Bayley, John. "New Novels." *Spectator,* 199 (1 November 1957), 586.

676. Brennan, Neil. *"At Lady Molly's."* *Epoch*, 11 (Fall 1958), 126-129.

677. Butcher, Fanny. Review of *At Lady Molly's*, in the *Chicago Sunday Tribune* (27 July 1958), p. 3.

* 678. Corke, Hilary. "New Novels." *Listener*, 58 (21 November 1957), 855.

679. Dolbier, Maurice. "Effervescent Comedy of English Society." *New York Herald Tribune Book Review*, 34 (27 July 1958), 3.

680. Fraser, G. S. "New Novels." *New Statesman*, 54 (2 November 1957), 582-583.

681. Fremantle, Anne. "Milestones on the Road." *Saturday Review*, 41 (26 July 1958), 18.

682. Grauel, George E. *"At Lady Molly's."* *Best Sellers*, 18 (1 August 1958), 161.

683. Hobson, Harold. "Society and the Novel." *Christian Science Monitor*, 50 (27 November 1957), 15.

684. Hughes, Riley. *"At Lady Molly's."* *Catholic World*, 188 (October 1958), 71.

685. Kiefer, H. C. *"At Lady Molly's."* *Arizona Quarterly*, 15 (Autumn 1959), 279-281.

686. McLaughlin, Richard. "Comedy of English Society Before Second World War." *Springfield Sunday Republican* (24 August 1958), p. 6D.

687. Mortimer, John. "Novels." *Encounter*, 10 (January 1958), 82-84. P. 83.

688. Powell, Dawn. "Somebody Else's Crowd." *Nation*, 187 (25 October 1958), 296.

689. Price, R. G. G. *"At Lady Molly's." Punch,* 233 (11 December 1957), 707.

690. Quinton, Anthony. Untitled book review. *London Magazine,* 5 (February 1958), 68-72. Pp. 68-70.

691. Rolo, Charles J. "Fiction Chronicle." *Atlantic,* 202 (September 1958), 80-82. P. 81.

692. Schlesinger, Arthur L., Jr. "Waugh a la Proust." *New Republic,* 139 (20 October 1958), 20-21.

693. Stern, James. "All Passion Spent." *New York Times Book Review* (27 July 1958), pp. 5, 12.

694. Webster, Harvey Curtis. "A Dance of British Eccentrics." *New Leader,* 42 (12 January 1959), 26-27.

695. Williams, David. "Widmerpool's Progress." *Manchester Guardian* (5 November 1957), p. 4.

* 696. Willis, Katherine Tappert. *"At Lady Molly's." Library Journal,* 83 (July 1958), 2053.

Casanova's Chinese Restaurant

697. Anon. "Between Proust and Waugh." *Time,* 76 (26 September 1960), 108, 110, 112.

698. —. *"Casanova's Chinese Restaurant." Booklist,* 57 (1 November 1960), 146.

699. —. "Modes of Perception." *TLS* (24 June 1960), p. 397.

700. —. "New Fiction." *The* (London) *Times* (23 June 1960), p. 15.

701. Bergonzi, Bernard. *"Casanova's Chinese Restaurant." Twentieth Century,* 168 (September 1960), 280-281.

702. Bliven, Naomi. "Books: The Marriage State." *New Yorker*, 36 (31 December 1960), 53-54.

703. Cosman, Max. "A Declining Class." *Commonweal*, 73 (25 November 1960), 238-239.

704. Dawson, Helen. "Briefing: *Casanova's Chinese Restaurant*." *Observer* (1 March 1970), p. 30.

705. De Mott, Benjamin. "Time Styles." *Hudson Review*, 13 (Winter 1960-1961), 602-611. P. 611.

706. Didion, Joan. "The Edge of the Precipice." *National Review*, 9 (19 November 1960), 315-316.

707. Dolbier, Maurice. "An English Social Comedy." *New York Herald Tribune Book Review*, 37 (18 September 1960), 6.

708. Greacen, Robert. Review of *Casanova's Chinese Restaurant*, in the *San Francisco Chronicle* (21 August 1960), p. 24.

709. Hicks, Granville. "The Personality of Paradox." *Saturday Review*, 43 (22 October 1960), 16.

710. Igoe, W. J. Review of *Casanova's Chinese Restaurant*, in the *Chicago Sunday Tribune Magazine of Books* (25 September 1960), p. 3.

711. Keown, Eric. "New Novels." *Punch*, 239 (20 July 1960), 103-104. P. 103.

712. Kermode, Frank. "The Interpretation of the Times." *Encounter*, 15 (September 1960), 71-76; reprinted in his *Puzzles and Epiphanies* (see First Part No. 60), pp. 121-130.

713. Maddocks, Melvin. "Anthony Powell's New Novel in 'The Music of Time'." *Christian Science Monitor*, 52 (6 October 1960), 15.

714. McLaughlin, Richard. "Powell Scores Again." *Springfield Sunday Republican* (23 October 1960), p. 4D.

715. Mizener, Arthur. "Life is Absurd and Also a Little Sad." *New York Times Book Review* (9 October 1960), p. 5.

716. Poore, Charles. "Books of The Times." *New York Times,* 110 (24 September 1960), 21.

717. Pritchett, V. S. "The Bored Barbarians." *New Statesman,* 59 (25 June 1960), 947-948; reprinted in his *The Living Novel and Later Appreciations.* New York: Random House, 1964, pp. 294-303; reprinted in his *The Working Novelist.* London: Chatto and Windus, 1965, pp. 172-180.

718. Raymond, John. "New Novels." *Listener,* 64 (7 July 1960), 33.

719. Shrapnel, Norman. "The artful rambler." *Guardian* (1 July 1960), p. 7.

720. Waugh, Evelyn. "Marriage á la mode—1936." *Spectator,* 204 (24 June 1960), 919.

The Kindly Ones

721. Anon. "Comic Opera (Act VI)." *Time,* 80 (12 October 1962), 108, 110.

722. —. "New Fiction." *The* (London) *Times* (28 June 1962), p. 15.

723. —. *"The Kindly Ones." Booklist,* 59 (15 October 1962), 165.

724. —. *"The Kindly Ones." Kirkus,* 30 (1 August 1962), 707.

725. —. *"The Kindly Ones." Virginia Quarterly Review,* 39

(Spring 1963), xlix.

726. Bergonzi, Bernard. "Unfair to Widmerpool?" *Guardian* (29 June 1962), p. 7.

727. Bliven, Naomi. "Ties That Bind." *New Yorker,* 39 (6 April 1963), 180-182, 185-188. Pp. 182, 185-188.

728. Fenwick, J. H. *"The Music of Time."* London Magazine, n.s. 2 (July 1962), 63-67.

729. Hartley, L. P. "Good Dog, Good Dog." *Time and Tide,* 43 (28 June 1962), 21-22.

730. Igoe, W. J. Review of *The Kindly Ones,* in the *Chicago Sunday Tribune of Books* (30 September 1962), p. 3.

731. Janeway, Elizabeth. "Far Away Someone Shot an Archduke." *New York Times Book Review* (30 September 1962), p. 5.

732. Karl, Frederick R. "Bearers of War and Disaster." *New Republic,* 147 (24 September 1962), 21-22.

733. McLaughlin, Richard. "Anthony Powell: Vision and Detachment." *Commonweal,* 77 (8 February 1963), 519.

734. Maddocks, Melvin. "Poise Among Shadows." *Christian Science Monitor,* 54 (27 September 1962), 11.

735. Mayne, Richard. "Incidental Music by Anthony Powell." *New Statesman,* 64 (6 July 1962), 17-18.

736. Phillipson, John S. *"The Kindly Ones."* Best Sellers, 22 (1 October 1962), 260.

737. Popkin, Henry. "On Meeting Old Mistresses." *Saturday Review,* 45 (29 December 1962), 37-38.

738. Price, R. G. G. "Counterpoint." *Punch,* 242 (27 June

1962), 989.

739. Saunders, Dero A. "A Delicious Sense of Uncertainty." *New York Herald Tribune Books,* 39 (30 September 1962), 13.

740. Scannell, Vernon. "New Novels." *Listener,* 67 (28 June 1962), 1128.

* 741. Symons, Julian. "Time's Laughing Stocks." *TLS* (29 June 1962), p. 476; reprinted as "A Long Way from Firbank," in his *Critical Occasions* (see First Part No. 116), pp. 74-79; replies to Symons' article by Hallam Edwardes, and John Carter, in *TLS* (13 July 1962), p. 509; response by Symons to both, in *TLS* (20 July 1962), p. 525.

742. Waugh, Evelyn. "Bioscope." *Spectator,* 208 (29 June 1962), 863-864.

743. Willis, Katherine Tappert. *"The Kindly Ones."* *Library Journal,* 87 (1 September 1962), 2920.

744. Wyndham, Francis. "Novels." *Encounter,* 19 (September 1962), 74-77. Pp. 74-76.

The Valley of Bones

745. Anon. "Déjà Vu." *Newsweek,* 64 (28 September 1964), 101.

746. —. "Musical Chairs." *Time,* 84 (28 August 1964), 96.

747. —. "New Fiction." *The* (London) *Times* (5 March 1964), p. 15.

748. —. "Nick Goes to War." *TLS* (5 March 1964), p. 189; reprinted in *T.L.S. Essays and Reviews from The Times Literary Supplement 1964.* London: Oxford University Press, 1965, pp. 105-107.

749. —. "Paperbacks: *The Valley of Bones.*" *The* (London) *Times* (13 April 1968), p. 23.

750. —. *"The Valley of Bones."* *Choice*, 1 (January 1965), 480.

751. Baro, Gene. "Of Man and Mars." *New York Times Book Review* (30 August 1964), pp. 4-5, 20.

752. Bergonzi, Bernard. "At Anthony Powell's." *New York Review of Books*, 3 (8 October 1964), 11-12.

753. Bliven, Naomi. "Military Merriment, Mental Marshlands." *New Yorker*, 40 (26 December 1964), 75-77. P. 75.

754. Curley, Daniel. "The Bones Begin to Stir." *New Leader*, 47 (23 November 1964), 22-23.

755. Davis, Robert Murray. *"The Valley of Bones."* *Books Abroad*, 39 (Summer 1965), 351.

756. De Mott, Benjamin. "Character Building: '64." *Harper's*, 229 (September 1964), 106, 108-109.

757. Fuller, Roy. *"The Valley of Bones."* *London Magazine*, n.s. 4 (May 1964), 86-88.

758. Getlein, Frank. Untitled book review. *Commonweal*, 81 (4 December 1964), 357.

759. Grauel, George E. *"The Valley of Bones."* *Best Sellers*, 24 (15 September 1964), 220-221.

760. Hartley, L. P. "Jenkins at War." *Spectator*, 212 (20 March 1964), 383.

761. Hicks, Granville. "This is the Army, Mr. Jenkins." *Saturday Review*, 47 (22 August 1964), 23-24.

762. Hope, Francis. "As If." *New Statesman*, 67 (6 March 1964), 371-372. P. 371.

763. Igoe, W. J. Review of *The Valley of Bones,* in the *Chicago Sunday Tribune Books Today* (13 September 1964), p. 8.

764. Jenkins, Roy. "Books of the Year." *Observer* (20 December 1964), p. 7.

765. Maddocks, Melvin. "Knights in a Chess Set." *Christian Science Monitor,* 56 (3 September 1964), 7.

766. Moore, Brian. "The secret behind Jenkins' sneer." *Book Week,* 1 (30 August 1964), 5, 13.

767. Poore, Charles. "The Army is Sometimes Like Civilian Life or More So." *New York Times,* 113 (27 August 1964), 31.

768. Price, R. G. G. "New Novels." *Punch,* 246 (11 March 1964), 396.

769. Pryce-Jones, Alan. Review of *The Valley of Bones,* in the *New York Herald Tribune* (1 September 1964), p. 21.

770. Radner, Sanford. "Anthony Powell and *The Valley of Bones.*" *English Record,* 15 (April 1965), 8-9.

771. Raven, Simon. "A novelist on the march." *Observer* (1 March 1964), p. 27.

772. Review of *The Valley of Bones,* in the *San Francisco Sunday Chronicle* (8 November 1964), p. 39.

773. Ross, M. Review of *The Valley of Bones,* in the *Listener* (12 March 1964), p. 443.

774. Shrapnel, Norman. "Jenkins in uniform." *Manchester Guardian Weekly,* 90 (12 March 1964), 11.

775. Soames, S. Review of *The Valley of Bones,* in the *Book-of-the-Month-Club News* (August 1964), p. 10.

776. Willis, Katherine Tappert. *"The Valley of Bones."* *Library Journal*, 89 (1 October 1964), 3774.

The Soldier's Art

777. Anon. "New Fiction." *The* (London) *Times* (15 September 1966), p. 16.

778. —. *"The Soldier's Art."* *Booklist*, 63 (15 May 1967), 981.

779. —. *"The Soldier's Art."* *Choice*, 4 (June 1967), 423-424.

780. —. *"The Soldier's Art."* *Kirkus*, 35 (15 January 1967), 80.

781. —. *"The Soldier's Art."* *New Yorker*, 43 (3 June 1967), 145.

782. —. *"The Soldier's Art."* *Publishers' Weekly*, 191 (23 January 1967), 256.

783. —. *"The Soldier's Art."* *Virginia Quarterly Review*, 43 (Summer 1967), cv, cx.

784. —. "The War of Total Paper." *Time*, 89 (3 March 1967), 102, 104.

785. —. "Twenty for the top shelf." *Manchester Guardian Weekly*, 95 (15 December 1966), 10.

786. —. "War Games." *TLS* (15 September 1966), p. 853; reprinted in *T.L.S. Essays and Reviews from The Times Literary Supplement 1966.* London: Oxford University Press, 1967, pp. 74-75.

787. Brockway, J. Review of *The Soldier's Art*, in *Books and Bookmen*, 12 (January 1967), 51.

788. Corbett, Edward P. J. *"The Soldier's Art."* *America*, 116 (29 April 1967), 657-658.

789. Davis, D. M. Review of *The Soldier's Art,* in the *National Observer,* 6 (27 March 1967), p. 19.

790. Dolbier, M. Review of *The Soldier's Art,* in the *World Journal Tribune,* 1 (10 March 1967), 28.

791. Garis, Robert. "Varieties of Will." *Hudson Review,* 20 (Summer 1967), 325-334. Pp. 331-334.

792. Grandsen, K. W. "Taste of the Old Time." *Encounter,* 27 (December 1966), 106-108.

793. Graver, Lawrence. "The Virtues of Verbosity." *New Republic,* 156 (22 April 1967), 22-25.

794. Gross, John. "A Question of Upbringing." *New York Review of Books,* 8 (18 May 1967), 34-36.

795. Haney, Patrick. "Snobbery in the Grand Manner." *Denver Quarterly,* 2 (Summer 1967), 146-148.

796. Hicks, Granville. "Detour from the Darkening Path." *Saturday Review,* 50 (18 March 1967), 23-24.

797. Hill, William B. *"The Soldier's Art." America,* 116 (6 May 1967), 702.

798. Igoe, W. J. Review of *The Soldier's Art,* in the *Chicago Sunday Tribune Books Today,* 4 (2 April 1967), 5.

799. Jacobsen, Josephine. *"The Soldier's Art." Commonweal,* 86 (12 May 1967), 239.

800. Janeway, Elizabeth. "More Music." *New York Times Book Review* (19 March 1967), p. 4.

801. McGuinness, Frank. Untitled book review. *London Magazine,* n.s. 6 (October 1966), 113-116. Pp. 113-115.

802. McQuade, Kate. *"The Soldier's Art." Library Journal,*

92 (15 February 1967), 797.

803. Maddocks, Melvin. "A specialist in gray humor." *Christian Science Monitor,* 59 (16 March 1967), 15.

804. Morris, Robert K. "Dancing in Cadence." *Nation,* 204 (29 May 1967), 697-699.

805. Morton, Charles W. *"The Music of Time."* *Atlantic,* 219 (May 1967), 110-111.

806. Poore, Charles. "The Music of Time in Battle Dress." *New York Times,* 116 (8 March 1967), 43.

807. Pryce-Jones, Alan. "Powell's elegiac art." *Book Week,* 4 (9 April 1967), 14, 16.

808. Raven, Simon. "Officers and cads." *Observer* (11 September 1966), p. 27.

809. Ryan, Frank L. *"The Soldier's Art."* *Best Sellers,* 27 (1 April 1967), 9-10.

810. Seymour-Smith, Martin. "Jenkins Marches On." *Spectator,* 217 (16 September 1966), 353.

811. Trevor, William. "Widmerpool militant." *Manchester Guardian Weekly,* 95 (22 September 1966), 11.

812. Zimmerman, Paul D. "Bottom Brass." *Newsweek,* 69 (13 March 1967), 113-114.

The Military Philosophers

813. Anon. "Briefly Noted." *New Yorker,* 45 (5 July 1969), 76.

814. —. "Dancing in the Dark." *TLS* (17 October 1968), p. 1170; reprinted in *T.L.S. Essays and Reviews from The*

Times Literary Supplement 1968. London: Oxford University Press, 1969, pp. 183-185.

815. —. "Powell's Piano Concertos." *Time,* 93 (28 March 1969), 90, 92.

816. —. "*The Military Philosophers.*" *Booklist,* 65 (15 April 1969), 943.

817. —. "*The Military Philosophers.*" *Kirkus,* 37 (15 January 1969), 68.

818. —. "*The Military Philosophers.*" *Publishers' Weekly,* 195 (13 January 1969), 84.

819. Beichman, Arnold. "*The Military Philosophers.*" *Commonweal,* 90 (30 May 1969), 326-327.

820. Braine, John. "The River Flows." *National Review,* 21 (6 May 1969), 443-445.

821. Cruttwell, Patrick. "Dancing along." *Book World,* 3 (6 April 1969), 11.

822. Curley, Daniel. "A Strained Passage." *New Leader,* 52 (31 March 1969), 20-22.

823. Gross, John. "Lieutenants and Luftmenschen." *New York Review of Books,* 12 (24 April 1969), 40-43. Pp. 40-41.

824. Hicks, Granville. "Literary Horizons." *Saturday Review,* 52 (8 March 1969), 28.

825. Hope, Francis. "Marching Orders." *New Statesman,* 76 (18 October 1968), 503-504.

826. Janeway, Elizabeth. "*The Military Philosophers.*" *New York Times Book Review* (9 March 1969), pp. 1, 42.

827. Jebb, Julian. "Enter Pamela Flitton, avenging angel."

The (London) *Times* (19 October 1968), p. 23.

828. Maddocks, Melvin. "A Different Drummer." *Atlantic,* 223 (March 1969), 141-143.

829. Marsh, Pamela. "The soldier is first of all a man." *Christian Science Monitor,* 61 (27 February 1969), 7.

830. Mayne, Richard. "Muzak of Time." *Listener,* 80 (24 October 1968), 555.

831. Pfaff, William. Untitled book review. *Commonweal,* 91 (5 December 1969), 317-318. P. 318.

832. Poore, Charles. "Many Lions, Few Unicorns." *New York Times,* 118 (13 March 1969), 45.

833. Pritchard, William H. "Anthony Powell's Serious Comedy." *Massachusetts Review,* 10 (Autumn 1969), 812-819.

834. Raven, Simon. "Around the battlements." *Observer* (13 October 1968), p. 30.

835. Review of *The Military Philosophers,* in the *National Observer,* 8 (31 March 1969), 17.

836. Ryan, Frank L. *"The Military Philosophers." Best Sellers,* 28 (15 March 1969), 508-509.

837. Shrapnel, Norman. "The Widmerpool symphony." *Guardian Weekly,* 99 (24 October 1968), 15.

838. Sokolov, Raymond A. "The Good Soldier." *Newsweek,* 73 (24 March 1969), 106, 108.

839. Tube, Henry. "Facing the Music." *Spectator,* 221 (18 October 1968), 547-548.

840. Willis, Katherine Tappert. *"The Military Philosophers." Library Journal,* 94 (15 March 1969), 1163.

Books Do Furnish A Room

841. Anon. *"Books Do Furnish A Room; a novel."* *Booklist*, 68 (15 October 1971), 183.

842. —. *"Books Do Furnish A Room."* *British Book News* (April 1971), p. 341.

843. —. *"Books Do Furnish A Room."* *Choice*, 9 (April 1972), 215-216.

844. —. *"Books Do Furnish A Room."* *Kirkus*, 39 (1 July 1971), 697.

845. —. *"Books Do Furnish A Room."* *Publishers' Weekly*, 200 (5 July 1971), 48.

846. —. "Notable." *New Republic*, 165 (23 October 1971), 28.

847. —. "Time marches on." *TLS* (19 February 1971), p. 199; reprinted in *TLS Essays and Reviews from the Times Literary Supplement 1971.* London: Oxford University Press, 1972, pp. 202-204.

848. Bailey, Paul. "Sniffing the Scandal." *London Magazine*, n.s. 11 (August/September 1971), 147-150.

849. Bayley, John. "Conducting the Music." *Listener*, 85 (18 February 1971), 213.

850. Beichman, Arnold. "Reshuffling the giddy-heads." *Christian Science Monitor*, 63 (28 October 1971), 11.

851. Bliven, Naomi. "Publish and perish." *New Yorker*, 47 (30 October 1971), 150, 153-154.

852. Broyard, Anatole. "Good-by to the Novel of Manners." *New York Times*, 120 (8 September 1971), 43.

853. Dawson, Helen. "Briefing: *Books Do Furnish A Room.*"

Observer (7 January 1973), p. 30.

854. Eby, Cecil. "A fox-trot to the music of time." *Book World*, 5 (12 September 1971), 13.

855. Fuson, Ben W. *"Books Do Furnish a Room."* *Library Journal*, 96 (August 1971), 2546.

856. Hill, William B. *"Books Do Furnish a Room."* *America*, 125 (20 November 1971), 432.

857. Jenkins, Roy. "Books of the Year." *Observer* (19 December 1971), p. 17.

858. Larkin, Philip. "Mr. Powell's Mural." *New Statesman* (19 February 1971), 243-244.

859. Mallet, Gina. *"Books Do Furnish A Room."* *Saturday Review*, 54 (11 September 1971), 43.

860. Mano, D. Keith. "Uses of the Novel." *National Review*, 23 (24 September 1971), 1062-1063.

861. May, Derwent. "Heroic Curiosity." *Encounter*, 36 (March 1971), 71-75. Pp. 71-72.

862. Pfaff, William. Untitled book review. *Commonweal*, 95 (3 December 1971), 235-236. P. 236.

863. Porterfield, Christopher. "Respectfully Submitted." *Time*, 98 (27 September 1971), 98.

864. Ratcliffe, Michael. "The silent nightmare of X. Trapnel." *The* (London) *Times* (15 February 1971), p. 10.

865. Review of *Books Do Furnish A Room,* in *Books and Bookmen*, 16 (April 1971), 42.

866. Ryan, Frank L. *"Books Do Furnish A Room."* *Best Sellers*, 31 (15 September 1971), 260.

867. Shrapnel, Norman. "Mystery tour." *Guardian Weekly*, 104 (27 February 1971), 19.

868. Sokolov, Raymond A. "The Music of Time Marches on." *New York Times Book Review* (10 October 1971), p. 42.

869. Wade, Rosalind. "Quarterly Fiction Review." *Contemporary Review*, 219 (July 1971), 45-48. P. 48.

870. Wall, Stephan. "Back to the literary life." *Observer* (14 February 1971), p. 24.

871. Waugh, Auberon. "Auberon Waugh on the Music of Time." *Spectator*, 226 (20 February 1971), 258-259.

Temporary Kings

872. Anon. "Degrees of decay." *TLS* (22 June 1973), p. 709.

873. —. *"Temporary Kings."* *Booklist*, 70 (1 December 1973), 369.

874. —. *"Temporary Kings."* *British Book News* (August 1973), p. 556.

875. —. *"Temporary Kings."* *Kirkus*, 41 (15 August 1973), 908.

876. —. *"Temporary Kings."* *Publishers' Weekly*, 204 (3 September 1973), 50.

877. —. "Top shelf of the year." *Guardian*, 109 (29 December 1973), 17.

878. Ayer, A. J. "Books of the Year." *Observer* (16 December 1973), p. 33.

879. Beichman, Arnold. "A dance to time's music: Powell's new novel." *Christian Science Monitor*, 66 (19 December 1973), B5.

880. Broyard, Anatole. " 'The Music of Time': Adagio." *New York Times,* 123 (12 October 1973), 41.

881. Chazen, Leonard. "Remembrance of things past, in the homestretch." *New York Times Book Review* (14 October 1973), p. 46.

882. De Feo, Ronald. "Dancing In the Dark." *National Review,* 25 (7 December 1973), 1367-1368.

883. Fuller, Roy. "First Eleven." *Listener,* 89 (21 June 1973), 839-840.

884. Hill, George. "Critics' Choice." *The* (London) *Times* (29 November 1973), p. IV.

885. —. "Fiction." *The* (London) *Times* (21 June 1973), p. 14.

886. Jebb, Julian. "Danse Macabre." *New Statesman,* 85 (22 June 1973), 931-932.

887. Jenkins, Roy. "Books of the Year." *Observer* (16 December 1973), p. 33.

888. McSweeney, Kerry. "The Editor's Column." *Queen's Quarterly,* 81 (Summer 1974), 324-327.

889. Michener, Charles T. "Peeping Toms." *Newsweek,* 82 (29 October 1973), 102-104.

890. Morris, Robert K. "Penultimate Pavane in Venice." *Nation,* 217 (10 December 1973), 632-633.

891. Nye, Robert. "Come Dancing with Anthony Powell." *Books and Bookmen,* 18 (August 1973), 52-53.

892. O'Hara, T. *"Temporary Kings." Best Sellers,* 33 (1 December 1973), 389.

893. Pickering, Sam, Jr. "The Valley of the Shadow." *Sewanee*

Review, 82 (Spring 1974), xxii, xxiv, xxvi.

894. Piper, David. "Critics' Choice." *The* (London) *Times* (29 November 1973), p. V.

895. Porterfield, Christopher. "Jenkins Ear Again." *Time,* 102 (22 October 1973), 105-106.

896. Portis, Rowe. *"Temporary Kings." Library Journal,* 98 (August 1973), 2337.

897. Raven, Simon. "A game of Musical chairs." *Observer* (17 June 1973), p. 33.

898. Review of *Temporary Kings,* in the *National Observer,* 13 (12 January 1974), 21.

899. Russell, John. "More Music of Time." *New Republic,* 169 (27 October 1973), 30.

900. Schrapnel, Norman. "Lord Widmerpool's world." *Guardian,* 108 (30 June 1973), 26.

901. Stanton, Lillian. Review of *Temporary Kings,* in the *Georgia Review,* 28 (Summer 1974), 371-374.

902. Starr, Roger. "The Eleventh Movement." *Saturday Review/World,* 1 (20 November 1973), 18-21.

Hearing Secret Harmonies

903. Amis, Kingsley. "The final cadence." *Observer* (7 September 1975), p. 21.

904. Anon. "Curtain calls." *Economist,* 256 (13 September 1975), 119.

905. —. *"Hearing Secret Harmonies." British Book News* (January 1976), p. 70.

906. —. "Notable." *Time,* 107 (17 May 1976), 80, 82.

907. —. "The Last Chord." *Guardian* (13 September 1975), p. 15.

908. Bayley, John. "A family and its fictions." *TLS* (12 September 1975), p. 1010.

909. Bell, Pearl K. "A Dance completed." *New Leader,* 59 (10 May 1976), 16-17.

910. Brennan, Neil. "The Winding Up of Widmerpool." *Commonweal,* 103 (7 May 1976), 310-312.

911. Brownjohn, Alan. "And the Dance goes on." *Encounter,* 46 (February 1976), 58-64.

912. Dawson, S. W. "Nicholas in Wonderland." *English,* 25 (Spring 1976), 80-84.

913. De Mott, Benjamin. "Ask at the house." *Atlantic,* 237 (April 1976), 108, 110.

914. Frayn, Michael. "The End of the Dance." *Observer* (7 September 1975), p. 17.

915. Fuller, Edmund. "Anthony Powell's Fifty-Year Saga." *Wall Street Journal,* 187 (27 April 1976), 22.

916. James, Clive. "Books of the Year." *Observer* (14 December 1975), p. 19.

917. Jebb, Julian. "Anthony Powell's dreams." *Listener,* 94 (11 September 1975), 347-348.

918. Jenkins, Roy. "Books of the Year." *Observer* (14 December 1975), p. 19.

919. Lejeune, Anthony. "An Acquired Taste." *National Review,* 28 (11 June 1976), 633-634.

920. Luckett, Richard. "The end of the line." *Spectator,* 235 (13 September 1975), 349.

921. Morris, Robert K. "Powell's Dance to the Grave." *Nation,* 222 (19 June 1976), 758-760.

922. Muggeridge, Malcolm. "A Valley of Lost Things." *New Statesman,* 90 (12 September 1975), 308-309.

923. —. "Books of the Year." *Observer* (14 December 1975), p. 19.

924. Naipaul, Shiva. "A sense of achievement." (London) *Sunday Times* (7 September 1975), p. 35.

* 925. O'Hara, T. *"Hearing Secret Harmonies."* *Best Sellers,* 36 (July 1976), 110.

926. Steegmuller, Francis. "The Last of the Dance." *Harper's,* 252 (April 1976), 94, 96, 98.

927. Towers, Robert. "The end of the dance." *New York Times Book Review* (11 April 1976), pp. 1-3.

928. Tucker, James. "The Music of Time." *New Review,* 2 (September 1975), 63-64.

929. Wood, Michael. "An Epic in a Whisper." *Saturday Review/World,* 3 (17 April 1976), 30-32.

930. —. "The dance stops." *New Society* (25 September 1975), pp. 705-706.

931. Worsley, T. C. "All through Jenkins' ear." *Financial Times* (11 September 1975), p. 29.

The Garden God and *The Rest I'll Whistle*

932. Broyard, Anatole. "A Novelist Glimpsed at Play." *New*

York Times, 121 (17 February 1972), 35.

933. Luddy, Thomas E. *"The Garden God* and *The Rest I'll Whistle."* Library Journal, 97 (1 May 1972), 1737.

Barnard Letters

934. Anon. *"Barnard Letters."* Saturday Review, 147 (2 February 1929), 152.

Novels of High Society from the Victorian Age

935. Anon. *"Novels of High Society from the Victorian Age."* Spectator, 179 (5 September 1947), 314.

John Aubrey and His Friends

936. Anon. *"John Aubrey and His Friends."* Choice, 2 (July-August 1965), 300.

937. —. *"John Aubrey and His Friends."* Kirkus, 17 (1 April 1949), 193.

938. —. "The Man Who Noticed." TLS (11 December 1948), p. 696.

939. —. "Two-Worlder." Time, 53 (9 May 1949), 110, 113-114.

940. Ashley, Maurice. "An Eccentric Scholar." Spectator, 181 (10 December 1948), 768, 770.

941. Daves, Charles. Review of John Aubrey and His Friends, in Seventeenth-Century News, 23 (Autumn 1965), 37-38.

942. Halsband, Robert. *"John Aubrey and His Friends."* Saturday Review of Literature, 32 (25 June 1949), 35.

943. Macaulay, Rose. Review of *John Aubrey and His Friends,* in the *Observer* (19 December 1948), p. 3.

944. Ogg, David. Review of *John Aubrey and His Friends,* in the *Listener,* 40 (9 December 1948), 893.

945. Review of *John Aubrey and His Friends,* in the *London Sunday Times* (12 December 1948), p. 3.

946. Stern, James. " 'Elegant, Cavalier.' " *New York Times Book Review* (15 May 1949), p. 5.

947. Trevor-Roper, H. R. "A Virtuoso." *New Statesman and Nation,* 37 (1 January 1949), 15-16.

948. Willis, Katherine Tappert. *"John Aubrey and His Friends."* *Library Journal,* 89 (1 December 1964), 4795.

949. Young, B. A. "Space-Time." *Punch,* 245 (2 October 1963), 507.

Brief Lives and Other Selected Writings of John Aubrey

950. Anon. "John Aubrey." *Manchester Guardian* (9 September 1949), p. 4.

* 951. Pritchett, V. S. "Books in General." *New Statesman and Nation,* 38 (27 August 1949), 222, 224.

JEAN RHYS
(Born in Dominica, West Indies 1894)

I. PRIMARY WORKS: NOVELS

1. *Postures.* London: Chatto and Windus, 1928; as *Quartet,* New York: Simon and Schuster, 1929; London: Deutsch, 1969 (this ed. reprinted in New York: Vintage, 1974); New York: Harper and Row, 1971; Harmondsworth: Penguin, 1973; as *Quatuor.* Trans. Viviane Forrester. Paris: Denoël, 1973.

2. *After Leaving Mr. Mackenzie.* London: J. Cape, 1931; New York: Knopf, 1931; London: Deutsch, 1969; Harmondsworth: Penguin, 1971; New York: Harper and Row, 1972; New York: Vintage, 1974.

3. *Voyage in the Dark.* London: Constable, 1934, 1936; New York: Morrow, 1935; London: Deutsch, 1967; New York: Norton, 1968; Harmondsworth: Penguin, 1969; New York: Popular Library, 1975; as *Voyage dans les ténébres.* Trans. René Daillie. Paris: Denoël, 1974; as *Reis Door Het Duister.* Trans. Henriëtte Van Eyk. Antwerp and Utrecht: A. W. Bruna, 1969.

4. *Good Morning, Midnight.* London: Constable, 1939; London: Deutsch, 1967; Don Mills, Ontario: Collins, 1967; Harmondsworth: Penguin, 1969; New York: Harper and Row, 1970; New York: Vintage, 1974; as *Bonjour Minuit.* Trans. Jacqueline Bernard. Paris: Denoël, 1969; as *Goedemorgen, Middernacht.* Trans. Max Schuchart. Utrecht: A. W. Bruna, 1969; as *Guten Morgen, Mitternacht.* Trans. Grete Felten. Hamburg:

Hoffmann and Campe, 1969; also München: Deutscher Taschenbuch-Verlag, 1971.

5. *Wide Sargasso Sea.* With introduction by Francis Wyndham. London: Deutsch, 1966; New York: Norton, 1967; Harmondsworth: Penguin, 1968, 1970, 1975; New York: Popular Library, 1975; as *Langt Over Havet.* Trans. Lotte Eskelund. Copenhagen: Fremad, 1967; as *Siintää Sargassomeri.* Trans. Eva Siikarla. Porvoo and Helsinki: Werner Söderström, 1968; as *Kreolerinnen Pâ Thornfield Hall.* Trans. Liv Malling. Oslo: H. Aschehoug, 1969; as *Széles Sargasso-Tenger.* Trans. Dezsö Tandori. Budapest: Európa Kiadó, 1971; as *La Prisonniére des Sargasses.* Trans. Yvonne Davet. Paris: Denoël, 1971; as *Široko Sargaško Morje.* Trans. Olga Šiftar. Murska Sobota (Yugoslavia): Pomurska Založba, 1971.

PRIMARY WORKS: SHORT STORIES

6. *The Left Bank and Other Stories.* With introduction by Ford Madox Ford. London: J. Cape, 1927; New York: Harper, 1927; Freeport, New York: Books for Libraries Press, 1970.

Contents: "Illusion"—"A Spiritualist"—"From a French prison"—"In a café"—"Tout Montparnasse and a lady"—"Mannequin"—"In the Luxemburg Gardens"—"Tea with an artist"—"Trio"—"Mixing cocktails."—"Again the Antilles"—"Hunger"—"Discourse of a lady standing a dinner to a down-and-out friend"—"A night"—"In the rue de l'Arrivee"—"Learning to be a mother"—"The blue bird"—"The grey day"—"At the Villa d' Or"—"La grosse Fifi"—"Vienne."

7. *Tigers are Better-Looking, with a Selection from The Left Bank.* London: Deutsch, 1968; Harmondsworth: Penguin, 1973; New York: Harper and Row, 1974; New York: Popular Library, 1976; as *Les Tigres sont plus beaux á voir.* Trans. Pierre Leyris. Paris: Mercure de

France, 1969; as *Die Dicke Fifi.* Trans. Grete Felten. Hamburg: Hoffmann and Campe, 1971.

Contents: "Till September Petronella"—"The Day They Burned the Books"—"Let Them Call It Jazz"—"Tigers are Better-Looking"—"Outside the Machine"—"The Lotus"—"A Solid House"—"The Sound of the River"—"Preface to a Selection of Stories from *The Left Bank*"—"Illusion"—"From a French Prison"—"Mannequin"—"Tea with an Artist"—"Mixing Cocktails"—"Again the Antilles"—"Hunger"—"La Grosse Fifi"—"Vienne."

8. "My dear darling Mr. Ramage." *The* (London) *Times* (28 June 1969), p. 19.

9. "I Spy a Stranger." *Penguin Modern Stories 1.* Ed. Judith Burnley. Harmondsworth: Penguin, 1969, pp. 53-67.

10. "Temps Perdi." *Penguin Modern Stories 1.* Harmondsworth: Penguin, 1969, pp. 69-88.

11. "Sleep It Off Lady." *New Review,* 1 (June 1974), 45-49.

* 12. "Kikimora." *New Yorker,* 52 (2 August 1976), 23-24.

PRIMARY WORKS: OTHER

13. "My day." *Vogue,* 165 (February 1975), 186-187. An auto-biographical account.

14. "On Not Shooting Sitting Birds." *New Yorker,* 52 (26 April 1976), 35. Personal narrative: autobiographical.

II. GENERAL SECONDARY STUDIES, INTERVIEWS, BIOGRAPHICAL SKETCHES, AND MISCELLANEOUS ITEMS

General references to Rhys's work also appear in the First Part of this bibliography. See the following numbers there: 61, 66, 97.

15. Alvarez, A. "Best Living English Novelist." *New York Times Book Review* (17 March 1974), pp. 6-7.

16. Anon. "Bursaries Awarded to Writers." *The* (London) *Times* (11 December 1967), p. 10. On the Art Council's award of £1,200 to Rhys.

17. —. "Neurotic Women." *TLS* (20 July 1967), p. 644. Review of *Voyage in the Dark,* and *Good Morning, Midnight.*

18. —. "Paperbacks." *Observer* (28 September 1975), p. 22. Short review of Rhys's *Voyage in the Dark* and *Good Morning, Midnight.*

19. —. "Rhys, Jean." *Contemporary Authors: A Bio-Bibliographical Guide to Current Authors and Their Works.* Vols. 25-28. Ed. Carolyn Riley. Detroit: Gale Research Company, 1971, p. 608.

20. —. "Rhys, Jean." *Contemporary Literary Criticism: Excerpts from Criticism of the Works of Today's Novelists, Poets, Playwrights, and Other Creative Writers.* Vol. 2. Ed. Carolyn Riley, and Barbara Harte. Detroit, Michigan: Gale Research Company, 1974, pp. 371-373.

21. —. "Rhys, Jean." *Current Biography Yearbook 1972.* Ed. Charles Moritz. New York: H. W. Wilson, 1972, pp. 364-367.

22. —. "Rhys, Jean." *The Concise Encyclopaedia of Modern World Literature.* Ed. Geoffrey Grigson. London: Hutchinson, 1963, pp. 369-370.

23. Babakhanian, Grace Schneck. "Expatriation and Exile as Themes in the Fiction of Jean Rhys." Diss. Illinois at Urbana-Champaign, 1976. *Dissertation Abstracts,* 37A (1976), 291-292.

24. Bailey, Paul. "Bedrooms in hell." *Observer* (18 May 1969), p. 30. Review of Rhys's *Quartet* and *After Leaving Mr. Mackenzie.*

25. Bernstein, Marcelle. "The inscrutable Miss Jean Rhys." *Observer* (1 June 1969), p. 40.

26. Bogataj, Katarina. "Nekdanja in današnja Jane Eyre." *Proster in Cas* (Yugoslavia), 5 (1973), 640-656.

27. Braybrooke, Neville. "Between Dog and Wolf." *Spectator,* 219 (21 July 1967), 77-78; reprinted in *Contemporary Novelists.* Ed. James Vinson. London and Chicago: St. James Press, 1972, pp. 1062-1064.

28. —. "The Return of Jean Rhys." *Caribbean Quarterly,* 16, No. 4 (December 1970), 43-46.

29. Cantwell, M. "I'm a person at a masked ball without a mask." *Mademoiselle,* 79 (October 1974), 170-171 ff. An interview.

30. Carter, Hannah. "Fated to be Sad." *Guardian* (8 August 1968), p. 5. An interview.

31. Cole, Laurence. "Jean Rhys." *Books and Bookmen* (January 1972), pp. 20-21.

32. De Kerchove, Arnold. "John Updike, Jean Rhys, André Gide." *Revue générale Belge* (1970-1973), 91-97.

33. Hall, John. "Jean Rhys." *Guardian* (10 January 1972), p. 8. An interview.

34. Lane, Margaret. "Life and hard times." *Spectator,* 222 (16 May 1969), 649-650. Review of *Quartet* and *After Leaving Mr. Mackenzie.*

35. Mellown, Elgin W. "Characters and Themes in the Novels of Jean Rhys." *Contemporary Literature,* 13 (Autumn 1972), 458-475.

36. Moss, Howard. "Going to Pieces." *New Yorker,* 50 (16 December 1974), 161-162, 165-166. A comprehensive article on all of her work.

37. Nye, Robert. "Women in a man's world." *Guardian Weekly,* 100 (22 May 1969), 15. Review of Rhys's *Quartet,* and *After Leaving Mr. Mackenzie.*

38. P. H. S. *"The Times* Diary: Second big award for Miss Rhys." *The* (London) *Times* (14 December 1967), p. 10.

* 39. Pooter. Untitled comments. *The* (London) *Times* (16 December 1967), p. 19. On the relation between Rhys and Ford Madox Ford.

40. Raban, Jonathan. "Living with Loose Ends." *New Review,* 2 (October 1975), 51-56. Pp. 53-54. On the novels of Jean Rhys in relation to family life.

41. Review of *After Leaving Mr. Mackenzie* and *Good Morning, Midnight,* in the *Village Voice,* 19 (6 June 1974), 35.

42. Shuttleworth, Martin. "Mrs. Micawber." *Punch,* 253 (16 August 1967), 253. A short general survey of her work.

43. Thurman, Judith. "The Mistress and the Mask." *Ms,* 4 (January 1976), 50-52, 81. On all of her novels.

44. Turner, Alice K. "Jean Rhys Rediscovered: How it Happened." *Publishers' Weekly,* 206 (1 July 1974), 56, 58.

45. Wakeman, John, and Stanley J. Kunitz, eds. "Jean Rhys," in their *World Authors 1950-1970.* New York: H. W. Wilson Company, 1975, pp. 1206-1207.

46. Webb, W. L. "Lately prized." *Guardian* (14 December 1967), p. 6. A biographical-critical sketch following her winning the £1,000 W. H. Smith award.

47. Wyndham, Francis. "Introduction to Jean Rhys." *London Magazine,* 7 (January 1960), 15-18.

III. STUDIES AND REVIEWS OF INDIVIDUAL WORKS

References to individual books by Rhys also appear in the First Part of this bibliography. See the following numbers there: 160, 177, 189, 315, 321.

Postures

or

Quartet

48. Anon. "Books in Brief: *Postures." Nation and Athenaeum,* 44 (6 October 1928), 26.

49. —. "Latin Quarter Rotters Characters of This Yarn." *New York World,* 69 (10 February 1929), 11 M.

50. —. "Poignant Tragedy." *New York Times Book Review* (10 February 1929), p. 8.

51. —. *"Postures." TLS* (4 October 1928), p. 706.

52. —. *"Quartet." Kirkus,* 39 (1 February 1971), 136.

53. —. *"Quartet." New York Times Book Review* (13 October 1974), pp. 44-45.

54. —. *"Quartet." Publishers' Weekly,* 199 (15 February 1971), 72.

55. —. *"Quartet." Publishers' Weekly,* 205 (1 July 1974), 85.

56. —. *"Quartet." Saturday Review of Literature,* 5 (20 April 1929), 936.

57. Gorman, Herbert. "The Unholy Four." *Books,* 5 (10 February 1929), 7.

58. Hazzard, Shirley. "Marya knew her fate and couldn't avoid it." *New York Times Book Review* (11 April 1971), p. 6.

59. Loercher, Diana. " 'When a gel must cut loose.' " *Christian Science Monitor,* 63 (20 May 1971), 4.

60. Lovett, Robert Morss. *"Quartet."* *Bookman,* 69 (April 1929), 193-194.

61. Matthews, T. S. "The Cocktail Hour." *New Republic,* 58 (17 April 1929), 258-259.

62. Raynor, Vivien. "Woman as Victim." *Book World,* 5 (23 May 1971), 7.

63. Review of *Quartet,* in the *Boston Evening Transcript* (20 March 1929), p. 2.

64. Ringer, Agnes. *"Quartet."* *Library Journal,* 96 (August 1971), 2547.

65. Van de Water, F. Review of *Quartet,* in the *New York Evening Post* (2 February 1929), p. 9.

Voyage in the Dark

66. Anon. "Briefly Noted." *New Yorker,* 44 (24 August 1968), 119.

67. —. "Paperbacks: *Voyage in the Dark."* *The* (London) *Times* (14 June 1969), p. 23.

68. —. "Recommended Novels." *Saturday Review,* 158 (1 December 1934), 468.

69. —. *"Voyage in the Dark."* *Kirkus,* 36 (1 February 1968),

140.

70. —. *"Voyage in the Dark."* Publishers' Weekly, 193 (8 January 1968), 65.

71. —. *"Voyage in the Dark."* TLS (1 November 1934), p. 752.

72. Britten, Florence Haxton. "Recent Leading Fiction: *Voyage in the Dark." New York Herald Tribune Books*, 11 (17 March 1935), 10.

73. Collier, Carmen P. *"Voyage in the Dark."* Best Sellers, 28 (1 May 1968), 58-59.

74. Hawthorne, Hazel. *"Voyage in the Dark."* New Republic, 82 (10 April 1935), 260.

75. Review of *Voyage in the Dark,* in the *Library Journal,* 93 (1 May 1968), 1919.

76. T. P., Jr. *"Voyage in the Dark."* Saturday Review of Literature, 11 (16 March 1935), 556.

After Leaving Mr. Mackenzie

77. Anon. *"After Leaving Mr. Mackenzie."* Kirkus, 39 (15 December 1971), 1332.

78. —. *"After Leaving Mr. Mackenzie."* New Republic, 68 (16 September 1931), 134.

79. —. *"After Leaving Mr. Mackenzie."* New Yorker, 48 (8 April 1972), 130.

80. —. *"After Leaving Mr. Mackenzie."* Publishers' Weekly, 200 (20 December 1971), 39.

81. —. *"After Leaving Mr. Mackenzie."* TLS (5 March 1931),

p. 180.

82. —. "Paperbacks." *Observer* (20 February 1974), p. 23.

83. —. "Twice-as-Naturalism." *New York Times Book Review* (28 June 1931), p. 6.

84. Bell, Pearl K. "Women Cast Adrift." *New Leader,* 55 (20 March 1972), 14-15.

85. Clemons, Walter. *"After Leaving Mr. Mackenzie."* *Newsweek,* 79 (6 March 1972), 77.

86. Dawson, Margaret Cheney. "Unbearable Justice." *New York Herald Tribune Books,* 7 (28 June 1931), 7.

87. Gilboy, J. Thomas. *"After Leaving Mr. Mackenzie."* *Best Sellers,* 31 (1 March 1972), 532.

88. Gilman, Lelde. *"After Leaving Mr. Mackenzie."* *Library Journal,* 97 (1 February 1972), 517.

89. Grahm, Gladys. "A Bedraggled Career." *Saturday Review of Literature,* 8 (25 July 1931), 5.

90. Levin, Martin. *"After Leaving Mr. Mackenzie."* *New York Times Book Review* (27 February 1972), p. 52.

91. Naipaul, V. S. "Without a Dog's Chance." *New York Review of Books,* 18 (18 May 1972), 29-31.

92. Review of *After Leaving Mr. Mackenzie,* in the *Boston Evening Transcript* (29 August 1931), p. 1.

93. Stone, Geoffrey. *"After Leaving Mr. Mackenzie."* *Bookman,* 74 (September 1931), 84-85.

94. Theroux, Paul. *"After Leaving Mr. Mackenzie."* *Book World,* 6 (13 February 1972), 6.

95. Weigle, Edith. Review of *After Leaving Mr. Mackenzie,* in the *Chicago Daily Tribune* (11 July 1931), p. 9.

Good Morning, Midnight

96. Anon. *"Good Morning, Midnight." Kirkus,* 38 (1 February 1970), 131.

97. —. *"Good Morning, Midnight." Publishers' Weekly,* 197 (26 January 1970), 268.

98. —. "Lost Years." *TLS* (22 April 1939), p. 231.

99. —. "Recommended New Novels: *Good Morning, Midnight." TLS* (15 July 1939), p. iv.

100. Blackburn, Sara. "Women's lot." *Book World,* 4 (5 April 1970), 6.

101. Broyard, Anatole. "A Difficult Year for Hats." *New York Times,* 123 (26 March 1974), 39.

102. Leonard, John. "What Men Don't Know About Women." *New York Times,* 119 (12 May 1970), 37.

103. Levin, Martin. *"Good Morning, Midnight." New York Times Book Review* (22 March 1970), p. 39.

104. Mair, John. "New Novels." *New Statesman and Nation,* 17 (22 April 1939), 614, 616. P. 614.

105. O'Brien, Kate. "Fiction." *Spectator,* 162 (16 June 1939), 1062.

106. Raskin, Barbara. "Classic Female." *New Republic,* 163 (4 July 1970), 27.

107. Ricks, Christopher. "Female and Other Impersonators." *New York Review of Books,* 15 (23 July 1970), 8, 10,

12-13.   Includes review of *Good Morning, Midnight.*

108. Wolff, Geoffrey. "Rhys: Memories of love." *Newsweek,* 75 (1 June 1970), 91-92.

Wide Sargasso Sea

109. Allen, Walter. "Bertha the Doomed." *New York Times Book Review* (18 June 1967), p. 5.

110. Anon. "A Fairy-Tale Neurotic." *TLS* (17 November 1966), p. 1039.

111. —. "Briefing: *Wide Sargasso Sea.*" *Observer* (29 September 1968), p. 22.

112. —. "fiction of the month." *Guardian* (2 December 1966), p. 7.

113. —. "New Fiction." *The* (London) *Times* (17 November 1966), p. 16.

114. —. Untitled book review. *Nation,* 205 (2 October 1967), 317.

115. —. *"Wide Sargasso Sea."* *Booklist,* 63 (15 July 1967), 1182.

116. —. *"Wide Sargasso Sea."* *Publishers' Weekly,* 191 (3 February 1967), 75-76.

117. Athill, Diana. "Jean Rhys, and the writing of *Wide Sargasso Sea.*" *Bookseller* (20 August 1966), pp. 1378-1379.

118. Braybrooke, Neville. "Shadows and Substance." *Spectator,* 217 (28 October 1966), 560-561.

119. Casey, Genevieve M. *"Wide Sargasso Sea."* *Best Sellers,* 27 (15 May 1967), 75.

120. Corke, Hilary. "New Fiction." *Listener*, 77 (19 January 1967), 103.

121. Frazer, Elizabeth. *"Wide Sargasso Sea." Library Journal*, 92 (15 May 1967), 1951.

122. Froshaug, Judy. "The bookmakers." *Nova* (September 1967), pp. 4-5.

123. Harrison, Max. "BBC Symphony Orchestra." *The* (London) *Times* (9 December 1971), p. 13. On the musical version—*Memories of Morning: Night* (by Gordon Crosse) based upon the text of the novel.

124. Hearne, John. "The *Wide Sargasso Sea:* a West Indian Reflection." *Cornhill*, no. 1080 (Summer 1974), 323-333.

125. Hope, Francis. "The First Mrs. Rochester." *New Statesman*, 72 (28 October 1966), 638-639.

126. Kersh, Gerald. "Second Time Around." *Saturday Review*, 50 (1 July 1967), 23.

127. Knowler, J. Review of *Wide Sargasso Sea*, in *Books and Bookmen*, 12 (December 1966), 84.

128. Luengo, Anthony E. *"Wide Sargasso Sea* and the Gothic Mode." *World Literature Written in English*, 15 (April 1976), 229-245.

129. MacInnes, Colin. "Nightmare in Paradise." *Observer* (30 October 1966), p. 28.

130. Ramchand, Kenneth. "Terrified consciousness." *Journal of Commonwealth Literature*, 7 (July 1969), 8-19.

131. Ross, Alan. Untitled book review. *London Magazine* n.s. 6 (November 1966), 99, 101.

The Left Bank and Other Stories

132. Aiken, Conrad. Review of *The Left Bank and Other Stories,* in the *New York Evening Post* (1 October 1927), p. 10.

133. Anon. "A Mistress of the *Conte.*" *New York Herald Tribune Books,* 4 (6 November 1927), 16.

134. —. "Miss Rhys's Short Stories." *New York Times Book Review* (11 December 1927), pp. 28, 30.

135. —. *"The Left Bank."* *Nation and Athenaeum,* 41 (25 June 1927), 424.

136. —. *"The Left Bank and Other Stories."* *New Statesman,* 29 (30 April 1927), 90.

137. —. *"The Left Bank."* *Saturday Review of Literature,* 4 (5 November 1927), 287.

138. —. *"The Left Bank."* *Spectator,* 138 (30 April 1927), 772.

139. —. *"The Left Bank and Other Stories."* *TLS* (5 May 1927), p. 320.

140. L. S. M. *"The Left Bank and Other Stories."* *New Republic,* 52 (16 November 1927), 345.

141. Review of *The Left Bank and Other Stories,* in the *Boston Evening Transcript* (9 November 1927), p. 7.

142. Wyndham-Lewis, D. B. "Hinterland of Bohemia." *Saturday Review,* 143 (23 April 1927), 637.

Tigers Are Better-Looking

143. Allen, Bruce. *"Tigers Are Better-Looking."* *Library Journal,* 99 (15 November 1974), 2983.

144. Anon. "Losing Battles." *TLS* (2 May 1968), p. 466.

145. —. *"Tigers Are Better-Looking..."* *Booklist*, 71 (1 December 1974), 367.

146. —. *"Tigers Are Better-Looking."* *Kirkus*, 42 (15 August 1974), 899.

147. —. *"Tigers Are Better-Looking."* *Publishers' Weekly*, 206 (26 August 1974), 299.

148. Bailey, Paul. Untitled book review. *London Magazine*, n.s. 8 (June 1968), 110-112. Pp. 110-111.

149. Baker, R. Review of *Tigers Are Better-Looking*, in *Books and Bookmen*, 13 (June 1968), 34.

150. Byatt, A. S. "Trapped." *New Statesman*, 75 (29 March 1968), 421-422. P. 422.

151. Heppenstall, Rayner. "Bitter-Sweet." *Spectator*, 220 (5 April 1968), 446-447.

152. Hope, Francis. "Did you once see Paris plain?" *Observer* (31 March 1968), p. 29.

153. Jebb, Julian. "Sensitive survivors." *The* (London) *Times* (30 March 1968), p. 21.

154. Johnson, Diane. "Overdrawn at the Left Bank of the World." *Book World* (3 November 1974), p. 1.

155. Leiter, Robert. *"Tigers Are Better-Looking."* *New Republic*, 171 (7 December 1974), 22-24.

156. Sullivan, Mary. "All Underdogs." *Listener*, 79 (25 April 1968), 549.

157. Tyler, Ralph. "Luckless Heroines, Swinish Men." *Atlantic*, 235 (January 1975), 81-84.

Penguin Modern Stories 1

* 158. Tuohy, Frank. "Good news." *The* (London) *Times* (2 August 1969), p. 20.

ALAN SILLITOE
(Born in Nottingham 1928)

I. PRIMARY WORKS: NOVELS

1. *Saturday Night and Sunday Morning.* London: W. H. Allen, 1958; Toronto: Smithers, 1958; New York: Knopf, 1959; London: Pan Books, 1960, 1972; with introduction by Sillitoe and commentary and notes by David Craig. Heritage of literature series. London and Harlow, Essex, 1968; New York: New American Library, 1973; as *Lördagskväll Och Söndagsmorgon.* Stockholm: Tiden, 1960; as *Lørdag Kveld og Søndag Morgen.* Trans. Finn Aasen. Oslo: Gyldendal, 1961; as *Samedi Soir, Dimanche Matin.* Trans. Henri Delgove. Paris: Editions du Seuil, 1961, 1963, 1968; as *Lørdag Aften-Søndag Morgen.* Trans. Vagn Grosen. Copenhagen: Gyldendal, 1961, 1963, 1967, 1971; as *Samstag Nacht und Sonntag Morgen.* Trans. Gerda von Uslar. Reinbeck and Hamburg: Rowohlt 1961, 1967; also Frankfurt: Büchergilde Gutenberg, 1964; also Zürich: Diogenes-Verlag, 1970; also Berlin: Verlag Volk u. Welt, 1972, 1974; as *Zaterdagavond en Zondagmorgen.* Trans. Hans Edinga. Amsterdam: Contact, 1961, 1965, 1967, 1968; also Antwerp: Contact, 1964; as *Sabato Sera, Domenica Mattina.* Trans. Floriana Bossi. Turin: Einaudi, 1961; as *Lauantai-illasta Sunnuntaiaamuun.* Trans. Erkki Haglund. Helsinki: Otava, 1962; as *Subotom Uveče—Nedeljom Ujutro.* Trans. Ljerka Radović. Beograd: Kosmos, 1962; as *Z Soboty na Niedziele.* 2nd ed. Trans. Jadwiga Milnikiel. Warsaw: Ksiazka i Wiedza, 1963, 1966; as *V Soboto Zvečer in V Nedeljo Zjutra.* Trans. Marjan Tavčar. Ljubljana: Prešernova družba, 1963; as *Mozaé*

Shabbat Uvoger Yom Alef. Trans. Rahél Aharoni. Mer-
havya: Sifriyyat Po'alim, 1963; as *Sábado à Noite E
Domingo de Manhã.* Trans. José de Sá Caetano. Lisbon:
Portugália, 1963; as *Sábado y Domingo.* Trans. Mariano
Sánchez Ventura. n.p. (Mexico): Joaquín Mortiz, 1965;
as *Cumartesi Gecesi ve Pazar Sabahi.* Trans. Aysegül
Günkut. Istanbul: Ağaoğlu Yayinevi, 1965; as *Sîmbătă
Noapte si Duminică Dimineată.* Trans. Vintilă Corbul.
Bucuresti (Romania): Editura pentru literatură univer-
sală, 1966; as *V Sobotu Večer, V Nedel'u Ráno.* Trans.
Jozef Kot. Bratislava (Czechoslovakia): Slov. spis.,
1966; as *V Sobotu Večer, V Neděli Ráno.* Trans. Petr
Pujman. Prague: Svoboda, 1967; as *Doyô No Yoru to
Nichiyô No Asa.* Trans. Nagakawa Reiji. Tokyo: Kawade shobô shinsha, 1968; as *Dissabte a la nit i diu-
menge.* Trans. Antoni Pigrau. Barcelona: Edicions 62,
1969; with *Loneliness of the long-distance runner* as
*Hosszutáviuto magány osságaszombat este, vasárnap
reggel.* Trans. Árpád Göncz. Budapest: Alföldy Ny,
1970; also Budapest: Európa Kiadó, 1970.

2. *The General.* London: W. H. Allen, 1960; New York:
Knopf, 1961; London: Pan Books, 1962, 1970; New
York: Avon, 1968; as *Counterpoint.* London: Pan,
1967; as *Le général.* Trans. Henri Delgove and Claude
Durand. Paris: Editions du Seuil, 1965; as *Shôgun.*
Trans. Sekiguchi Isao. Tokyo: Hayakawa shobô, 1970.

3. *Key to the Door.* London: W. H. Allen, 1961; New York:
Knopf, 1962; New York: New American Library, 1963;
London: Pan Books, 1963; London: Macmillan, 1969;
as *Az ajtó Kulcsa.* Trans. Miklós Vasárhelyi. Budapest:
Europa Kiadó, 1963; as *Kl'úč od domu.* Trans. Eugen
Klinger. Bratislava (Czechoslovakia): SVKL, 1963; as
Ključ ot Dveri. Trans. N. Dehtereva, et. al. Moscow:
Hudož. lit., 1964; also Moscow: Progress, 1964, 1966,
1969; as *Ključ za Vratata.* Trans. Aleksandăr Stefanov
and Dimitri Ivanov. Sonfija (Yugoslavia): Nar. Kultura,
1965; as *Klucz do Drzwi.* Trans. Jadwiga Milnikiel.
Warsaw: Ksiazka i Wiedza, 1965; as *Klíč Ke Dveřím.*

Trans. Emanuel and Emanuela Tilsch. Prague: Statní nakladatelství Krásné literatury a umění, 1965; as *Ključ vid Dverej.* Trans. Galyna Bušnyna. Kiev (Russia): Dnipro, 1965; as *Duru Raktas.* Trans. Juozas Butenas. Vilnjus (Russia): Vaga, 1966; as *Le Chiavi di Casa.* Trans. Vincenzo Mantovanni. Torino (Italy): Einaudi, 1966; as *Schlüssel zur Tür.* Trans. Stephan Hermlin and Heinz Kamnitzer. Berlin: Verl. Volk u. Welt, 1966; as *Ukse võti.* Trans. Valda Rand. Tallinn: Eêsti raamat, 1967; as *Durvju Atslēga.* Trans. Ilga Melnbárde. Riga (Russia): Liesma, 1969.

4. *The Death of William Posters.* London: W. H. Allen, 1965; New York: Knopf, 1965; London: Pan Books, 1967; London: Macmillan, 1969; as *La Mort de William Posters.* Trans. Ramón Folch i Camarasa. Barcelona: Edicions 62, 1966; as *De Dood Van William Posters.* Trans. Jean A. Schalekamp. Amsterdam: Contact, 1967; as *Smărtta na Uiljam Poustărz.* Trans. Aleksandăr Hrusanov. Plovdiv (Bulgaria): Hr. G. Danov, 1968; as *William Posters No Shi.* Trans. Hashiguchi Minoru. Tokyo: Shûeisha, 1969; as *Śmierć Williama Postersa.* Trans. Jadwiga Milnikiel. Warsaw: Ksiazka i Wiedza, 1969; as *Der Tod des William Posters.* Trans. Peter Naujack. Zürich: Diogenes-Verlag, 1969; also Frankfurt: Fischer-Taschenbuch—Verlag, 1972; as *La Muerte de William Posters.* Trans. Andrés Bosch. Barcelona: Lumen, 1970.

5. *A Tree on Fire.* London: Macmillan, 1967; Garden City, New York: Doubleday, 1968; London: Pan Books, 1969; as *Boom in Brand.* Trans. Jean A. Schalekamp. Amsterdam: Contact, 1970; as *Él Árbol en Llamas.* Trans. Juan Ribalta. Barcelona: Lumen, 1972; as *Moeru Ki.* Trans. Suzuki Kenzô. Tokyo: Shûeisha, 1972; as *Drzewo W Ogniu.* Trans. Jadwiga Milnikiel. Warsaw: Ksiazka i Wiedza, 1972.

6. *A Start in Life.* London: W. H. Allen, 1970; New York: Scribners, 1971; London: Pan Books, 1972; as *Ein Start ins Leben.* Trans. Günter Eichel and Anna von

Cramer-Klett. Zürich: Diogenes-Verlag, 1971.

7. *Travels in Nihilon.* London: W. H. Allen, 1971; New York: Scribners, 1972; London: Pan Books, 1973; as *Nihilon.* Trans. Fritz Güttinger. Zürich: Diogenes-Verlag, 1973.

8. *Raw Material.* London and New York: W. H. Allen, 1972; New York: Scribners, 1973; rev. ed. London: Pan Books, 1974.

9. *The Flame of Life.* London: W. H. Allen, 1974.

10. *The Widower's Son.* London: W. H. Allen. Expected date of publication is 22 November 1976.

PRIMARY WORKS: SHORT STORIES

11. *The Loneliness of the Long-Distance Runner.* London: W. H. Allen, 1959; Toronto: Smithers, 1959; New York: Knopf, 1960; with the poem "The Rats". London: Pan Books, 1961, 1968; New York: New American Library, 1965?, 1971; with *Billy Liar,* by Keith Waterhouse. Heritage of Literature series. London and Essex, Harlow: Longmans, 1966; with *Sanctuary,* by Theodore Dreiser, and related poems. Ed. Roy Bentley. Agincourt, Ontario: Book Society of Canada, 1967; as *Ensom Løber og andre noveller.* Trans. Vagn Grosen and Klaus Rifbjerg. Copenhagen: Gyldendal, 1962, 1967; as *La soledad del corredor de fondo.* Trans. Baldomero Porta. Barcelona: Editorial Seix Barral, 1962, 1969, 1971; as *Odinokij-begun.* Trans. R. Rajt—Kovaleva, et al. Moscow: Mol. gvardija, 1963; as *La Solitude du coureur de fond.* Trans. Henri Delgove. Paris: Editions du Seuil, 1963, 1974; also Lausanne: La Guilde du livre, 1966; as *La Solitudine del Maratoneta.* Trans. Vincenzo Mantovani. Troino: Einaudi, 1964; as *De Eenzaamheid van de Langeafstandsloper.* Trans. Jean A. Schalekamp. Amsterdam: Contact, 1964; as *Samotność Długodystan-*

sowca. Trans. Maria Skibniewska. Warsaw: Państw. Instytut Wydawn, 1964; as *Samotnijat Begač Na Dǎlgo Razstojanie.* Trans. Violeta Ticin. Sofija: Nar. mladež, 1965; as *Die Einsamkeit Des Langstreckenläufers und andere Erzählungen.* Trans. Günther Klotz and Hedwig Jolenberg. Zürich: Diogenes Verl, 1967, 1974; also Berlin: Verl. Volk and Welt, 1969, 1971; also München: Deutscher Taschenbuch–Verl, 1969, 1971, 1973; as *Gargabalnieka Vientuliba.* Trans. Maija Andersone. Riga (Russia): Liesma, 1968; with other stories in *Chôkyori Sôsha No Kodoku.* Trans. Maruya Saiichi and Kôno Ichirô. Tokyo: Shûeisha, 1969; as *Die Lumpensammler-stochter.* Trans. Wulf Teichmann. Zürich: Diogenes-Verlag, 1973.

Contents: "The Loneliness of the Long-Distance Runner"–"Uncle Ernest"–"Mr. Raynor The School Teacher"–"The Fishing-Boat Picture"–"Noah's Ark"–"On Saturday Afternoon"–"The Match"–"The Disgrace of Jim Scarfedale"–"The Decline and Fall of Frankie Buller."

12. *The Ragman's Daughter and Other Stories.* London: W. H. Allen, 1963; New York: Knopf, 1964; London: Pan Books, 1966, 1970; "The good women," from *The Ragman's Daughter* in *Tiblid Naised.* Trans. V. Kivilo. Tallin: Gaz.-žurn. izd., 1963; with *The Loneliness of the Long-Distance Runner,* as *Osamělost prespolního běžce.* Trans. Josef Škvorecký and Petr Pujman. Prague: Statní nakladatelství Krásné literatury a umění, 1965; as *De Dochter van de Voddenman.* Trans. Jean A. Schalekamp. Amsterdam: Contact, 1965; as *Córka Szmaciarza.* Trans. Jadwiga Milnikiel. Warsaw: Ksiażka i Wiedza, 1966; as *La fille du chiffonnier.* Trans. Guy and Gérard Durand. Paris: Editions du Seuil, 1967; with other stories in *Kuzuya No Musume.* Trans. Kôno Ichirô and Hashiguchi Minoru. Tokyo: Shûeisha, 1969.

Contents: "The Ragman's Daughter"–"The Other John Peel"–"The Firebug"–"The Magic Box"–"The Bike"–

"To Be Collected"—"The Good Women."

13. *Guzman, Go Home, and Other Stories.* London: Macmillan, 1968; Garden City, New York: Doubleday, 1969; London: Pan Books, 1970; as *Guzman Kaere.* Trans. Hashiguchi Minoru. Tokyo: Shûeisha, 1970; as *Guzman, Do Domu.* Trans. Jadwiga Milnikiel. Warsaw: Ksiazka i Wiedza, 1971; as *Guzman, Go Home.* Trans. Anna von Cramer-Klett. Wels (Austria): Welsermühl, 1971; also Zürich: Diogens-Verlag, 1971; as *Váyase, Guzmán.* Trans. Ariel Bignami. Buenos Aires: Centro Editor de America Latina, 1973.

Contents: "Revenge" — "Chicken" — "Canals" — "The Road"—"The Rope Trick"—"Isaac Starbuck"—"Guzman, Go Home."

14. *A Sillitoe Selection: Eight short stories.* Selected and edited by Michael Marland, with a specially written introduction by Sillitoe. Harlow, Essex: Longmans, 1968.

Contents: "The Bike"—"The Ragman's Daughter"—"Noah's Ark"—"The Firebug"—"On Saturday Afternoon"—"Uncle Ernest"—"The Fishing-boat Picture"—"The Decline and Fall of Frankie Buller." This book includes a twelve-inch L. P. record of Sillitoe reading "The Bike" and "On Saturday Afternoon".

15. *Men, Women and Children.* London: W. H. Allen, 1973; New York: Scribners, 1974.

Contents: "Mimic"—"Pit Strike"—"Before Snow Comes" —"Enoch's Two Letters"—"The View"—"A Trip to Southwell"—"The Chiker"—"The End of Enoch?"—"Scenes from the Life of Margaret."

16. "The Devil's Almanack." *New Review*, 2 (August 1975), 39-42; reprinted in *Prairie Schooner*, 50 (Spring 1976), 1-11.

PRIMARY WORKS: PLAYS

17. *Saturday Night and Sunday Morning,* 1960 (screenplay).

18. *The Loneliness of the Long-Distance Runner,* 1961. London: Woodfall Films, 1962 (mimeographed filmscript).

19. *All Citizens are Soldiers,* with Ruth Fainlight. Adaptation of a play by Lope de Vega (produced Stratford upon Avon, 1967). London: Macmillan, 1969; Chester Springs, Pennsylvania: Dufour, 1969.

20. *The Ragman's Daughter,* 1970 (screenplay).

21. *This Foreign Field* (produced in London, 1970).

PRIMARY WORKS: POETRY

22. *Without Beer or Bread.* Dulwich Village: Outposts Publicatons, 1957.

Contents: "Left as on dead"—"Shadows"—"Opposites" —"Anthem"—"Poem Written in Majorca"—"Toni Moreno"—"Icarus"—"Guide to the Tiflis railway"—"To Ruth"—"Poem (Out of my thousand voices)."

23. *The Rats and Other Poems.* London: W. H. Allen, 1960.

Contents: "The Rats"—"Left as one Dead"—"When I am a Child"—"You Had a Dream Last Night"—"Perplexed, Placed as I Am"—"O Why Grow You Afraid"— "Spermed on Midsummer Days"—"On Ruth's First Swim in the Mediterranean, 1952"—"Sonnet: Love"— "To Ruth"—"Out of My Thousand Voices"—"Icarus" — "Ulysses" — "Telemachus" — "Carthage" — "The Wild Moon"—"The Seasons"—"Moon Poem"—"Toni Moreno"—"A Child's. Drawing"—"Islands"—"The Arc" —"The One Too Many"—"Poem Written on a Twin-brother's Release from a Siberian Prison Camp"—"The

Escapist"—"Rock of Ages"—"Pictures of Loot"—"Autumn in Majorca"—"Shadow"—"Reflections on a Dead Bluebottle"—"Dead Lilac"—"Poem Written in Majorca" —"Opposites"—"Fragment to End."

24. *A Falling Out of Love and Other Poems.* London: W. H. Allen, 1964.

Contents: "Cabo Finisterre"—"Poem Left by a Dead Man"—"A Falling Out of Love"—"Full Bawd"—"Left as a Desert"—"The Rebels"—"Woods"—"Full Moon Through a Telescope"—"Semipalatinsk"—"Two Cities" — "Suicide" — "Storm" — "Housewife" — "Stars" — "Eve"—"Yes"—"Russian Folk Song"—"Poem"—"March Birth"—"Lake District Cottage"—"The Desert"—"Thirteen Lines"—"Say Sheffield"—"Atomic Goodnight"—"A Dead Man's Grave"—"The Shopshire Woman"—"Car Fights Cat"—"Ruth"—"Strategy and Statement"—"Epitaph"—"Convalescence"—"In Summer and South"—"Frog Poem"—"Friend Died"—"Autumn Nightfire"—"One Day See"—"Truth"—"Sane Man's Image"—"Guide to the Tiflis Railway."

25. *Shaman and Other Poems.* London: Turret, 1968.

Contents: "Night"—"Tree"—"Made for Each Other" —"Altamira"—"Pander"—"Ditchling Beacon"—"Shaman" — "Baby" — "We" — "Samenessess" — "Mixed-up Mystic Thoughts of a Midwestern Missle Man"—"He who continually travels..."—"I saw a swastika scrawled on a wall in Irkutsk..."—"Ride it, ride it out..."—"Parsley Hair..."—"Those stupid little trumpets of the Lord..."—"House"—"A wild cat savaged my hand..."—"The river has burst its banks"—"Poem"—"Death of Ehrenburg" —"Survival"—"Poet"—"Last Poem."

26. *Love in the Environs of Voronezh and Other Poems.* London: Macmillan, 1968; Garden City, New York: Doubleday, 1969.

Contents: contains all of the poems, with different titles, at times, of *Shaman and Other Poems* with the one exception of "I saw a swastika scrawled on a wall in Irkutsk" not included here. Also contains "First Poem" — "Suicide" — "Window" — "Eagledream" — "The Demon Lover"—"Love's Mansion"—"Romeo"—"Mercutio's Pintable Death"—"End"—"Cancer"—"Sonja's Dead Horse"—"Gambler"—"Against the Moon and Love"— "To Burn Out Love"—"Lizard"—"The Knight in Panther's Skin"—"Empty Quarter"—"Smile"—"Gulf of Bothnia"—"Eurasia: Jetnotes"—"Siberian Lake."

27. *Poems,* with Ruth Fainlight, and Ted Hughes. London: Rainbow Press, 1971.

Contents of Sillitoe's contribution: "The Fall"—Chain" —"Alchemist"—"Silence and Stillness"—"Who Died of Love?"—"Poem Written on a Speeding Train, for the Hereford College of Education."

28. *Barbarians and other poems.* London: Turrett, 1973, 1974.

Contents: "Kettle"—"Barbarians"—"Learning Hebrew" —"Fish of the Zodiacs"—"View from Misk Hill"—"Hunger"—"Autumn 1971"—"Open Plan."

29. *Storm: new poems.* London: W. H. Allen, 1974.

Contents: "Chain"—"Love"—"Hephzibah"—"Naked"— "I Love You"—"Lover's Plea"—"Sea Talk"—"Last Thoughts"—"Ghosts"—"Goodbye Kursk"—"Toasting"— "W"—"Railway Station"—"Open Plan"—"Full Moon's Tongue"—"Who Died of Love?"—"Lovers"—"Plague-Meeting"—"Situation"—"Place without a Name"—"Spanish New Year"—"View from Misk Hill"—"February Poems I-X"—"Silence and Stillness"—"The Weight of Summer"—"Rose"—"Hunger"—"Storm (at Bellagio)"— "Fox"—"Odours"—"The Dead"—"Pilgrim"—"The Fall" —"Autumn 1971"—"Creation"—"Lamp Post"—"Signal Box" — "Barbarians" — "Somme" — "Alchemist" —

"Synagogue in Prague 1963"—"Irkutsk 1963"—"Zodiac Fish"—"A Few Lines on Malvern Abbey"—"Learning Hebrew"—"Poem Written on the Hereford Train."

PRIMARY WORKS: OTHER

30. "Both Sides of the Street." *TLS* (8 July 1960), p. 435. On the values, responsibilities, and goals of the working class novelist, especially on his struggle against the Mass Media. Response is made by Edwin Brock in *TLS* (15 July 1960), p. 449. Additional responses are made by Jim Darby, and John Hyde Preston in *TLS* (22 July 1960), p. 465.

31. "Novel or Play?" *Twentieth Century*, 169 (February 1961), 206-211. On his desire to write plays.

32. With Doris Lessing and others. "Revolt in Cuba." *The* (London) *Times* (19 April 1961), p. 13. A letter of protest against the American invasion of Cuba.

33. "Late Starter." *The* (London) *Times* (18 May 1961), p. 19. On what he has read.

34. Untitled book review. *Listener*, 66 (27 July 1961), 144-145. Review of Edna Nixon's *Voltaire and the Calas Case.*

35. "Ximbombas." *New Statesman*, 62 (22 December 1961), 954. An account of a festive Christmas experience in Malaga.

36. "Introduction," to *Riceyman Steps* by Enoch Arnold Bennett. London: Thomas Nelson and Sons, 1961; London: Pan Books, 1964.

37. "Introduction," to *The Old Wive's Tale* by Enoch Arnold Bennett. London: Thomas Nelson and Sons, 1961; London: Pan Books, 1964.

38. "Cheating Eichmann." *Spectator,* 211 (4 October 1963), 429-430. Review of H. Flender's *Rescue in Denmark,* and W. Warmburnn's *The Dutch under German Occupation.*

39. "Drilling and Burring." *Spectator,* 212 (3 January 1964), 11-12. On his first job as a factory worker.

40. "Inside the Whale." *Spectator,* 212 (31 January 1964), 149. Review of Laurens van der Post's *Journey into Russia.*

41. "Poor People." *Anarchy,* 38 (April 1964).

42. *The Road to Volgograd* (travel). London: W. H. Allen, 1964; New York: Knopf, 1964; London: Pan Books, 1966; London: Macmillan, 1969; as *Dorogna na Volgograd.* Trans. N. Dehtereva. Moscow: Pravda, 1964.

43. "The wild horse." *Twentieth Century,* 173 (Winter 1964/65), 90-92. On violence in fiction.

44. "The Boy Revolutionary." *New Statesman,* 69 (18 June 1965), 972-974. Review of Richard O'Connor's *Jack London,* and *The Bodley Head Jack London.* Vol. 3, ed. by Arthur Calder-Marshall.

45. *The City Adventures of Marmalade Jim* (juvenile). Illustrated by Dorothy Rice. London: Macmillan, 1967; as *Prygody Kota Dzima-Marmeladyka.* Trans. Ivan Leščenko. Kiev: Veselka, 1972.

46. "Sent to Approved School." *The* (London) *Times* (24 November 1969), p. 11. A letter to the Editor. Sillitoe protests the law that puts boys away for four years if found guilty of truancy.

47. "Bad form, old boy—and so it was." *The* (London) *Times* (8 April 1972), p. 7. On why he objects to government questionnaires. Response by J. D. Hammond in *The*

Times (13 April 1972), p. 19.

48. "WAG." *TLS* (20 July 1973), p. 834. A letter to the Editor. A protest against R. H. Gruner's thoughts on the Writer's Action Group.

49. "The Arab-Israel conflict." *The* (London) *Times,* p. 19. A protest against Arab military efforts to destroy Israel.

50. "When will the Russians see that humanity is good for them?" *The* (London) *Times* (10 June 1974), p. 14. "Alan Sillitoe on the basic freedom to choose a place to live."

51. "My Israel." *New Statesman,* 88 (20 December 1974), 890-892. On several favorable responses to Israel.

52. Untitled letter to the Editor. *Books and Bookmen,* 20 (January 1975), 5; reply by Colin Wilson immediately follows, pp. 5-6; response to Colin Wilson by Alan Sillitoe in *Books and Bookmen,* 20 (April 1975), 5-6; response by Alan Sillitoe and others in *Books and Bookmen,* 20 (May 1975), 5-7. On Colin Wilson's comments regarding the number of Jews exterminated by Hitler.

53. *Mountains and Caverns.* London: W. H. Allen, 1975.

II. GENERAL SECONDARY STUDIES, INTERVIEWS, BIOGRAPHICAL SKETCHES, AND MISCELLANEOUS ITEMS

General references to Sillitoe's work also appear in the First Part of this bibliography. See the following numbers there: 2, 9, 10, 11, 12, 16, 17, 19, 23, 28, 29, 31, 32, 34, 35, 36, 37, 38, 40, 42, 44, 45, 50, 53, 55, 56, 72, 75, 76, 77, 78, 80, 82, 85, 89, 94, 95, 96, 100, 101, 104, 107, 109, 110, 119, 125, 127, 131, 158, 171, 199, 206, 213, 258, 262, 266, 305, 308.

54. Anon. "Alan Sillitoe." *The* (London) *Times* (6 February 1964), p. 15. An interview.

55. —. "Briton pleads for gaoled writers." *The* (London) *Times* (12 September 1967), p. 5.

56. —. "First Novel Award." *The* (London) *Times* (7 April 1959), p. 6. A notice that The Authors' Club Award will be given to Sillitoe for his *Saturday Night and Sunday Morning.*

57. —. "Sillitoe, Alan." *World Authors 1950-1970.* Ed. John Wakeman and Stanley J. Kunitz. New York: H. W. Wilson, 1975, pp. 1302-1305.

58. —. "Silver Quill for New Novelist: Mr. Alan Sillitoe Looks Forward to Wilder Travels." *The* (London) *Times* (23 April 1959), p. 9. A biographical sketch based upon an interview.

59. —. "Wrong age by writer." *The* (London) *Times* (19 November 1971), p. 2. On Sillitoe's being fined for failing

to fill in a census form correctly. He gave his age as 101.

60. Atherton, Stanley S. "Alan Sillitoe's Battleground." *Dalhousie Review*, 48 (1968), 324-331.

61. Biester, Hanne-Lore. "Alan Sillitoe und die Sowjetunion." *Zeitschrift für Anglistik und Amerikanistik*, 17 (1969), 60-74.

62. Burns, Johnnie Wade. "An Examination of Elements of Socialist Realism in Five Novels of Alan Sillitoe." Diss. George Peabody College for Teachers, 1975. *Dissertation Abstracts*, 36A (1975), 2213-2214.

63. Dixon, Terrell F. "Expostulation and a Reply: The Character of Clegg in Fowles and Sillitoe." *Notes on Contemporary Literature*, 4, No. 2 (1974), 2-4.

64. Gindin, James. "Alan Sillitoe's Jungle." *Texas Studies in Literature and Language*, 4 (Spring 1962), 35-48.

65. —. Untitled comments. *Contemporary Novelists.* London and Chicago: St. James Press, 1972, pp. 1132-1134.

66. Hajek, Igor. "Morning Coffee with Sillitoe." *Nation*, 208 (27 January 1969), 122-124. An interview.

67. Hennessy, Brendan. "Alan Sillitoe Interviewed." *Transatlantic Review*, No. 41 (Winter-Spring 1972), pp. 108-113.

68. Hurrell, John Dennis. "Alan Sillitoe and the Serious Novel." *Critique*, 4, No. 1 (1961), 3-16.

69. Klotz, Günther. "Alan Sillitoe's Heroes." *Essays in Honour of William Gallacher.* Ed. Erika Lingner, et. al. Berlin: Humboldt University, 1966, pp. 259-263.

70. Le Franc, Bolivar. "Sillitoe at forty." *Books and Bookmen*, 14 (June 1969), 21-22, 24. An interview.

71. Lefranc, M. "Alan Sillitoe: An Interview." *Études Anglaises,* 26 (January-March 1973), 35-48.

72. Lockwood, Bernard. "Four Contemporary British Working-Class Novelists: A Thematic and Critical Approach to the Fiction of Raymond Williams, John Braine, David Storey and Alan Sillitoe." Diss. Wisconsin, 1966. *Dissertation Abstracts,* 28A (1967), 1081.

73. Nardella, Anna Ryan. "The Existential Dilemmas of Alan Sillitoe's Working-Class Heroes." *Studies in the Novel,* 5 (Winter 1973), 469-482.

74. Norman, Barry. "Alan Sillitoe avoids the complacency trap." *The* (London) *Times* (26 October 1972), p. 12. An interview.

75. P. H. S. "Very alive." *The* (London) *Times* (21 July 1969), p. 4. A discussion with Sillitoe about his play, *This Foreign Field.*

76. Peel, Marie. "The loneliness of Alan Sillitoe." *Books and Bookmen,* 19 (December 1973), 42-46. On all of his work.

77. Penner, Allen Richard. *Alan Sillitoe.* New York: Twayne, 1972.

78. —. "The Political Prologue and Two Parts of a Trilogy: *The Death of William Posters* and *A Tree on Fire." University Review,* 35 (1968), 11-20.

79. Rosselli, John. "A Cry from the Brick Streets." *Reporter,* 23 (10 November 1960), 37, 40, 42. On Sillitoe and his working-class novels.

80. Sauter, Josef-Hermann. "Interview mit Alan Sillitoe." *Weimarer Beiträge,* 19, No. 12 (1973), 44-59.

81. Simmons, Michael K. "The 'In-Laws' and 'Out-Laws' of

Alan Sillitoe." *Ball State University Forum*, 14 (Winter 1973), 76-79.

82. Splendore, Paula. " 'Gioventu,' Lavore e rabbia in tre romanzi inglesi d'oggi." *Annali Istituto Universitario Orientale, Napoli, Sezione Germanica*, 11 (1968), 195-207.

83. Vizioli, Paulo. "Alan Sillitoe, a experiência do romance proletário." *O Estado de São Paulo, Suplemento Literário*, 10 (November 1974), 5.

84. Wexler, Alexanda. "Der abgeschnittene Kopf." *Deutsche Rundschau*, 88 (1962), 50-55. Includes comments on Sillitoe.

85. Wood, Ramsay. "Alan Sillitoe: The Image Shedding the Author." *Four Quarters*, 21 (November 1971), 3-10.

III. STUDIES AND REVIEWS OF
INDIVIDUAL WORKS

References to individual books by Sillitoe also appear in the First Part of this bibliography. See the following numbers there: 156, 157, 166, 200, 207, 215, 216, 221, 222, 223, 227, 234, 235, 248, 251, 252, 260, 268, 270, 296, 310, 321, 344, 346.

Saturday Night and Sunday Morning

86. Anon. "A Pop Theatre Crib from Pop Religion. Prince of Wales Theatre: *Saturday Night and Sunday Morning.*" *The* (London) *Times* (2 February 1966), p. 15.

87. —. "Blessings in Disguise." *TLS* (7 November 1958), p. 646.

88. —. "New Leases of Life?" *TLS* (2 September 1960), p. 562.

89. —. *"Saturday Night and Sunday Morning." Booklist,* 56 (1 September 1959), 29.

90. —. *"Saturday Night and Sunday Morning." Reporter,* 21 (15 October 1959), 56.

91. —. "Sillitoe Novel on the Stage. Musical Without Songs. Nottingham Playhouse: *Saturday Night and Sunday Morning.*" *The* (London) *Times* (16 April 1964), p. 6.

92. Baro, Gene. Review of *Saturday Night and Sunday Morning,* in the *New York Herald Tribune Book Review* (16 August 1959), p. 6.

93. Bradbury, Malcolm. "Beating the World to the Punch." *New York Times Book Review* (16 August 1959), pp. 4-5.

94. Curley, Thomas F. "A Disturbing Look at British Life." *Commonweal,* 70 (4 September 1959), 478-479.

95. Fenby, George. "The Organic Self (A Study of Selected English Working-Class Fiction)." Diss. Connecticut, 1973. *Dissertation Abstracts,* 33A (1973), 6352-6353.

96. Howe, Irving. "The Worker as a Young Tough." *New Republic,* 141 (24 August 1959), 27-28.

97. Kingston, Jeremy. "Theatre." *Punch,* 250 (9 February 1966), 206. Review of stage production of novel.

98. McKinney, Joan. Review of *Saturday Night and Sunday Morning,* in the *San Francisco Chronicle* (29 November 1959), p. 29.

99. Meighan, Matthew H. *"Saturday Night and Sunday Morning."* *Best Sellers,* 19 (1 September 1959), 174-175.

100. Mott, Schuyler. *"Saturday Night and Sunday Morning."* *Library Journal,* 84 (July 1959), 2216.

101. O'Callaghan, John. *"Saturday Night and Sunday Morning."* *Guardian* (16 April 1964), p. 9. Review of the play based on the book.

102. Osgerby, J. R. "Alan Sillitoe's *Saturday Night and Sunday Morning."* *Renaissance and Modern Essays.* Ed. G. R. Hibbard. London, 1966, pp. 215-230.

103. Price, Martin. "Six Recent Novels." *Yale Review,* n.s. 49 (September 1959), 124-132. Pp. 127-129.

* 104. Staples, Hugh B. *"Saturday Night and Sunday Morning:* Alan Sillitoe and the White Goddess." *Modern Fiction*

Studies, 10 (Summer 1964), 171-181.

105. West, Anthony. "On the Inside Looking In." *New Yorker,* 35 (5 September 1959), 103-104.

106. Yaffe, James. "Many Moods Have These Europeans. 4. England." *Saturday Review,* 42 (5 September 1959), 17.

The General

107. Allen, Walter. "The Fable and the Moral." *New Statesman,* 59 (21 May 1960), 765.

108. Anon. "A Weakness for Music." *TLS* (20 May 1960), p. 317.

109. —. "New Fiction." *The* (London) *Times* (26 May 1960), p. 17.

110. —. *"The General."* *Booklist,* 57 (1 February 1961), 323.

111. Coleman, John. "Music Week." *Spectator,* 204 (27 May 1960), 778.

112, Cosman, Max. "A Rebel of Uncertain Cause." *Commonweal,* 73 (17 February 1961), 535-536.

113. Dennis, Nigel. "Symphony of Errors." *New York Times Book Review* (22 January 1961), p. 4.

114. Foster, Richard. "What is Fiction For?" *Hudson Review,* 14 (Spring 1961), 142-149. Pp. 144-145.

115. Harcourt, Peter. *"The General."* *Twentieth Century,* 168 (July 1960), 90-92.

116. McDonough, James P. *"The General."* *Best Sellers,* 20 (1 March 1961), 457.

117. McKinney, Joan. Review of *The General,* in the *San Fran-*

cisco Chronicle (29 January 1961), p. 27.

118. Moon, Eric. *"The General."* *Library Journal,* 86 (1 February 1961), 596.

119. Paulding, Gouverneur. "A War, an Orchestra, a Taut Situation." *New York Herald Tribune Book Review,* 37 (22 January 1961), 29.

120. Penner, Allen R. *"The General:* Exceptional Proof of a Critical Rule." *Southern Humanities Review,* 4 (1970), 135-143.

121. Perrott, Roy. "Art v. authority." *Manchester Guardian Weekly,* 82 (26 May 1960), 11.

122. —. "Art Versus Power." *Guardian* (20 May 1960), p. 9.

123. Phinney, A. W., Jr. "British: Sillitoe Tries a Parable." *Christian Science Monitor,* 53 (26 January 1961), 5.

124. Richardson, Joanna. "New Novels." *Punch,* 238 (8 June 1960), 817-818.

125. Ross, T. J. "From the Netherworld of the Future." *New Republic,* 144 (6 February 1961), 25.

* 126. Solotaroff, Theodore. "Fiction Chronicle." *Partisan Review,* 28 (March-April 1961), 301-308. Pp. 302-304.

Key to the Door

127. Allen, Walter. "In the World of the Bottom Dogs." *New York Times Book Review* (25 March 1962), p. 5.

128. Anon. "Anatomy of a Radical." *Time,* 79 (6 April 1962), 100.

129. —. "Briefly Noted." *New Yorker,* 38 (22 September

1962), 177.

130. —. *"Key to the Door."* *Kirkus,* 30 (15 January 1962), 71.

131. —. "New Fiction." *The* (London) *Times* (19 October 1961), p. 15.

132. —. "Scenes from Provincial Life." *TLS* (20 October 1961), p. 749.

133. Barrett, William. "England, My England." *Atlantic,* 209 (May 1962), 122-124.

134. Beck, Warren. Review of *Key to the Door,* in the *Chicago Sunday Tribune* (18 March 1962), p. 4.

135. Booth, Wayne C. "Yes, But Are They Really Novels?" *Yale Review,* n.s. 51 (Summer 1962), 630-637. Pp. 634-635.

* 136. Coleman, John. "The Unthinkables." *New Statesman,* 62 (27 October 1961), 610, 612.

137. G. B. *"Key to the Door."* *New York Herald Tribune Books,* 38 (8 April 1962), 6-7.

138. Howe, Irving. "In Fear of Thinking." *New Republic,* 146 (28 May 1962), 25-26.

139. Hynes, Samuel. "A Quality of Honesty." *Commonweal,* 76 (6 April 1962), 46-47.

140. Kiniery, Paul. *"Key to the Door."* *Best Sellers,* 22 (1 April 1962), 8.

141. Koningsberger, Hans. "Dropped Aitches in Malaya." *Saturday Review,* 45 (24 March 1962), 26.

142. McDowell, Frederick P. W. "Self and Society: Alan Sillitoe's *Key to the Door.*" *Critique,* 6, No. 1 (Spring

1963), 116-123.

143. McMichael, George. Review of *Key to the Door,* in the *San Francisco Chronicle* (27 May 1962) p. 29.

144. Moon, Eric. *"Key to the Door." Library Journal,* 87 (15 February 1962), 786.

145. Penner, Allen Richard. "Dantesque Allegory in Sillitoe's *Key to the Door." Renascence,* 20 (Winter 1968), 79-85, 103.

146. Raven, Simon. "Two Kinds of Jungle." *Spectator,* 207 (20 October 1961), 551-552. P. 551.

147. Review of *Key to the Door,* in the *Springfield Republican* (8 August 1962), p. 4d.

148. Weatherby, W. J. "Mr. Sillitoe takes another look." *Manchester Guardian Weekly,* 85 (26 October 1961), 11.

149. —. "Too much love." *Guardian* (20 October 1961), p. 7.

The Death of William Posters

150. Aldridge, John W. "Frank Dawley's Dilemma." *New York Times Book Review* (29 August 1965), p. 26.

151. Anon. "Briefing: *The Death of William Posters." Observer* (18 June 1967), p. 18.

152. —. "Briefly Noted." *New Yorker,* 41 (20 November 1965), 242, 244.

153. —. "Destructive Dialectic." *Newsweek,* 66 (16 August 1965), 82.

154. —. "Hitching Out of Reality." *TLS* (13 May 1965), p. 365.

155. —. "New Fiction." *The* (London) *Times* (13 May 1965), p. 15.

156. Burgess, Eve. "New Novels." *Punch,* 248 (9 June 1965), 870.

157. Coleman, John. "On the Run." *Observer* (9 May 1965), p. 26.

158. Corke, Hilary. "Stories and Symbols." *Listener,* 73 (27 May 1965), 797.

159. Davenport, John. "Zentimental Journey." *Spectator,* 214 (14 May 1965), 639-641. Pp. 640-641.

160. Green, Martin. "Advertisements for himself." *Book Week,* 2 (22 August 1965), 4, 16.

161. Kermode, Frank. "Rammel." *New Statesman,* 69 (14 May 1965), 765-766.

162. Leslie, Andrew. "Long-distance escapism." *Manchester Guardian Weekly,* 92 (13 May 1965), 11.

163. McGuinness, Frank. "Selected Books." *London Magazine,* n.s. 5 (August 1965), 102-105. Pp. 102-104.

164. Moon, Eric. "Against the Establishment." *Saturday Review,* 48 (21 August 1965), 27.

165. Morgan, Derek. "The Desert of Freedom." *Reporter,* 33 (23 September 1965), 59-60.

166. Pérez-Minik, Domingo. "El 'William Posters' de Alan Sillitoe." *Insula,* 26 (May 1971), 7.

167. Thompson, Donald E. *"The Death of William Posters." Library Journal,* 90 (15 September 1965), 3626.

A Tree on Fire

168. Anon. *"A Tree on Fire." Choice,* 6 (April 1969), 218.

169. —. "Anglo-Apocalyptic." *TLS* (9 November 1967), p. 1053.

170. Burrows, Miles. "Ceremonies of Experience." *New Statesman,* 74 (10 November 1967), 644-645.

171. Clive, George. "Time for decision." *Spectator,* 219 (10 November 1967), 579-580. P. 579.

172. Doyle, Paul A. *"A Tree on Fire." Best Sellers,* 28 (15 August 1968), 209-210.

173. Jackson, Katherine Gauss. *"A Tree on Fire." Harper's,* 237 (September 1968), 101.

174. Jebb, Julian. "Rant before passion." *The* (London) *Times* (11 November 1967), p. 22.

175. McGuinness, Frank. Untitled book review. *London Magazine,* n.s. 7 (November 1967), 91-93. Pp. 91-92.

176. Millar, Neil. "Fierce burnings in private wildernesses." *Christian Science Monitor,* 60 (6 September 1968), 9.

177. Pryce-Jones, Alan. "Anguished puritan." *Book World,* 2 (25 August 1968), 8.

178. Shrapnel, Norman. "Mightier than the sword." *Manchester Guardian Weekly,* 97 (16 November 1967), 11.

179. Tannenbaum, Earl. *"A Tree on Fire." Library Journal,* 93 (August 1968), 2899.

180. Williams, David. "New Fiction." *Punch,* 253 (8 November 1967), 721.

181. Wolfe, Peter. "Happenings and Harangues." *Saturday Review,* 51 (17 August 1968), 25-26.

182. Yurick, Sol. "Rite of Passage." *New York Times Book Review* (22 September 1968), p. 34.

A Start in Life

183. Anon. "A naturalist no more." *TLS* (18 September 1970), p. 1026.

184. —. *"A Start in Life."* *Booklist,* 68 (15 October 1971), 183.

185. —. *"A Start in Life."* *British Book News* (November 1970), p. 901.

186. Clark, John R. *"A Start in Life."* *Saturday Review,* 54 (16 October 1971), 69.

187. Coleman, John. "Novels or whatever." *Observer* (13 September 1970), p. 28.

188. Ewart, Gavin. "Hams in Cider." *London Magazine,* n.s. 10 (December 1970), 99-102. P. 99.

189. Farrell, J. G. "Girls and boys." *Spectator,* 225 (10 October 1970), 407.

190. Graver, Lawrence. "A bastard from Nottingham tells his story." *New York Times Book Review* (26 September 1971), p. 2.

191. Howes, Victor. "Long Distance operator." *Christian Science Monitor,* 63 (7 October 1971), 7.

192. Lovering, Joseph P. *"A Start in Life."* *Best Sellers,* 31 (15 January 1972), 468-469.

193. Moon, Eric. *"A Start in Life."* *Library Journal,* 96 (August

1971), 2548.

194. Scannell, Vernon. "A Real Bastard." *New Statesman*, 80 (18 September 1970), 343.

195. Theroux, Paul. "Novels." *Book World*, 5 (10 October 1971), 2.

196. Watrin, J. "Alan Sillitoe's *A Start in Life.*" *Revue des Langues Vivantes*, 38 (1972), 508-516.

197. Williams, David. "Short distance runner." *The* (London) *Times* (24 September 1970), p. 14.

Travels in Nihilon

198. Anon. "Nothing doing." *TLS* (17 September 1971), p. 1105.

199. —. *"Travels in Nihilon."* *British Book News* (January 1972), p. 85.

200. Blackburn, Sara. "Four novels: dewinding, competing, indulging and breaking free." *New York Times Book Review* (15 October 1972), p. 2.

201. Boston, Richard. "News from nowhere." *Observer* (12 September 1971), p. 28.

202. Burroway, Janet. "Limping Westward." *New Statesman*, 82 (17 September 1971), 369-370. P. 370.

203. Evans, R. Daniel. *"Travels in Nihilon."* *Best Sellers*, 32 (15 September 1972), 281-282.

204. Jones, D. A. N. "Local Authorities." *Listener*, 86 (16 September 1971), 578.

205. Nye, Robert. "Upside-down Utopia." *Guardian*, 105 (25

September 1971), 21.

206. Smith, Michael Kalen. *"Travels in Nihilon." Library Journal*, 97 (1 November 1972), 3618.

207. Wagner, Geoffrey. "From Sublime to Sickening." *National Review*, 24 (10 November 1972), 1254-1255. P. 1254.

208. Waugh, Auberon. "Auberon Waugh on class fictions." *Spectator*, 227 (2 October 1971), 479.

209. Weeks, Edward. *"Travels in Nihilon." Atlantic*, 230 (October 1972), 134.

Raw Material

210. Amis, Martin. "Circling Around." *Observer* (5 November 1972), p. 38.

211. Anon. "On the anvil." *TLS* (3 November 1972), p. 1305.

212. —. *"Raw Material." Choice*, 11 (April 1974), 261.

213. —. *"Raw Material." New Yorker*, 49 (31 December 1973), 59-60.

214. —. *"Raw Material." Publishers' Weekly*, 204 (10 September 1973), 41-42.

215. Compton, D. G. *"Raw Material." Books and Bookmen*, 18 (January 1973), 96-97.

216. Johnson, B. S. "Truth and Lies." *New Statesman*, 84 (27 October 1972), 608-609.

217. Jones, D. A. N. "Brown Studies." *Listener*, 88 (26 October 1972), 557.

218. Pearson, Gabriel. "Unfinished business." *Guardian*, 107

(11 November 1972), 25.

219. Portis, Rowe. *"Raw Material."* *Library Journal,* 98 (1 December 1973), 3578.

220. Schnee, Phillip H. *"Raw Material."* *Best Sellers,* 33 (15 January 1974), 462.

The Flame of Life

221. Anon. *"The Flame of Life."* *British Book News* (February 1975), p. 141.

222. Davies, Russell. "Trouble at the dacha." *TLS* (29 November 1974), p. 1336.

223. Mellors, John. "Brotherly lust." *Listener,* 92 (5 December 1974), 753-754. P. 754.

224. Peel, Marie. "Tomorrow to fresh fields." *Books and Bookmen,* 20 (May 1975), 49-50.

225. Quigly, Isabel. "Sweet smell." *Financial Times* (28 November 1974), p. 30.

* 226. Richardson, Maurice. "Bores and super-bores." *Observer* (1 December 1974), p. 34.

The Loneliness of the Long-Distance Runner

227. Anon. "Borstal and Cambridge." *TLS* (2 October 1959), p. 557.

228. —. "Borstal Boy's Hatred of Normal People." *The* (London) *Times* (27 April 1961), p. 18. Review of a radio adaptation of the title story.

229. —. "New Fiction." *The* (London) *Times* (8 October 1959),

p. 15.

230. —. "Notes from the Underground." *Time,* 75 (18 April 1960), 116, 119.

231. —. *"The Loneliness of the Long-Distance Runner."* Booklist, 56 (15 April 1960), 511.

232. Baro, Gene. "Tales of British Working Class Life." *New York Herald Tribune Book Review,* 36 (29 May 1960), 6.

233. Boroff, David. "Glimpses of a Shabby Gaiety." *Saturday Review,* 43 (16 April 1960), 27.

234. Bradbury, Malcolm. "Beneath the Veneer, Pure Animal Life." *New York Times Book Review* (10 April 1960), p. 5.

235. Coleman, John. "Resign the Living." *Spectator,* 203 (25 September 1959), 416.

236. Cosman, Max. "Disapproval with Compassion." *Commonweal,* 72 (29 April 1960), 131.

237. Denny, N. "The Achievement of the Long-Distance Runner." *Theoria,* No. 24 (1965), pp. 1-12.

238. Hough, Graham. "New Novels." *Listener,* 62 (1 October 1959), 542.

239. Johnson, Pamela Hansford. "New Novels." *New Statesman,* 58 (3 October 1959), 448-449.

240. McClarren, Robert R. *"The Loneliness of the Long-Distance Runner."* Library Journal, 85 (15 February 1960), 783.

241. McKinney, Joan. Review of *The Loneliness of the Long Distance Runner,* in the *San Francisco Chronicle* (1 May 1960), p. 30.

242. O'Rourke, Elizabeth. *"The Loneliness of the Long Distance Runner." Best Sellers,* 20 (1 May 1960), 58.

243. Penner, Allen R. "Human Dignity and Social Anarchy: Sillitoe's 'The Loneliness of the Long-Distance Runner'." *Contemporary Literature,* 10 (Spring 1969), 253-265.

244. Perrott, Roy. "Life through the eyes of the odd man out." *Guardian* (25 September 1959), p. 7.

245. Price, R. G. G. "New Fiction." *Punch,* 237 (14 October 1959), 315.

* 246. Pritchett, V. S. "Saints and Rogues." *Listener,* 68 (6 December 1962), 957-959. P. 959.

247. Updike, John. "Voices from Downtroddendom." *New Republic,* 142 (9 May 1960), 11-12.

248. West, Anthony. "Puppets and People." *New Yorker,* 36 (11 June 1960), 144-146. Pp. 145-146.

249. Wyndham, Francis. Untitled book review. *London Magazine,* 7 (March 1960), 65-68. Pp. 65-66.

The Ragman's Daughter

250. Aldridge, John W. "Room at the Bottom." *Book Week,* 1 (12 January 1964), 1, 16.

251. Anon. "Laureate of the Losers." *Time,* 83 (7 February 1964), 106.

252. —. *"The Ragman's Daughter and Other Stories." Virginia Quarterly Review,* 40 (Spring 1964), lx.

253. Bowen, John. "What Is There New to Learn From the View of 'Them' and 'Us'?" *New York Times Book Review* (12 January 1964), pp. 4-5.

254. Brooke, Jocelyn. "New Fiction." *Listener,* 70 (24 October 1963), 667.

255. Furbank, P. N. "Rags and Riches." *Encounter,* 22 (February 1964), 80-82. Pp. 81-82.

256. Green, Benny. "Cinema." *Punch,* 263 (1 November 1972), 636. Review of the movie version of the book.

257. Grumbach, Doris. *"The Ragman's Daughter." Critic,* 22 (February 1964), 91.

258. Kauffmann, Stanley. "Nothing to Lose But Your Chains." *New York Review of Books,* 2 (5 March 1964), 8.

259. Miller, Karl. "Sillitoe and Son." *New Statesman,* 66 (18 October 1963), 530.

260. Moon, Eric. "Pegasus in the Grime." *Saturday Review,* 47 (25 January 1964), 39.

261. Price, R. G. G. "New Fiction." *Punch,* 245 (16 October 1963), 577-578. P. 578.

262. Richler, Mordecai. "Proles on Parade." *Spectator,* 211 (25 October 1963), 535.

263. Storey, David. "Which revolution?" *Manchester Guardian Weekly,* 89 (24 October 1963), 10.

* 264. Tannenbaum, Earl. *"The Ragman's Daughter and Other Stories." Library Journal,* 89 (1 February 1964), 657.

265. Wilkie, Brian. "Grim and Funny." *Commonweal,* 80 (27 March 1964), 20-21.

Guzman, Go Home, and Other Stories

266. Anon. "Fiction round-up: *Guzman, Go Home." The*

(London) *Times* (21 December 1968), p. 19.

267. —. "Love and War." *TLS* (24 October 1968), p. 1193.

268. Dawson, Helen. "Breifing: *Guzman, Go Home.*" *Observer* (20 September 1970), p. 24.

269. Hislop, Alan. "Life as a series of lost directions." *New York Times Book Review* (14 December 1969), pp. 44-45. P. 45.

270. Hough, Carolyn A. *"Guzman, Go Home and Other Stories."* *Library Journal,* 94 (15 September 1969), 3085.

271. Scannell, Vernon. "I am Yours." *New Statesman,* 76 (1 November 1968), 588.

272. Sterne, Richard Clark. *"Guzman, Go Home and Other Stories."* *Saturday Review,* 52 (22 November 1969), 86.

Men, Women and Children

273. Anon. *"Men, Women and Children."* *Booklist,* 71 (1 December 1974), 367.

274. —. *"Men, Women and Children."* *British Book News* (January 1974), p. 77.

275. —. *"Men, Women and Children."* *Choice,* 11 (December 1974), 1480.

276. —. "Tales of integrity and experience." *TLS* (19 October 1973), p. 1269.

277. Cunningham, Valentine. "Ninety-Five Tales." *Listener,* 90 (8 November 1973), 638.

278. D. M. "Not so simple." *Observer* (11 November 1973), p. 36.

279. Doyle, Paul A. *"Men, Women and Children."* *Best Sellers,* 34 (15 September 1974), 282.

280. Feinstein, Elaine. "Unashamed Humanism." *London Magazine,* n.s. 13 (February/March 1974), 137-140. P. 138.

281. Levin, Martin. *"Men, Women and Children."* *New York Times Book Review* (22 September 1974), p. 40.

282. Nolan, Robert J. *"Men, Women and Children."* *Library Journal,* 99 (15 September 1974), 2178.

283. Nordell, Roderick. *"Men, Women and Children."* *Christian Science Monitor,* 66 (21 August 1974), 11.

284. Shrapnel, Norman. "Simplicity is difficult." *Guardian,* 109 (20 October 1973), 24.

All Citizens Are Soldiers

285. Peter, John. "Clumsy echo of old play." *The* (London) *Times* (20 June 1967), p. 6.

This Foreign Field

286. Bryden, Ronald. "Lunatic infidelity." *Observer* (29 March 1970), p. 24.

287. Wardle, Irvine. "Agrarian takeover." *The* (London) *Times* (25 March 1970), 17.

The Rats and Other Poems

288. Anon. "The Poet and His Hate." *TLS* (6 January 1961), p. 5.

289. Blackburn, Thomas. "Poetic Knowledge." *New Statesman,*

60 (24 December 1960), 1016.

290. Davie, Donald. "Kinds of Mastery." *Spectator,* 206 (10 February 1961), 193-194. P. 194.

291. Furbank, P. N. "New Poetry." *Listener,* 65 (26 January 1961), 195.

292. Kell, Richard. "Passion and vistavision." *Manchester Guardian Weekly,* 84 (26 January 1961), 11.

A Falling Out of Love and Other Poems

293. Alvarez, A. "O My America!" *Observer* (4 October 1964), p. 27.

294. Ricks, Christopher. "Sprawling." *New Statesman,* 68 (25 September 1964), 448-450. P. 449.

Love in the Environs of Voronezh and Other Poems

295. Anon. *"Love in the Environs of Voronezh."* *Virginia Quarterly Review,* 45 (Summer 1969), xcvi.

296. Foster, Jane. *"Love in the Environs of Voronezh."* *Library Journal,* 94 (15 April 1969), 1806-1807.

297. Howes, Victor. "Alan Sillitoe—the novelist as a poet." *Christian Science Monitor,* 61 (24 February 1969), 9.

298. Kramer, Aaron. *"Love in the Environs of Voronezh."* *Library Journal,* 94 (1 March 1969), 1001.

299. Seymour-Smith, Martin. "From bad to verse." *Spectator,* 221 (20 September 1968), 397-398.

Barbarians and Other Poems

300. Anon.   "Ovaltine lids and other observations." *TLS* (24 May 1974), p. 554.

The Road to Volgograd

301. Anon.   "For the Tourist." *TLS* (25 June 1964), p. 555.

302. Brockway, James.   "Alan Sillitoe: *The Road to Volgograd.*" *Tirade,* 8 (1964), 598-600.

303. Gross, John.   "A Month in the Country." *New Statesman,* 67 (19 June 1964), 959-960.

304. Hingley, Ronald.   "Innocent Abroad." *Spectator,* 212 (26 June 1964), 857-858.

305. Ivsky, Oleg.   *"Road to Volgograd."* *Library Journal,* 90 (15 January 1965), 247.

306. Pisko, Ernest S.   "Two Reports on the Soviets." *Christian Science Monitor,* 56 (31 December 1964), 5.

307. Richardson, Joanna.   "Moscow and Rome." *Punch,* 247 (5 August 1964), 208.

308. Roberts, Henry L.   "The shades of red." *Book Week,* 2 (28 March 1965), 14-15. P. 14.

The City Adventures of Marmalade Jim

309. Anon.   "Faraway Places—and Pictures to Show the Way." *TLS* (30 November 1967), pp. 1148-1149. P. 1148.

310. Gillott, Jacky.   "Hens, jellies and wild things." *The* (London) *Times* (21 October 1967), p. 21.

Mountains and Caverns

311. Amis, Martin. "Being Serious in the Fifties." *New States-man*, 90 (7 November 1975), 577-578.

312. Anon. *"Mountains and Caverns."* British Book News (January 1976), p. 21.

C[HARLES] P[ERCY] SNOW
(Born in Leicester 1905)

I. PRIMARY WORKS: EARLY NOVELS

1. *Death Under Sail.* London: Heinemann, 1932, 1933, 1936, rev. ed. 1959; Garden City, New York: Doubleday, 1932; Harmondsworth: Penguin, 1963; as *Śmierć Pod Żaglami.* Trans. Jadwiga Milnikiel. Warsaw: Iskry, 1961; as *Yacht Senjô No Satsujin.* Trans. Sakurai Masuo. Tokyo: Kôbundo, 1964; as *Smert Pid Vitrylamy.* Trans. Galyns'ka and M. Pinčevs'kyj. Kiev: Dnipro, 1965; as *Jarimat Al-Yakht.* Trans. 'Abd al-Mun'im Sádiq. al-Qahirah: al-Dār al-Qawmíyah, 1966; as *Morte A Vele Spiegate.* Trans. Marina Valente. Milano: Rizzoli, 1967; as *Mord Unterm Segel.* Trans. Liselotte Mickel. Stuttgart: Deutsche Verlaganst, 1971; also Hamburg: Rowohlt,1974; as *Le barreur solitaire.* Trans. Alexandre Ralli. Paris: Bourgois, 1972.

2. *New Lives for Old* (published anonymously). London: Victor Gollancz, 1933, 1935.

3. *The Search.* London: Victor Gollancz, 1934; New York and Indianapolis, Indiana: Bobbs-Merrill, 1935; rev. ed. London: Macmillan, 1958, 1959; New York: Scribner, 1959, 1967; New York: New American Library, 1960; Harmondsworth: Penguin, 1965; as *Poiski.* Trans. B. Gribanov. Moscow: Progress, 1964.

Strangers and Brothers Series:

4. *Strangers and Brothers.* London: Faber and Faber, 1940, 1944; London: Macmillan, 1951, 1953, 1958; New York: Macmillan, 1958; New York: Scribner, 1960, 1963, 1972; Harmondsworth: Penguin, 1962, 1968; as *George Passant.* Harmondsworth: Penguin, 1973; as *Extraños y Hermanos.* Trans. Rosa S. de Naveira. Barcelona: Plaza and Janés, 1962; as *Fremde und Brüder.* Trans. Grete Felten. Stuttgart: Deutsche Verlaganst, 1964.

5. *The Light and the Dark.* London: Faber and Faber, 1947; New York: Macmillan, 1948, 1961; London: Macmillan, 1951, 1952, 1957, 1958; New York: Scribner, 1961, 1964; Harmondsworth: Penguin, 1962, 1968, 1973; as *Die Lichten und die Dunklen Gewalten.* Trans. Walter Puchwein. Wien: Zsolnay, 1948; as *La Lumière et les Tenèbres.* Trans. Renée Villoteau. Paris: R. Laffont, 1951; as *Jasnośc I Mrok.* Trans. Henry K. Kreczkowski. Warsaw: Pánstw. Instytut Wydawn, 1961.

6. *Time of Hope.* London: Faber and Faber, 1949; New York: Macmillan, 1950; London: Macmillan, 1951, 1958; New York: Scribner, 1961, 1966; New York: Harper, 1961; Harmondsworth: Penguin, 1962, 1970; as *Jahre der Hoffnung.* Trans. Edmund Th. Kauer. Vienna: Zsolnay, 1951; as *Le Temps de L'espoir.* Trans. Renée Villoteau. Paris: R. Laffont, 1952; as *Zeit der Hoffnung.* Trans. Grete Felten. Stuttgart: Deutsche Verlaganst, 1960; also Stuttgart and Salzburg: Europäischer Buchklub, 1963; also Zürich: Buchclub Ex Libris, 1963; as *A Reménység Kora.* Trans. Peter Nagy. Budapest: Európa, 1962; as *Pora Nadežd.* Trans. V. Vasilev and T. Kudrjavceva. Moscow: Izd. inostr. lit., 1962; as *Czas Nadziel.* Trans. Jadwiga Milnikiel. Warsaw: Państw. Instytut Wydawn, 1963.

7. *The Masters.* London: Macmillan, 1951, 1954, 1958, 1972; New York: Macmillan, 1951; Harmondsworth:

Penguin, 1956, 1969, 1972; Garden City, New York: Doubleday, 1959; New York: Scribner, 1960, 1965; as *Die Lehre.* Trans. Georg Goyert. München: Desch, 1952; as *Rektorsvalet.* Trans. Jane Lundblad. Stockholm: Norstedt, 1954; as *Profesoři.* Trans. Eliška Hornátová. Prague: Státní nakladatelstvi Krásné literatury a umění, 1963; as *Universitarii.* Trans. Veronica Suteu. Bucarest: Editura pentru literatură universală, 1967.

8. *The New Men.* London and Toronto: Macmillan, 1954, 1958, 1960; New York: Scribner, 1955, 1961, 1965; Harmondsworth: Penguin, 1959, 1970; as *De Nya Männen.* Trans. Jane Lundblad. Stockholm: Norstedt, 1956; as *Gli Uomini Nuovi.* Trans. Maria Rosaria Schisano. Torino: Einaudi, 1965; also Milano: Club degli editori, 1965; as *Nueve hombre del siglo xx.* Trans. Mercedes García Arenal, et. al. Madrid: Alianza Editorial, 1969; as *Entscheidung in Barford.* Trans. Grete Felten. Berlin: Verl. Volk and Welt, 1970; also Stuttgart: Deutsche Verlagsant, 1970.

9. *Homecomings.* London: Macmillan, 1956; Harmondsworth: Penguin, 1962, 1966; as *Homecoming.* New York: Scribner, 1956, 1965; as *Hemkomster.* Trans. Gemma Snellman. Stockholm: Norstedt, 1960; as *Wege Nach Haus.* Trans. Grete Felten. Stuttgart: Deutsche Verlagsant, 1962; as *Vozvraščenija Domoj.* Trans. N. Emeljannikova. Moscow: Hudož. lit., 1964; as *Zavråštanija U Doma.* Trans. Todor Vălčev. Sofija (Bulgaria): Nar. Kultura, 1966.

10. *The Conscience of the Rich.* London: Macmillan, 1958, 1960; New York: Scribner, 1958, 1960; Harmondsworth: Penguin, 1961, 1970; as *Das Gewissen der Reichen.* Trans. Dorothea and Rolf Michaelis. Stuttgart: Deutsche Verlagsant, 1961.

11. *The Affair.* London: Macmillan, 1960; New York: Scribner, 1960, 1962; Harmondsworth: Penguin, 1962, 1970;

as *Delo*. Trans. V. Efanova. Moscow: Goslitizdat, 1962; as *Il Caso Howard*. Trans. Vincenzo Mantovani. Torino: Einaudi, 1962; as *Affaeren*. Trans. Anton Kjaedegaard. Copenhagen: Gyldendal, 1963; as *L'affaire Howard*. Trans. Suzanne Desternes. Paris: R. Laffont, 1963; as *De Zaak-Howard*. Trans. G. Messelaar. Amsterdam: Contact, 1963; as *Affären*. Trans. Erik Frykman. Stockholm: Norstedt, 1963; as *Die Affäre*. Trans. Grete Felten. Stuttgart: Deutsche Verlagsant, 1963; also Berlin and Darmstadt: Buch-Gemeinschaft, 1965; as *Sprawa Howarda*. Trans. Zofia Kierszys. Warsaw: Państw. Instytut Wydawn, 1964; as *Afera*. Trans. Gordana Bunčic. Zagreb (Yugoslavia): Zora, 1970.

12. *Corridors of Power*. London and Toronto: Macmillan, 1964; New York: Scribner, 1964; New York: Bantam Books, 1965; Harmondsworth: Penguin, 1966, 1967, 1970; as *Koridori Na Vlastta*. Trans. Ženi Božilova. Sofija (Bulgaria): NSOF, 1967; as *Maktens Korridorer*. Trans. Gunnar Barklund. Stockholm: Norstedt, 1967; as *Korridore de Macht*. Trans. Grete Felten. Berlin: Verl. Volk and Welt, 1967; also Stuttgart: Deutsche Verlagsanst, 1967; as *Võimu Telgitagused*. Trans. U. Lehtsalu. Tallin: Eêsti raamat, 1968; as *Varas Gaiteni*. Trans. Vanda Vikane. Riga: Liesma, 1968.

13. *The Sleep of Reason*. London: Macmillan, 1968; New York: Scribner, 1969; Harmondsworth: Penguin, 1970.

14. *Last Things*. London: Macmillan, 1970; New York: Scribner, 1970; Harmondsworth: Penguin, 1972.

15. *Strangers and Brothers*. Omnibus ed. 3 vols. London: Macmillan, 1972. Contains entire eleven novels of series.

PRIMARY WORKS: LATER NOVELS

16. *The Malcontents*. London: Macmillan, 1972; New York: Scribner, 1972; Harmondsworth: Penguin, 1975.

17. *In Their Wisdom.* London: Macmillan, 1974; New York: Scribner, 1974.

PRIMARY WORKS: PLAYS

18. *The View Over the Park* (produced in London, 1950).

19. *Family Party,* with Pamela Hansford Johnson. London: Evans, 1951.

20. *Spare the Rod,* with Pamela Hansford Johnson. London: Evans, 1951.

21. *The Best Foot Forward,* with Pamela Hansford Johnson. London: Evans, 1951.

22. *The Pigeon with the Silver Foot,* with Pamela Hansford Johnson. London: Evans, 1951; Acting ed., 1960.

23. *The Supper Dance,* with Pamela Hansford Johnson. London: Evans, 1951.

24. *To Murder Mrs. Mortimer,* with Pamela Hansford Johnson. London: Evans, 1951.

25. With William Gerhardi. *The Fool of the Family* (produced in London, 1964).

26. *The Public Prosecutor,* with Pamela Hansford Johnson (produced in London, 1967). An adaptation of a play by Georgi Dzhagarov. Trans. Marguerite Alexieva. London: Peter Owen, 1969; Seattle, Washington: University of Washington Press, 1969.

PRIMARY WORKS: OTHER

27. With A. M. Taylor. "Infra-Red Investigations of Molecular Structure—Part I. Apparatus and Technique." *Proceed-*

ings of the Royal Society of London: Series A, 124 (June 1929), 442-452.

28. With F. I. G. Rawlings, and E. K. Rideal. "Infra-Red Investigations of Molecular Structure. Part II—The Molecule of Nitric Oxide." *Proceedings of the Royal Society of London: Series A,* 124 (June 1929), 453-464.

29. With E. K. Rideal. "Infra-Red Investigations of Molecular Structure. Part III—The Molecule of Carbon Monoxide." *Proceedings of the Royal Society of London: Series A,* 125 (October 1929), 462-483.

30. With E. K. Rideal. "Infra-Red Investigations of Molecular Structure—Part IV. The Overtone of Nitric Oxide." *Proceedings of the Royal Society of London: Series A,* 126 (January 1930), 355-359.

31. With Francis Ian Gregory Rawlins. "Colours of Inorganic Salts." *Nature,* 125 (8 March 1930), 349-350.

32. With T. M. Lowry. "The Optical Rotatory Power of Quartz on either side of an Infra-Red Absorption Band." *Proceedings of the Royal Society of London: Series A,* 127 (May 1930), 271-278.

33. "Science of the Year." *Bookman,* 85 (December 1933), 159-161. On the importance of Blackett's discovery of a positive electron.

34. "Rejuvenation promises end of old age." *Pictorial Review,* 35 (May 1934), 4 ff.

35. With E. Eastwood. "Absorption Spectra of Aldehydes." *Nature,* 133 (16 June 1934), 908-909.

36. With F. P. Bowden. "Physico-chemical Studies of Complex Organic Molecules. Part I—Monochromatic Irradiation." *Proceedings of the Royal Society of London: Series B,* 115 (June 1934), 261-273.

37. "Infra-red Investigations of Molecular Structure. Part V—The Simplest Kind of Polyatomic Molecule." *Proceedings of the Royal Society of London: Series A,* (July 1930), 294-316.

38. With E. Eastwood. "Sources of Error in Absorption Spectroscopy." *Nature,* 135 (2 February 1935), 186.

39. With E. Eastwood. "Electronic Spectra of Polyatomic Molecules. I—Saturated Aldehydes; II—Acrolein." *Proceedings of the Royal Society of London: Series A,* 149 (April 1935), 434-466.

40. "Enjoyment of science." *Spectator,* 156 (12 June 1936), 1074-1075; reprinted in *Living Age,* 351 (November 1936), 205-208; reprinted in *C. P. Snow: A Spectrum* (see main entry), pp. 6-8. On the mental enjoyment of science in the minds of scientists.

41. "A False Alarm in Physics." *Spectator,* 157 (16 October 1936), 628-629. On a scientific experiment which almost upset the law of conservation of energy.

42. "What we need from applied science." *Spectator,* 157 (20 November 1936), 904; reprinted in *C. P. Snow: A Spectrum* (see main entry), pp. 9-10. Science needs to be applied to the common good, "to improve the innate quality of the human race."

43. "Superfluity of Particles." *Spectator,* 157 (4 December 1936), 984-985. On the different parts of an atom.

44. "The Humanity of Science." *Spectator,* 158 (16 April 1937), 702-703. Review of A. V. Hill's *What Science Stands For.*

45. "Controlling Reproduction." *Spectator,* 159 (22 October 1937), 678-679.

46. "The Brightest Things in the Universe." *Spectator,* 160

(28 January 1938), 124-125. On the astronomer
Zwicky's discovery of supernova.

47. "Science in a Modern World." *Discovery*, n.s. 1 (October
1938), 317-321. A report on a meeting of the British
Association held at Cambridge, in August, 1938. On
"Science and War," "Science and Society," and "Science and Education."

48. "Science and Conscience: A Letter from Mr. Richard
Aldington." *Discovery*, n.s. 1 (December 1938), 421-
424. Snow replies to Aldington, pp. 422-424. Snow defends science, and scientists.

49. *Richard Aldington: An Appreciation.* London: Heinemann, 1938.

50. "Scientific Prophecies." *Discovery*, n.s. 2 (January 1939),
1-2. On the certainty of scientific progress.

51. "Blueprint of the Future of Science." *Discovery*, n.s. 2
(March 1939), 107-111. Review of J. D. Bernal's *The
Social Function of Science*.

52. "The First Excitement That Knowledge Gives." *Discovery*,
2 (April 1939), 161-162; reprinted in *C. P. Snow: A
Spectrum* (see main entry), p. 11. On his mental excitement at the age of nine as he read about the nature of
the atom in Arthur Mee's *Children's Encyclopaedia*.

53. "Science and Air Warfare." *Discovery*, n.s. 2 (May 1939),
215-217. On the exaggerations of dangers by air warfare.

54. "Race, Nations, Class: Lessons of Genetics." *Discovery*,
n.s. 2 (June 1939), 271-274. A presentation of quota-
tions from, and comments on C. H. Waddington's *An Introduction to Modern Genetics*.

55. "A New Attempt to Explain Modern Physics." *Discovery*,
n.s. 2 (July 1939), 329-331. A survey of the best books

on science for the layman.

56. "A New Means of Destruction?" *Discovery,* n.s. 2 (September 1939), 443-444. On the possible creation of what Snow calls the "Uranium bomb" (i.e., the Atom Bomb). A further note on its unlikely possibility appears in *Discovery,* n.s. 2 (October 1939), 529. Response is made by D. W. F. M. in *Discovery,* n.s. 2 (November 1939), 573.

57. "Lord Rutherford." *Spectator,* 163 (13 October 1939), 512, 514. Review of A. S. Eve's biography, *Rutherford.*

58. *"The Fate of Homo Sapiens."* *Discovery,* n.s. 2 (October 1939), 499-501. Review of book by H. G. Wells.

59. "Against Destructiveness." *Discovery,* n.s. 2 (November 1939), 557-558. On the need to continue civilized pursuits during the war then beginning.

60. *"Rutherford."* *Discovery,* n.s. 2 (November 1939), 611, 613. Review of A. S. Eve's biography.

61. "The Truth of Genetics." *Discovery,* n.s. 2 (December 1939), 617-619. Review of Amram Scheinfeld's *You and Heredity.*

62. "Stretches of Time." *Discovery,* n.s. 3 (January 1940), 1-2. On the short amount of time man has been on earth. On the vast amount of possible time for man in the future.

63. "Scientists and War Discoveries." *Discovery,* n.s. 3 (February 1940), 59-60. A comparison is made between English and German methods of scientific values.

64. "The End of *Discovery."* *Discovery,* n.s. 3 (March 1940), 117-118.

65. *Writers and Readers of the Soviet Union.* Watford, Hertfordshire: Farleigh Press, 1943.

66. "Careers." *Political Quarterly*, 15 (October 1944), 310-317.

67. "The Mathematician on Cricket." *The Saturday Book.* Ed. Leonard Russell. London: Hutchinson, 1948.

68. "Cult of the Atrocious." London *Sunday Times* (16 October 1949), p. 3; reprinted in *C. P. Snow: A Spectrum* (see main entry), pp. 12-13. Negative review of E. Flaiano's *Mariam*, A. West's *On a Dark Night*, U. Sinclair's *One Clear Call*, and W. Faulkner's *Intruder in the Dust.*

69. "The Wisdom of Niels Bohr." *The Saturday Book.* Ed. Leonard Russell. London: Hutchinson, 1949, pp. 180-184.

70. "Books and Writers." *Spectator*, 185 (22 September 1950), 320; reprinted in *C. P. Snow: A Spectrum* (see main entry), pp. 14-16. On the decline of the aesthetic novel. He disagrees with Henry Green's predictions about the future of the novel. Snow supports the conventional use of scene, narrative, and commentary as the best ways to write novels.

71. "Books and Writers." *Spectator*, 186 (19 January 1951), 82; reprinted in *C. P. Snow: A Spectrum* (see main entry), pp. 17-19. Review of Ada Leverson's *Love's Shadow* and *The Limit*, and Ronald Firbank's *Three Novels: Caprice, Vainglory, Inclinations.* Attacks "moment-to-moment" writing as too shallow, emotionally as well as intellectually.

72. "A Novel Revised." *Spectator*, 187 (27 July 1951), 136, 138; reprinted in *C. P. Snow: A Spectrum* (see main entry), pp. 20-21. Review of Edward Sackville-West's *Simpson.*

73. "Professional Exploration." *Spectator*, 188 (25 April 1952), 554, 556. Review of *West African Explorers*, ed. by C. Howard.

74. "Valedictory." London *Sunday Times* (28 December 1952), p. 7; reprinted in *C. P. Snow: A Spectrum* (see main entry), pp. 22-23. Attacks "moment-by-moment" writing, and, on the other hand, supports traditional methods.

75. "The Novelist's Methods." *Spectator,* 190 (27 February 1953), 254, 256. Review of A. A. Mendilow's *Time and the Novel.*

76. "A Writer of Quality." *Spectator,* 190 (27 March 1953), 384-385. Review of two novels by Edith Wharton: *The House of Mirth,* and *The Age of Innocence.*

77. "Reflections on Mr. Dean's Report." *Spectator,* 192 (12 March 1954), 283-284; reprinted in *C. P. Snow: A Spectrum* (see main entry), pp. 24-26. Review of Gordon Dean's *Report on the Atom.*

78. "Using Science." *New Statesman and Nation,* 47 (20 March 1954), 374, 376. Review of J. D. Bernal's *Science and Industry in the Nineteenth Century,* and the Manchester Joint Research Council's *Industry and Science.*

79. "Scientists in America." *Spectator,* 193 (2 July 1954), 29-30. Review of Don K. Prince's *Government and Science.*

80. "Phase of Expansion." *Spectator,* 193 (1 October 1954), 406. Review of Ernest Watkins's *Prospect of Canada.*

81. "The Well-endowed." *New Statesman and Nation,* 48 (25 December 1954), 850-851. On Canada and its resources.

82. "Story tellers for the Atomic Age." *New York Times Book Review* (30 January 1955), pp. 1, 28-29. On the negative reaction of modern novelists to science. On the novel of sensibility, and cultural suicide. On the new relationship between scientists and novelists because of the Bomb.

83. "The Irregular Right." *Nation*, 182 (24 March 1956), 238-239; reprinted in *C. P. Snow: A Spectrum* (see main entry), pp. 27-29. On the lack of a radical intelligentsia in England; on the almost total domination by the Establishment.

84. "Industrial Dynamo." *New Statesman and Nation*, 51 (16 June 1956), 702-703. Review of J. M. Cohen's *The Life of Ludwig Mond.*

85. "The Mind of the Mathematician." *New Statesman and Nation*, 52 (25 August 1956), 219-220. Review of Norbert Wiener's autobiography, *I am a Mathematician.*

86. "New Minds for the New World." *New Statesman and Nation*, 52 (1 September 1956), 279.

87. "The Trusted Rebel." *New Statesman and Nation*, 53 (9 February 1957), 175-176. Review of W. H. G. Armytage's *Sir Richard Gregory.*

88. "London Diary." *New Statesman and Nation*, 53 (23 February 1957), 226-227; also in same volume, (2 March 1957), 266-267; reprinted in part in his *C. P. Snow: A Spectrum* (see main entry), p. 34. On several aspects of London activities and people.

89. *"Dickens at Work."* *New Statesman*, 54 (27 July 1957), 119-120; reprinted in his *C. P. Snow: A Spectrum* (see main entry), pp. 35-37. Review of book by J. Butt and K. Tillotson.

90. With Angus Wilson and others. "Hungarian Writers On Trial." *The* (London) *Times* (29 October 1957), p. 11. A letter to the Editor. A protest.

91. "The Changing Nature of Love." *Mademoiselle*, 46 (February 1958), 105, 180-181; reprinted in his *C. P. Snow: A Spectrum* (see main entry), pp. 38-41. On the passing of romantic love in favor of what he calls "Knowledgeable

love." On the problems and dangers of modern marriage as a result of the changing perspective.

92. "The Men of Fission." *Holiday,* 23 (April 1958), 95, 108, 110-112, 114; reprinted in *C. P. Snow: A Spectrum* (see main entry), pp. 42-47. On the atomic scientists at Harwell.

93. "Not the Whole Truth." *New Statesman,* 55 (14 June 1958), 771-772. Review of Robert Jungk's *Brighter than a Thousand Suns.*

94. "Challenge to the Intellect." *TLS* (15 August 1958), p. iii; reprinted in his *C. P. Snow: A Spectrum* (see main entry), pp. 48-52. An attack on the aesthetic "theory" of the anti-novel. The bulk of modern novels (excepting those written by serious British novelists) are written in extreme reaction to social forces, especially "the impact of the scientific revolution on the literary sensibility." Proust and Joyce are discussed as best representing "the polarization of the novel form." The British novelist has rejected heavy symbolism, and naturalism. There is a brief discussion of the development of the British novel. Snow refers to Amis, Greene, Hartley, Lessing, Powell, and Wilson (among others).

95. "The Habit of Truth." *New Republic,* 139 (18 August 1958), 26; reprinted in his *C. P. Snow: A Spectrum* (see main entry), p. 53. Review of J. Bronowski's *Science and Human Values.*

96. "New Men for a New Era." London *Sunday Times* (24 August 1958), p. 12; reprinted in his *C. P. Snow: A Spectrum* (see main entry), pp. 54-56. Under the threat of over-population, men who have subdued their egos are now forming together in groups so as to meet new, upcoming social needs.

97. "American Literature: Which Side of the Atlantic: The Writer's Choice." *New Statesman,* 56 (6 September

1958), 287-288. Snow discusses the pros and cons of writing in America and England. His favor goes to England which he claims has a known audience for the writer; the American writer, on the other hand, does not know the nature of his audience.

98. "Science and Hope: The Future of Man." *Nation,* 187 (13 September 1958), 124-125. On technological and social progress. On the ability of man to survive, even after a possible H-Bomb war.

99. "The Atomic Pioneers." *New Republic,* 139 (27 October 1958), 18-19; reprinted in his *C. P. Snow: A Spectrum* (see main entry), pp. 57-58. Review of Robert Jungk's *Brighter than a Thousand Suns.*

100. "Act in Hope." *New Statesman,* 56 (15 November 1958), 698-700. Review of J. D. Bernal's *World Without War.*

101. "The Age of Rutherford." *Atlantic,* 202 (November 1958), 76-81; reprinted in his *C. P. Snow: A Spectrum* (see main entry), pp. 59-65; reprinted in his *Variety of Men* (see main entry), pp. 3-20. A biographical account of Rutherford, and a discussion of the general attitudes of scientists during the 1920's and 1930's.

102. "The Missing Scientists." *Reporter,* 20 (19 February 1959), 38-39. Review of Eleazar Lipsky's *The Scientists.*

103. "Lessons from Cambridge." *New Statesman,* 57 (21 March 1959), 406-408. Review of *The Victoria History of the County of Cambridge, Vol. III. The City and the University of Cambridge,* ed. by J. P. C. Roach.

104. "Lord Cherwell." *New Statesman,* 58 (26 September 1959), 398-399. Review of R. F. Harrod's *The Prof.*

105. "Coriolanus of the Intellectuals." *Encounter,* 13 (November 1959), 66-68. Review of Jacques Barzun's *The House of Intellect.*

106. *The Two Cultures and the Scientific Revolution.* Cambridge (England): University Press, 1959; London: Macmillan, 1959; New York: Cambridge University Press, 1959, 1962; as *Futatsu No Bunka to Kagaku Kakumei.* Trans. Makinosuke Matsui. Tokyo: Misuzu shobô, 1960; as *De To Kulturer.* Trans. Ragnar Kvam. Oslo: Cappelen, 1960, 1963; as *De Tvá Kulturerna.* Trans. Claes-A. and Lillemor Wachtmeister. Malmö (Sweden): Cavefors, 1961; also Uppsala: Studentförenig, 1961; as *Los Dos Culturas y la Revolución Científica.* Trans. Maria Raquel Bengolca. Buenos Aires: Sur, 1963; as *Les Dues Cultures I la Revolució Científica.* Trans. Jordi Solé-Turá. Barcelona: Edicíons 62, 1965; as *Les Deux Cultures: Supplément aux 'Deux Cultures.'* Trans. Claude Noël. Paris: J.-J. Pauvert, 1968.

107. "Why Not Fall Into Line?" *The* (London) *Times* (10 February 1960), p. 11. A letter to the Editor. On the liberal quality of a Russian book exhibition.

108. "The 'Two-Cultures' Controversy: Afterthoughts." *Encounter,* 14 (February 1960), 64-68. A reply to critics of "The Two Cultures" first published in *Encounter,* 1959.

109. With Rosamond Lehmann, Angus Wilson, and others. "Spanish Prisoners." *The* (London) *Times* (1 March 1960), p. 11. A protest letter against the Spanish government's arrest of author Luis Goytisolo, and others.

110. "Billiard-Room Talks." London *Sunday Times* (6 March 1960), p. 18; reprinted in his *C. P. Snow: A Spectrum* (see main entry), pp. 68-69. An exhcnge of letters between Leonard Russell and Snow. Snow discusses the theme (justice) of his novel, *The Affair.*

* 111. "The Moral Grandeur of Einstein." *New Statesman,* 59 (26 March 1960), 453-454.

112. "The Moral Un-Neutrality of Science." *Science,* 133 (27

January 1961), 256-259; reprinted as *The Moral Un-Neutrality of Science.* Peace Education Program. Philadelphia (?): American Friends Service Committee, 1961; reprinted in his *C. P. Snow: A Spectrum* (see main entry), pp. 70-77. Orig. a lecture delivered before the American Association for the Advancement of Science, December 27, 1960.

113. "Whether We Live or Die." *Life,* 50 (3 February 1961), 90-92, 94, 97-98, 100, 102, 104. An account of the conflict between two scientists—Sir Henry Tizard and F. A. Lindemann—over the development of radar, and on the decision to undertake stategic bombing.

114. "Science, Politics, and the Novelist; Or the Fish and the Net." *Kenyon Review,* 23 (Winter 1961), 1-17; reprinted in his *C. P. Snow: A Spectrum* (see main entry), pp. 83-91. An attack on academic literary criticism. On the novel as an international art form. On the birth and subsequent effect of the stream of consciousness novel. On the polar differences between Joyce and Proust, and the contemporary British novelist's choice of the latter over the former. On the inability of New Criticism to deal with the architectonics of the novel. On the themes of science and politics in his own work, and the inability of the stream of consciousness technique to handle them.

115. "Scientists at War." *The* (London) *Times* (8 April 1961), p. 9. A letter to the Editor. On the Tizard-Lindemann disagreement over the priority to be given to the development of radar.

116. *"All Souls and Appeasement."* *Listener,* 65 (27 April 1961), 747. Review of A. L. Rowse's book.

117. "Both Cultures." *New Statesman,* 61 (21 April 1961), 630. Review of J. Bronowski's *Science and Human Values.*

118. "The Pressures of Society." *TLS* (9 June 1961), p. 351.

Review of *The Writer's Dilemma.*

119. "Miasma, Darkness and Torpidity." *New Statesman,* 62 (11 August 1961), 186-187. Review of George Elder Davie's book on Scottish universities, *The Democratic Intellect.*

120. With Sidney Hook, H. Stuart Hughes, and Hans J. Morgenthau. "Western Values and Total War." *Commentary,* 32 (October 1961), 277-304. A slightly abridged transcript of a round-table discussion held before a selected audience at the Institute of Human Relations.

121. "A Quarter Century: Its Great Delusions." *Look,* 25 (19 December 1961), 116, 119-120, 122, 124, 126. Snow discusses Western man's delusions caused by the technological revolution.

122. "Englishmen of Power and Place on the Road That Led to Munich." *New York Times Book Review* (24 December 1961), p. 3; reprinted in his *C. P. Snow: A Spectrum* (see main entry), pp. 94-95. Review of A. L. Rowse's *Appeasement: A Study in Political Decline, 1933-39.*

123. "The Literati and the Scientists." *The Fate of Man.* Ed. Clarence Crane. New York: Braziller, 1961.

124. "Introduction," to *The Jew in a Gentile World.* Ed. Arnold Rogow. New York: Macmillan, 1961; reprinted in part in *C. P. Snow: A Spectrum* (see main entry), pp. 92-93.

125. "Italo Svevo: Forerunner of Cooper and Amis." *Essays and Studies by Members of the English Association,* 14 (1961), 7-16.

126. Editor, with Pamela Hansford Johnson. *Winter's Tales 7: Stories from modern Russia.* London: Macmillan, 1961; as *Stories from Modern Russia.* New York: St. Martins Press, 1962.

127. *Science and Government.* Godkin Lectures at Harvard

University, 1960. Cambridge, Massachusetts: Harvard University Press, 1961; London: Oxford University Press, 1961; Toronto: S. J. R. Saunders, 1961; with a new appendix. Cambridge, Massachusetts: Harvard University Press, 1962; also New York: The New American Library, 1962, 1965; also London: Four Square Books, 1963; as *Kagaku To Seiji.* Trans. Natsuo Shumuta. Tokyo: Otowa Shobô, 1961; as *Politik Hinter Verschlossenen Türen.* Trans. Grete and Karl E. Felten. Stuttgart: Deutsche Verlaganst, 1961; as *Videnskab Og Stat.* Trans. Bjarne Nørretranders. Copenhagen: Gyldendal, 1962; as *Vitenskap Og Statsstyre.* Trans. Ragnar Kvam. Oslo: Cappelen, 1962; as *Ciencia y Gobierno.* Trans. Manual Escalera. Barcelona: Seix y Barral, 1963; as *Scienza E Governo.* Trans. Luciano De Maria. Torino: Einaudi, 1966; as *Valdstjórn Og Vísindi.* Trans. Baldur Símonarson. Reykjavík (Iceland): Hio islenzka bokmenntafélag, 1970.

128. With Malcolm Muggeridge. "Conversation Piece." *Encounter,* 18 (February 1962), 90-93. Extract from a 1962 (?) transcript of Granada T.V.'s "Appointment with C. P. Snow." Conversation concentrates on the Two Cultures.

129. "The Cold War and the West." *Partisan Review,* 29 (Winter 1962), 81-83. Snow responds to seven questions on the subject of the Cold War.

130. "C. P. Snow on American Education." *School and Society,* 90 (5 May 1962), 209. Excerpts from Snow's statements made on a Hartford, Connecticut radio program, "Yale Reports." Snow discusses the poor quality of America's primary and secondary schools. Students are not asked to do hard work.

131. *Magnanimity. Rectorial address delivered before University of St. Andrews, 13th April, 1962.* St. Andrews, Scotland: University of St. Andrews Students Representative Council, 1962; London: Macmillan, 1962.

132. *A Postscript to Science and Government.* Cambridge, Massachusetts: Harvard University Press, 1962; London: Oxford University Press, 1962.

133. *Recent Thoughts on the Two Cultures. An oration delivered at Birkbeck College, London, 12th December, 1961, in celebration of the 138th anniversary of the foundation of the college.* London: Birkbeck College, 1962.

134. "Preface," to *Francis Brett Young,* by Jessica Brett Young. London: Heinemann, 1962.

135. With others. "House of Lords Reform: Opportunity for Parliament." *The* (London) *Times* (28 March 1963), p. 13. A letter to the Editor.

136. "Education and Sacrifice." *New Statesman,* 65 (17 May 1963), 746-750. An abbreviated version of Snow's Richmond Lecture given on May 1, 1963 at Cambridge.

137. *C. P. Snow: A Spectrum: Science, Criticism, Fiction.* Ed. Stanley Weintraub. New York: Scribner, 1963.

138. "Higher education in America." *NEA Journal,* 53 (April 1964), 11.

139. "A down-to-earth aerial act." *Book Week,* 2 (29 November 1964), 3. Review of J. Robert Oppenheimer's *The Flying Trapeze: Three Crises for Physicists.*

140. "Books of the Year." *Observer* (20 December 1964), p. 7. Snow picks his three favorite books of 1964.

141. *Two Cultures: and, A Second Look* (rev. ed. of *The Two Cultures and the Scientific Revolution*). London and New York: Cambridge University Press, 1964, 1969; New York and Toronto: New American Library, 1964, 1970 (?); as *Le Due Culture.* Trans. Adriano Carugo. Milano: Feltrinelli, 1964; as *Futatsu No Bunka To*

Kagaku Kakumei. Rev. ed. Trans. Matsui Makinosuke. Tokyo: Misuzu Shobô, 1965, 1967; as *De Två Kulturerna: en ny genomgång.* Trans. Claes A. and Lillemor Wachtmeister, and Roland Adlerberth. Malmö (Sweden): Cavefors, 1965; also Stockholm: Seelig, 1965; as *Duas Culturas.* Trans. Idalina Pina Amaro. Lisbon: Dom Quixote, 1965; as *De To Kulturer.* Trans. Ane Munk-Madsen. Copenhagen: Vinten, 1966; as *Die Zwei Kulturen.* Trans. Grete and Karl E. Felten. Stuttgart: Klett, 1967; as *Dve Kulture I Ponovo O Njima.* Trans. Aleksandar I. Spasić. Beograd: Narodni univerzitet "Braća Stamenković," 1971.

142. "Preface," to *The half-world of American Culture: a miscellany,* ed. by Carl Bode. Carbondale: Southern Illinois University Press, 1965.

143. Consulting Editor, with René Dubos and Henry Margenau, to *Energy,* by Mitchell Wilson and the editors of *Life.* Amsterdam: Time-Life International, 1965.

144. "Introduction," to *A London Childhood* by John Holloway. London: Routledge and Kegan Paul, 1966; New York: Scribner's, 1967.

145. With William Golding and others. "War in Vietnam." *The* (London) *Times* (23 May 1967), p. 9. A letter to the Editor. Snow and three others oppose the British Government's support of the American policy in Vietnam.

146. "George F. Kennan: too extraordinary for his own good." *Book World,* 1 (5 November 1967), 1. Review of Kennan's *Memoirs, 1925-1950.*

147. "Charl'z Snou—chitatelyam nashego zhurnala." *Vestnik Moskovskogo universiteta: Filologiya,* 5 (1967), 59-60.

148. *Variety of Men.* London: Macmillan, 1967; New York: Scribner, 1967; Harmondsworth: Penguin, 1969; as *Ogni Sorta di Gente.* Trans. Marcella Bonsanti. Bari

(Italy): De Donato, 1968; as *Ningen Kono Tayô Naru-mono.* Trans. Umeda Toshio and Inoue Teruo. Tokyo: Kinokuniya shoten, 1970.

Contents: "Rutherford"—"G. H. Hardy"—"H. G. Wells" —"Einstein"—"Lloyd George"—"Winston Churchill"— "Robert Frost"—"Dag Hammarskjöld"—"Stalin."

149. "Foreword," to *A Mathematician's Apology,* by Godfrey Harold Hardy. London: Cambridge University Press, 1967.

150. "Soviet scientific impresario." *Book World,* 2 (8 September 1968), 4. Review of *Peter Kapitsa on Life and Science,* trans. by Albert Parry.

151. "Georgi Dzhagarov, or the Problems of a Liberal Communist." *London Magazine,* n.s. 8 (September 1968), 79-95. On the moral position of the Bulgarian, anti-Stalinist writer. On Dzhagarov's play, *The Public Prosecutor.*

152. "Liberal Communism: The Basic Dogma, the Scope for Freedom, the Danger in Optimism." *Nation,* 207 (9 December 1968), 617-623. An introduction to Georgi Dzhagarov's play, *The Public Prosecutor.*

153. "The defense of Leningrad, one of the most horrible and heroic episodes in history." *New York Times Book Review* (26 January 1969), pp. 1, 42. Review of Harrison E. Salisbury's *The 900 Days: The Siege of Leningrad.*

154. "Views from Earth on the Odyssey into Space." *Look,* 33 (4 February 1969), 77. Snow discusses the voyage of Apollo 8.

155. "Study of teaching of gifted children." *The* (London) *Times* (15 May 1969), p. 6. Snow wishes to see greater contacts between gifted people.

156. "The gene drain." *Spectator,* 222 (16 May 1969), 665. A

letter to the editor. Snow predicts that biogenetics will become as large a controversy as Darwinism. Negative response is made by Israel Shahak in *Spectator*, 222 (30 May 1969), 733. Reply to both is made by E. J. Mishan in *Spectator*, 222 (14 June 1969), 797.

157. "Hint of Joy amidst the Misery." *Life*, 67 (1 August 1969), 8. Review of Lovat Dickson's *H. G. Wells*.

158. "The Moon Landing." *Look*, 33 (26 August 1969), 68-70, 72. Snow discusses his reasons why he thinks the space program is a failure.

159. "Out of the Air: Sam would have said it." *Listener*, 82 (18 September 1969), 376. Snow comments on J. B. Priestley.

160. "Books of the Year." *Observer* (21 December 1969), p. 17. Snow chooses his three top selections.

161. *The State of Siege.* New York: Scribner, 1969; Oxford: Oxfam, 1970.

162. "Less Fun than Machiavelli." *New Statesman*, 79 (9 January 1970), 50. Review of Jeremy Bray's *Decision in Government.*

163. "The Djilas enigma." *Financial Times* (15 January 1970), p. 8. Review of Milovan Djilas's *The Unperfect Society.*

164. "Too big for their palettes?" *Financial Times* (22 January 1970), p. 8. Review of Jean Gimpel's *The Cult of Art.*

165. "Our prose heritage." *Financial Times* (5 February 1970), p. 24. Review of Vols. 1 and 2 of *The Pelican Book of English Prose.*

166. "Tolstoy at 80." *Financial Times* (13 February 1970), p. 26. Review of Leo Tolstoy's *The Law of Love and the Law of Violence.*

167. "One day in August." *Financial Times* (20 February 1970), p. 8. Review of Masuji Ibuse's novel, *Black Rain.*

168. "A G. K. C. revival?" *Financial Times* (26 February 1970), p. 12. Review of *G. K. Chesterton,* a selection from his non-fictional prose, selected by W. H. Auden.

169. "How it all began." *Financial Times* (5 March 1970), p. 10. Review of *The French Right from de Maistre to Maurras,* ed. by J. S. McClellan, and *Gobineau: Selected political writings,* ed. by Michael D. Biddies.

170. "In the time of the Doges." *Financial Times* (12 March 1970), p. 12. Review of Maurice Rowdon's *The Fall of Venice.*

171. "The Bible into Modern English." *Financial Times* (19 March 1970), p. 30. Review of *The New English Bible with the Apocrypha.*

172. "Wilde's importance." *Financial Times* (26 March 1970), p. 12. Review of *The Artist as Critic: Critical Writings of Oscar Wilde,* ed. by Richard Ellmann.

173. "Our very own Chekhov." *Financial Times* (2 April 1970), p. 28. Review of *Chekhov: Stories 1889-91,* translated and ed. by Ronald Hingley.

174. "The novelist on himself." *Financial Times* (9 April 1970), p. 28. Review of *The Collected Edition of Graham Greene: Vols. 1-4.*

175. "Inside the cabinet." *Financial Times* (16 April 1970), p. 8. Review of Stephen Roskill's *Hankey: Man of Secrets: Vol. I, 1877-1918,* and Patrick Gordon Walker's *The Cabinet.*

176. "From a garden in Florence." *Financial Times* (23 April 1970), p. 28. Review of Harold Acton's *More Memoirs of an Aesthete.*

177. "The case of Mr. Krim." *Financial Times* (30 April 1970), p. 14. Review of Seymour Krim's *Views of a Near-sighted Cannoneer.*

178. "Thriller writer on Wall Street." *Financial Times* (8 May 1970), p. 14. Review of Emma Lathen Gollancz's *Murder to Go.*

179. "Snapshot album." *Financial Times* (14 May 1970), p. 12. Review of Frank Tuohy's *Fingers in the Door.*

180. "Huxley heritage." *Financial Times* (28 May 1970), p. 30. Review of Julian Huxley's *Memories.*

181. "Salute to Dickens." *Financial Times* (4 June 1970), p. 12. Review of Angus Wilson's *The World of Charles Dickens,* and A. E. Dyson's *The Inimitable Dickens.*

182. "How 'equal' are we really?" *Daily Telegraph* (5 June 1970), color supplement, pp. 14-17.

183. "The old creature." *Financial Times* (18 June 1970), p. 14. Review of *Letters of Arnold Bennett: Vol. III, 1916-1931,* by James Hepburn.

184. "Chaos of clear ideas." *Financial Times* (25 June 1970), p. 8. Review of *The Bodley Head Bernard Shaw: Collected Plays with their prefaces Vol. I* and *Shaw: An Autobiography 1856-1898,* selected by Stanley Weintraub.

185. "Brotherly love." *Financial Times* (2 July 1970), p. 12. Review of Ruth Michaelis-Jena's *The Brothers Grimm.*

186. "A man of our time." *Financial Times* (9 July 1970), p. 26. Review of Saul Bellow's *Mr. Sammler's Planet.*

187. "The case of Leavis and the serious case." *TLS* (9 July 1970), pp. 737-740. On inaccuracies in Leavis' critical attacks upon him. On the quality of English education.

On the different natures of science and humanist culture.

188. "Inside the nightmare." *Financial Times* (16 July 1970), p. 24. Review of *The Diplomatic Diaries of Oliver Harvey, 1937-40*, ed. by John Harvey.

189. "Poet's last dance." *Financial Times* (23 July 1970), p. 22. Review of W. B. Yeats and Margot Ruddock's correspondence, *Ah, Sweet Dancer*, ed. by Roger McHugh.

190. "The brave and the free." *Financial Times* (30 July 1970), p. 8. Review of Peter Green's *The Year of Salamis*.

191. "Wise dumb ox." *Financial Times* (6 August 1970), p. 8. Review of Ellen Moers's *Two Dreisers: the Man and the Novelist*.

192. "Quest for the truth." *Financial Times* (21 August 1970), p. 8. Review of Colin Cross's *Who Was Jesus*.

193. "Sweet smell of success." *Financial Times* (27 August 1970), p. 8. Review of Nicholas Monsarrat's *Life is a Four-Letter Word: Vol. II Breaking Out*.

194. "World's eye view." *Financial Times* (3 September 1970), p. 8. Review of Arnold Toynbee's *Cities on the Move*.

195. "Almost too exquisite." *Financial Times* (10 September 1970), p. 10. Review of *The Bodley Head Max Beerbohm*, ed. by David Cecil.

196. "Captain Hook." *Financial Times* (17 September 1970), p. 10. Review of Janet Dunbar's *J. M. Barrie: The Man Behind the Image*.

197. "The insider." *Financial Times* (1 October 1970), p. 24. Review of *Maurice Baring Restored*, ed. by Paul Horgan.

198. "Never before." *Financial Times* (8 October 1970), p. 26. Review of Alvin Toffler's *Future Shock*.

199. "Architect of evil." *Financial Times* (15 October 1970), p. 30. Review of Albert Speer's *Inside the Third Reich*.

200. "Playing a fish." *Financial Times* (22 October 1970), p. 27. Review of Ernest Hemingway's *Islands in the Stream*.

201. "Man of honour." *Financial Times* (29 October 1970), p. 22. Review of Edgar Johnson's *Sir Walter Scott: The Great Unknown*.

202. "Zuckmayer's zest." *Financial Times* (5 November 1970), p. 14. Review of Carl Zuckmayer's *A Part of Myself*.

203. "Pepys deciphered." *Financial Times* (12 November 1970), p. 15. Review of *The Diary of Samuel Pepys: Volumes 1-3*, ed. by Robert Latham and William Matthews.

204. "Pam's progress." *Financial Times* (19 November 1970), p. 14. Review of Jasper Ridley's *Lord Palmerston*.

205. "Seasonal sleuths." *Financial Times* (26 November 1970), p. 32. Review of Yseult Bridges's *Poison and Adelaide Bartlett, Two Studies in Crime, How Charles Bravo Died*, and *Saint-With Red Hands*.

206. "Books to give." *Financial Times* (26 November 1970), p. 33. Snow suggests Wilson's *The World of Charles Dickens* among three other books as a good Christmas gift.

207. With his son, Philip Snow. "Hope for America." *Look*, 34 (1 December 1970), 30, 33-34, 36, 41. Snow talks about the American people—our power structure, our fear of revolution, the "communication gap," racism, American universities, the space program, and pollution.

208. "Mailer's orbit." *Financial Times* (4 December 1970), p. 10. Review of Norman Mailer's *A Fire on the Moon*.

209. "That sweet city." *Financial Times* (10 December 1970),

p. 8. Review of Dacre Balsdon's *Oxford Now and Then,* and Charles Fenby's *The Other Oxford.*

210. "Mind of Mann." *Financial Times* (18 December 1970), p. 22. Review of Thomas Mann's *Joseph and His Brethren,* his *Stories of a Lifetime: Volumes One and Two,* and *Letters of Thomas Mann 1889-1942.*

211. "Dickens and the public service." *Dickens 1970: Centenary Essays.* London: Chapman and Hall, 1970, pp. 125-149.

212. "Shakespeare." *Financial Times* (1 January 1971), p. 10. Review of S. Schoenbaum's *Shakespeare's Lives.*

213. "Royal lady." *Financial Times* (14 January 1971), p. 26. Review of David Green's *Queen Anne,* and Mollie Gillen's *The Prince and his Lady.*

214. "Who is speaking, please?" *Financial Times* (21 January 1971), p. 12. Review of *Kruschev Remembers* with an Introduction, Commentary and Notes by Edward Crankshaw.

215. "At Los Alamos." *Financial Times* (4 February 1971), p. 12. Review of Thomas McMahon's *A Random State.*

216. "The white and the red." *Financial Times* (12 February 1971), p. 27. Review of Mikhail Bulgakov's *The White Guard,* and Andrei Platonov's *The Fierce and Beautiful World.*

217. "Minds of the Ministers." *Financial Times* (25 February 1971), p. 14. Review of Cameron Hazlehurst's *Politicians at War July 1914 to May 1915.*

218. "Literary Lover." *Financial Times* (4 March 1971), p. 24. Review of Robert T. Fitzhugh's *Robert Burns: The Man and the Poet.*

219. "Man of Steel." *Financial Times* (11 March 1971), p. 14. Review of Joseph Frazier Wall's *Andrew Carnegie.*

220. "C. P. Snow." *The* (London) *Times* (13 March 1971), p. 17. Snow discusses "the personal history behind" his *Strangers and Brothers* sequence.

221. "Syracuse shambles." *Financial Times* (20 March 1971), p. 10. Review of Peter Green's *Armada from Athens,* and Wolfgang Leppmann's *Winckelmann.*

222. "The airy mountain." *Financial Times* (25 March 1971), p. 14. Review of Christ Bonington's *Annapurna South Face.*

223. "Brown study." *Financial Times* (1 April 1971), p. 24. Review of George Brown's *In My Way.*

224. "Black-shirt leanings." *Financial Times* (8 April 1971), p. 26. Review of Alastair Hamilton's *The Appeal of Fascism.*

225. "Facing the music." *Financial Times* (15 April 1971), p. 26. Review of Gerda Charles's *The Destiny Waltz.*

226. "Romantic hawk." *Financial Times* (22 April 1971), p. 30. Review of Peregrine Worsthorne's *The Socialist Myth.*

227. "Blind to Byron." *Financial Times* (29 April 1971), p. 16. Review of Leslie A. Marchand's *Byron,* and *Spencer at Waterloo* ed. by Beatrice Madan.

228. "Establishment Editor." *Financial Times* (13 May 1971), p. 12. Review of Donald McLachlan's *In the Chair: Barrington-Ward of the Times.*

229. "Bohemian and bourgeois." *Financial Times* (20 May 1971), p. 12. Review of Joanna Richardson's *Verlaine,* and T. C. Duncan-Eaves and Ben D. Kimpel's *Samuel*

Richardson.

230. "Mr. Lonelyhearts." *Financial Times* (3 June 1971), p. 12. Review of Jay Martin's *Nathaniel West: The Art of His Life.*

231. "Creed like wildfire." *Financial Times* (10 June 1971), p. 26. Review of Robert M. Grant's *Augustus to Constantine.*

232. "The likes of us." *Financial Times* (17 June 1971), p. 24. Review of Richard Faber's *Proper Stations: A Study of class in Victorian fiction,* P. J. Keating's *The Working Classes in Victorian Fiction,* and *Working-class Stories of the 1890's.*

233. "Meeting of Minds." *Financial Times* (24 June 1971), p. 14. Review of *The Born-Einstein Letters* with commentaries by Max Born.

234. "Calling a halt." *Financial Times* (1 July 1971), p. 12. Review of Duncan Williams's *Trousered Apes: A Study in the Influence of Literature on Contemporary Society.*

235. "Third party." *Financial Times* (8 July 1971), p. 26. Review of Michael Joseph's *Katherine Mansfield: The Memories of E. M.*

236. "Raffles, Wimsey and Co." *Financial Times* (15 July 1971), p. 28. Review of Colin Watson's *Snobbery with Violence.*

237. "With the Norsemen to Vinland." *Financial Times* (22 July 1971), p. 10. Review of Samuel Eliot Morison's *The European Discovery of America: The Northern Voyages AD 500-1600.*

238. "Angry African." *Financial Times* (29 July 1971), p. 10. Review of Yambo Ouologuem's *Bound to Violence.*

239. "Sentiment and sarcasm." *Financial Times* (5 August 1971), p. 10. Review of Leo Rosten's *People I Have Loved, Known, or Admired.*

240. "Cubitt's London." *Financial Times* (12 August 1971), p. 10. Review of Hermione Hobhouse's *Thomas Cubitt, Master Builder.*

241. "Marcel's way." *Financial Times* (19 August 1971), p. 20. Review of *Marcel Proust: 1871-1922, a Centenary Volume* ed. by Peter Quennell.

242. "Two aspects of science's giant." *Life,* 71 (20 August 1971), 14. Review of Ronald W. Clark's *Einstein: The Life and Times.*

243. "Political heroine." *Financial Times* (26 August 1971), p. 8. Review of *Lloyd George: A Diary by Frances Stevenson,* ed. by A. J. P. Taylor.

244. "Wolfe's clothing." *Financial Times* (2 September 1971), p. 10. Review of Malcolm Lowry's *October Ferry to Gabriola,* ed. by Margerie Lowry.

245. "Light on Ike." *Financial Times* (9 September 1971), p. 24. Review of Stephan E. Ambrose's *The Supreme Commander: The War Years of General Dwight D. Eisenhower.*

246. "Classical virtues." *Financial Times* (16 September 1971), p. 10. Review of Lord Robbins's *Autobiography of an Economist.*

247. "Discomfort of the lucky language." *The* (London) *Times* (25 September 1971), p. 10. On the many foreign translations of English books, but that the reverse situation is not mutual. Snow makes three points on how the English might produce more and better translations of foreign writers. Response by Peter du Sautoy in *The Times* (28 September 1971), p. 13; responses by Peter

Owen, and Kathleen Nott in *The Times* (29 September 1971), p. 15; reply by Snow to Peter du Sautoy in *The Times* (1 October 1971), p. 17; response to Snow's original article is made by Arladne Nicolaeff which immediately follow's Snow's reply letter; response to Snow's article is made by A. R. W. Room in *The Times* (4 October 1971), p. 13; responses by Peter Owen, and Gillon Aitken to A. R. W. Room in *The Times* (6 October 1971), p. 15.

248. "Humans without hope." *Financial Times* (30 September 1971), p. 36. Review of Wallace Stegner's *Angle of Repose*, and Mary McCarthy's *Birds of America*.

249. "Open windows." *Financial Times* (7 October 1971), p. 28. Review of E. M. Forster's novel, *Maurice*.

250. "Steiner's manifesto." *Financial Times* (14 October 1971), p. 14. Review of George Steiner's *In Bluebeard's Castle: Some notes towards the Redefinition of Culture.*

251. "In the communities of the elite." *TLS* (15 October 1971), p. 1249. An examination of modern elites (i.e., specialists): athletes, administrators, scientists, artists, and academic scholars. On the need for a greater literary understanding of these elites.

252. "Family figures." *Financial Times* (21 October 1971), p. 10. Review of Christopher Isherwood's *Kathleen and Frank.*

253. "Grandiose failure." *Financial Times* (28 October 1971), p. 34. Review of Martin Gilbert's *Winston S. Churchill: Vol. III, 1914-16.*

254. "Beyond Barchester." *Financial Times* (4 November 1971), p. 16. Review of James Pope-Hennessy's *Anthony Trollope*, and Ruth Robert's *Trollope: artist and novelist.*

255. "Careering along." *Financial Times* (11 November 1971), p. 24. Review of *The Diaries of Sir Alexander Cadogan 1938-45*, ed. by David Dilks.

256. "To end it..." *Financial Times* (18 November 1971), p. 16. Review of A. Alvarez's *The Savage God: A Study of Suicide.*

257. "Yorkshire Pakistanis at school." *Financial Times* (25 November 1971), p. 14. Review of Rachel Scott's *A Wedding Man is Nicer than Cats, Miss.*

258. "Relations and friends." *Financial Times* (2 December 1971), p. 28. Review of Chaim Bermant's *The Cousinhood.*

259. "Books as presents." *Financial Times* (2 December 1971), p. 28. Snow praises Gerda Charles's *The Destiny Waltz,* and *A Slanting Light.*

260. "Generous social critic." *Financial Times* (9 December 1971), p. 12. Review of Glen St. J. Barclay's *Twentieth Century Nationalism,* and two books by John Vaizey: *Capitalism,* and *Social Democracy.*

261. "Aimless elite." *Financial Times* (16 December 1971), p. 12. Review of R. Prawer Jhabvaia's *An Experience of India.*

262. "Emily 'the major'." *Financial Times* (23 December 1971), p. 17. Review of Winifred Gerin's *Emily Brontë: A biography.*

263. "Captive audiences." *Financial Times* (30 December 1971), p. 8. Review of *In God's Name: examples of preaching in England 1534-1662,* ed. by John Chandos.

264. "Testimony of Four Peers: C. P. Snow." *Esquire,* 76 (December 1971), 159, 282. Snow answers *Esquire's* question, "Do the Claims of Conscience Outweigh the Duties

of Citizenship?"

265. *Public Affairs.* London: Macmillan, 1971; New York: Scribner, 1971.

Contents: "Prologue"—"The Two Cultures and the Scientific Revolution (1959)"—"The Two Cultures: a Second Look (1963)"—"The Case of Leavis and the Serious Case (1970)"—"Science and Government (1960)"—"Appendix to 'Science and Government' (1962)"—"The Moral Un-neutrality of Science (1960)"—"The State of Siege (1968)"—"Epilogue."

266. "Leader of the BEF." *Financial Times* (6 January 1972), p. 20. Review of J. R. Colville's *Man of Valour: Field Marshall Lord Gort, V. C.*

267. "L. B. J. at large." *Financial Times* (20 January 1972), p. 12. Review of Lyndon Baines Johnson's *The Vantage Point.*

268. "Blissful dawn." *Financial Times* (27 January 1972), p. 12. Review of Wiktor Woroszylski's *The Life of Mayakovsky.*

269. "Modern revolutionaries." *Financial Times* (3 February 1972), p. 22. Review of Jason Epstein's *The Great Conspiracy Trial,* Tariq Ali's *The Coming British Revolution,* and Theresa Hayter's *Hayter of the Bourgeosie.*

270. "Friend to Burgess." *Financial Times* (17 February 1972), p. 22. Review of Goronwy Rees's *A Chapter of Accidents.*

271. "Family ritual." *Financial Times* (24 February 1972), p. 28. Review of Chaim Raphael's *A Feast of History,* and Cecil Roth and Bezalel Narkiss's *Jewish Art.*

272. "Where power lies." *Financial Times* (2 March 1972), p. 24. Review of George Mallaby's *Each in His Office:*

Studies of Men in Power.

273. "Triumph and fall." *Financial Times* (9 March 1972), p. 32. Review of Madeline Bingham's *Sheridan.*

274. "Elder scientists." *Financial Times* (16 March 1972), p. 24. Review of Emilio Segre's *Enrico Fermi: Physicist,* and J. D. Bernal's *The Extension of Man.*

275. "Paying the piper." *Financial Times* (23 March 1972), p. 32. Review of Michael Foss's *The Age of Patronage,* and Tim Chilcott's *A Publisher and His Circle.*

276. "The Drabble Touch." *Financial Times* (30 March 1972), p. 34. Review of Margaret Drabble's *The Needle's Eye.*

277. "Little grey cells." *Financial Times* (6 April 1972), p. 24. Review of Julian Symons's *Bloody Murder: From the Detective Story to the Crime Novel: A History.*

278. "El Draque." *Financial Times* (13 April 1972), p. 36. Review of George Malcolm Thomson's *Sir Francis Drake.*

279. "Two critics." *Financial Times* (20 April 1972), p. 14. Review of Edmund Wilson's *Upstate,* and A. E. Dyson's *Between Two Worlds.*

280. "Our man on the spot." *Financial Times* (27 April 1972), p. 34. Review of C. L. Sulzberger's *The Last of the Giants.*

281. "Innocent but determined." *Financial Times* (4 May 1972), p. 24. Review of *Fanny Burney, Journals and Letters: Volumes I and II.*

282. "Ford the talent spotter." *Financial Times* (11 May 1972), p. 29. Review of Arthur Mizener's *The Saddest Story.*

283. "The decent society." *Financial Times* (25 May 1972), p. 36. Review of Robert Rhodes James's *Ambitions and*

Realities: British Politics 1964-1970.

284. "Shrewd spinster." *Financial Times* (1 June 1972), p. 32. Review of Jane Aiken Hodge's *The Double Life of Jane Austen.*

285. "Too many too soon." *Financial Times* (8 June 1972), p. 32. Review of Dennis Gabor's *The Mature Society,* and Liam Hudson's *The Cult of the Fact.*

286. "First lady's fears." *Financial Times* (15 June 1972), p. 14. Review of Joseph P. Lash's *Eleanor and Franklin.*

287. "As if John Gunther had written 'Inside Science'." *New York Times Book Review* (18 June 1972), p. 4. Review of Mitchell Wilson's *Passion to Know.*

288. "Great robust girl." *Financial Times* (22 June 1972), p. 14. Review of Emile Zola's *Nana.*

289. "Absentee presence." *Financial Times* (29 June 1972), p. 33. Review of A. J. P. Taylor's *Beaverbrook.*

290. "Behind the best-sellers." *Financial Times* (6 July 1972), p. 33. Review of Erskine Childers's *The Riddle of the Sands,* and three books by Patrick Hamilton: *The Light Went Out: a biography, Hangover Square,* and *The Slaves of Solitude;* and Claud Cockburn's *Best-Seller.*

291. "Blitzed American." *Financial Times* (13 July 1972), p. 23. Review of *The London Observer: The Journal of Raymond E. Lee, 1940-1941,* ed. by James Lentze.

292. "Two discoveries." *Financial Times* (20 July 1972), p. 31. Review of Cynthia Ozick's *The Pagan Rabbi,* and Nicholas Wollaston's *The Tale Bearer.*

293. "Napolean of the novel." *Financial Times* (3 August 1972), p. 31. Review of Leon Edel's *Henry James: The Master, 1901-1916.*

294. "Snobs and sinners." *Financial Times* (10 August 1972), p. 19. Review of Barbara Hardy's *The Exposure of Luxury: Radical Themes in Thackery.*

295. "Englishman among Yankees." *Financial Times* (17 August 1972), p. 12. Review of Edward Dicey's *Spectator of America.*

296. "Boys and girls and bricks." *Financial Times* (24 August 1972), p. 14. Review of John Searle's *The Campus War.*

297. "All the military conspirators." *Financial Times* (31 August 1972), p. 7. Review of Guy Chapman's *The Dreyfus Trials.*

298. "Perchance not to dream." *Financial Times* (7 September 1972), p. 12. Review of Anthony Storr's *The Dynamics of Creation.*

299. "Death of a boy." *Financial Times* (14 September 1972), p. 31. Review of Chingiz Aitmatov's *The White Steamship.*

300. "Odour of man." *Financial Times* (28 September 1972), p. 14. Review of J. H. Plumb's *The Making of a Statesman: Vol. II, The Kings Minister.*

301. "Tempestuous lady." *Financial Times* (5 October 1972), p. 14. Review of Christopher Sykes's *Nancy.*

302. "Victorian will-power." *Financial Times* (12 October 1972), p. 16. Review of Cecil Woodham-Smith's *Queen Victoria: Her Life and Times, Vol. I, 1819-1861.*

303. "Orwell up for air." *Financial Times* (19 October 1972), p. 28. Review of Peter Stansky and William Abraham's *The Unknown Orwell.*

304. "Clear-sighted Swede." *Financial Times* (26 October 1972), p. 14. Review of Gunnar Hagglof's *Diplomat.*

305. "Duke after Battle of Waterloo." *Financial Times* (2 November 1972), p. 30. Review of Elizabeth Longford's *Wellington: Vol. II Pillar of State.*

306. "Mao then and now." *Financial Times* (9 November 1972), p. 29. Review of Han Suyin's *The Morning Deluge: Mao Tse-tung and the Chinese Revolution, 1883-1954.*

307. "Soldier at Savoy Hill." *Financial Times* (16 November 1972), p. 14. Review of Andrew Boyle's *Only the Wind Will Listen: Reith of the BBC.*

308. "High-fliers and others." *Financial Times* (23 November 1972), p. 33. Review of Nigel Grant's *Soviet Education,* and John Hajnal's *The Student Trap.*

309. "Boy meets girl." *Financial Times* (7 December 1972), p. 32. Review of Derek and Julia Parker's *The Compleat Lover.*

310. "Scaling Parnassus." *Financial Times* (15 December 1972), p. 34. Review of *The New Oxford Book of English Verse* ed. by Helen Gardner; and *British Poetry Since 1960: A Critical Survey* ed. by M. Schmidt and G. Lindop.

311. "Bennett's hidden self." *Financial Times* (21 December 1972), p. 29. Review of *Arnold Bennett in Love,* ed. by George and Jean Beardmore.

312. "Teddy's boys." *Financial Times* (28 December 1972), p. 10. Review of Donald Read's *Edwardian England 1901-15,* and Keith Middlemass's *The Life of King Edward VII.*

313. "Humane bravery of Bobs." *Financial Times* (4 January 1973), p. 26. Review of W. H. Hannah's *Bobs.*

314. "Come into the garden, Maud." *Financial Times* (11 January 1973), p. 10. Review of *Memoirs—W.B. Yeats,* ed. by

Denis Donoghue.

315. "Sicilian splendours." *Financial Times* (19 January 1973), p. 12. Review of Raleigh Trevelyan's *Princes Under the Volcano.*

316. "Planters' punches." *Financial Times* (25 January 1973), p. 12. Review of Richard S. Dunn's *Sugar and Slaves.*

317. "Good-living P.M." *Financial Times* (1 February 1973), p. 14. Review of John Wilson's *C.B.: A Life of Sir Henry Campbell-Bannerman.*

318. "Seeing red." *Financial Times* (15 February 1973), p. 34. Review of David Caute's *The Fellow-Travellers,* and Sebastian Haffner's *Failure of a Revolution: Germany, 1918-19.*

319. "Waving the flag." *Financial Times* (22 February 1973), p. 29. Review of Peter Grosvenor and James McMillan's *The British Genius.*

320. "Women and gurus." *Financial Times* (1 March 1973), p. 29. Review of Iris Murdoch's *The Black Prince,* and R. Prawer Jhabvala's *A New Dominion.*

321. "Führer's kinks." *Financial Times* (8 March 1973), p. 30. Review of Walter Langer's *The Mind of Adolf Hitler.*

322. "Coming out." *Financial Times* (15 March 1973), p. 16. Review of R. A. Leeson's *Strike—A Live History 1887-1971.*

323. "Sages and plagues." *Financial Times* (22 March 1973), p. 34. Review of George Watson's *The English Ideology: Studies in the Language of Victorian Politics,* and Marc Bloch's *The Royal Touch.*

324. "Poets of our time." *Financial Times* (29 March 1973), p. 37. Review of *The Oxford Book of Twentieth Cen-*

tury English Verse chosen by Philip Larkin.

325. "Stylish soldier." *Financial Times* (5 April 1973), p. 32. Review of Nigel Nicholson's *Alex: The Life of Field-Marshal Alexander of Tunis*, and Melton S. Davis's *Who Defends Rome?*

326. "Crop of crimes." *Financial Times* (12 April 1973), p. 37. Review of Kingsley Amis's *Riverside Villas Murder*, Jean Stubbs's *Dear Laura*, P. D. James's *An Unsuitable Job for a Woman*, and Richard D. Altick's *Victorian Studies in Scarlet*.

327. "House and its head." *Financial Times* (19 April 1973), p. 39. Review of Meriol Trevor's *The Arnolds*.

328. "Second chamber sallies." *Financial Times* (26 April 1973), p. 12. Review of Viscount Massereene and Ferrard's *The Lords*.

329. "Pert maidens." *Financial Times* (3 May 1973), p. 16. Review of Heinrich Boll's *Group Portrait with a lady*, and Vladimir Nabokov's *Transparent Things*.

330. "Cruel climate." *Financial Times* (10 May 1973), p. 20. Review of Morris Fraser's *Children in Conflict*.

331. "Explorer's World." *Financial Times* (17 May 1973), p. 31. Review of Tim Jeal's *Livingstone*, Cecil Northcott's *David Livingstone*, Ian Anstruther's *I Presume*, and *Livingstone*, ed. by Bridgial Pachai.

332. "Good man and foes." *Financial Times* (24 May 1973), p. 20. Review of John Williams's *Stoner*.

333. "Bullitt on target." *Financial Times* (1 June 1973), p. 16. Review of *For the President*, ed. by Orville H. Bullitt.

334. "The Protector." *Financial Times* (7 June 1973), p. 17. Review of Antonia Fraser's *Cromwell*, and C. V. Wedg-

845

wood's *Oliver Cromwell.*

335. "H. G. sees it through." *Financial Times* (21 June 1973), p. 36. Review of Norman and Jeanne Mackenzie's *The Time Traveller: The Life of H. G. Wells.*

336. "Welsh wizard from Criccieth." *Financial Times* (29 June 1973), p. 32. Review of John Grigg's *The Young Lloyd George,* and Michael Kinnear's *The Fall of Lloyd George.*

337. "How we quit India." *Financial Times* (5 July 1973), p. 39. Review of Dennis Kincaid's *British Social Life in India 1608-1937,* and *Wavell: The Viceroy's Journal,* ed. by Penderel Moon.

338. "Unto Caesar." *Financial Times* (12 July 1973), p. 18. Review of Michael Grant's *The Jews in the Roman World.*

339. "Over the sticks." *Financial Times* (19 July 1973), p.33. On Dick Francis.

340. "Mind of a spy." *Financial Times* (26 July 1973), p. 33. Review of Patrick Seale and Maureen McConville's *Philby: The Long Road to Moscow.*

341. "Wily statesman." *Financial Times* (3 August 1973), p. 12. Review of J. F. Bernard's *Talleyrand.*

342. "Dry Canadian." *Financial Times* (9 August 1973), p. 10. Review of Lester B. Pearson's *Memoirs 1897-1948: Through Diplomacy to Politics.*

343. "Surgery that cut two ways." *New York Times Book Review* (12 August 1973), pp. 3-4. Review of I. S. Cooper's *The Victim Is Always the Same.*

344. "Peasant power in turbulent times." *Financial Times* (16 August 1973), p. 12. Review of M. Mollat and P. Wolff's *The Popular Revolutions of the Late Middle Ages.*

345. "Restless spirit." *Financial Times* (23 August 1973), p. 26. Review of Joanna Richardson's *Enid Starkie.*

346. "Victoriana." *Financial Times* (30 Augst 1973), p. 10. Review of *The Victorian City. Volumes I and II,* ed. by H. J. Dyos and Michael Wolff.

347. "Man from Missouri." *Financial Times* (6 September 1973), p. 19. Review of Margaret Truman's *Harry S. Truman.*

348. "Suicide of the old world." *Financial Times* (13 September 1973), p. 30. Review of Maurice Paléologue's *An Ambassador's Memoirs 1914-1917.*

349. "Crimes of a killer." *Financial Times* (20 September 1973), p. 33. Review of John Bingham's *The Hunting Down of Peter Manuel.*

350. "London pride." *Financial Times* (27 September 1973), p. 14. Review of Bernard Donoghue and G. W. Jones's *Herbert Morrison: Portrait of a Politician.*

351. "Parliament men and peers." *Financial Times* (4 October 1973), p. 31. Review of David Cecil's *The Cecils of Hatfield House,* and Wendy Hinde's *George Canning.*

352. "Nye's Manna." *Financial Times* (18 October 1973), p. 18. Review of Michael Foot's *Aneurin Bevan: A Biography. Vol. Two 1945-60.*

353. "Old Times." *Financial Times* (25 October 1973), p. 33. Review of Jacquetta Hawkes's *The First Great Civilizations.*

354. "Attitudes of Aldous." *Financial Times* (1 November 1973), p. 34. Review of Sybile Bedford's *Aldous Huxley Vol. I. 1894-1939.*

355. "Imperial dilemma." *Financial Times* (7 November 1973),

p. 40.   Review of James Morris's *Heaven's Command.*

356. "The real Alexander." *Financial Times* (15 November 1973), p. 33.   Review of Robin Lane Fox's *Alexander the Great.*

357. "Boer blockbuster." *Financial Times* (22 November 1973), p. 30.   Review of Ronald Harwood's *Articles of Faith,* and Willaim Trevor's *Elizabeth Alone.*

358. "Versatile courtier." *Financial Times* (29 November 1973), p. 16.   Review of Robert Halsband's *Lord Hervey: Eighteenth Century Courtier.*

359. "Rumbold's realism." *Financial Times* (21 December 1973), p. 21.   Review of Martin Gilbert's *Sir Horace Rumbold.*

360. "Mind of the Great Cham." *Financial Times* (3 January 1974), p. 36.   Review of *Johnson As Critic,* ed. by John Wain.

361. "Extravagant Poe." *Financial Times* (10 January 1974), p. 32.   Review of Daniel Hoffman's *Poe Poe Poe Poe Poe Poe Poe,* and *Comic Tales of Edgar Allan Poe,* ed. by Angus Wolfe Murray.

362. "The English on tour." *Financial Times* (17 January 1974), p. 8.   Review of Charles Dickens's *Pictures from Italy,* and *Abroad,* compiled by Alan Wykes.

363. "Supreme story-teller." *Financial Times* (24 January 1974), p. 25.   Review of Anthony Curtis's *The Pattern of Maugham.*

364. "Background to Trollope." *Financial Times* (31 January 1974), p. 25.   Review of *What I Remember: Thomas Adolphus Trollope,* ed. by Herbert van Thal.

365. "The Faces of Maugham: a portrait for his centenary—

introduced by Anthony Curtis." *Listener*, 91 (7 February 1974), 170. On Maugham's character.

366. "Brio and Bayonets." *Financial Times* (7 February 1974), p. 26. Review of Peter Nichol's *Italia, Italia;* and Max Gallo's *Mussolini's Italy.*

367. "Re-fighting old battles." *Financial Times* (14 February 1974), p. 25. Review of Ronald Lewin's *Churchill as Warlord.*

368. "Portraits of people." *Financial Times* (1 March 1974), p. 28. Review of A. O. J. Cockshut's *Truth to Life.*

369. "Love in a cruel climate." *Financial Times* (8 March 1974), p. 29. Review of Hester W. Chapman's *Anne Boleyn.*

370. "Maiden lady." *Financial Times* (15 March 1974), p. 30. Review of Hilary Spurling's *Ivy When Young: The Early Life of Ivy Compton-Burnett 1884-1919.*

371. "Fallible father." *Financial Times* (21 March 1974), p. 15. Review of Gore Vidal's *Burr.*

372. "Things do get better." *Financial Times* (29 March 1974), p. 38. Review of P. B. Medawar's *The Hope of Progress.*

373. "Boys will be boys." *Financial Times* (4 April 1974), p. 32. Review of Henry de Montherlant's *The Boys.*

374. "Bounds of possibility." *Financial Times* (11 April 1974), p. 32. Review of William W. Bartley's *Wittgenstein,* and *The Freud-Jung Letters,* ed. by William McGuire.

375. "Victorian values." *Financial Times* (18 April 1974), p. 18. Review of R. McLean's *Victorian Publishers' Book Bindings in Cloth and Leather,* R. D. Altick's *Victorian People and Ideas,* and *William Morris: Ornamentations and Illustrations* (from *The Kelmscott Chaucer*).

376. "Old China hand." *Financial Times* (25 April 1974), p. 19. Review of John Peter Davies's *Dragon by the Tail.*

377. "When to conserve?" *Financial Times* (2 May 1974), p. 28. Review of John Passmore's *Man's Responsibility for Nature.*

378. "How Maundy made money." *Financial Times* (10 May 1974), p. 34. Review of Tom Cullen's *Maundy Gregory: Purveyor of Honours.*

379. "Long collonades." *Financial Times* (16 May 1974), p. 14. Review of Rudolf Wittkower's *Palladio and English Palladianism*, and Alfonso Lowe's *La Serenissima.*

380. "Wisdom of a warden." *Financial Times* (24 May 1974), p. 16. Review of Sir William Hayter's *A Double Life.*

381. "Public servants private face." *Financial Times* (31 May 1974), p. 38. Review of Stephen Roskill's *Hankey: Man of Secrets. Vol. III 1931-36.*

382. "Causes of mirth." *Financial Times* (6 June 1974), p. 30. Review of Richard Boston's *An Anatomy of Laughter*, and Ann Thwaite's *Waiting for the Party: The Life of Frances Hodgson Burnett.*

383. "The real Tolstoy." *Financial Times* (13 June 1974), p. 26. Review of Edward Crankshaw's *Tolstoy.*

384. "Whigs and woman." *Financial Times* (27 June 1974), p. 14. Review of Sonia Keppel's *The Sovereign Lady.*

385. "Foreman on the job." *Financial Times* (11 July 1974), p. 26. Review of Margaret Drabble's *Arnold Bennett*, and *Arnold Bennett: The Evening Standard Years*, ed. by Andrew Mylett.

386. "Smiley comes back." *Financial Times* (19 July 1974), p. 19. Review of John LeCarre's *Tinker Sailor Soldier*

Spy.

387. "Fathoming the Führer." *Financial Times* (25 July 1974), p. 24. Review of Joachim C. Fest's *Hitler.*

388. "Acting like artists." *Financial Times* (1 August 1974), p. 14. Review of Stanley Weintraub's *Whistler,* Roy McMullen's *Victorian Outsider,* and Phillip Henderson's *Swinburne.*

389. "Ringside views." *Financial Times* (8 August 1974), p. 12. Review of Phillip Mason's *A Matter of Honour,* and Peter Mudford's *Birds of a Different Plumage.*

390. "Long arm." *Financial Times* (15 August 1974), p. 22. Review of *Essays in the History of Publishing,* ed. by Asa Briggs.

391. "Savage lines." *Financial Times* (22 August 1974), p. 22. Review of H. M. Atherton's *Political Prints in the Age of Hogarth,* and Richard Fitzgerald's *Art and Politics.*

392. "Ourselves observed." *Financial Times* (30 August 1974), p. 22. Review of *Britain Through American Eyes,* ed. by Henry Steele Commager.

393. "Radical Wife." *Financial Times* (5 September 1974), p. 13. Review of Claire Tomalin's *The Life and Death of Mary Wollstonecraft.*

394. "Great Van a wit." *Financial Times* (12 September 1974), p. 23. Review of Madeleine Bingham's *Masks and Facades: Sir John Vanbrugh, the Man in His Setting.*

395. "Priestley: one hell of a lot of talent...a birthday portrait by Paul Bailey." *Listener,* 92 (12 September 1974), 335-338. P. 335. Snow comments on Priestley.

396. "Aldous concluded." *Financial Times* (19 September 1974), p. 29. Review of Sybille Bedford's *Aldous Hux-*

ley: Vol. Two, 1939-1963.

397. "Happily ill." *Financial Times* (26 September 1974), p. 32. Review of George Pickering's *Creative Malady.*

398. "Royals aboard." *Financial Times* (4 October 1974), p. 14. Review of Richard Hough's *Louis and Victoria: the First Mountbattens.*

399. "Dawn of civilization." *Financial Times* (17 October 1974), p. 23. Review of Kenneth Clark's *Another Part of the Wood,* and *Henry Moore Drawings* selected and introduced by Kenneth Clark.

400. "Political ego." *Financial Times* (24 October 1974), p. 39. Review of Patrick Devlin's *Too Proud to Fight.*

401. "B.B." *Financial Times* (31 October 1974), p. 34. Review of Andrew Boyle's *Poor, Dear Brendan.*

402. "In search of Eden." *Financial Times* (14 November 1974), p. 16. Review of Thor Heyerdahl's *Fatu-Hiva: Back to Nature?*

403. "The invisible woman." *Financial Times* (28 November 1974), p. 30. Review of Gordon N. Ray's *H. G. Wells and Rebecca West.*

404. "Sam the strong." *Financial Times* (5 December 1974), p. 34. Review of John Wain's *Samuel Johnson.*

405. "Magnificent Manchu." *Financial Times* (12 December 1974), p. 12. Review of Jonathan D. Spence's *Emperor of China: Self-Portrait of K'ang Hsi.*

406. "Seeker of sensation." *Financial Times* (19 December 1974), p. 10. Review of Kenneth Robinson's *Wilkie Collins,* and *Wilkie Collins—The Critical Heritage* ed. by Norman Page.

407. "Old-time cricket." *Financial Times* (2 January 1975), p. 8. Review of Brodribb's *The Croucher.*

408. "My Book for 1975." *Financial Times* (2 January 1975), p. 8. Snow hopes for a serious critical study of Balzac to be done.

409. "Ruling clan." *Financial Times* (9 January 1975), p. 19. Review of Christopher Hibbert's *The Rise and Fall of the House of the Medici.*

410. "World ago." *Financial Times* (16 January 1975), p. 11. Review of Charles Ritchie's *The Siren Years: Undiplomatic Diaries 1937-1945.*

411. "Lion rampant." *Financial Times* (23 January 1975), p. 30. Review of Susan Chitty's *The Beast and the Monk: A Life of Charles Kingsley,* and Brenda Colioms's *Charles Kingsley: the Lion of Eversley.*

412. Review of Rayner Heppenstall's *Reflections of the Newgate Calendar. Financial Times* (6 February 1975), p. 24.

413. "Dostoevsky, crime and punishment." *Financial Times* (13 February 1975), p. 28. Review of Leonid Grossman's *Dostoevsky.*

414. "Parochial spires." *Financial Times* (27 February 1975), p. 32. Review of Phillip Rieff's *Fellow Teachers,* and *The Universities in the Nineteenth Century,* ed. by Michael Sanderson.

415. "The U. S. and the flight from reason." *Intellect,* 103 (February 1975), 278.

416. "Faraway princess." *Financial Times* (6 March 1975), p. 26. Review of Robert Gibson's *The Land Without a Name: Alain-Fournier and His World.*

417. "Browning versions." *Financial Times* (16 March 1975),

p. 16. Review of William Irvine and Park Honan's *The Book, The Ring and The Poet: A Biography of Robert Browning.*

418. "Impossible Gogol." *Financial Times* (20 March 1975), p. 30. Review of Henri Troyat's *Gogol.*

419. "Mr. President's mistress." *Financial Times* (27 March 1975), p. 40. Review of Fawn M. Brodie's *Thomas Jefferson: an Intimate History.*

420. "Raffles rides again." *Financial Times* (3 April 1975), p. 34. Review of Barry Perowne's *Raffles Revisited,* E. W. Hornung's *Raffles: The Amateur Cracksman,* and E. W. Hornung's *Raffles: The Black Mask.*

421. "A drop of arsenic." *Financial Times* (10 April 1975), p. 32. Review of Robin Odell's *Exhumation of a Murder.*

422. "All in miniature." *Financial Times* (17 April 1975), p. 16. Review of James Pope-Hennessy's *The Houses of Parliament,* Roy Strong's *Nicholas Hilliard,* Madeline Bingham's *The Making of Kew,* and David Holloway's *Derby Day.*

423. "Hardy quest." *Financial Times* (17 April 1975), p. 34. Review of Robert Gittings's *Young Thomas Hardy.*

424. "Tum-tum." *Financial Times* (1 May 1975), p. 32. Review of Kinley Robey's *The King, the Press and the People,* Gordon Brook-Shepherd's *Uncle of Europe,* John Pearson's *Edward the Rake,* and Dennis Judd's *Edward VII.*

425. "Victim of the system." *Financial Times* (9 May 1975), p. 16. Review of David L. Lewis's *Prisoners of Honour,* and Anthony Farra-Hockley's *Goughie.*

426. "Case for the cliffhanger." *Financial Times* (15 May 1975), p. 18. Review of David Lippincott's *The Voice of Armaggedon,* and Glendon Swarthout's *The Shootlist.*

427. "In love with nature." *Financial Times* (22 May 1975), p. 34. Review of Robert Franklin's *Queen Wolf,* Annie Dillard's *Pilgrim at Tinker Creek,* and Alan Cottrell's *Portrait of Nature.*

428. "A look at the other place." *Financial Times* (29 May 1975), p. 12. Review of Janet P. Morgan's *The House of Lords and the Labour Government 1964-70.*

429. "Worldling of genius." *Books and Bookmen,* 20 (May 1975), 11. Review of Milo Keynes's *Essays on John Maynard Keynes.*

430. "In and out of the wilderness." *Financial Times* (5 June 1975), p. 34. Review of Martin Gilbert's *Winston S. Churchill: Volume IV,* and A. J. Sylvester's *Life with Lloyd George,* ed. by Colin Cross.

431. "In search of man." *Financial Times* (12 June 1975), p. 35. Review of Sonia Cole's *Leaky's Luck.*

432. "What you will." *Financial Times* (19 June 1975), p. 28. Review of Michael Black's *The Literature of Fidelity.*

433. "Playing to win." *Financial Times* (27 June 1975), p. 18. Review of John Arlott's *The Oxford Companion to Sports and Games.*

434. *"H. G. J. Moseley: The Life and Letters of an English Physicist 1887-1915."* *Books and Bookmen,* 20 (June 1975), 64-65. Review of J. L. Heilbron's biography.

435. "Solidarity and single-mindedness of the Cecils." *Financial Times* (3 July 1975), p. 10. Review of Kenneth Rose's *The Later Cecils.*

436. "Parson who loved cream." *Financial Times* (10 July 1975), p. 14. Review of Piers Brendon's *Hawker of Morwenstow.*

437. "In balk in the Balkans." *Financial Times* (17 July 1975), p. 10. Review of Anthony Hope's *Sophy of Kravonia,* and W. W. Jacob's *Selected Short Stories.*

438. "Policeman and psychopath." *Financial Times* (24 July 1975), p. 12. Review of James McLevy's *The Casebook of a Victorian Detective* (ed. by George Scott-Moncrieff), and Stanley Ellin's *Stronghold.*

439. "Satirical Spinster." *Financial Times* (31 July 1975), p. 20. Review of Douglas Bush's *Jane Austen,* and *Sandition* by Jane Austen and another Lady.

440. "Super summit." *Financial Times* (7 August 1975), p. 19. Review of Charles M. Lee Jr.'s *Meeting at Potsdam.*

441. "So are they all, all honourable men." *Financial Times* (22 August 1975), p. 8. Review of Maurice Cowling's *The Impact of Hitler.*

442. "Scottish power house." *Financial Times* (28 August 1975), p. 17. Review of David Daniell's *The Interpreter's House: A Critical Assessment of the Work of John Buchan.*

443. "Father of the Revolution." *Financial Times* (4 September 1975), p. 11. Review of Jean Matrat's *Robespierre,* and George Rudé's *Robespierre.*

444. "Pursuit of Nancy." *Financial Times* (11 September 1975), p. 29. Review of Harold Acton's *Nancy Mitford: a memoir.*

445. "Wrath of Reith." *Financial Times* (18 September 1975), p. 16. Review of *The Reith Diaries* ed. by Charles Stuart.

446. "Don's saga." *Financial Times* (26 September 1975), p. 16. Review of J. C. Masterman's *On the Chariot Wheel.*

447. "Handfuls of dust." *Financial Times* (2 October 1975),

p. 16. Review of Christopher Sykes's *Evelyn Waugh.*

448. "Boisterous and magnanamous peer." *Financial Times* (9 October 1975), p. 12. Review of Lord Hailsham's *The Door Wherein I Went.*

449. "Deaths and entrances." *Financial Times* (17 October 1975), p. 12. Review of Agatha Christie's *Curtain: Poirot's Last Case,* Nicolas Freeling's *What Are the Bugles Blowing for?,* and *The Continental Op* by Dashiell Hammett (ed. by Steven Marcus).

450. "Mind and body." *Financial Times* (30 October 1975), p. 29. Review of Ronald W. Clark's *The Life of Bertrand Russell.*

451. "In old New York." *Financial Times* (7 November 1975), p. 14. Review of R. W. B. Lewis's *Edith Wharton: a biography,* and Margot Peters's *Unquiet Soul.*

452. "Mud into myth." *Financial Times* (13 November 1975), p. 23. Review of Paul Fussel's *The Great War and Modern Memory,* and *The Ordeal of Alfred M. Hale: The memoirs of a soldier servant,* ed. by Paul Fussel.

453. "The Corridors of DNA." *New York Review of Books,* 22 (13 November 1975), 3-4. Review of Anne Sayre's *Rosalind Franklin and DNA.*

454. "Those conquering heroes." *Financial Times* (20 November 1975), p. 28. Review of Rita McWilliams Tullberg's *Women at Cambridge,* Ruth Adam's *A Woman's Place, 1910-1975,* and *The Victorian Public School* ed. by Brian Simon and Ian Bradley.

455. "English as she is spoke." *Financial Times* (4 December 1975), p. 29. Review of F. E. Halliday's *The Excellency of the English Tongue,* Basil Cottle's *The Plight of English,* A. P. Cowie and R. Mackin's *Oxford Dictionary of Curret Idiomatic English, Vol. I,* and *Words* by King-

sley Amis and 13 others.

456. "Primevil powers." *Financial Times* (11 December 1975), p. 10. Review of Adrian J. Desmond's *The Hot-Blooded Dinosaurs: A Revolution in Palaeontology.*

457. "No 10 people." *Financial Times* (18 December 1975), p. 16. Review of Robert Blake's *The Office of Prime Minister,* and *The Most Gracious Speeches to Parliament 1900-74,* compiled and ed. by F. S. W. Craig.

458. "Civil servant of God." *Financial Times* (31 December 1975), p. 13. Review of T. H. L. Parker's *John Calvin.*

459. "P. L. R." *New Review,* 2 (December 1975), 12-13. Snow publishes his speech before the House of Lords on a bill to aid writers financially.

460. "Introduction," to *The Case-Book of Sherlock Holmes,* by Arthur Conan Doyle. London: Cape, 1975.

461. *Trollope.* London: Macmillan, 1975; as *Trollope: His Life and Art.* New York: Scribners, 1975.

462. "Scottish connection." *Financial Times* (8 January 1976), p. 20. Review of Ludovick Kennedy's *A Presumption of Innocence: The Amazing Case of Patrick Meehan.*

463. "Natural force." *Financial Times* (16 January 1976), p. 29. Review of J. H. Huizinga's *The Making of a Saint.*

464. "Blasting off." *Financial Times* (29 January 1976), p. 25. Review of *George Orwell: The Critical Heritage* ed. by Jeffrey Myers, and *Enemy Salvoes: Selected Literary Criticism of Wyndham Lewis* ed. by C. J. Fox.

465. "Digging up clues." *Financial Times* (5 February 1976), p. 16. Review of two books by Georges Simenon: *Maigret and the Black Sheep* and *Three Beds in Manhattan;* H. F. R. Keating's *Murder Must Appetise,* and *Crime on Her*

Mind ed. by Michelle B. Slung.

466. "A French Churchill." *Financial Times* (12 February 1976), p. 15. Review of Edgar Holt's *The Tiger: The Life of Georges Clemenceau.*

467. "Beast watching." *Financial Times* (19 February 1976), p. 29. Review of Cynthia Moss's *Portraits in the Wild: Animal Behavior in East Africa.*

468. "Power of Pitt." *Financial Times* (4 March 1976), p. 24. Review of Stanley Ayling's *The Elder Pitt.*

469. "Cuban master." *Financial Times* (12 March 1976), p. 12. Review of Alejo Carpentier's *Reasons of State.*

470. "Twenty years inside." *Financial Times* (23 March 1976), p. 15. Review of Albert Speer's *Spandau: The Secret Diaries.*

471. "Son of Burr." *Financial Times* (1 April 1976), p. 28. Review of Gore Vidal's *1876,* Paul Theroux's *The Family Arsenal,* and Paul Theroux's *Fong and the Indians.*

472. "Players' King." *Financial Times* (23 April 1976), p. 20. Review of Raymund FitzSimons's *Edmund Kean.*

473. "On the Floss." *Financial Times* (29 April 1976), p. 37. Review of Ruby V. Redinger's *George Eliot: The Emergent Self.*

474. "Success saga." *Financial Times* (7 May 1976), p. 12. Review of *Steinbeck: A Life in Letters,* ed. by Elaine Steinbeck and Robert Wallsten.

475. "Doctor in the house." *Financial Times* (13 May 1976), p. 32. Review of Ronald Hingley's *A New Life of Anton Chekhov.*

476. "Master players." *Financial Times* (21 May 1976), p. 37.

Review of two biographical sketches, Gerald Broadribb's *Maurice Tate,* and Trevor Bailey's *Sir Gary.*

477. "Croissants for the Master." *Financial Times* (27 May 1976), p. 12. Review of Céleste Albaret's *Monsieur Proust.*

478. "Eye-opener about Oscar." *Financial Times* (3 June 1976), p. 12. Review of H. Montgomery Hyde's *Oscar Wilde.*

479. "Shrewd observer." *Financial Times* (10 June 1976), p. 25. Review of W. Averell Harriman and Elie Abel's *Special Envoy to Churchill and Stalin: 1941-1946.*

480. "Frenchman in the lab." *Financial Times* (18 June 1976), p. 19. Review of Maurice Goldsmith's biography, *Frederic Joliot-Curie.*

481. "From Agincourt onwards." *Financial Times* (1 July 1976), p. 12. Review of John Keegan's *The Face of Battle,* and *The War Lords,* ed. by Sir Michael Carver.

482. "When we were very young." *Financial Times* (9 July 1976), p. 29. Review of Samuel Hynes's *The Auden Generation,* Elizabeth Salter and Allanah Harper's *Edith Sitwell: Fire of the Mind,* and *The Very Rich Hours of Adrienne Monnier,* translated by Richard McDougall.

483. "Sour face of success." *Financial Times* (15 July 1976), p. 25. Review of Catherine Dupré's *John Galsworthy,* and John Galsworthy's *Ten Best Plays.*

* 484. "Exit Nero." *Financial Times* (22 July 1976), p. 12. Review of Rex Stout's *A Family Affair,* and Matthew Vaugham's *The Discretion of Dominick Ayres.*

II. GENERAL SECONDARY STUDIES, INTERVIEWS, BIOGRAPHICAL SKETCHES, NOTICES OF AWARDS AND HONORS, AND MISCELLANEOUS ITEMS

General references to Snow's work also appear in the First Part of this bibliography. See the following numbers there: 1, 6, 7, 12, 16, 17, 18, 23, 25, 27, 29, 31, 32, 34, 35, 36, 37, 38, 40, 43, 45, 46, 49, 55, 56, 57, 60, 64, 65, 66, 71, 75, 76, 77, 78, 80, 81, 84, 86, 89, 90, 95, 96, 98, 101, 103, 104, 105, 107, 110, 111, 112, 116, 118, 121, 122, 123, 124, 125, 127, 132, 133, 136, 140, 142, 143, 153, 159, 171, 191, 199, 210, 211, 214, 225, 226, 231, 236, 238, 241, 250, 262, 266, 285, 293, 305, 313, 334.

485. Allen, Walter. "Mr. Leavis Pays His Respects to Mr. Snow." *New York Times Book Review* (1 April 1962), p. 10.

486. —. Untitled comments. *Contemporary Novelists.* Ed. James Vinson. London and Chicago: St. James Press, 1972, pp. 1153-1155.

487. Anikin, G. V. "Teoriya romana v literaturno-kriticheskikh stat'yakh Charl'za Persi Snou." *Uchenye Zapiski Ural'-skogo universiteta, Sverdlovsk,* 98 (1970), 100-112.

488. Anon. "A Question of Brains." *TLS* (23 March 1962), p. 201; replies by J.H. Kells, and I.C. Robinson, in *TLS* (30 March 1962), p. 217; reply by R.H. Stringer, in *TLS* (6 April 1962), p. 233; reply by Edmund Fuller, in *TLS* (13 April 1962), p. 249. On the Snow-Leavis controversy.

489. —. "A Snow Job?" *Newsweek,* 59 (5 March 1962), 52.

On the Tizard-Lindermann controversy.

490. —. "Adding up Einstein." *Newsweek*, 55 (11 April 1960), 82. A summary of Snow's thoughts on Einstein, supported mainly by quotes from Snow.

491. —. "Britain's lead in desalination." *The* (London) *Times* (12 May 1965), p. 16. An account of Snow's remarks on the activities of The Committee on Desalination Research.

492. —. " 'Business Lunches Waste Time.' " *The* (London) *Times* (29 January 1965), p. 7. An account of Snow's statements at a lunch given by the Business Equipment Trade Association in London.

493. —. "Can science save Britain's industry?" *Business Week*, No. 1862 (8 May 1965), pp. 113-114, 116, 118, 121. A biographical article, with concentration on Snow's view of the problems of British industry.

494. —. "C. P. Snurd on banality." *Private Eye*, 1 (May 1962), 5.

495. —. "Chubb Fellow." *New Yorker*, 37 (16 December 1961), 44-45. On Snow as a Chubb Fellow at Yale. Snow talks about his novels and writing habits.

496. —. "Civil Servants' Science Talks: Bringing Together 'Two Cultures'." *The* (London) *Times* (6 May 1964), p. 9. On a government experiment inspired by Snow's ideas on the Two Cultures.

497. —. "Decision on the Bombing of Germany: British Scientists 'Overruled'." *The* (London) *Times* (2 December 1960), p. 13. An account of Snow's Godkin lectures given at Harvard.

498. —. "Deluded Materialists?" *Newsweek*, 59 (15 January 1962), 20, 23. An account of Snow's statements on

American beliefs.

499. —. "Disaster to learning and science." *The* (London) *Times* (14 December 1967), p. 8. An account of Snow's worry over the secret plans of administrators.

500. —. "Endeavouring too much at once." *The* (London) *Times* (29 February 1968), p. 5. On Britain's "lamentable" record on financing scientific applications.

501. —. "Engineers Need Higher Status: Lord Snow Urges New Effort." *The* (London) *Times* (25 March 1966), p. 7.

502. —. "Familiar and Unfamiliar: Some Faces of Labor." *Newsweek*, 64 (2 November 1964), 51. A biographical sketch.

503. —. "Fiction." *Saturday Review*, 54 (25 December 1971), 33. Includes short comments on *The Sleep of Reason* and *Last Things.*

504. —. "Glum Snow Job?" *Senior Scholastic*, 93 (6 December 1968), 23. On Snow's lecture at Westminster College in Fulton, Missouri.

505. —. "Greater opportunities for arts in the regions." *The* (London) *Times* (23 March 1972), p. 14. Brief comment on Regional arts associations.

506. —. "Growth rate warning by Lord Snow." *The* (London) *Times* (5 February 1965), p. 8. On industrial growth.

507. —. "Harsh decisions must be carried through." *The* (London) *Times* (2 August 1966), p. 6. An account of Snow's views on the need for government to strongly enforce its decisions.

508. —. "High priority sought for national system of nursery schools." *The* (London) *Times* (11 July 1974), p. 10. Snow opposes teachers on strike, and defends elitism.

509. —. "Higher education target being exceeded." *The* (London) *Times* (2 December 1965), p. 8. An account of Snow's remarks on the need for universities to serve society better, i.e., by giving society the people it desires.

510. —. "In the Name of Obedience." *Nation,* 192 (7 January 1961), 3. On Snow's address to the American Association for the Advancement of Science.

511. —. "Interview with C. P. Snow." *Review of English Literature,* 3 (July 1962), 91-108.

512. —. "Interview with C. P. Snow and Pamela Hansford Johnson." *Publishers' Weekly,* 176 (30 November 1959), 28-29.

513. —. "James Tait Black Prize Awards." *The* (London) *Times* (2 March 1955), p. 10. A notice of Snow's winning the award for *The New Men,* and *The Masters* (in sequence).

514. —. "Latest appointments." *The* (London) *Times* (9 February 1971), p. 14. Announcement of Snow's appointment to the Arts Council of Great Britain.

515. —. "Latest appointments." *The* (London) *Times* (5 February 1974), p. 14. Mentions Snow's retirement from the Arts Council of Great Britain.

516. —. "Libraries With 'Atmosphere of a Gaol.': Usefulness Killed in Colleges." *The* (London) *Times* (20 September 1961), p. 5. Includes an account of Snow's ideas on what is really valuable in libraries.

517. —. "Lord Attlee on Atom Bomb Statement." *The* (London) *Times* (28 March 1961), p. 6. An account of Snow's reaction to Lord Attlee.

518. —. "Lord Eccles urging Arts Council not to support filthy, blasphemous plays." *The* (London) *Times* (4 February 1971), p. 6. Snow discusses censorship.

519. —. "Lord Snow." *The* (London) *Times* (31 October 1964), p. 8. On Snow's being gazetted as *Baron* Snow.

520. —. "Lord Snow Advocates Women Engineers." *The* (London) *Times* (23 March 1965), p. 16. An account of Snow's statements made at Rugby College of Engineering Technology.

521. —. "Lord Snow Foresees a New Revolution Soon." *The* (London) *Times* (14 April 1966), p. 6. An account of Snow's address to the Historical Association in London. On the cybernectic revolution.

522. —. "Lord Snow in Maiden Speech Tilts at Coterie Rule." *The* (London) *Times* (19 November 1964), p. 12.

523. —. "Lord Snow Joins Youth Theatre Council." *The* (London) *Times* (16 January 1967), p. 12.

524. —. "Lord Snow: No Regrets and a New Book." *The* (London) *Times* (9 April 1966), p. 5. An account of Snow's remarks about his experience while serving as Parliamentary Secretary.

525. —. "Lord Snow right to send his son to Eton." *The* (London) *Times* (11 February 1965), p. 14.

526. —. "Lord Snow to aid Post Office." *The* (London) *Times* (3 December 1969), p. 1.

527. —. "Lord Snow to Retire." *The* (London) *Times* (31 March 1966), p. 12. A notice of Snow's resignation as Parliamentary Secretary to the Ministry of Technology.

528. —. "Lord Snow Told to Set an Example." *The* (London) *Times* (18 February 1965), p. 17. On Snow's sending his son to Eton.

529. —. "Lord Snow urges wider search for management." *The* (London) *Times* (19 November 1964), p. 6. An account

of Snow's maiden speech as Parliamentary Secretary in the Ministry of Technology.

530. —. "Magnanimity in the Modern Society: Sir Charles Snow on Decline." *The* (London) *Times* (14 April 1962), p. 5. An account of Snow's inaugural address as Rector of St. Andrews.

531. —. "Modern Polonius." *Time*, 77 (3 February 1961), 78. Comments on Snow's *Time of Hope*, and *The Light and the Dark*.

532. —. "More graduate recruits." *The* (London) *Times* (25 July 1968), p. 13. On England's Civil Service's inability to attract some of the most competent people.

533. —. "More Than Politics Needed: Sir C. Snow on 'Great Turning Point'." *The* (London) *Times* (5 September 1961), p. 6. An account of Snow's address to the council of the International Federation of Library Associations. Snow speaks of his anxiety over the problem of nuclear disarmament. Response by Lord Hinchingbrooke in *The Times* (12 September 1961), p. 11; reply by Snow in *The Times* (14 September 1961), p. 13.

534. —. "Mr. Cousins 'Unfairly Attacked'." *The* (London) *Times* (4 December 1965), p. 6. An account of Snow's remarks to the Association of Scientific Workers on England's need for computer specialists.

535. —. "Need for a plan on the use of leisure time." *The* (London) *Times* (4 November 1965), p. 16. An account of Snow's remarks on scientific administrators.

536. —. "Negotiations favoured." *The* (London) *Times* (19 June 1968), p. 6. Snow comments on Britain's relations with Rhodesia.

537. —. "Not Quite 'U'." *The* (London) *Times* (15 December 1964), p. 5. An account of Snow's statements on

England's need for better teachers of science, and its need for more women to become engineers.

538. —. "Nuclear tests underground." *The* (London) *Times* (9 March 1967), p. 22. An account of Snow's statement regarding Britain's "wrong calculation in ever investing in nuclear arms."

539. —. "Obsessed with the academic obstacle race." *The* (London) *Times* (11 February 1965), p. 14. An account of Snow's ideas on education in England.

540. —. "Operation Snow Removal." *National Review*, 12 (27 March 1962), 194. On the Snow-Leavis controversy.

541. —. "Opinion: A State of Siege." *Time*, 92 (22 November 1968), 17. A reaction to Snow's John Findlay Green lecture at Westminster College, Fulton, Missouri; on the subject of possible future famine.

542. —. "Our new president." *Library Association Record*, 62 (December 1960), 389-390.

543. —. "Parliament: House of Commons." *The* (London) *Times* (2 July 1963), p. 14. A report of Snow's statements on "Investigating the causes of typhoid outbreaks" and "Tourists advised to be vaccinated."

544. —. "Peers want College of Arms left alone: Bill rejected." *The* (London) *Times* (11 May 1973), p. 14. An account of Snow's opposition to the bill.

545. —. "People are talking about...Sir Charles Snow and Lady Snow." *Vogue*, 137 (1 March 1961), 140-141.

546. —. "Poor Nations Need Common Effort, Says Sir C. Snow." *The* (London) *Times* (14 July 1964), p. 6. An account of Snow's address to the Tagore India Centre in London.

547. —. "Preparing society for age of less work." *The* (London) *Times* (3 March 1966), p. 16. An account of Snow's remarks on computers.

548. —. "Provincial claims for opera and ballet." *The* (London) *Times* (22 March 1973), p. 14. On the hardships and sacrifices artists must be willing to face.

549. —. "Random effect of university cuts." *The* (London) *Times* (3 November 1965), p. 18. An account of Snow's remarks regarding a moratorium on university building.

550. —. "Roman Catholic attitude to birth control must shift." *The* (London) *Times* (11 February 1971), p. 8. On world population relative to the food supply and natural resources.

551. —. "Russian Honour for Sir Charles Snow." *The* (London) *Times* (26 March 1963), p. 14. On Snow's having conferred upon him the honorary degree of doctor of philological sciences by the Rostov-on-Don University.

552. —. "Science or classics: how far to influence the choice?" *The* (London) *Times* (3 December 1964), p. 16. An account of what Snow intends to do as the Parliamentary Secretary in the Ministry of Technology.

553. —. "Sir Charles Snow and Mr. Levin: Snow v. Associated Newspapers Ltd. and Another." *The* (London) *Times* (1 August 1963), p. 8. On Snow's charging Mr. Levin and people concerned with *The Daily Mail* with libel.

554. —. "Sir C. Snow Calls for Business School." *The* (London) *Times* (7 May 1963), p. 7. An account of Snow's address to Cambridge University's Balance Group.

555. —. "Sir C. Snow Given Post in Technology Ministry." *The* (London) *Times* (20 October 1964), p. 12. A notice of Snow's becoming Parliamentary Secretary in the Ministry.

556. —. "Sir C. Snow Gives Arts Warning." *The* (London) *Times* (8 December 1962), p. 5. An account of his address to a literary luncheon given in his honor.

557. —. "Sir Charles Snow on Nuclear Peril: Scientists' Duty." *The* (London) *Times* (28 December 1960), p. 8.

558. —. "Sir C. Snow on Oxbridge Snobbery." *The* (London) *Times* (2 May 1963), p. 7. An account of Snow's Richmond lecture at Downing College, Cambridge.

559. —. "Sir C. Snow Resigns Directorship." *The* (London) *Times* (24 October 1964), p. 6. A notice of his resigning from the board of directors of the English Electric Company.

560. —. "Sir C. Snow's Eye Operation Fails." *The* (London) *Times* (1 May 1962), p. 6. On Snow's loss of sight in his left eye. Another operation took place in November and is reported in *The Times* (under the title "Sir Charles Snow") on 10 November 1962, p. 8; and under the title "Sir C. Snow's Sight Saved" on 13 November 1962, p. 12.

561. —. "Sir C. Snow's New Post." *The* (London) *Times* (30 March 1963), p. 10. On Snow's being elected a director of the London branch of the University of Chicago Press.

562. —. "Snow, C(harles) P(ercy)." *Contemporary Authors: A Bio-Bibliographical Guide to Current Authors and Their Works.* Ed. Barbara Harte and Carolyn Riley. Detroit, Michigan: Gale Research Company, 1969, pp. 1073-1076. See Vols. 5-8, first revision.

563. —. "Snow, C(harles) P(ercy)." *Current Biography: Who's News and Why 1954.* Ed. Marjorie Dent Candee. New York: H. W. Wilson, 1954, pp. 584-585.

564. —. "Snow, C(harles) P(ercy)." *Current Biography Yearbook 1961.* Ed. Charles Moritz. New York: H. W.

Wilson, 1962, pp. 431-434.

565. —. "Snow, Charles Percy." *Twentieth Century Authors: First Supplement.* Ed. Stanley J. Kunitz. New York: H. W. Wilson, 1955, pp. 932-934.

566. —. "Snow wants school for talented." *The* (London) *Times* (7 October 1967), p. 4. An account of Snow's address to Ithaca College, New York.

567. —. "Snow's War." *Nation,* 207 (9 December 1968), 612. On Snow's warning of the danger of overpopulation.

568. —. "Specter of Famine." *Commonweal,* 89 (13 December 1968), 367-368. On Snow's lecture at Westminster College in Fulton, Missouri.

569. —. "Strategy remains forward defence." *The* (London) *Times* (7 July 1966), p. 7. An account of Snow's remarks on "polycentrism."

570. —. "Students Welcome Sir Charles Snow." *The* (London) *Times* (13 April 1962), p. 14. On the celebration activities at St. Andrews.

571. —. "Sunny Snow." *Time,* 79 (20 April 1962), 51-52. On his installation as 30th Lord Rector of St. Andrew's University.

572. —. "Talks on assistance for authors." *The* (London) *Times* (24 June 1965), p. 16. An account of Snow's remarks on why writers (especially middle-aged ones) needed government help.

573. —. "Technology and Humanism" *TLS* (29 July 1965), pp. 641-642. On Snow as a cult-figure.

574. —. "The Many-sided Life of Sir Charles Snow." *Life,* 50 (7 April 1961), 134-136. Includes a survey of Snow's opinion on many issues of the day.

575. —. "The New Year Honours." *The* (London) *Times* (1 January 1957), p. 4, col. 1. Notice of Snow's receiving "Knights Bachelor."

576. —. "The Two Tyrannies." *The* (London) *Times* (25 October 1963), p. 13. Response by W. L. Bragg in *The Times* (31 October 1963), p. 13.

577. —. "Tribute to Lord Snow." *The* (London) *Times* (7 April 1966), p. 8. The publication of a letter from Prime Minister Wilson to Snow on the latter's retirement from the Ministry of Technology.

578. —. "TV Channel for Education?: Too Much Dirt." *The* (London) *Times* (21 January 1965), p. 12. An account of Snow's views on the quality of TV programs.

579. —. "Two Cultures 'Are Drawing Closer'." *The* (London) *Times* (27 March 1965), p. 10. An account of Snow's remarks made while answering questions at a conference of the Institute of Public Relations.

580. —. "Two Western Cultures." *Time*, 74 (6 July 1959), 59.

581. —. "University News: Cambridge." *The* (London) *Times* (14 July 1960), p. 7. A notice of Snow's appointment to one of two Extraordinary Fellowships.

582. —. "University News: Cambridge." *The* (London) *Times* (8 February 1966), p. 12. A notice of Snow's being elected into honorary fellowship at Christ College.

583. —. "University News: Liverpool." *The* (London) *Times* (13 January 1960), p. 14. A notice that Snow will receive the honorary degree of L.L.D. on April 30.

584. —. "University News: St. Andrews." *The* (London) *Times* (15 November 1962), p. 15. On Snow's gift of £430 to the Students' Representative Council.

585. —. "University News: Sir C. Snow Rector of St. Andrews." *The* (London) *Times* (13 November 1961), p. 14.

586. —. "University Salute to Sciences: Degree Ceremony at Liverpool." *The* (London) *Times* (2 May 1960), p. 7. Includes notice of Snow's receiving the honorary degree of Doctor of Laws.

587. —. "Unwrapped." *The* (London) *Times* (10 December 1965), p. 13. An account of Snow's remarks on the cost and delivery of parcels in England.

588. —. "Vital Role of Fish as A.D. 2000 Food: Lord Snow's Warning." *The* (London) *Times* (1 June 1965), p. 16.

589. —. "Walking the Corridors of Power." *Newsweek,* 64 (28 December 1964), 25. An interview.

590. —. "Why are Jews successful?" *Christianity Today,* 13 (25 April 1969), 31. A discussion of Snow's ideas on the subject.

591. —. "Wider Field Wanted for Harwell." *The* (London) *Times* (16 February 1965), p. 8. An account of Snow's inspection of the various divisions of Harwell.

592. Arsenescu, Adina. "C. P. Snow." *Orizont,* 2 (February 1969), 51-54.

593. Ashton, Thomas L. "Realism and the Chronicle: C. P. Snow's *Cinéma Vérité." South Atlantic Quarterly,* 72 (Autumn 1973), 516-527.

594. Balliett, Whitney. "The Author." *Saturday Review,* 38 (8 January 1955), 9. A biographical sketch of Snow.

595. Bannon, Barbara A. "Authors and editors." *Publishers' Weekly,* 195 (14 April 1969), 25-27.

596. Beker, Miroslav. "Svijet C. P. Snowa." *Forum* (Zagreb),

7-8 (1966), 618-628.

597. Bergonzi, Bernard. "The World of Lewis Eliot." *Twentieth Century,* 167 (March 1960), 214-225; response by Peter Fison in *Twentieth Century,* 167 (June 1960), 568-571.

598. Bernard, Kenneth. "C. P. Snow and Modern Literature." *University Review* (Kansas City), 31 (March 1965), 231-233.

599. Brogan, Denis. "Inequality and Mr. Short." *Spectator,* 222 (18 April 1969), 505. Includes discussion of Snow's remarks on the "superiority of Jewish genes."

600. Buckley, Vincent. "C. P. Snow: How Many Cultures?" *Melbourne Critical Review,* 5 (1962), 102-107.

601. Buckley, William F., Jr. "The Voice of Sir Charles." *National Review,* 12 (22 May 1962), 358. On Snow's relation to communism.

602. Butler, John. "Snow in the Tropics: A Parody of C. P. Snow." *Transition,* 7 (December/January 1968), 31-33.

603. Calisher, Hortense. "Can There Be an American C. P. Snow?" *Reporter,* 15 (1 November 1956), 39-43. On the sequence novel; on the work of Snow, especially *Time of Hope,* and *Homecoming.*

604. Caute, David. "A writer's prospect—IX." *London Magazine,* 7 (February 1960), 40-46.

605. Coleman, Terry. "A various man." *Guardian Weekly,* 103 (19 September 1970), 15. An interview.

606. —. "Flummery rampant on a field of Snow." *Guardian* (8 September 1970), p. 7. An interview.

607. Cooper, William. "The World of C. P. Snow." *Nation,* 184 (2 February 1957), 104-105.

608. Corke, Hilary. "The Dog That Didn't Bark." *New Republic*, 148 (13 April 1963), 27-30. Response by Alexander H. Sackton, and Andre Schiffrin appear in *New Republic*, 148 (4 May 1963), 36-37. On the Snow-Leavis controversy.

609. Cornelius, David K., and Edwin Saint Vincent. *Cultures in Conflict: perspectives on the Snow-Leavis controversy.* Chicago: Scott, Foresman, 1964.

610. Cousins, Norman. "Third culture." *Saturday Review*, 49 (7 May 1966), 42.

611. Dallmayr, Fred R. "Political Science and the 'Two Cultures'." *Journal of General Education*, 19 (January 1968), 269-295.

612. Davis, Robert G. *C. P. Snow.* New York and London: Columbia University Press, 1965.

613. Dobree, Bonamy. "The Novels of C. P. Snow." *Literary Half-Yearly*, 4 (January 1963), 28-34.

614. Dolbier, M. "Building bridges between two cultures." *New York Herald Tribune Book Review* (2 March 1958), p. 2.

615. Downs, H. "Let's all be eggheads." *Science Digest*, 59 (May 1966), 90-93.

616. Dunkley, Chris. "11 Snow novels dramatized for BBC radio." *The* (London) *Times* (14 January 1971), p. 16.

617. Dutfield, K. T. "The Art of Science." *TLS* (7 November 1963), p. 907. A letter to the editor, about C. P. Snow on D. H. Lawrence.

618. Eisely, Loren. "The illusion of the two cultures." *American Scholar*, 33 (Winter 1963/1964), 387-399.

619. Elman, Richard M. "C. P. Snow's Disconcerting Narrator."
New Leader, 44 (3 April 1961), 24-25. Snow's narrator,
Lewis Eliot, is discussed in relation to *Time of Hope*, and
The Light and the Dark.

620. Faulkner, Peter. "William Morris and the Two Cultures."
Journal of the William Morris Society, 2 (Spring 1966),
9-12.

621. Fiedler, Leslie A. "Poetry, Science and the End of Man."
Tri-Quarterly (Fall 1964), pp. 7-14.

622. Fietz, Lothar. "Cambridge und die Diskussion um das
Verhältnis von Literatur und Naturwissenschaft." *Lit-
eratur-Kultur-Gesellschaft in England und Amerika:
Aspekte und Forschungsbeiträge. Friedrich Schubel
zum 60. Geburtstag.* Frankfurt: Diesterweg, 1966,
pp. 113-127.

623. Finkelstein, Sidney. "The Art and Science of C. P. Snow."
Mainstream, 14 (September 1961), 31-57.

624. Fison, Peter. "A Reply to Bernard Bergonzi's 'The World
of Lewis Eliot'." *Twentieth Century*, 167 (June 1960),
568-571.

625. Foster, Kenelm. "Snow against the poets." *Blackfriars*,
45 (May 1964), 224-226.

626. Fowler, Albert. "The Negative Entropy of C. P. Snow."
Approach, 58 (Winter 1966), 7-13.

627. Fraser, G. S. "C. P. Snow." *The Politics of Twentieth-
Century Novelists.* Ed. George A. Panichas. New York:
Hawthorn Books, 1971, pp. 124-133.

628. Fuller, Edmund. "C. P. Snow: Spokesman of Two Communities," in his *Books with Men Behind Them*. New
York: Random House, 1962, pp. 102-134. On the
novels and *The Two Cultures and the Scientific Revolu-*

tion.

629. Gale, George. "Saying the unsayable." *Spectator,* 225 (25 July 1970), 65-66. P. 65. Includes comments on Snow's ideas on the superiority of Jews due to gene differences.

630. Gardner, A. "A Literary owl who doesn't give a hoot." *Saturday Review,* 44 (4 March 1961), 53-54.

631. Glicksberg, Charles I. *Modern Literary Perspectivism.* Dallas, Texas: Southern Methodist University Press, 1970. Includes brief comments on Snow.

632. Goodwin, Donald Francis. "The Fiction of C. P. Snow." Diss. Iowa, 1966. *Dissertation Abstracts,* 27A (1967), 3009.

633. Graves, Nora Calhoun. "The Two Culture Theory in C. P. Snow's Novels." Dissertation at the University of South Mississippi, 1967; reprinted as book with same title. Hattiesburg, Mississippi: University and College Press of Mississippi, 1971.

634. Greacen, Robert. "The World of C. P. Snow." *Texas Quarterly,* 4 (Autumn 1961), 266-274.

635. —. *The World of C. P. Snow.* With a bibliography by Bernard Stone. Lowestoft: Scorpion Press, 1962; reprinted New York: London House and Maxwell, 1963.

636. Green, Martin. *Science and the Shabby Curate of Poetry: Essays about the two cultures.* London: Longmans, Green, 1964; New York: Norton, 1965.

637. Greenberg, D. S. "Reaction to Snow: scientists' role in public affairs draws increasingly heavy criticisms." *Science,* 142 (4 October 1963), 13, 34-35. Discussions follow in *Science:* 143 (3 January 1964), 7; 143 (14 February 1964), 638.

638. Gulliver, Antony F. "The Political Novels of Trollope and Snow." Diss. Connecticut, 1969. *Dissertation Abstracts,* 30 A (1969), 684.

639. Halio, Jay L. "C. P. Snow's Literary Limitations." *Northwest Review,* 5 (Winter 1962), 97-102.

640. Hall, William F. "The Humanism of C. P. Snow." *Wisconsin Studies in Contemporary Literature,* 4 (Spring-Summer 1963), 199-208.

641. Hamilton, Kenneth. "C. P. Snow and Political Man." *Queen's Quarterly,* 69 (Autumn 1962), 416-427. Reply to E. W. Mandel.

642. Hand, Harry E. "The Paper Curtain: The Divided World of Snow and Leavis Revisited." *Journal of Human Relations* (Wilberforce, Ohio), 14 (1966), 351-363.

643. Hartley, Anthony. "The Inevitable Oligarchy." *Twentieth Century,* 162 (October 1957), 303-308. Includes several references to Snow's ideas about the subject of power.

644. Heppenstall, Rayner. *The Fourfold Tradition.* London: Barrie and Rockliff, 1961; New York: New Directions, 1961, pp. 224-246.

645. Hicks, Granville. "Politician in a Nuclear Quandary." *Saturday Review,* 47 (12 September 1964), 33-34. On Snow's *Strangers and Brothers* sequence. A contrast to Powell's long sequence is made.

646. Hodgson, P. E. "Culture and Subculture." *Month,* 217 (March 1964), 177-181.

647. Hoff, Harry Summerfield. *C. P. Snow,* by William Cooper (pseud.). London: Longmans, Green, 1959; rev. ed., 1962.

648. Hollis, Christopher. "Snows of Tomorrow Year." *Specta-*

tor, 214 (26 February 1965), 254. Short poem on Snow's sending his son to Eton.

649. Howe, Edel. *The Modern Psychological Novel.* Rev. ed. New York: Grosset and Dunlap, 1961. Includes comments on Snow.

650. Ivasheva, Valentina. "Illusion and Reality (About the Works of C. P. Snow)." *Inostrannaja Literatura*, No. 6 (June 1960), pp. 198-203.

651. —. "Meeting Charles Snow." *Soviet Literature*, No. 8 (1963), pp. 180-182. On the popularity of Snow's novels in the Soviet Union.

652. —. "V Koridorakh vlasti." *Raduga* (Moscow), 8 (1968), 159-174. ("In the corridors of power")

* 653. Jaffa, Herbert C. "C. P. Snow, Portrait of Man as an Adult." *Humanist*, 24 (September-October 1964), 148-150.

654. Johnson, Gerald W. "Footnote to a Current Dialogue." *American Scholar*, 32 (Winter 1962-63), 66-72. On the Snow-Leavis controversy.

655. Johnson, Pamela Hansford. "Three Novelists and the Drawing of Character: C. P. Snow, Joyce Cary and Ivy Compton-Burnett." *Essays and Studies, 1950* (The English Association), 3 (1950), 82-99.

656. Karl, Frederick R. *C. P. Snow: The Politics of Conscience.* Carbondale: Southern Illinois University Press, 1963.

657. Kazin, Alfred. "A Gifted Boy from the Midlands." *Reporter*, 20 (5 February 1959), 37-39. On Snow's *Strangers and Brothers* sequence.

658. Ketels, Violet B. "Shaw, Snow, and the New Men." *Personalist*, 47 (October 1966), 520-531.

659. Knipe, Michael. "Lord Snow on racial factor in success." *The* (London) *Times* (2 April 1969), p. 4. On genetic differences between races.

660. Kvam, Ragnar. "Ny engelsk prosa." *Samtiden,* 69 (November 1960), 549-557. On Snow, Colin Wilson, and Durrell.

661. Leavis, F. R. *English Literature in Our Time and The University: The Clark Lectures 1967.* London: Chatto and Windus, 1969, pp. 28, 44, 55, 96, 171, 181.

662. —. *Nor Shall My Sword: Discourses on Pluralism, Compassion and Social Hope.* London: Chatto and Windus, 1972; New York: Barnes and Noble, 1972, pp. 20, 29, 41-74, 139-140, 158, 164, 167, 171-172, 176-177, 182-183, 187-188, 194, 216-217.

663. —. "Two Cultures? The Significance of C. P. Snow." *Melbourne Critical Review,* 5 (1962), 90-101; reprinted in *Spectator,* 208 (16 March 1962), 297-303; reprinted as *Two Cultures? The Significance of C. P. Snow. With an essay on Sir Charles Snow's Rede Lecture,* by Michael Yudkin. London: Chatto and Windus, 1962; reprinted New York: Random House, 1963; reprinted in his *Nor shall my sword: discourses on pluralism, compassion and social hope.* London: Chatto and Windus, 1972; reprinted New York: Barnes and Noble, 1972, pp. 41-74.

664. MacArthur, Brian. "Lord Snow on the danger of neglecting most gifted pupils." *The* (London) *Times* (8 March 1969), p. 8. An account, with support of several quotes from Snow's address, of the inaugural Claysemore lecture.

665. Macdonald, Alastair. "Imagery in C. P. Snow." *University Review* (Kansas), 32 (June 1966), 303-306; 33 (October 1966), 33-38.

666. McElheny, V. K. "Snow returns to writing." *Science,* 152

(6 May 1966), 745.

667. Mandel, E. W. "Anarchy and Organization." *Queen's Quarterly*, 70 (Spring 1963), 131-141. A rejoinder to Kenneth Hamilton.

668. —. "C. P. Snow's Fantasy of Politics." *Queen's Quarterly*, 69 (Spring 1962), 24-37.

669. Margolis, H. "Intellectual life in England: Leavis views C. P. Snow; Boothby views Leavis." *Science*, 135 (30 March 1962), 1114-1115.

670. Marsden, Dennis. "Lord Snow's Middle-class Dilemma." *Twentieth Century*, 173 (Spring 1965), 6-14. On Snow and education.

671. Martin, Graham. "Novelists of Three Decades: Evelyn Waugh, Graham Greene, C. P. Snow." *The Modern Age. Pelican Guide to English Literature.* Harmondsworth and Baltimore: Penguin, 1961.

672. Mayne, Richard. "The Club Armchair." *Encounter*, 21 (November 1963), 76-82. Comments on all of Snow's work.

673. Millar, Ronald. "My relationship with C. P. Snow: Ronald Millar interviewed by Quentin Lloyd." *Time and Tide*, 43 (13-20 September 1962), 16.

674. —. *The Affair. The New Men. The Masters: Three Plays based on the novels and with a preface by C. P. Snow.* London: Macmillan, 1964.

675. —. "The Play of the Book." *TLS* (19 September 1968), p. 1053. On how Millar came to write *The Affair* into the form of a play. He also discusses *The New Men* and *The Masters* as plays.

676. Millgate, Michael. "Structure and Style in the Novels of

C. P. Snow." *Review of English Literature,* 1 (April 1960), 34-41.

677. Moskin, J. Robert. "A Conversation with C. P. Snow." *Saturday Review/World,* 1 (6 April 1974), 20-22, 47. An interview.

678. Murray, Byron O. "C. P. Snow: Grounds for Reappraisal." *Personalist,* 47 (January 1966), 91-101.

679. Neuman, Robert Roland. "Structure and Meaning in the Strangers and Brothers Novel Sequence of C. P. Snow." Diss. Marquette, 1973. *Dissertation Abstracts,* 34A (1973), 2646.

680. Newquist, Roy. *Counterpoint.* New York: Simon and Schuster, 1964, pp. 554-560.

681. Nott, Kathleen. "The Type to Which the Whole Creation Moves? Further Thoughts on the Snow Saga." *Encounter,* 18 (February 1962), 87-88, 94-97. Comments on Snow's *Science and Government,* and several of his novels:

682. Novak, Robert L. "The New Man, The Lewis Eliot Man: A Study of the Narrator in C. P. Snow's Novel Sequence, Strangers and Brothers." Diss. Oklahoma, 1972. *Dissertation Abstracts,* 33A (1972), 1175-1176.

683. O'Connor, Frank. "The Girl at the Gaol Gate." *Review of English Literature,* 1 (April 1960), 25-33. C. P. Snow's work is compared to the work of Irish novelist Mary Lavin.

684. —. *The Lonely Voice: A Study of the Short Story.* Cleveland and New York: The World Publishing Company, 1963, pp. 207-208. Comparison between C. P. Snow and Irish writers.

685. Olssen, E. A. "Plato, Sir Charles Snow and the Arts Profes-

sor." *Comment,* 3 (January 1962), 12-15.

686. P.H.S. "Grade One." *The* (London) *Times* (29 March 1971), p. 12. On the television series of the *Strangers and Brothers* sequence.

687. —. "Intellectuals go for EEC." *The* (London) *Times* (17 May 1971), p. 12. An account of Snow's favoring Great Britain's entry into the Common Market.

688. —. "Snow job." *The* (London) *Times* (11 August 1971), p. 10. An account of Snow's being interviewed in Russia. Snow discusses the advantages Russian writers have over English writers.

689. —. "Snow's TV saga." *The* (London) *Times* (12 August 1970), p. 6. An interview, in which Snow discusses negotiations then going on to do a television series of his *Strangers and Brothers* sequence.

690. —. "Steam ahead." *The* (London) *Times* (13 August 1970), p. 6. An account of B.B.C. Radio's plans to adopt Snow's *Strangers and Brothers* sequence to radio production.

691. —. "The gloom of Lord Snow." *The* (London) *Times* (27 September 1968), p. 10. A biographical sketch, supported with some quotes from Snow on contemporary life, and his work.

692. Panter-Downes, Mollie. "Letter from London." *New Yorker,* 38 (24 March 1962), 167-170, 173-174. Pp. 173-174. Discusses Snow-Leavis controversy.

693. Parkhill-Rathbone, James. "The 'gravitas' of C. P. Snow." *Books and Bookmen,* 17 (November 1971), 6-8.

694. Petelkin, G., and Ja. Simkin. *Carl'z Persi Snou, pisatel' i čelovek.* Rostov na Donu: University Press, 1963.

695. Pickrel, Paul. "Two Novelists: Outsider and Insider." *Harper's*, 230 (June 1965), 116-118. On Dreiser and Snow.

696. Putt, S. Gorley. "Technique and culture: three Cambridge portraits." *Essays and Studies 1961* (English Association), pp. 17-31. Snow is one of the three.

697. —. "The Snow-Leavis Rumpus." *Antioch Review*, 23 (Fall 1963), 299-313.

698. Quoodle. "The Two Cultures." *Spectator*, 214 (19 February 1965), 225. Comment on Snow's sending his son to Eton.

699. Rabinovitz, Rubin. "C. P. Snow vs. the Experimental Novel." *Columbia University Forum*, 10 (Fall 1967), 37-41.

700. Ramakrishnaiah, C. "Possessive Love in *Strangers and Brothers:* A Study of C. P. Snow's Use of the Principle of Resonance in Developing the Theme." *Indian Journal of English Studies*, 11 (1970), 112-121.

701. Richardson, Kenneth Ridley. "Snow, C. P." *Twentieth Century Writing: A Reader's Guide to Contemporary Literature.* Ed. Kenneth Richardson. London: Newnes Books, 1969, pp. 571-574.

702. Roberts, Catherine. "Nightingales, Hawks, and the Two Cultures." *Antioch Review*, 25 (1965), 221-238.

703. Rousseau, G. S. "Are There Really Men of Both Cultures?" *Dalhousie Review*, 52 (1972), 351-372.

704. Saal, Rollene. "Sir Charles P. Snow." *Saturday Review*, 43 (7 May 1960), 15. A biographical sketch of his life and work.

705. Schenck, Hilbert, Jr. "Revisiting the 'Two Cultures'."

The Centennial Review of Arts and Science (Michigan State), 8 (1964), 249-261.

706. Schuchart, Max. "De Romankunst van C. P. Snow." *Book Van Nu,* 13 (March 1960), 130-131.

707. Seehase, Georg. "Humanistische Möglichkeiten im Kritischen Realismus von Charles Percy Snow." *Zeitschrift für Anglistik,* 20 (1972), 119-130.

708. Seigel, L. "C. P. Snow." *Wilson Library Bulletin,* 28 (January 1954), 404.

709. Šestakov, D. "Dva romana Čarl'za Snou." *Novyj mir,* 39 (May 1963), 262-265.

710. Shahak, Israel. "The gene drain." *Spectator,* 222 (2 May 1969), 596. A negative response to Snow's belief that genes may account for genetic superiority.

711. Shestakov, Dmitri. "What C. P. Snow Means to Us." *Soviet Literature,* No. 1 (1966), pp. 174-179.

712. Simpson, M. S. "The Snow affair." *Bulletin of the Atomic Scientists,* 19 (April 1963), 28-32.

713. Smith, LeRoy W. "C. P. Snow as Novelist: A Delimitation." *South Atlantic Quarterly,* 64 (Summer 1965), 316-331.

714. Smith, Peter J. "The gene drain." *Spectator,* 222 (18 April 1969), 502. Includes comment on Snow's belief that genes may account for high achievement among Jews.

715. Spender, Stephen. *The Struggle of the Modern.* London: Hamish Hamilton, 1963, pp. 55-57, 58, 59, 64-67, 82, 119.

716. Stanford, Derek. "A disputed master: C. P. Snow and His

Critics." *Month,* 29 (February 1963), 91-94.

717. —. "C. P. Snow: The Novelist as Fox." *Meanjin,* 19 (September 1960), 236-251.

718. —. "Sir Charles and the Two Cultures." *Critic,* 21 (October-November 1962), 17-21.

719. Stanford, Raney. "Personal Politics in the Novels of C. P. Snow." *Critique,* 2, No. 1 (1958), 16-28.

720. —. "The Achievement of C. P. Snow." *Western Humanities Review,* 16 (Winter 1962), 43-52.

721. Strickland, Geoffrey. "The question of tone: reflections on the Leavis-Snow controversy." *Delta,* 30 (Summer 1963), 16-21.

722. Swinden, Patrick. "The World of C. P. Snow." *Critical Quarterly,* 15 (Winter 1973), 297-313.

723. Tasker, John. *The Richmond Lecture: its purpose and achievement.* Swansea: Brymill Publishers, 1972.

724. Thale, Jerome. "C. P. Snow: the Art of Worldliness." *Kenyon Review,* 22 (Fall 1960), 621-634.

725. —. *C. P. Snow.* Edinburgh and London: Oliver and Boyd, 1964; reprinted New York: Scribners, 1965.

726. Trilling, Lionel. "Science, Literature and Culture: a comment on the Leavis-Snow controversy." *Commentary,* 33 (June 1962), 461-477; reprinted as "The Leavis-Snow Controversy," in his *Beyond Culture.* New York: Viking Press, 1965, pp. 145-177. A Discussion of Trilling's ideas appears in *Commentary,* 34 (November 1962), 447-448.

727. Trocsányi, Miklós. "C. P. Snow." *Az angol irodalom a huszadik században.* 2 vols. Budapest: Gondolat, 1970,

II, pp. 57-76.

728. Trumper, C. M. "Lewis Eliot novels by C. P. Snow." *Ontario Library Review,* 66 (November 1962), 225-226.

729. Turner, Ian. "Above the Snow Line: The Sociology of C. P. Snow." *Overland,* 18 (August 1960), 37-43.

730. Vogel, Albert W. "The Academic World of C. P. Snow." *Twentieth Century Literature,* 9 (October 1963), 143-152.

731. Wagner, Geoffrey. "Writer in the Welfare State." *Commonweal,* 65 (12 October 1956), 49-50. Comments on the *Stranger and Brothers* sequence.

732. Wall, Stephen. "The Novels of C. P. Snow." *London Magazine,* n.s. 4 (April 1964), 68-74.

733. Warman, Christopher. "Lord Snow predicts catastrophe by AD 2000." *The* (London) *Times* (17 December 1970), p. 3. An account of Snow's ideas on the "food population collision."

734. Watson-Watt, R. "Truth about Churchill's aide: a rebuttal to the Godkin lectures by C. P. Snow at Harvard." *Saturday Review,* 44 (4 March 1961), 49-53. Discussion follows in *Saturday Review,* 44 (1 April 1961), 44-45.

735. Webster, Harvey C. "The sacrifices of success." *Saturday Review,* 41 (12 July 1958), 8-10 ff.

736. Wollheim, Richard. "London Letter." *Partisan Review,* 29 (Spring 1962), 263-269. On the Snow-Leavis controversy.

737. Wren-Lewis, John. "Ten years under Snow." *New Statesman,* 76 (19 September 1969), 386.

III. STUDIES AND REVIEWS OF
INDIVIDUAL WORKS

References to individual books by Snow also appear in the First Part of this bibliography. See the following numbers there: 3, 48, 68, 138, 173, 176, 179, 181, 195, 196, 203, 215, 224, 243, 248, 251, 253, 254, 260, 267, 273, 278, 281, 282, 283, 288, 297, 303, 311, 330, 336, 337, 340, 341, 345.

Death Under Sail

738. Anderson, Isaac. "New Mystery Stories." *New York Times Book Review* (16 October 1932), p. 21.

739. Anon. *"Death Under Sail."* TLS (11 August 1932), p. 570.

740. —. "New Novels." *New Statesman and Nation,* 4 (30 July 1932), 133-134. P. 134.

741. Cuppy, Will. "Mystery and Adventure: *Death Under Sail."* *New York Herald Tribune,* 9 (18 September 1932), 10.

742. McManis, Rumana. Review of *Death Under Sail,* in the *New York Evening Post* (17 September 1932), p. 7.

743. Partridge, Ralph. "Detection and Crime." *New Statesman,* 58 (31 October 1959), 599-600. P. 600.

744. Pym, Christopher. "It's a Crime." *Spectator,* 203 (9 October 1959), 492, 494. P. 494.

745. Review of *Death Under Sail,* in the *Boston Evening Tran-*

script (5 October 1932), p. 3.

The Search

746. Anon. *"The Search."* *Publishers' Weekly,* 192 (17 July 1967), 71.

747. —. *"The Search."* *TLS* (6 September 1934), p. 602.

748. —. "Troubled Scientist's Aims and Ambitions." *Springfield Sunday Union and Republican* (30 June 1935), p. 5e.

749. Benét, William Rose. "A Scientist's Story." *Saturday Review of Literature,* 11 (13 April 1935), 622.

750. Bien, Peter. "Novel of Scientists in the Twenties." *New York Herald Tribune Book Review,* 35 (18 January 1959), 5.

751. Bremner, Marjorie. "Crime Sheet." *Twentieth Century,* 167 (January 1960), 90-92. P. 91.

752. Gransden, K. W. "People and Power." *Encounter,* 11 (December 1958), 88-91. P. 91.

753. Hamilton, Alex. Review of *The Search,* in *Books and Bookmen,* 10 (March 1965), 35.

754. J. N., and D. N. Review of *The Search,* in *Nature,* 134 (8 December 1934), 890.

755. Kiefer, H. C. *"The Search."* *Arizona Quarterly,* 15 (Winter 1959), 363-364.

756. Kiley, Frederick S. Review of *The Search,* in *Clearing House* (February 1961), p. 379.

757. McDonough, James P. *"The Search."* *Best Sellers,* 18 (15

January 1959), 401-402.

758. Owen, Ivon M. *"The Search." Tamarack Review,* 12 (Summer 1959), 101-102.

759. Quennell, Peter. "New Novels." *New Statesman and Nation,* 8 (15 September 1934), 329.

760. Raven, Simon. "Three out of Four." *Spectator,* 201 (10 October 1958), 496-497. P. 497.

761. Review of *The Search,* in the *Wisconsin Library Bulletin,* 31 (July 1935), 93.

762. Sherman, Beatrice. *"The Search* and Some Other Recent Works of Fiction." *New York Times Book Review* (14 April 1935), p. 6.

763. Tilden, David. "Some Recent Leading Fiction: *The Search." New York Herald Tribune Books,* 11 (28 April 1935), 12.

764. W. E. H. Review of *The Search,* in the *Boston Evening Transcript* (5 June 1935), p. 2.

Strangers and Brothers

765. Anon. *"Strangers and Brothers." Booklist,* 57 (1 November 1960), 147.

766. —. *"Strangers and Brothers." Bookmark,* 20 (December 1960), 68.

767. —. *"Strangers and Brothers." Christian Century,* 78 (11 January 1961), 51.

768. —. *"Strangers and Brothers." Kirkus,* 28 (15 July 1960), 576.

769. —. *"Strangers and Brothers." TLS* (26 October 1940),

p. 541.

770. Chamberlain, John. "The Uncertain Rebels." *Wall Street Journal*, 156 (11 November 1960), 6.

771. Davis, Robert Gorham. "Facing One's Self is Part of the Trial." *New York Times Book Review* (25 September 1960), p. 5.

772. Dobrée, Bonamy. *"Fiction."* *Spectator*, 165 (8 November 1940), 484, 486. P. 486.

773. Geismar, Maxwell. "The Birth of a Sequence." *Saturday Review*, 43 (1 October 1960), 19.

774. Harding, Walter. Review of *Strangers and Brothers*, in the *Chicago Sunday Tribune* (2 October 1960), p. 8.

775. Hawkins, Desmond. "Home and Away." *New Statesman and Nation*, 20 (23 November 1940), 520.

776. Hutchens, J. K. Review of *Strangers and Brothers*, in the *San Francisco Chronicle* (13 October 1960), p. 37.

777. Klein, Marcus. "The Pride of Power." *New Leader*, 44 (2 January 1961), 26-27.

778. Millgate, Michael. *"Strangers and Brothers."* *Commentary*, 30 (July 1960), 76-79.

779. Nordell, Rod. "Serious Novels: Snow and Hersey Raise Some Questions." *Christian Science Monitor*, 52 (29 September 1960), 11.

780. Review of *Strangers and Brothers*, in the *Wisconsin Library Bulletin*, 57 (January 1961), 49.

781. Spector, Robert Donald. "No. 1 in a Modern Master's Chronicle." *New York Herald Tribune Book Review* (2 October 1960), p. 5.

782. Walsh, William J. *"Strangers and Brothers." Best Sellers,* 20 (15 October 1960), 263-264.

783. Wermuth, Paul C. *"Strangers and Brothers." Library Journal,* 85 (15 September 1960), 3106.

The Light and the Dark

784. Algren, Nelson. Review of *The Light and the Dark,* in the *Chicago Sunday Tribune* (17 February 1948), p. 25.

785. Allen, Walter. "New Novels." *New Statesman and Nation,* 34 (6 December 1947), 455-456. P. 456.

786. Anon. "Briefly Noted." *New Yorker,* 23 (21 February 1948), 90.

787. —. "C. P. Snow Book Ban in S. Africa." *The* (London) *Times* (12 April 1965), p. 10.

788. —. *"The Light and the Dark." Kirkus,* 15 (15 December 1947), 679.

789. —. "The Steerforth Tradition." *TLS* (8 November 1947), p. 573.

790. Chapman, Hester W. "Fiction." *Spectator,* 179 (21 November 1947), 662, 664.

791. Chase, John W. "A Special Melancholy." *New York Times Book Review* (29 February 1948), p. 16.

792. Doyle, E. D. Review of *The Light and the Dark,* in the *San Francisco Chronicle* (22 February 1948), p. 11.

793. Farrelly, John. "Love affair." *New Republic,* 118 (23 February 1948), 24-25.

794. Fausset, Hugh I'A. "New Novels." *Manchester Guardian*

(7 November 1947), p. 3.

795. Feld, Rose. "Doomed Young Scholar." *New York Herald Tribune Weekly Book Review*, 24 (22 February 1948), 4.

796. Johnson, Lucy. Review of *The Light and the Dark*, in the *Book-of-the-Month-Club News* (February 1961), p. 8.

797. Jones, Howard Mumford. "Doubting Don." *Saturday Review of Literature*, 31 (27 March 1948), 17.

798. Phillipson, John S. *"The Light and the Dark."* *Best Sellers*, 20 (15 February 1961), 438.

799. Wasson, Donald. *"The Light and the Dark."* *Library Journal*, 73 (15 February 1948), 337.

Time of Hope

800. Anon. "A Provincial Childhood." *TLS* (30 September 1949), p. 629.

801. —. "Briefly Noted." *New Yorker*, 36 (29 July 1950), 71-72.

802. —. "Fiction." *Saturday Review*, 49 (26 November 1966), 40.

803. —. *"Time of Hope."* *Kirkus*, 18 (1 June 1950), 313.

804. Bannon, Barbara A. "Forecast of Paperbacks." *Publishers' Weekly*, 189 (27 June 1966), 102.

805. Garrigue, Jean. "Fiction Parade." *New Republic*, 123 (16 October 1950), 21.

806. Gerhardi, William. "English Odyssey." *Spectator*, 183 (30 September 1949), 438, 440.

807. Hass, V. P. Review of *Time of Hope,* in the *Chicago Sunday Tribune* (6 August 1950), p. 3.

808. Hilton, James. "Englishman, Born in 1905." *New York Herald Tribune Book Review,* 26 (16 July 1950), 10.

809. Review of *Time of Hope,* in the *Christian Science Monitor* (22 July 1950), p. 8.

810. Scott, J. D. "New Novels." *New Statesman and Nation,* 38 (8 October 1949), 402, 404.

811. Siggins, Clara M. *"Time of Hope." Best Sellers,* 20 (15 February 1961), 438-439.

812. Smith, Harrison. "Ardent, Tortured Barrister." *Saturday Review of Literature,* 33 (15 July 1950), 11-12.

813. Spacks, Barry. "Implacable Hopes." *Saturday Review,* 44 (1 April 1961), 18.

814. West, Herbert F. "Sensitive Youth." *New York Times Book Review* (16 July 1950), p. 18.

815. Willis, Katherine Tappert. *"Time of Hope." Library Journal,* 75 (July 1950), 1181-1182.

The Masters

816. Anon. "Briefly Noted." *New Yorker,* 27 (10 November 1951), 144.

817. —. "Mantle of the Master." *TLS* (20 July 1951), p. 449.

818. —. "Millar-Snow Play at the Savoy." *The* (London) *Times* (6 May 1963), p. 6.

819. —. *"The Masters." Booklist,* 48 (15 October 1951), 58.

820. —. *"The Masters."* *Kirkus,* 19 (15 August 1951), 450.

821. Barr, Donald. "Fellows of Cambridge." *New York Times Book Review* (16 December 1951), p. 17.

822. Bernt, H. H. *"The Masters."* *Library Journal,* 76 (15 September 1951), 1421.

823. Bloomfield, Paul. "Some Novels." *Manchester Guardian* (27 July 1951), p. 4.

824. Dent, Alan. "At the Play." *Punch,* 244 (12 June 1963), 862. Review of the stage production.

825. Downing, Francis. Review of *The Masters,* in *Commonweal,* 55 (21 December 1951), 283.

826. Jones, H. M. Review of *The Masters,* in the *New York Herald Tribune Book Review* (28 October 1951), p. 5.

827. Laski, Marghanita. "New Novels." *Spectator,* 187 (20 July 1951), 106.

828. Latham, Earl. "The Managerialization of the Campus." *Public Administration Review,* 19 (Winter 1959), 48-57.

829. Lehan, Richard. "The Divided World: *The Masters* Examined." *Six Contemporary Novels: Six Introductory Essays in Modern Fiction.* Ed. William O. S. Sutherland. Austin, Texas: University of Texas Department of English, 1962, pp. 46-57.

830. Millar, Ronald. *The Masters. A Play...Based on the novel by C. P. Snow.* London: Samuel French, 1964.

831. Noon, William T. "Satire, Poison and the Professor." *English Review,* 11 (Fall 1960), 54-55.

832. Proctor, Mortimer R. "The Cult of Oxford." *The English University Novel.* Berkeley and Los Angeles: University

of California Press, 1957; London: Cambridge University Press, 1957, pp. 179-180.

833. Review of *The Masters,* in *School and Society,* 75 (5 January 1952), 15.

834. Rodger, Ian. "Drama: Cambridge and Celts." *Listener,* 60 (21 August 1958), 281, 283. P. 281. Review of R. D. Smith's radio broadcast of the novel.

835. Scott, J. D. "New Novels." *New Statesman and Nation,* 42 (4 August 1951), 134-135. P. 134.

836. Smith, Harrison. "The Problems of Intellect." *Saturday Review of Literature,* 34 (3 November 1951), 17.

The New Men

837. Anon. "Briefly Noted." *New Yorker,* 30 (29 January 1955), 80.

838. —. "Life Among the A-Scientists." *Nation,* 180 (5 March 1955), 206.

839. —. "Of Bureaucratic Man." *TLS* (27 May 1954), p. 296.

840. —. "Science and Politics." *The* (London) *Times* (1 May 1954), p. 8.

841. —. "The Bomb Kept Under Control. Strand Theatre: *The New Men.*" *The* (London) *Times* (7 September 1962), p. 15. On the stage version of the novel.

842. —. *"The New Men."* *Booklist,* 51 (15 January 1955), 226.

843. —. *"The New Men."* *Kirkus,* 22 (15 December 1954), 813.

844. Ashe, Geoffrey. "Neutralism." *Commonweal,* 61 (4 February 1955), 485-486.

845. Berryman, John. "Days of Crisis in the Great Experiment." *New York Times Book Review* (9 January 1955), pp. 4-5.

846. Crane, Milton. Review of *The New Men,* in the *Chicago Sunday Tribune* (9 January 1955), p. 3.

847. Gröger, Erika. "Der bürgerliche Atomwissenschaftler im englisch-amerikanischen Roman von 1945 bis zur Gegenwart." *Zeitschrift für Anglistik und Amerikanistik,* 16 (1968), 25-48.

848. Hobson, Harold. "The Saga of Lewis Eliot." *Christian Science Monitor,* 31 (13 January 1955), 7.

849. Hodgart, Patricia. "New Novels." *Manchester Guardian* (4 May 1954), p. 4.

850. Johnson, Pamela Hansford. "Modern Fiction and the English Understatement." *TLS* (7 August 1959), p. iii.

851. Krutch, Joseph Wood. "Moral Dilemma of the Atomic Scientist." *New York Herald Tribune Book Review,* 31 (9 January 1955), 4.

852. Metcalf, John. "New Novels." *Spectator,* 192 (14 May 1954), 600.

853. Price, R. G. G. *"The New Men." Punch,* 226 (26 May 1954), 649.

854. Rettger, T. L. Review of *The New Men,* in the *Chemical and Engineering News,* 33 (27 June 1955), 2764.

855. Romilly, Giles. "New Novels." *New Statesman and Nation,* 47 (1 May 1954), 573-574. P. 573.

* 856. Smith, Harrison. "Morality vs. the Atomic Monster." *Saturday Review,* 38 (8 January 1955), 9.

857. Stéphane, Nelly. "Des Hommes Nouveaux ou un Monde

Nouveau?" *Europe,* 48 (July 1970), 198-203.

858. Symons, Julian. "On Bureaucratic Man," in his *Critical Occasions* (see First Part No. 116), pp. 68-73.

859. W. H. *"The New Men." Twentieth Century,* 156 (July 1954), 96.

860. Walbridge, Earle F. *"The New Men." Library Journal,* 80 (1 January 1955), 69-70.

861. Watson, Kenneth. "C. P. Snow and *The New Men." English,* 15 (Spring 1965), 134-139.

Homecomings
or
Homecoming

862. Anon. "Briefly Noted." *New Yorker,* 32 (3 November 1956), 208-209.

863. —. "Corridors of Power." *TLS* (7 September 1956), p. 524.

864. —. "Galsworthy's Ghost." *Time,* 68 (8 October 1956), 116, 118.

865. —. *"Homecoming." Booklist,* 53 (15 October 1956), 94-95.

866. —. *"Homecoming." Bookmark,* 16 (November 1956), 37.

867. —. *"Homecoming." Kirkus,* 24 (15 September 1956), 718.

868. —. "New Fiction." *The* (London) *Times* (13 September 1956), p. 13.

869. Bremner, Marjorie. *"Homecomings." Twentieth Century,* 160 (December 1956), 582, 584-585.

870. Cosman, Max. "Voices of Power." *Nation,* 183 (8 December 1956), 504-505.

871. Cranston, Maurice. "The Immediate Sense of Ordeal." *New Republic,* 135 (8 October 1956), 18.

872. Engle, Paul. Review of *Homecoming,* in the *Chicago Sunday Tribune* (7 October 1956), p. 4.

873. George, Daniel. "New Novels." *Spectator,* 197 (14 September 1956), 362, 364. P. 362.

874. Glauber, Robert H. "C. P. Snow's Number Six." *New York Herald Tribune Book Review,* 33 (7 October 1956), 2.

875. King, Carlyle. "Fiction Chronicle." *Tamarack Review,* 2 (Winter 1957), 70-76. P. 70-71.

876. Maddocks, Melvin. "In the Corridors of Power." *Christian Science Monitor,* 48 (11 October 1956), 11.

877. Mayne, Richard. "Snow: Major Read Ahead!" *New Statesman and Nation,* 52 (22 September 1956), 350-352. Pp. 350-351.

878. Price, R. G. G. *"Homecomings." Punch,* 231 (3 October 1956), 415.

879. Review of *Homecoming,* in *Saturday Review,* 48 (23 October 1965), 63.

880. Shrapnel, Norman. "Long Snow." *Manchester Guardian* (11 September 1956), p. 4.

881. Smith, Harrison. "Love and Precision." *Saturday Review,* 39 (13 October 1956), 15.

882. Stewart, J. I. M. Untitled book review. *London Magazine,* 4 (January 1957), 71, 73.

* 883. Sykes, Gerald. "Portrait of a Public Man." *New York Times Book Review* (7 October 1956), pp. 5, 44.

The Conscience of the Rich

884. Anon. "A Question of Creeds." *TLS* (28 March 1958), p. 165.

885. —. "Breaking Away from the Family Circle." *The* (London) *Times* (27 March 1958), p. 13.

886. —. *"The Conscience of the Rich."* *Booklist,* 54 (1 April 1958), 445.

887. —. *"The Conscience of the Rich."* *Bookmark,* 17 (March 1958), 146.

888. —. *"The Conscience of the Rich."* *Kirkus,* 25 (1 December 1957), 877.

889. Bremner, Marjorie. *"The Conscience of the Rich."* *Twentieth Century,* 163 (June 1958), 386-388.

890. Cosman, Max. "Wealth and Rebellion." *Nation,* 186 (15 March 1958), 240.

891. Crane, Milton. Review of *The Conscience of the Rich,* in the *Chicago Sunday Tribune* (23 February 1958), p. 12.

* 892. Curran, Charles. "The Two Worlds of C. P. Snow." *New Republic,* 138 (2 June 1958), 17-18.

893. Davis, Robert Gorham. "The Marches of London." *New York Times Book Review* (23 February 1958), p. 4.

894. Gardner, Helen. "The World of C. P. Snow." *New Statesman,* 55 (29 March 1958), 409-410.

895. Glauber, Robert H. "No. 7 in C. P. Snow's Notable Series."

New York Herald Tribune Book Review, 34 (23 February 1958), 5.

896. Green, James. "Two Generations Between the Two World Wars." *Commonweal,* 68 (27 June 1958), 332.

897. Kermode, Frank. "Sophisticated Quest." *Spectator,* 200 (11 April 1958), 464.

898. Kiefer, H. C. *"The Conscience of the Rich."* *Arizona Quarterly,* 14 (Autumn 1958), 261-264.

899. Larnen, Brendan. *"The Conscience of the Rich."* *Best Sellers,* 17 (1 March 1958), 408.

900. Maddocks, Melvin. *"Conscience of the Rich."* *Christian Science Monitor,* 50 (27 February 1958), 11.

901. Podhoretz, Norman. "England, My England." *New Yorker,* 34 (10 May 1958), 143-146.

902. Price, R. G. G. *"The Conscience of the Rich."* *Punch,* 234 (23 April 1958), 554.

903. Quigly, Isabel. "A Problematic Lot." *Encounter,* 11 (July 1958), 92-93. P. 92.

904. Redman, Ray. "The Complexities of Sir Charles." *Saturday Review,* 41 (22 February 1958), 19.

905. Rolo, Charles. " 'The Recording Novel.' " *Atlantic,* 201 (April 1958), 94-95.

906. Shrapnel, Norman. "Whose Day and Age?" *Manchester Guardian* (1 April 1958), p. 4; reprinted in *Manchester Guardian Weekly,* 79 (10 April 1958), 10.

907. Walbridge, Earle F. *"The Conscience of the Rich."* *Library Journal,* 83 (15 February 1958), 609.

908. Wyndham, Francis. Untitled book review. *London Magazine,* 5 (June 1958), 70-74. Pp. 70-72.

The Affair

909. Anon. "Briefly Noted." *New Yorker,* 36 (28 May 1960), 141-142.

910. —. "Old Friends in New Roles." *TLS* (15 April 1960), p. 237.

911. —. "Play Based on Novel by C. P. Snow." *The* (London) *Times* (17 July 1961), p. 14.

912. —. "Psychological Action at High Table." *The* (London) *Times* (22 September 1961), p. 16. Review of the Strand Theatre's stage production of the novel.

913. —. "Some Uncertainty About *The Affair.*" *The* (London) *Times* (25 September 1962), p. 14. A review of the American reviews of the play performed at the Henry Miller Theatre in New York.

914. —. *"The Affair."* Booklist, 56 (1 June 1960), 602.

915. —. *"The Affair."* Bookmark, 19 (May 1960), 204.

916. —. *"The Affair."* Christian Century, 77 (5 October 1960), 1156, 1158.

917. —. *"The Affair."* Kirkus, 28 (1 February 1960), 108.

918. —. "The Corridors of Power." *Time,* 75 (16 May 1960), 103-104.

919. —. Untitled report. *The* (London) *Times* (22 December 1962), p. 6, col. 4. On why Snow's play had to close three weeks before its planned conclusion in New York.

920. Bergonzi, Bernard. "All Decent." *Spectator,* 204 (15 April

1960), 548-549.

921. Bremner, Marjorie. *"The Affair."* *Twentieth Century*, 168 (July 1960), 89-90.

922. Bryant, Donald C. Review of *The Affair*, in the *American Association of University Professors Bulletin* (March 1961), p. 70.

923. Butcher, Fanny. Review of *The Affair*, in the *Chicago Sunday Tribune* (8 May 1960), p. 22.

924. Clancy, Joseph P. "The Corridors of Power." *Commonweal*, 72 (13 May 1960), 184-186.

925. Davis, Robert Gorham. "Up for Trial was Justice Itself." *New York Times Book Review* (8 May 1960), pp. 1, 24.

926. Dennis, Nigel. "Under the Combination Room." *Encounter*, 17 (December 1961), 51-53.

927. Furbank, P. N. "New Novels." *Listener*, 63 (14 April 1960), 678.

928. Glass, Bentley. Review of *The Affair*, in *Science* (26 May 1961), p. 1698.

929. Hicks, Granville. "A Matter of Justice." *Saturday Review*, 43 (7 May 1960), 15, 66.

930. Hogan, William. Review of *The Affair*, in the *San Francisco Chronicle* (9 May 1960), p. 35.

931. Hollander, John. "Two Worlds, Two Generations." *New Republic*, 142 (30 May 1960), 17-19.

932. Kashcheeva, V. "Rannee tvorchestvo Ch. P. Snou. Roman Poiski." *Moskovskii gosudarstvennyi pedagogicheskii institut imeni Lenian*, 304 (1968), 170-188.

933. Keown, Eric. "At the Play." *Punch,* 242 (10 January 1962), 113. Review of the stage production of the novel.

934. Kermode, Frank. "Beckett, Snow, and Pure Poverty." *Encounter,* 15 (July 1960), 73-77. Pp. 76-77.

935. Kiefer, H. C. *"The Affair."* *Arizona Quarterly,* 16 (Autumn 1960), 276-277.

936. Lodge, Robert A. *"The Affair."* *Best Sellers,* 20 (1 June 1960), 90.

937. Millar, Ronald. *The Affair: A play in three acts...From the novel by C. P. Snow.* London: Samuel French, 1963; as *"The Affair:* dramatization of novel by C. P. Snow." *Theatre Arts,* 47 (March 1963), 25-56.

938. Miller, Karl. Review of *The Affair,* in the *Observer* (10 April 1960), p. 21.

939. Millgate, Michael. "Strangers and Brothers." *Commentary,* 30 (July 1960), 76-79.

940. Miner, Earl. "C. P. Snow and the Realistic novel." *Nation,* 190 (25 June 1960), 554-555.

941. Nelson, Bryce E. *"The Affair."* *Audit,* 1 (March 1961), 11-15.

942. Nordell, Rod. "A Question of Justice Among Men of Affairs." *Christian Science Monitor,* 52 (12 May 1960), 8B.

943. Owen, Ivon M. *"The Affair."* *Tamarack Review,* 17 (Autumn 1960), 75-77.

944. Price, R. G. G. "New Novels." *Punch,* 238 (13 April 1960), 530.

945. Spector, Robert Donald. "In Cambridge, a Modern Dreyfus

Case." *New York Herald Tribune Book Review*, 36 (8 May 1960), 5.

946. Steiner, George. "The Master Builder." *Reporter*, 22 (9 June 1960), 41-43.

947. Waterhouse, Keith. "New Novels." *New Statesman*, 59 (16 April 1960), 566.

948. Webb, W. L. "Chronicler of the intelligentry." *Manchester Guardian Weekly*, 82 (21 April 1960), 11.

949. —. "Chronicling the intelligentry." *Guardian* (14 April 1960), p. 10.

950. Weeks, Edward. "A Study in Justice." *Atlantic*, 205 (June 1960), 166-167.

951. Wermuth, Paul C. *"The Affair." Library Journal*, 85 (15 March 1960), 1144-1145.

Corridors of Power

952. Adams, Robert. "Pomp and circumstance: C. P. Snow." *Atlantic*, 214 (November 1964), 95-98.

953. Anon. "Briefing: *Corridors of Power." Observer* (30 October 1966), p. 22.

954. —. "Briefly Noted." *New Yorker*, 40 (7 November 1964), 243-244.

955. —. "Living Newspaper." *Newsweek*, 64 (14 September 1964), 94.

956. —. "New Fiction." *The* (London) *Times* (5 November 1964), p. 15.

957. —. "Of Men and Decisions." *Time*, 84 (18 September

1964), 118.

958. —. "Outsiders or Insiders?" *Economist,* 213 (14 November 1964), 710-711.

959. —. " 'Pravda' Quotes from C. P.Snow Book." *The* (London) *Times* (7 December 1964), p. 8.

960. —. "Professors: Two Cultures in the Corridors." *Time,* 84 (20 November 1964), 102.

961. —. "The Realism of the Worldly." *TLS* (5 November 1964), p. 993; reprinted in *T.L.S. Essays and Reviews from The Times Literary Supplement 1964.* London: Oxford University Press, 1965, pp. 100-103.

962. Balogh, Thomas. "Books of the Year." *Observer* (20 December 1964), p. 7.

963. Boyle, Sir Edward. "Sir Edward Boyle, a former Cabinet Minister, gives an insider's opinion of 'Corridors of Power'." *Observer* (1 November 1964), p. 27.

964. Brock, Clifton. *"Corridors of Power."* *Library Journal,* 89 (1 September 1964), 3187.

965. Brown, Jim. Review of *Corridors of Power,* in the *Book-of-the-Month Club News* (August 1964), p. 2.

966. Buckmaster, Henrietta. "How to 'Push on Open Doors'." *Christian Science Monitor,* 56 (17 September 1964), 11.

967. Carlin, M. M. "In Defence of Psnow." *Spectator,* 213 (20 November 1964), 675. A translation of a Swahili translation of a German translation of a Russian article on this novel.

968. Crews, Frederick C. "Private Lives, Public Lives." *New York Review of Books,* 3 (5 November 1964), 13-15. Pp. 14-15.

969. Curley, Daniel. "Satan is Missing." *New Leader*, 47 (7 December 1964), 24-25.

970. Dolbier, M. Review of *Corridors of Power*, in the *New York Herald Tribune Book Review* (14 September 1964), p. 19.

971. Dollen, Charles. *"Corridors of Power."* *Best Sellers*, 24 (15 September 1964), 221-222.

972. Enright, D. J. "Easy lies the head." *New Statesman*, 68 (6 November 1964), 698-699; reprinted in his *Conspirators and Poets*. Chester Springs, Pennsylvania: Dufour, 1966, pp. 106-110.

973. Faverty, F. Review of *Corridors of Power*, in *Books Today* (13 September 1964), p. 10.

974. Fuller, Edmund. "C. P. Snow Deals with Nuclear Age Dilemma." *Wall Street Journal*, 164 (15 September 1964), 18.

975. Hart, Jeffrey. "To Wield the Scepter." *America*, 111 (26 September 1964), 354.

976. Huston, M. Review of *Corridors of Power*, in *San Francisco Sunday Chronicle* (13 September 1964), p. 26.

977. Johnson, Lucy. "Arms and Men." *Progressive*, 28 (December 1964), 46-47.

978. Ludlow, George. "The power of C. P. Snow." *Time and Tide*, 5 (11 November 1964), 20.

979. Macdonald, Alastair. "The Failure of Success." *Dalhousie Review*, 44 (Winter 1964-1965), 494-500.

980. —. Untitled book review. *Queen's Quarterly*, 72 (Spring 1965), 205.

981. Muggerdige, Malcolm. *"Corridors of Power." The Critic as Artist.* Ed. G. A. Harrison. New York: Liveright, 1972, pp. 267-272.

982. —. "Oh No, Lord Snow." *New Republic,* 151 (28 November 1964), 27-29.

983. Pickrel, Paul. "Heading Toward Postcivilization: Novelist Laureate." *Harper's,* 229 (October 1964), 126, 128.

984. Prescott, Orville. "A Novel About England's 'Closed' Politics." *New York Times,* 113 (14 September 1964), 31.

985. Price, R. G. G. "New Novels." *Punch,* 247 (18 November 1964), 784.

986. Pryce-Jones, Alan. "A structure built for business, not for living." *Book Week,* 2 (13 September 1964), 5, 15.

987. Schlesinger, Arthur, Jr. "When the Movers Meet the Shakers, Lewis Eliot Listens In." *New York Times Book Review* (14 September 1964), pp. 4, 28.

988. Shils, Edward. "The Charismatic Centre." *Spectator,* 213 (6 November 1964), 608-609.

989. Steiner, George. "Never the Whole Truth." *Reporter,* 31 (8 October 1964), 50-52.

990. Taylor, A. J. P. "Dark Corridors." *New Statesman,* 68 (6 November 1964), 698.

991. Wall, Stephen. "New Novels." *Listener,* 72 (5 November 1964), 732.

992. Walsh, J. "C. P. Snow: *Corridors of Power* is a novel about nuclear policy and politics, closed and open." *Science,* 146 (9 October 1964), 234-236.

993. Waugh, Auberon. "Over-Privileged Intellectuals." *National Review,* 16 (6 October 1964), 870-871.

994. Weightman, John. "It's tough at the top." *Observer* (1 November 1964), p. 27.

995. Weintraub, S. Review of *Corridors of Power*, in *Books Abroad*, 39 (Spring 1965), 219.

996. Wilkie, Brian. "C. P. Snow's Latest." *Commonweal*, 81 (2 October 1964), 48-49.

997. Williams, Raymond. "Public and private lives." *Manchester Guardian Weekly*, 91 (12 November 1964), 10.

The Sleep of Reason

998. Anon. "Generation on Trial." *Time*, 93 (10 January 1969), 72.

999. —. "Monsters at Bay." *TLS* (31 October 1968), p. 1217; reprinted in *T.L.S. Essays and Reviews from The Times Literary Supplement, 1968*. London: Oxford University Press, 1969, pp. 175-177.

1000. —. *"The Sleep of Reason."* *Booklist*, 65 (15 February 1969), 639.

1001. —. *"The Sleep of Reason."* *Kirkus*, 36 (1 November 1968), 1246.

1002. —. *"The Sleep of Reason."* *Publishers' Weekly*, 194 (11 November 1968), 42.

1003. Borowitz, Albert I. "The Snows on the Moors." *American Scholar*, 40 (Fall 1971), 708, 710, 712, 714, 716, 718, 720, 722, 724, 726, 728, 730, 732. All pages but 718, 720.

1004. Bradbury, Malcolm. "As the rot sets in." *Guardian Weekly*, 99 (7 November 1968), 15.

1005. Corbett, Edward P. J. *"The Sleep of Reason."* *America*, 120 (8 February 1969), 173-174.

1006. Dawson, Helen. "Briefing: *The Sleep of Reason."* *Observer* (8 November 1970), p. 27.

1007. Derrick, Christopher. "You Get Carried Away." *Tablet*, 222 (14 December 1968), 1246, 1248.

1008. Fuller, Edmund. "C. P. Snow's Efforts to Keep Reason Awake." *Wall Street Journal*, 173 (13 January 1969), 12.

1009. Fuller, Roy. "Restricted Vision." *Listener*, 80 (31 October 1968), 538-539.

1010. Hicks, Granville. "Literary Horizons." *Saturday Review*, 52 (11 January 1969), 78-79.

1011. Hill, William B. *"The Sleep of Reason."* 28 (15 January 1969), 425-426.

1012. Hope, Francis. "Just how good is Snow?" *Observer* (3 November 1968), p. 30.

1013. Jackson, Katherine Gauss. *"The Sleep of Reason."* *Harper's*, 238 (February 1969), 102.

1014. Jellinek, Roger. "Ombudsman to the World." *New York Times*, 118 (11 January 1969), 31.

1015. Johnson, Robert D. *"The Sleep of Reason."* *Library Journal*, 94 (15 February 1969), 781-782.

1016. Lobdell, J. C. Untitled book review. *National Review*, 21 (25 February 1969), 191.

1017. Maddocks, Melvin. " 'Take It Off!' Cry the C. P. Snow Fans." *Life*, 66 (17 January 1969), 8.

1018. Marsh, Pamela. "Lewis Eliot lectures his times: Freedom vs. responsibility." *Christian Science Monitor,* 61 (16 January 1969), 11.

1019. Monod, Sylvère. *"The Sleep of Reason."* *Études Anglaises,* 23 (July-September 1970), 350-352. In French.

1020. Muggeridge, Malcolm. "Books." *Esquire,* 72 (March 1969), 51-52, 54, 56. Pp. 54, 56.

1021. Park, Clara Claiborne. "The Snows of yesteryear, updated." *Book World,* 3 (5 January 1969), 3.

1022. Review of *The Sleep of Reason,* in the *National Observer,* 8 (13 January 1969), 23.

1023. Richardson, Jack. *"The Sleep of Reason."* *New York Times Book Review* (19 January 1969), pp. 5, 35.

1024. Steiner, George. "Last Step for Mrs. Brown." *New Yorker,* 45 (12 July 1969), 83-86, 89-91.

1025. Tomalin, Claire. "Decencies." *New Statesman,* 76 (1 November 1968), 587.

1026. Trevor, William. "Lewis Eliot and the avenging age of freedom." *The* (London) *Times* (2 November 1968), p. 22.

Last Things

1027. Anon. "Islands in the river." *Economist,* 237 (21 November 1970), Autumn Survey, xvii.

1028. —. *"Last Things."* *Booklist,* 67 (15 September 1970), 83-84.

1029. —. *"Last Things."* *British Book News* (January 1971), p. 84.

1030. —. *"Last Things."* *Kirkus,* 38 (15 June 1970), 656.

1031. —. *"Last Things."* *Publishers' Weekly,* 197 (15 June 1970), 58.

1032. —. *"Last Things."* *Publishers' Weekly,* 200 (4 October 1971), 61.

1033. —. "The world of power and groups." *TLS* (23 October 1970), pp. 1223-1224.

1034. Bonnet, Jacky. *"Last Things:* Snow's Refusal of Man's Tragic Individual Condition." *Les Langues Modernes,* 66 (1972), 302-304.

1035. Bradbury, Malcolm. "Snow's Bleak Landscape." *New Statesman,* 80 (30 October 1970), 566-567; reprinted in his *Possibilities* (see First Part No. 16), pp. 201-210.

1036. Corbett, Edward P. J. *"Last Things."* *America,* 123 (22 August 1970), 100.

1037. Dawson, Helen. "Briefing: *Last Things."* *Observer* (5 November 1972), p. 35.

1038. Edelman, Maurice. "The cycle closes in Snow-land." *Life,* 69 (21 August 1970), 8.

1039. Fuller, Edmund. "C. P. Snow Concludes His Awesome Project." *Wall Street Journal,* 176 (24 August 1970), 6.

1040. Graves, Nora Calhoun. "Literary Allusions in *Last Things."* *Notes on Contemporary Literature,* 1 (January 1971), 7-8.

1041. Griffin, Lloyd W. *"Last Things."* *Library Journal,* 95 (July 1970), 2521.

1042. Hawkes, Peter. "The day thou gavest." *Spectator,* 225

(7 November 1970), 563-564.

1043. Hill, William B. *"Last Things."* *America,* 123 (28 November 1970), 464.

1044. —. *"Last Things."* *Best Sellers,* 30 (15 September 1970), 226-227.

1045. Jones, D. A. N. "Inconclusive." *Listener,* 84 (29 October 1970), 598-599. Response by C. P. Snow in *Listener,* 84 (12 November 1970), 663. Response to C. P. Snow and D. A. N. Jones by Morris Shapira in *Listener,* 84 (26 November 1970), 738. Response to Morris Shapira in *Listener,* 84 (10 December 1970), 817.

1046. Jones, Richard. "The End of the C. P. Snow Affair." *Atlantic Monthly,* 226 (September 1970), 112-117.

1047. Jones-Davies, Margaret. *"Last Things."* *Études Anglaises,* 25 (April-June 1972), 331-333. In French.

1048. LeCarre, John. "Vocation in a world of pain." (London) *Sunday Times* (25 October 1970), p. 27.

1049. Levenston, E. A. "Interrupted and Interruption Sentences." *English Studies,* 55 (October 1974), 409-420. Pp. 414-420.

1050. Maddocks, Melvin. "Lord of Limbo." *Time,* 96 (24 August 1970), 62.

1051. Mallet, Gina. "Boiler room in the ship of state." *Book World,* 4 (23 August 1970), 5.

1052. Morris, Robert K. "Thematic Skeletons Fleshed Out with Plot and Character." *Saturday Review,* 53 (22 August 1970), 43-45, 55.

1053. O'Connor, John J. "Suggestions for Christmas Book

Giving: *Last Things."* *Wall Street Journal,* 176 (8 December 1970), 22.

1054. Parker, Dorothy L. "A monument completed." *Christian Science Monitor,* 62 (27 August 1970), 11.

1055. Raymond, John. "Eliot comes through." *Financial Times* (22 October 1970), p. 27.

1056. Review of *Last Things,* in the *National Observer,* 9 (31 August 1970), 17.

1057. Saal, Rollene W. "Pick of the Paperbacks." *Saturday Review,* 53 (25 April 1970), 36.

1058. Scott, Paul. "No news from the other world." *The* (London) *Times* (22 October 1970), p. 8.

1059. Shapiro, Charles. "Political Fates." *Novel: A Forum on Fiction,* 5, No. 1 (Fall 1971), 87-89. Pp. 88-89.

1060. Shrapnel, Norman. "Great intimations." *Guardian Weekly,* 103 (31 October 1970), 19.

1061. Sokolov, Raymond A. "Strangers and Brothers." *Newsweek,* 76 (17 August 1970), 88, 90.

1062. Weightman, John. "End of the corridor." *Observer* (25 October 1970), p. 34.

1063. Weintraub, Stanley. "An elegiac ending to C. P. Snow's 11-novel cycle." *New York Times Book Review* (23 August 1970), pp. 4, 14, 16.

1064. —. *"Last Things:* C. P. Snow eleven novels after." *Mosaic,* 4, No. 3 (1971), 135-141.

1065. Wood, Michael. "End of the Line." *New York Review of Books,* 16 (11 March 1971), 41-44. Pp. 41-42.

The Malcontents

1066. Amis, Martin. "Generation gap." *Observer* (2 July 1972), p. 31.

1067. Anon. "Briefly Noted." *New Yorker,* 48 (13 May 1972), 145-146.

1068. —. "Paperbacks." *Observer* (22 June 1975), p. 23.

1069. —. "Reasonable revolutionaries." *TLS* (30 June 1972), p. 737.

1070. —. *"The Malcontents." British Book News* (September 1972), pp. 816-817.

1071. —. *"The Malcontents." Choice,* 9 (July-August 1972), 648.

1072. —. *"The Malcontents." Kirkus,* 40 (1 March 1972), 280.

1073. —. *"The Malcontents." Publishers' Weekly,* 201 (6 March 1972), 56.

1074. Blumberg, Myrna. "Moral Passports." *New Statesman,* 84 (7 July 1972), 26-27.

1075. Broyard, Anatole. "New Tricks for an Old Don." *New York Times,* 121 (26 April 1972), 43.

1076. Caute, David. "Snow blindness." *Guardian,* 107 (8 July 1972), 19.

1077. Frakes, J. R. "Sketches in poster-paints." *Book World,* 6 (7 May 1972), 13.

1078. Hill, William B. *"The Malcontents." Best Sellers,* 32 (15 May 1972), 95.

1079. Hobson, Harold. "Snow's Summer cloud." *Christian*

Science Monitor, 64 (17 May 1972), 13.

1080. Jones, D. A. N. "Fils à papa." *Listener*, 87 (29 June 1972), 873-874.

1081. Morris, Robert K. "C. P. Snow: Nevertheless." *Nation*, 214 (29 May 1972), 696-697.

1082. P. H. S. "Snow drifts." *The* (London) *Times* (14 December 1971), p. 12.

1083. Parker, Robert Anthony. *"The Malcontents."* *America*, 126 (10 June 1972), 618-619.

1084. Porterfield, Christopher. "Notable." *Time*, 99 (12 June 1972), 89-90.

1085. Review of *The Malcontents*, in the *New Leader*, 55 (29 May 1972), 16.

1086. Schlueter, Paul. "Unconvincing Radicals." *Christian Century*, 89 (1 November 1972), 1105-1107.

1087. Thwaite, Anthony. "In the comfortably ruminative Snow manner." *New York Times Book Review* (7 May 1972), p. 5.

1088. Waugh, Auberon. "C. P. Snow: shows promise." *Spectator*, 229 (8 July 1972), 54.

1089. Weber, Brom. *"The Malcontents."* *Saturday Review*, 55 (17 June 1972), 76-77.

1090. Weeks, Edward. *"The Malcontents."* *Atlantic*, 229 (June 1972), 110-111.

1091. Williams, David. "Good intentions on strange ground." *The* (London) *Times* (29 June 1972), p. 12.

In Their Wisdom

1092. Anon. "A matter of money." *TLS* (11 October 1974), p. 1109.

1093. —. "Briefly Noted." *New Yorker,* 50 (13 January 1975), 90.

1094. —. "Full fathom five..." *Economist,* 253 (30 November 1974), Autumn Survey, 4, 6-8. P. 8.

1095. —. *"In Their Wisdom." Booklist,* 71 (1 November 1974), 269.

1096. —. *"In Their Wisdom." Choice,* 12 (March 1975), 78.

1097. —. *"In Their Wisdom." Kirkus,* 42 (1 September 1974), 963.

1098. —.*"In Their Wisdom." Publishers' Weekly,* 206 (30 September 1974), 52-53.

1099. Crain, Jane Larkin. *"In Their Wisdom." Saturday Review,* 2 (11 January 1975), 26.

1100. Cunningham, Valentine. "Money Talks." *New Statesman,* 88 (18 October 1974), 546. Negative reply to the review by J. J. Dawtry in *New Statesman,* 88 (1 November 1974), 619.

1101. Fuller, Edmund. "Absorbing Battle Over a Man's Will." *Wall Street Journal,* 185 (28 January 1975), 16.

1102. Gray, Larry. *"In Their Wisdom." Library Journal,* 99 (1 November 1974), 2873.

1103. Hill, William B. *"In Their Wisdom." Best Sellers,* 34 (1 March 1975), 528-529.

1104. Jones, D. A. N. "In their enclaves." *New Review,* 1

(November 1974), 76.

1105. Maddocks, Melvin. "Cash and Curry." *Time,* 104 (25 November 1974), 123, E19.

1106. O'Hara, J. D. "C. P. Snow: Like Chinese water torture, the persistent drip of platitudes." *New York Times Book Review* (27 October 1974), p. 7.

1107. Oka, Takashi. "C. P. Snow's lovingly crafted new novel." *Christian Science Monitor,* 67 (30 January 1975), 10.

1108. Parker, Derek. "Fiction." *The* (London) *Times* (10 October 1974), p. 13.

1109. Parkhill-Rathbone, James. "The public and private faces of C. P. Snow." *Books and Bookmen,* 20 (March 1975), 55-56.

1110. Shrapnel, Norman. "Life and love above the Snow-line." *Guardian Weekly,* 111 (19 October 1974), 20.

1111. Story, Jack Trevor. "Lid off the Lords." *Listener,* 92 (10 October 1974), 482.

1112. Symons, Julian. *"In Their Wisdom."* *Critic,* 33 (March/ April 1975), 73.

1113. Thwaite, Anthony. "A matter of money." *Observer* (13 October 1974), p. 29.

1114. Weeks, Edward. *"In Their Wisdom."* *Atlantic,* 234 (December 1974), 124-125.

View Over the Park

1115. Anon. *"View Over the Park."* *The* (London) *Times* (31 August 1950), p. 6.

The Fool of the Family

1116. Anon. "Sir Charles Snow's Play with Mr. Gerhardi." *The* (London) *Times* (19 May 1964), p. 16.

The Two Cultures and the Scientific Revolution

1117. Allen, Walter, A. C. B. Lovell, J. H. Plum, David Riesman, Bertrand Russell, Sir John Cockcroft, and Michael Ayrton. " 'The Two Cultures': A Discussion of C. P. Snow's Views." *Encounter*, 13 (August 1959), 67-73.

1118. Allen, Walter. "Shorter Review." *New Statesman*, 57 (6 June 1959), 806.

1119. Anon. "Attack on the 'Two Cultures' of C. P. Snow: Work Criticized by Dr. Leavis." *The* (London) *Times* (1 March 1962), p. 12.

1120. —. "The Scientific Nightingale." *Spectator*, 211 (4 October 1963), 406-407.

1121. —. "The Two Cultures." *TLS* (22 May 1959), p. 305.

1122. —. *"The Two Cultures and the Scientific Revolution."* *Bookmark*, 19 (January 1960), 90.

1123. —. "Two cultures reaffirmed." *Scientific America*, 209 (December 1963), 67.

1124. Barnett, H. G. Review of *The Two Cultures and the Scientific Revolution*, in the *Northwest Review*, 3 (Summer 1960), 95-98.

1125. Bernal, J. D., Ian Parsons, Geoffrey Wagner, T. T. Roe, Michael Ayrton, Sarah Gainham, Peter Green, Remington Rose, A. M. Mimardiere, P. A. Bill, Margot C. Heinemann, J. Bodington, G. N. A. Guinness, J. F. L. Long, Oswald Harland, and Bernard Miles. "The Two

Cultures." *Spectator,* 208 (23 March 1962), 365-367.
A collection of letters on the Snow-Leavis controversy.

1126. Carr, W. I. "Literature and Society." *Caribbean Quarterly,* 7 (June 1962), 76-93.

1127. Clark, G. A. Review of *The Two Cultures and the Scientific Revolution,* in *Ethics,* 71 (October 1960), 72.

1128. Collins, Frederic W. "Where There is no Understanding." *New Republic,* 142 (11 April 1960), 17-18.

1129. Conquest, Robert, Lord Boothby, J. H. Plumb, Lovat Dickson, and Robert Harvey. "The Two Cultures." *Spectator,* 208 (30 March 1962), 395-396. A collection of letters on the Snow-Leavis controversy.

1130. Dixon, John R. "Two semantic cultures." *Etc.,* 23 (March 1966), 77-83.

1131. Editorial. "The Two Cultures." *Spectator,* 208 (30 March 1962), 387-388.

1132. Fallers, L. "C. P. Snow and the third culture." *Bulletin of the Atomic Scientists,* 17 (October 1961), 306-310. Discussion follows in vol. 18 (February 1962), 31-32.

1133. Gardiner, C. Wrey. " 'The Two Cultures.' " *Encounter,* 13 (July 1959), 87.

1134. Gerhardi, William, J. D. Scott, Dame Edith Sitwell, Lord Boothby, Susan Hill, Denis Lant, Stephen Toulmin, G. Reichardt, Anthony Storr, Ronald Millar, G. S. Fraser, Peter Jay, C. R. O. Jones, M. S. Deol, Sir Oliver Scott, Arnold L. Haskell, and Gavin Ewart. "Sir Charles Snow, Dr. F. R. Leavis, and The Two Cultures." *Spectator,* 208 (16 March 1962), 329-333.

1135. Green, Martin. "A literary defence of *The Two Cultures.*"

Critical Quarterly, 4 (Summer 1962), 155-162; reprinted *Kenyon Review*, 24 (Autumn 1962), 731-739; reprinted in his *Science and the Shabby Curate of Poetry*, pp. 1-30.

1136. —. "The Great Threat." *Commonweal*, 71 (12 February 1960), 552.

1137. Huxley, Julian. "The Two Cultures and Education." *Encounter*, 14 (June 1960), 91-93.

1138. Jurczak, Chester A. "Humanities or Science." *Duquesne Review*, 8 (Fall 1962), 3-11.

1139. Kreuzer, Helmut. "Literarische und Szientifische Intelligenz." *Sprache im Technischen Zeitalter*, No. 24 (October 1967), pp. 305-323; reprinted in *Literarische und naturwissenschaftliche Intelligenz: Dialog über die 'zwei Kulturen.'* Ed. Helmut Kreuzer, et. al. Stuttgart: Klett, 1969.

1140. Lekachman, Robert. "Some Reflections on Modern Ignorance." *Columbia University Forum*, 3 (Spring 1960), 27-30.

1141. Lengyel, E. "The two cultures and the abyss in between." *The Humanities in the age of science*. Ed. C. Angoff. Rutherford, New Jersey: Fairleigh Dickinson University Press, 1968, pp. 101-115.

1142. Maddox, John. "The Significance of C. P. Snow." *Guardian* (20 March 1962), p. 6.

1143. Maldonado Denis, Manuel. " 'Las dos cultures' de C. P. Snow." *Asomante*, 18, No. 3 (1962), 20-25.

1144. Marcus, Steven. "Intellectuals, Scientists, and the Future." *Commentary*, 29 (February 1960), 165-169.

1145. Nott, Kathleen. "Whose Culture?" *Listener*, 67 (12 April 1962), 631-632; 67 (19 April 1962), 677-678.

1146. Polanyi, Michael. " 'The Two Cultures.' " *Encounter,* 13 (September 1959), 61-64.

1147. Quoodle. *"Spectator's Notebook."* *Spectator,* 212 (21 February 1964), 237. On the Snow-Leavis controversy.

1148. Raimirez, J. Roland E. "The Rich and the Poor: Some Observations on C. P. Snow." *Duquesne Review,* 8 (Fall 1962), 16-22.

1149. Ray, Cyril. "Postscript..." *Spectator,* 208 (16 March 1962), 349-350. On the *Spectator's* publication of F. R. Leavis's attack on Snow's 'Two Cultures.'

1150. Read, Herbert. "Mood of the Month—X." *London Magazine,* 6 (August 1959), 39-43. Negative reply by C. P. Snow in *London Magazine,* 6 (October 1959), 57-59; a favorable reply immediately follows by Frederick Anyon, p. 59. Response by Herbert Read to C. P. Snow appears in *London Magazine,* 6 (November 1959), 73-74.

1151. Review of *The Two Cultures and the Scientific Revolution,* in the (Iowa) *Journalism Quarterly* (Autumn 1960), p. 608.

1152. Roskill, S. W., Richard Rees, Charles E. Raven, Robert Kabak, and Neville Denny. "The Two Cultures." *Spectator,* 208 (6 April 1962), 442. A collection of letters on the Snow-Leavis controversy.

1153. Shreiber, Kurt C. "C. P. Snow and Education for Tomorrow." *Duquesne Review,* 8 (Fall 1962), 13-15.

1154. Sisk, John P. "Writers and Scientists: The Two Cultures." *Ramparts,* 1 (September 1962), 17-22.

1155. Starbuck. "Sparking Plugs." *Spectator,* 211 (1 November 1963), 551.

1156. —. *"Spectator's* Notebook: Snowballing." *Spectator,* 208 (6 April 1962), 433. On the Snow-Leavis controversy over the 'Two Cultures.'

1157. Waddington, C. H. "Humanists and Scientists: A Last Comment on C. P. Snow." *Encounter,* 14 (January 1960), 72-73.

1158. Wilson, J. Tuzo. "Two Worlds of the Modern Mind That Seldom Meet." *New York Times Book Review* (3 January 1960), pp. 3, 14.

1159. Wollheim, Richard. "Grounds for Approval." *Spectator,* 203 (7 August 1959), 168-169.

Stories From Modern Russia
or
Winter's Tales 7

1160. Allen, Gay Wilson. "Reality in a Monolithic State." *Saturday Review,* 45 (7 April 1962), 28.

1161. Anon. "Briefly Noted." *New Yorker,* 38 (14 April 1962), 184.

1162. —. "New Fiction." *The* (London) *Times* (7 December 1961), p. 18.

1163. —. *"Winter's Tales 7."* *Booklist,* 58 (1 May 1962), 609.

1164. —. *"Winter's Tales 7."* *Kirkus,* 30 (15 February 1962), 194.

1165. —. "Without Fireworks." *Newsweek,* 59 (2 April 1962), 89.

1166. —. "Without Pretentions." *TLS* (8 December 1961), p. 877.

1167. Belknap, Robert L. Review of *Winter's Tales 7,* in the *Russian Review* (October 1962), p. 393.

1168. Blum, Julius. Review of *Winter's Tales 7,* in the *Slavic and East European Journal* (Summer 1964), p. 204.

1169. Bryden, Ronald. "With a Difference." *Spectaor,* 207 (15 December 1961), 908.

1170. Conquest, Robert. "Snow on their Boots." *London Magazine,* n.s. 1 (January 1962), 82-84.

1171. —. "The Snows and Burintern Solidarity." *New Leader,* 45 (11 June 1962), 24-25.

1172. FitzGibbon, Constantine. Review of *Winter's Tales 7,* in *Time and Tide* (14 December 1961), p. 2119.

1173. Friedberg, Maurice. Review of *Winter's Tales 7,* in the *Slavic Review* (March 1963), p. 179.

1174. Futrell, Michael. Untitled book review. *Listener,* 67 (25 January 1962), 185.

1175. Gross, John. "From Russia, with Love." *New Statesman,* 62 (15 December 1961), 931-932. P. 931.

1176. H. B. H. *"Stories From Modern Russia."* *Springfield Sunday Republican* (15 April 1962), p. 4D.

1177. Hayward, Max. "Facts of Soviet life and literature." *Guardian* (8 December 1961), p. 7.

1178. Janeway, Elizabeth. Review of *Winter's Tales 7,* in the *Chicago Sunday Tribune* (6 May 1962), p. 2.

1179. Lask, Thomas. "Books of The Times." *New York Times,* 111 (9 April 1962), 27.

1180. Lemon, Lee T. "From Many Places." *Prairie Schooner,*

36 (Summer 1962), 190-194. P. 192.

1181. Neiswender, Rosemary. *"Stories From Modern Russia: Winter's Tales 7."* Library Journal, 87 (15 March 1962), 1152-1153.

1182. Pisko, Ernest S. "Fair and Warmer?" *Christian Science Monitor,* 54 (19 April 1962), 7.

1183. Price, R. G. G. "New Fiction." *Punch,* 242 (3 January 1962), 79-80. P. 80.

1184. Review of *Winter's Tales 7,* in the *Wisconsin Library Bulletin,* 58 (July 1962), 240.

1185. Rugoff, Milton. "The 'Individual' vs. the 'System'." *New York Herald Tribune Books,* 38 (22 April 1962), 10.

1186. Slonim, Marc. "In Russia, At Long Last, It's Spring." *New York Times Book Review* (15 April 1962), pp. 1, 30-31. Pp. 30-31.

* 1187. Swetland, Anita. Review of *Winter's Tales 7,* in the *Humanist* (November-December 1962), p. 203.

Science and Government

1188. Anon. "A Partial View." *TLS* (14 April 1961), p. 226; reply by C. P. Snow, in *TLS* (21 April 1961), p. 249.

1189. —. "General." *New Yorker,* 37 (22 April 1961), 179-180.

1190. —. *"Science and Government."* Booklist, 57 (15 April 1961), 514.

1191. —. *"Science and Government."* Bookmark, 20 (April 1961), 168.

1192. Barraclough, Geoffrey. "Salesmen in Power." *Spectator,* 206 (14 April 1961), 521.

1193. Calder, Ritchie. "Clash of Titans." *Nation,* 192 (15 April 1961), 323-324.

1194. Cowen, Robert C. "C. P. Snow on Natural Science and Public Policy: Beware 'the Euphoria of Gadgets; the Euphoria of Secrets'." *Christian Science Monitor,* 53 (6 April 1961), 9.

1195. Crossman, R. H. S. "Secret Decisions." *Encounter,* 16 (June 1961), 86-90. Response made by Robert Strausz-Hupé. *Encounter,* 17 (August 1961), 85.

1196. Deininger, Whitaker T. "Unsilent Snow." *Christian Century,* 78 (7 June 1961), 712-713.

1197. Harrison, Gordon. "A Scientific Duel and Its Moral." *New York Herald Tribune Book Review,* 37 (9 April 1961), 29.

1198. Jenkins, O. Review of *Science and Government,* in the *Carleton Miscellany,* 2 (Summer 1961), 104-109.

1199. Johnson, Paul. "Jupiter Complex." *New Statesman,* 61 (7 April 1961), 549-550.

1200. Jones, M. Review of *Science and Government,* in *Science and Society,* 26 (Winter 1962), 58-63.

1201. Lekachman, Robert. Review of *Science and Government,* in the *Political Science Quarterly,* 76 (September 1961), p. 465.

1202. Lewis, J. D. Review of *Science and Government,* in the *American Political Science Review,* 55 (December 1961), 912.

1203. Maddox, John. "The Higher Politics of Science." *Man-*

chester Guardian Weekly, 84 (13 April 1961), 10.

1204. Moon, Eric. *"Science and Government." Library Journal,* 86 (15 May 1961), 1894.

1205. Perlman, David. Review of *Science and Government,* in the *San Francisco Chronicle* (16 April 1961), p. 22.

1206. Review of *Science and Government,* in *Foreign Affairs,* 39 (July 1961), 697.

1207. Review of *Science and Government,* in the *Wisconsin Library Bulletin,* 57 (July 1961), 242.

1208. Strauss, Lewis L. "Who Should Have Power to Decide?" *New York Times Book Review* (2 April 1961), pp. 1, 14.

1209. Weeks, Edward. "Decision Makers." *Atlantic,* 207 (April 1961), 108.

1210. Weisberger, B. A. Review of *Science and Government,* in the *Chicago Sunday Tribune* (2 April 1961), p. 3.

A Postscript to Science and Government

1211. Anon. "Two-World Communication." *TLS* (27 July 1962), p. 535.

1212. Hengist, Philip. "Accomodation Through Mutual Terror." *Punch,* 243 (12 December 1962), 875.

1213. Toulmin, Stephen. "Scientist-Overlord." *Spectator,* 209 (27 July 1962), 104-105.

Two Cultures: and, A Second Look

1214. Anon. "Snow's Second Look." *New Statesman,* 67 (6

March 1964), 370-371.

1215. —. *"The Two Cultures: and A Second Look."* TLS (3 July 1969), p. 738.

1216. Bartley, Robert. "C. P. Snow's New-Found Optimism." *Wall Street Journal,* 163 (22 May 1964), 10.

1217. Fairlie, Henry. "Cults not Cultures." *Spectator,* 211 (1 November 1963), 554.

1218. Kemeny, John G. "The Tower of Babel revisited." *Book Week,* 2 (1 November 1964), 14.

1219. Review of *The Two Cultures: and, A Second Look,* in *Scientific American,* 210 (June 1964), 134.

1220. Walsh, J. "C. P. Snow: second thoughts on the two cultures likely to keep the pot boiling." *Science,* 142 (8 November 1963), 653-654.

Variety of Men

1221. Adams, J. Donald. "Characterized by Singularity." *Saturday Review,* 50 (27 May 1967), 34.

1222. Agius, Ambrose. *"Variety of Men."* *Best Sellers,* 27 (1 May 1967), 60-61.

1223. Angoff, Allan. *"Variety of Men."* *Library Journal,* 92 (15 March 1967), 1151.

1224. Anon. "Books: A Guide for Christmas Giving—*Variety of Men."* *Wall Street Journal,* 170 (4 December 1967), 20.

1225. —. "Nine Characters Find an Author." *TLS* (18 May 1967), p. 411.

1226. —. *"Variety of Men."* *Booklist,* 63 (1 July 1967), 1130.

1227. —. *"Variety of Men."* *Kirkus,* 35 (1 March 1967), 327.

1228. —. *"Variety of Men."* *New Yorker,* 43 (27 May 1967), 152.

1229. —. *"Variety of Men."* *Publishers' Weekly,* 191 (13 February 1967), 70.

1230. —. "Voyeurs of Power." *Economist,* 223 (27 May 1967), 919.

1231. Bates, Lewis. "The Future-Makers." *Punch,* 252 (24 May 1967), 773.

1232. Bedient, Calvin. "The Gaze Behind the Lens." *Nation,* 205 (17 July 1967), 59-60. P. 60.

1233. Cockburn, Claud. "Mates." *New Statesman,* 73 (26 May 1967), 721-722. P. 722.

1234. Comfort, Alex. "Snow men." *Manchester Guardian Weekly,* 96 (25 May 1967), 10.

1235. D. W. "Portrait Galleries." *Tablet,* 221 (24 June 1967), 695-697.

1236. Fuller, Edmund. "C. P. Snow Discusses Nine Men of History." *Wall Street Journal,* 169 (18 May 1967), 16.

1237. Hook, Sidney. Review of *Variety of Men,* in the *New Leader,* 50 (28 August 1967), 16.

1238. Igoe, W. J. Review of *Variety of Men,* in *Books Today,* 4 (28 May 1967), 3.

1239. Maddocks, Melvin. "Behind the Scenes at Snow's Power-ama." *Life,* 62 (5 May 1967), 10.

1240. Maloff, Saul. "Living with Spin." *Newsweek,* 69 (24 April 1967), 101A, 102.

1241. Manthorne, Jane. *"Variety of Men."* *Horn Book,* 43 (December 1967), 769.

1242. Martin, Kingsley. "Influences and others." *Listener,* 77 (8 June 1967), 754, 756. P. 756.

1243. Muggeridge, Malcolm. "Mr. Worldly Wiseman." *Observer* (21 May 1967), p. 26.

1244. Nordell, Roderick. "Snapshots from one man's album." *Christian Science Monitor,* 59 (4 May 1967), B11.

1245. Review of *Variety of Men,* in *Catholic Library World,* 39 (November 1967), 237.

1246. Review of *Variety of Men,* in the *National Observer,* 6 (5 June 1967), 21.

1247. Ryan, A. P. "Mad Dons and Clergymen." *The* (London) *Times* (18 May 1967), p. 15.

1248. Taylor, A. J. P. "Old Men Remember." *New York Review of Books,* 9 (3 August 1967), 14-17. Pp. 15-17.

1249. Turner, Arthur C. "Ten from Three Worlds." *New York Times Book Review* (23 April 1967), p. 3.

1250. Wain, John. "E Pluribus Unum." *New Republic,* 156 (27 May 1967), 25-26, 28.

1251. Waugh, Auberon. "Men of Power." *Spectator,* 218 (16 June 1967), 709-710.

The State of Siege

1252. Anon. *"The State of Siege."* *Booklist,* 66 (1 September

1969), 14-15.

1253. —. *"The State of Siege."* Choice, 7 (April 1970), 264.

1254. —. *"The State of Siege."* Kirkus, 37 (1 March 1969), 293.

1255. —. *"The State of Siege."* Publishers' Weekly, 195 (17 March 1969), 53.

1256. Garrett, T. M. *"The State of Siege."* Best Sellers, 29 (15 June 1969), 125.

1257. Haseltine, R. W. *"The State of Siege."* Library Journal, 94 (15 May 1969), 1975.

1258. Mudrick, Marvin. "The End of the World or Else." *Hudson Review*, 22 (Fall 1969), 551-560. Pp. 555-556.

1259. Review of *The State of Siege*, in *Christian Century*, 86 (21 May 1969), 713.

1260. Review of *The State of Siege*, in *Science Books*, 5 (December 1969), 203.

Public Affairs

1261. Anon. "It's that culture-gap again." *TLS* (19 November 1971), p. 1448.

1262. —. *"Public Affairs."* Booklist, 68 (15 January 1972), 405.

1263. —. *"Public Affairs."* British Book News (March 1972), pp. 186-187.

1264. —. *"Public Affairs."* Choice, 9 (March 1972), 133.

1265. —. *"Public Affairs."* Kirkus, 39 (1 September 1971), 1008.

1266. —. *"Public Affairs."* Publishers' Weekly, 200 (20 September 1971), 46.

1267. Boytinck, Paul W. *"Public Affairs."* Library Journal, 96 (1 December 1971), 4018.

1268. Casey, John. "Snowballs." Spectator, 227 (27 November 1971), 770-772.

1269. Clairborne, Robert. *"Public Affairs."* New York Times Book Review (26 December 1971), pp. 2-3, 13.

1270. Crick, Bernard. "The More It Snows." New Statesman, 82 (29 October 1971), 591-592.

1271. Dunn, John. "Science and C. P. Snow." Listener, 86 (11 November 1971), 656-657.

1272. Fishlock, David. "Moguls at Work." Financial Times (28 October 1971), p. 34.

1273. Fuller, Edmund. "Lord Snow's Humane Advices." Wall Street Journal, 179 (3 January 1972), 6.

1274. Hampshire, Stuart. "Priorities of progress." Observer (31 October 1971), p. 32.

1275. —. "Suspect Sages." New York Review of Books, 19 (21 September 1972), 12-13.

1276. McAleer, John J. *"Public Affairs."* Best Sellers, 31 (15 January 1972), 465.

1277. March, R. H. Review of Public Affairs, in the Bulletin of the Atomic Scientists, 28 (March 1972), 133.

1278. Review of Public Affairs, in Science Books, 8 (May

1972), 13.

1279. Steiner, George. "Imagining Science." *Listener,* 86 (18 November 1971), 686-688.

1280. Weintraub, Stanley. "A Sage's Summa." *New Republic,* 165 (27 November 1971), 23-25.

Trollope

1281. Anon. *"Trollope."* *British Book News* (January 1976), pp. 61-62.

1282. —. *"Trollope: His Life and Art."* *Kirkus,* 43 (15 September 1975), 1110.

1283. —. *"Trollope: His Life and Art."* *New Yorker,* 51 (12 January 1976), 91.

1284. —. *"Trollope: His Life and Art."* *Publishers' Weekly,* 208 (20 October 1975), 68.

1285. Barber, John. "Drama from the melting Snow." *Daily Telegraph Magazine* (10 March 1975), p. 9.

1286. Brookes, Gerry H. "Trollope Illustrated." *Prairie Schooner,* 50 (Summer 1976), 182-183.

1287. Cary, Cecile Williamson. *"Trollope: His Life and Art."* *Antioch Review,* 34 (Spring 1976), 374-375.

1288. Dennis, Nigel. "Keeping the Secret." *New York Review of Books,* 22 (11 December 1975), 34-35.

1289. Fuller, Edmund. "Fresh Recognition for an Enduring Author." *Wall Street Journal,* 186 (15 December 1975), 12.

1290. Gersh, Gabriel. *"Trollope: His Life and Art."* *Western*

Humanities Review, 30 (Spring 1976), 175-177.

1291. Green, Benny. "Snow bound." *Spectator,* 235 (18 October 1975), 511.

1292. Miller, J. Hillis. "The Truth About Trollope." *Yale Review,* 65 (Spring 1976), 450-455.

1293. Raban, Jonathan. "The Secrets of Survival." *New Statesman,* 90 (24 October 1975), 505-506.

1294. Review of *Trollope,* in *Book World* (31 August 1975), p. 2.

1295. Review of *Trollope,* in the *Guardian Weekly,* 113 (26 October 1975), p. 27.

1296. Review of *Trollope,* in the *New Republic,* 173 (25 October 1975), 30.

1297. Wade, Rosalind. "A Fresh Assessment of Trollope." *Contemporary Review,* 228 (February 1976), 108-109.

1298. Wall, Stephen. "Snow's Trollope." *Observer* (19 October 1975), p. 27.

1299. Wildman, John Hazard. "Trollope: Reemphasis of a Reputation." *Southern Review,* 12 (April 1976), 419-421.

MURIEL [SARAH] SPARK
(Born in Edinburgh 1918)

I. PRIMARY WORKS: NOVELS

1. *The Comforters.* London: Macmillan, 1957; Philadelphia, Pennsylvania: Lippincott, 1957; Harmondsworth: Penguin, 1963; New York: Avon, 1965; as *Die Tröster.* Trans. Peter Naujack. Zürich: Diogenes Verlag, 1963; also Berlin: Ullstein, 1968.

2. *Robinson.* London: Macmillan, 1958; Philadelphia, Pennsylvania: Lippincott, 1958, 1963; New York: Avon, 1964, 1969; Harmondsworth: Penguin, 1964; as *Robinson.* Trans. Elizabeth Gilbert. Zürich: Diogenes Verlag, 1962; also Frankfurt: Ullstein, 1967; as *Robinson.* Trans. Cármen Cienfuegos. Santiago: Zig-Zag, 1969; as *Mr. Robinson.* Trans. Mária Borbás. Budapest: Kozmosz, 1972.

3. *Memento Mori.* London: Macmillan, 1959; Philadelphia, Pennsylvania: Lippincott, 1959; New York: Time, Inc., 1959, 1964; New York: Meridian Books, 1960; Harmondsworth: Penguin, 1961; New York: Avon, 1966, 1971, 1973; as *Memento Mori.* Trans. Peter Naujack. Zürich: Diogenes Verl, 1960, 1972; also Frankfurt and Hamburg: Fischer Bucherei, 1963; also Stuttgart and Hamburg: Bücherbund, 1964; as *Memento Mori.* Trans. Christopher Maaløe. Copenhagen: Schønberg, 1960; as *Memento Mori.* Trans. Ingebourg von Rosen. Stockholm: Norstedt, 1960; as *Memento Mori.* Trans. Augusta Mattioli. Milano: A. Mondadori, 1963; as *Memento Mori.* Trans. Ilona Róna. Budapest: Európa Kiadó,

1963; as *Memento Mori.* Trans. Katje Vranken. Amsterdam: Contact, 1963, 1968; as *Memento Mori.* Trans. Magdeleine Paz. Paris: R. Laffont, 1964; as *Memento Mori.* Trans. J. B. Cuyás Boira. Andorra la Vella: Andorra, 1969; as *Memento Mori.* Trans. Krystyna Tarnowska. Warsaw: Państw. Instytut Wydawn, 1970; as *Memento Mori.* Trans. Peter Naujack. Wels (Austria): Welsermühl, 1972.

4. *The Ballad of Peckham Rye.* London: Macmillan, 1960; Philadelphia, Pennsylvania: Lippincott, 1960; Harmondsworth: Penguin, 1963, 1970; with *The Comforters* and *Memento Mori* as *A Muriel Spark Trio.* Philadelphia, Pennsylvania: Lippincott, 1962; with *The Bachelors* as *Two by Muriel Spark.* New York: Dell, 1964; with *Memento Mori.* New York: Modern Library, 1966; as *Die Ballade von Peckham Rye.* Trans. Elisabeth Schnack. Zürich: Diogenes Verlag, 1961, 1974; as *Balladen om Djävulens Sändebud.* Trans. Ingebourg von Rosen. Stockholm: Norstedt, 1965; as *Balladen om Djäevelens Sendebud.* Trans. Christopher Maaløe. Copenhagen: Spektrum, 1967; as *Balada Z Předměstí.* Trans. Heda Kovályová. Prague: Odeon, 1970.

5. *The Bachelors.* London and Toronto: Macmillan, 1960; New York: St. Martin's Press, 1960; Philadelphia, Pennsylvania: Lippincott, 1961; Harmondsworth: Penguin, 1963; as *Junggesellen.* Trans. Elisabeth Schnack. Zürich: Diogenes Verlag, 1961; also Reinbek: Rowohlt, 1968; as *De Vrijgezellen.* Amsterdam: Contact, 1962, 1963, 1967; also Amsterdam: Querido, 1966, 1969; as *Dokushinsha.* Trans. Akio Kudo. Tokyo: Shinchôsha, 1962; as *Ungkarlarna.* Trans. Ingebourg von Rosen. Stockholm: Norstedt, 1962.

6. *The Prime of Miss Jean Brodie.* London and Toronto: Macmillan, 1961; Philadelphia, Pennsylvania: Lippincott, 1962; New York: Dell, 1964, 1966; Harmondsworth: Penguin, 1965, 1969; as *Die lehrerin.* Trans. Peter Naujack. Zürich: Diogenes Verlag, 1962; also Reinbek and

Hamburg: Rowohlt, 1969; as *Le bel âge de Miss Brodie.* Trans. Magdeleine Paz. Paris: R. Laffont, 1962; as *Miss Jean Brodies Bästa År.* Trans. Ingebourg von Rosen. Stockholm: Norstedt, 1963; also Stockholm: Vingförl, 1964; as *Gli anni in fiore della Signorina Brodie.* Trans. Ida Omboni. Verona: A. Mondadori, 1964; as *Juffrouw Brodies Beste Jaren.* Trans. W. A. C. Whitlau. Amsterdam and Antwerp: Contact, 1965; as *El Punt Dolc de la Senyoreta Brodie.* Trans. Manuel de Pedrolo. Barcelona: Edicions 62, 1967; as *La Primavera de Una Solterona.* Trans. Augusto Gubler. Santiago: Zig-Zag, 1969; as *Pelnia Zycia Panny Brodie.* Trans. Zofia Uhrynowska. Warsaw: Panst. Inst. Wydawn, 1972.

7. *The Girls of Slender Means.* London and Toronto: Macmillan, 1963; New York: Knopf, 1963; New York: St. Martin's Press, 1963; New York: Avon, 1963; Harmondsworth: Penguin, 1966, 1975; with *Memento Mori.* London: Reprint Society, 1965; as *Mädchen mit begrenzten moglich Keiten.* Trans. Kyra Stromberg. Reinbek and Hamburg: Rowohlt, 1964, 1970; as *Ubemidlede piker fra gode hjem.* Trans. Carl Frederik Prytz. Oslo: Gyldendal, 1964; as *Fattiga Flickor.* Trans. Ingebourg von Rosen. Stockholm: Norstedt, 1964; as *Les demoiselles de petite fortune.* Trans. Magdeleine Paz. Paris: R. Laffont, 1965; as *Le ragazze di pochi mezzi.* Trans. Luisa Pantaleoni. Milano and Verona: A. Mondadori, 1966; as *Meisjes Met Een Smalle Beurs.* Trans. Katja Vranken. Amsterdam and Antwerp: Contact, 1966; as *Piger I Trange Kår.* Trans. Christopher Maaløe. Copenhaen: Spektrum, 1968; as *Las señoritas de escasos medios.* Trans. Andres Bosch. Barcelona: Editorial Lumen, 1968.

8. *The Mandelbaum Gate.* London and Toronto: Macmillan, 1965; New York: Knopf, 1965; Harmondsworth: Penguin, 1967, 1970; as *La porta di Mandelbaum.* Trans. Ettore Capriolo. Milano: A. Mondadori, 1966; also Milano: Club degli editori, 1967; as *Mandelbaumporten.* Trans. Olov Jonason. Helsingfors (Sweden): H. Schildts,

1966; also Stockholm: Norstedt, 1966; as *Mandelbaum—Porten.* Trans. Mogens Boisen. Copenhagen: Spektrum, 1966; as *Mandelbaumin Portti.* Trans. Juhani Jaskari. Porvoo and Helsinki: Werner Söderström, 1966; as *De Mandelbaumpoort.* Trans. H. W. J. Schaap. Amsterdam: Contact, 1966, 1969; as *Das Mandelbaumtor.* Reinbek and Hamburg: Rowohlt, 1967; as *La porte Mandelbaum.* Trans. Pierre Marly, Marie-Christine and Robert Mengin. Paris: Buchet-Chastel, 1968.

9. *The Public Image.* London: Macmillan, 1968; New York: Knopf, 1968; Harmondsworth: Penguin, 1970; as *In den Augen der Öffentlichkeit.* Trans. Christian Ferber. Reinbek and Hamburg: Rowohlt, 1968; as *L'image publique.* Trans. Marie-Christine and Robert Mengin. Paris: Buchet-Chastel, 1969; as *I Publikum Øjne.* Trans. Christopher Maaløe. Copenhagen: Gyldendal, 1969; as *De Image van een Filmster.* Trans. H. W. J. Schaap. Amsterdam: Contact, 1969; as *Ansiktet Utåt.* Trans. Ingebourg von Rosen. Stockholm: Norstedt, 1969; as *La imagen pública.* Trans. Andrés Bosch. Barcelona: Editorial Lumen, 1970; as *Lice Za Publikata.* Trans. Zivko Kefalov. Sofia (Bulgaria): Nar. Kultura, 1971; as *A Közönség Bálványa.* Trans. Istvan Bart. Budapest: Európa Kiadó, 1971; as *Na Publika.* Trans. V. Murav'ev, et. al. Moscow: Mol. gvardija, 1971.

10. *The Driver's Seat.* London: Macmillan, 1970; New York: Knopf, 1970; Harmondsworth: Penguin, 1974; New York: Bantam, 1975; as *Identikit:* Trans. Masolino d'Amico. Milano: Bompiani, 1971; as *Førersaedet.* Trans. Christopher Maaløe. Copenhagen: Gyldendal, 1971; as *Förarsätet.* Trans. Erik Sandin. Stockholm: Norstedt, 1971; as *Untenseki.* Trans. Fukamachi Mariko. Tokyo: Hayakawa shobô, 1972.

11. *Not to Disturb.* London: Macmillan, 1971; New York: Viking Press, 1972; Harmondsworth: Penguin, 1974.

12. *The Hothouse by the East River.* London: Macmillan,

1973; New York: Viking Press, 1973.

13. *The Abbess of Crewe.* London: Macmillan, 1974; New York: Viking Press, 1974.

14. *The Takeover.* London: Macmillan, 1976; New York: Viking, 1976.

PRIMARY WORKS: SHORT STORIES

15. "Ladies and Gentlemen." *Chance,* No. 3 (April 1953); reprinted *Transatlantic Review,* 9 (Spring 1962), 107-114; reprinted *Harper's,* 231 (July 1965), 60-64.

16. *The Go-Away Bird and Other Stories.* London: Macmillan, 1958; Philadelphia, Pennsylvania: Lippincott, 1960, 1961; Harmondsworth: Penguin, 1963; as *Der Seraph und der Sambesi und andere Erzahlungen.* Trans. Peter Naujack and Elisabeth Schnack. Zurich: Diogenes Verlag, 1963; as *Tachisare Tori.* Trans. Ebizuka Hiroshi. Tokyo: Sakai shoten, 1966; with other short stories by Spark, as *De Zwarte Madonna en andere Verhalen.* Trans. Johan and Frans Van der Woude. Amsterdam: Contact, 1970.

Contents: "The Black Madonna"—"The Pawnbroker's Wife"—"The Twins"—"Miss Pinkerton's Apocalypse"— " 'A Sad Tale's Best for Winter' "—"The Go-Away Bird" —"Daisy Overend"—"You Should Have Seen the Mess"— "Come Along, Marjorie"—"The Seraph and the Zambesi" —"The Portobello Road."

17. *The Seraph and the Zambesi.* Philadelphia, Pennsylvania: Lippincott, 1960.

18. *Voices at Play: Stories and Ear-Pieces* (includes radio plays). London: Macmillan, 1961, 1965; Philadelphia, Pennsylvania: Lippincott, 1961, 1962; New York: St. Martin's Press, 1961; Harmondsworth: Penguin, 1966.

Contents (Radio Plays): "The Danger Zone"—"The Dry River Bed"—"The Interview." (Short Stories): "The Ormolu Clock"—"The Curtain Blown by the Breeze"—"The Dark Glasses"—"Bang-bang You're Dead"—"A Member of the Family"—"The Father's Daughters"—"The Party Through the Wall."

19. "Gentile Jewesses." *New Yorker,* 39 (22 June 1963), 31-34; reprinted in *Winter's Tales 9.* Ed. A. D. Maclean. London: Macmillan, 1963; New York: St. Martin's Press, 1963, pp. 235-246.

20. *Collected Stories: 1.* London: Macmillan, 1967; New York: Knopf, 1968.

Contents: Contains all of the stories found in her *The Go-Away Bird and Other Stories,* as well as the following: "The Curtain Blown by the Breeze"—"Bang-bang You're Dead"—"The Playhouse Called Remarkable"—"The Leaf-Sweeper"—"The Ormolu Clock"—"The Dark Glasses"—"A Member of the Family"—"The House of the Famous Poet"—"The Father's Daughters"—"Alice Long's Dachshunds."

PRIMARY WORKS: PLAYS

21. *Doctors of Philosophy* (produced in London, 1962). London: Macmillan, 1963; New York: Knopf, 1966.

PRIMARY WORKS: POETRY

22. "On Seeing the Picasso-Matisse Exhibition, London, December, 1945." *The Poetry Review,* 37, No. 2 (April- May 1946), 165-166.

23. "Spring Hat 1946." *The Poetry Review,* 37, No. 4 (August-September 1946), 328.

24. "The Victoria Falls." *The Poetry Review,* 37, No. 4 (August-September 1946), 285.

25. "The Well." *The Poetry Review,* 38, No. 1 (January-February 1947), 82-86.

26. "Autumn." *Poetry Review,* 38, No. 2 (March-April 1947), 155-156.

27. "Leaning Over an Old Wall." *The Poetry Review,* 38, No. 2 (March-April 1947), 106.

28. "The Robe and the Song." *The Poetry Review,* 38, No. 3 (May-June 1947), 192-193; reprinted in *Poems I Remember.* Ed. Christmas Humphries. London: Michael Joseph, 1960.

29. "Birthday." *The Poetry Review,* 38, No. 4 (July-August 1947), 270.

30. "Cadmus." *The Poetry Review,* 38, No. 5 (September-October 1947), 379.

31. "The Bells at Bray." *The Poetry Review,* 38, No. 5 (September-October 1947), 353.

32. "Omega." *The Poetry Review,* 38, No. 6 (November-December 1947), 519.

33. "You Dreamer." *Canadian Poetry Magazine,* 11 (March 1948), 23.

34. "Invocation to a child." *Poetry Quarterly,* 10, No. 1 (Spring 1948), 22.

35. "A Letter to Howard." *Poetry Quarterly,* 10, No. 3 (Autumn 1948), 152-153.

36. "The Beads." *Poetry Quarterly,* 11, No. 3 (Autumn 1949), 144-145.

37. "The Voice of One Lost Sings Its Gain." *Poetry Quarterly*, 11, No. 4 (Winter 1949), 221.

38. "Indian Feathers." *Variegation*, 4 (Autumn 1949), 4.

39. "Variations on intuition." *Variegation*, 4, No. 2 (1949), 16.

40. Translator, with Derek Stanford, of Apollinaire's "Poem XVII" from *Shadows of My Love*. *Poetry Quarterly*, 12, No. 3 (Autumn 1950), 149.

41. "Portrait." *Recurrence*, 2, No. 2 (1951), 7.

42. "No Need for Shouting." *Poetry Quarterly*, 13, No. 1 (Spring 1951), 24.

43. "Birthday Acrostic." *Poetry Quarterly*, 13, No. 2 (Summer 1951), 68.

44. *The Fanfarlo and Other Verse.* Aldington, Kent: Hand and Flower Press, 1952.

    Contents: "The Fanfarlo"—"The Grave That Time Dug"—"Elementary"—"Elegy in a Kensington Churchyard"—"The Yellow Book"—"Like Africa"—"We Were Not Expecting the Prince Today"—"Evelyn Cavallo"—"From a Love Cycle"—"The Rout"—"Persicos Odi"—"Four People in a Neglected Garden"—"Against the Transcendentalists."

45. "My Kingdom for a Horse." *TLS* (28 August 1953), p. xvi.

46. "Conversations." *TLS* (30 December 1955), p. 786.

47. "Domestic Dawn." *Saturday Review*, 40 (13 April 1957), 30.

48. "The Strange Case of the Card-Party." *Experiment*, 7 (Winter 1957), 201.

49. *Collected Poems I.* London: Macmillan, 1967; New York: Knopf, 1968.

Contents: "Elementary"—"Against the Transcendentalists"—"The Ballad of the Fanfarlo"—"The Grave that Time Dug"—"Elegy in a Kensington Churchyard"—"The Yellow Book"—"Like Africa"—"We Were Not Expecting the Prince Today"—"Evelyn Cavallo"—"A Tour of London: I. Daybreak Composition; II. Kensington Gardens; III. What the Stranger Wondered; IV. Day of Rest; V. Suburb; VI. The House; VII. Man in the Street"—"The Rout"—"Four People in a Neglected Garden"—"On the Lack of Sleep"—"The Pearlminers"—"Omens"—"My Kingdom for a Horse"—"Intermittence"—"Complaint in a Wash-out Season"—"Litany of Time Past"—"The Fall" —"Faith and Works"—"Conundrum"—"Note by the Wayside"—"The Messengers"—"Fruitless Fable"—"Bluebell Among the Sables"—"A Visit"—"Industriad"—"Communication"—"Verlain Villanelle"—"Edinburgh Villanelle" — "Holy Water Rondel" — "Shipton-under-Wychwood"—"Conversations"—"The Card Party"—"Chrysalis" —"The Nativity: I. The Conversation of the Three Wise Men; II. The Conversation of the Shepherds; III. The Conversation at the Inn; IV. The Conversation of the Angels"—"Sisera"—"Canaan"—"Persicos Odi (Horace, i.xxxviii, in the Jacobean mode)"—"To Lucius Sestius in the Spring (Horace i, iv)"—"Winter Poem (Horace i, ix)"—"Prologue and Epilogue after Catullus: I. Nox est perpetua una dormienda; II. Furi et Aureli comites Catulli."

PRIMARY WORKS: OTHER

50. "Editorial: The Catholic View." *The Poetry Review*, 38, No. 6 (November-December 1947), 402-405. A defence of modern poetry.

51. "Editorial: Criticism, Effect and Morals." *The Poetry Review*, 39, No. 1 (January-February 1948), 3-6. On the

qualities needed in a critic of contemporary poetry.

52. "Editorial: Reassessment." *The Poetry Review*, 39, No. 2 (April-May 1948), 103-104. On the need for a reassessment of the Classics, and literary criticism.

53. "Reassessment—II." *The Poetry Review*, 39, No. 3 (August-September 1948), 234-236. On "how the values and criteria of the poet himself relate to his work."

54. "A pamphlet from the U.S." *The Poetry Review*, 39, No. 4 (October-November 1948), 318. In praise of *Poetry Awards*.

55. "Poetry and the other Arts." *The Poetry Review*, 39, No. 5 (December-January 1948-1949), 390.

56. *"Beyond the Terminus of Stars* by Hugo Manning." *Poetry Quarterly*, 11, No. 2 (Summer 1949), 122-123.

57. "Cecil Day Lewis." *Poetry Quarterly*, 11, No. 3 (Autumn 1949), 162-168. Review of his *Poems 1943-1947.*

58. "Three Vintages." *Poetry Quarterly*, 11, No. 4 (Winter 1949), 252-256. Review of books of poetry by Edith Sitwell, Louis MacNeice, and Kathleen Raine.

59. "Poetry or Exam Paper?" *Poetry Quarterly*, 12, No. 1 (Spring 1950), 62. Letter to the editor on a particular translation of Rilke's *The Lay of Love and Death of Cornet Christopher Rilke.*

60. Editor, with Derek Stanford. *Tribute to Wordsworth: A Miscellany of Opinion for the Centenary of the Poet's Death.* Foreword by Herbert Read. London: Wingate, 1950; London: T. Brun, 1950; Port Washington, New York: Kennikat Press, 1970; Folcroft, Pennsylvania: Folcroft, 1974.

61. "What You Say, and How You Say It." *Poetry Quarterly,*

12, No. 4 (Winter 1950-1951), 234-237. Review of books by six contemporary writers, including two anthologies.

62. "Psychology and Criticism." *TLS* (25 May 1951), p. 325. A letter to the editor, in defense of the use of psychology in critical-biography.

63. "The Stricken Deer." *Poetry Quarterly*, 13, No. 2 (Summer 1951), 89-90. Review of Norman Nicholson's *William Cowper.*

64. *"The Apple and the Spectroscope."* *Poetry Quarterly*, 13, No. 3 (Autumn 1951), 139-144. Review of book by T. R. Henn.

65. *Child of Light: A Reassessment of Mary Wollstonecraft Shelly.* Hadleigh, Essex: Tower Bridge Publications, 1951; London: Macmillan, 1963.

* 66. "A Post Romantic." *Poetry Quarterly*, 14, No. 2 (Summer 1952), 59-60. Review of *The Poems of Arthur Hough Clough*, ed. by H. F. Lowry, et. al.

* 67. Editor. *A Selection of Poems*, by Emile Brontë. London: Grey Walls Press, 1952; London: British Book Centre, 1953.

68. *Emily Brontë: Her Life and Work*, with Derek Stanford. London: Peter Owen, 1953, 1960, 1966; London: British Book Centre, 1953; London: House and Maxwell, 1960; London: Transatlantic Arts, 1963; New York: Coward-McCann, 1966.

69. *John Masefield.* London: Peter Nevill, 1953; London: Macmillan, 1962; Philadelphia, Pennsylvania: R. West, n.d.

* 70. Editor, with Derek Stanford. *My Best Mary: The Selected Letters of Mary Wollstonecraft Shelly.* London: Win-

945

gate, 1953; New York: Roy Publications, 1954; Folcroft, Pennsylvania: Folcroft, 1974; Philadelphia, Pennsylvania: R. West, n.d.

* 71. Editor. *The Brontë Letters.* London: Peter Nevill, 1954; as *The Letters of the Brontës: A Selection.* Norman, Oklahoma: University of Oklahoma Press, 1954; London: Macmillan, 1966.

* 72. Editor, with Derek Stanford. *Letters of John Henry Newman.* London: Peter Owen, 1957; Westminster, Maryland: Newman Press, 1957.

* 73. *"Ronald Knox."* *Twentieth Century,* 167 (January 1960), 83-85. Review of Evelyn Waugh's biography.

* 74. "How I Became a Novelist." *John O'London's Weekly,* 3 (1 December 1960); reprinted in *Books and Bookmen* (November 1961), p. 9.

75. "Edinburgh-born." *New Statesman,* 64 (10 August 1962), 180. On her being a constitutional exile from Edinburgh; on the importance of the word *nevertheless;* and on the influence of Edinburgh upon her character.

76. "Author and Critic." *TLS* (4 October 1963), p. 787; reply by Derek Stanford in *TLS* (11 October 1963), p. 807; reply by Jon Wynne-Tyson immediately follows Stanford's; response to Stanford and Wynne-Tyson by Erica Marx in *TLS* (18 October 1963), p. 827; reply to Miss Marx by Wynne-Tyson in *TLS* (25 October 1963), p. 857. Miss Spark's letter to the editor expresses strong disapproval to Derek Stanford's book on her.

77. "Poetry and Politics." *Parliamentary Affairs,* 16 (Autumn 1963), 445-454.

78. "Memento mori for Bluebell." *Book Week,* 2 (27 December 1964), 2, 7. On her cat, Bluebell.

79. "The Quest for Lavishes Ghast." *Esquire,* 62 (December 1964), 216, 218. On her frantic search for the meaning of the phrase "Lavishes ghast."

80. "The Brontës as Teachers." *New Yorker,* 41 (22 January 1966), 30-33.

81. "Exotic Departures." *New Yorker,* 42 (28 January 1967), 31-32. On how London "apparitions of 1952 have become...an established social reality" in 1967. On youth and boredom.

82. With Graham Greene, V. S. Naipaul, and Auberon Waugh. "Biafra's Rights." *The* (London) *Times* (13 November 1968), p. 11. A letter to the Editor.

83. *The Very Fine Clock* (juvenile). Drawings by Edward Gorey. New York: Knopf, 1968; London: Macmillan, 1969; as *Die sehr gute Uhr.* Trans. Gerd Hoffmans. Zurich: Diogenes Verlag, 1971.

84. "The Desegregation of Art." *Month,* 5 (May 1972), 152-153.

85. "My Vote." *Observer* (6 October 1974), p. 23. On why she might vote for the Liberal Party.

II. GENERAL SECONDARY STUDIES, INTERVIEWS, BIOGRAPHICAL SKETCHES, AND MISCELLANEOUS ITEMS

General references to Spark's work also appear in the First Part of this bibliography. See the following numbers there: 10, 12, 14, 16, 17, 23, 29, 31, 32, 35, 36, 40, 55, 56, 58, 59, 62, 64, 70, 71, 72, 75, 78, 80, 85, 90, 93, 94, 96, 98, 101, 107, 114, 115, 125, 126, 127, 141, 143, 236, 238, 298, 299, 308, 318, 319.

* 86. Anon. *"A Muriel Spark Trio."* *Best Sellers,* 22 (1 September 1962), 217. Review of *The Comforters, Memento Mori,* and *The Ballad of Peckham Rye.*

87. —. "Literary Prize for Muriel Spark." *The* (London) *Times* (12 February 1966), p. 10. A notice of her winning the James Tait Black Memorial Prize for her *The Mandelbaum Gate.*

88. —. "Prime of Mrs. Spark." *Observer* (27 September 1970), p. 36. Profile of Muriel Spark in Rome.

89. —. "Sideights." *Contemporary Authors: A Bio-Bibliographical Guide to Current Authors and Their Works.* Ed. Barbara Harte and Carolyn Riley. Detroit, Michigan: Gale Research, 1963, pp. 1083-1084.

90. —. "The Order of the British Empire." *The* (London) *Times* (2 January 1967), p. 15, col. 4. A notice of Spark's receiving the O.B.E. honor.

91. Armstrong, George. "George Armstrong Talks to Muriel

Spark." *Guardian,* (30 September 1970), p. 8.

92. Baldanza, Frank. "Muriel Spark and the Occult." *Wisconsin Studies in Contemporary Literature,* 6 (Summer 1965), 190-203.

93. Bradbury, Malcolm. "Muriel Spark's fingernails." *Critical Quarterly,* 14 (Autumn 1972), 241-250; reprinted in his *Possibilities* (see First Part No. 16), pp. 247-255.

94. Byatt, A. S. "Whittled and Spiky Art." *New Statesman,* 74 (15 December 1967), 848. On her *Collected Stories,* and *Collected Poems.*

95. Davison, Peter. "The Miracles of Muriel Spark." *Atlantic,* 222 (October 1968), 139-142. On several of Spark's works, especially *Collected Poems: 1, Collected Stories: 1,* and *The Public Image.*

96. Dobie, Ann B. "Muriel Spark's Definition of Reality." *Critique,* 12, No. 1 (1970), 20-27.

97. —, and Carl Wooton. "Spark and Waugh: Similarities by Coincidence." *Midwest Quarterly,* 13 (1972), 423-434.

98. Dolbier, Maurice. " 'I'm Very Fierce...When I Start.' " *New York Herald Tribune Books,* 38 (11 February 1962), 7. An interview.

99. Engelborghs, Maurits. "Britse 'Lady Novelists'." *Dietsche Warande en Belfort* (Antwerp), No. 4 (1969), pp. 286-292. On Spark and Edna O'Brien.

100. Fielding, Gabriel. "Sex, Symbolism and Modern Literature." *Critic,* 26 (August-September 1967), 18, 20-22. Pp. 20-21.

101. Gillham, Ian. "Keeping it short." *Listener,* 84 (24 September 1970), 411-413. An interview.

102. Graude, Luke. "Gabriel Fielding, New Master of the Catholic Classic?" *Catholic World,* 197 (June 1963), 172-179. Pp. 175-176.

103. Greene, George. "A Reading of Muriel Spark." *Thought,* 43 (1968), 393-407.

104. Grosskurth, Phyllis. "The World of Muriel Spark: Spirits or Spooks?" *Tamarack Review,* 39 (Spring 1966), 62-67.

105. Hamilton, Alex. "Muriel Spark." *Guardian* (8 November 1974), p. 10. An interview.

106. Hazzard, Shirley. " 'A Mind Like a Blade.' " *New York Times Book Review* (29 September 1968), pp. 1, 62. Review of Spark's *Collected Stories,* and *The Public Image.*

107. Hengist, Philip. "Muriel Spark." *Punch,* 245 (31 July 1963), 175-176. Review of several of Spark's works.

* 108. Holland, Mary. "The Prime of Muriel Spark." *Observer Colour Supplement* (17 October 1965), pp. 8-10.

109. Hoyt, Charles Alva. "Muriel Spark: The Surrealist Jane Austen." *Contemporary British Novelists.* Ed. Charles Shapiro (see First Part No. 107), pp. 125-143.

110. Hynes, Joseph. "After Marabar: Reading Forster, Robbe-Grillet, Spark." *Iowa Review,* 5, No. 1 (1974), 120-126.

111. Hynes, Samuel. "Prime of Muriel Spark." *Commonweal,* 75 (23 February 1962), 562-568.

112. Jacobsen, Josephine. "A Catholic Quartet." *Christian Scholar,* 47 (1964), 139-154. Includes comments on Spark.

113. Jones, Jacqueline Ann. "The Absurd in the Fiction of Muriel Spark." Diss. Pennsylvania, 1974. *Dissertation*

Abstracts, 36A (1975), 317-318.

114. Kemp, Peter. *Muriel Spark.* Novelists and Their World Series. London: Elek, 1974; New York: Harper, 1975.

115. Kennedy, Alan. "Cannibals, Okapis, and Self-Slaughter in the Novels of Muriel Spark," in his *The Protean Self* (see First Part No. 58), 151-211.

116. Kermode, Frank. "God's Plots." *Listener,* 78 (7 December 1967), 759-760. Review of Spark's *Collected Poems.* Vol. I, and *Collected Stories.* Vol. I.

117. —. "House of Fiction: Interviews with Seven English Novelists." *Partisan Review,* 30 (Spring 1963), 61-82. Pp. 79-82.

* 118. —. "The Prime of Miss Muriel Spark." *New Statesman,* 66 (27 September 1963), 397-398; reprinted in his *Continuities* (see First Part No. 59), 202-207.

119. Keyser, Barbara Elizabeth Yarbrough. "The Dual Vision of Muriel Spark." Diss. Tulane, 1971. *Dissertation Abstracts,* 32A (1972), 4005.

120. Laffin, Gerry Starr. "Unresolved Dualities in the Novels of Muriel Spark." Diss. Wisconsin, 1973. *Dissertation Abstracts,* 34A (1974), 4268.

121. Leclaire, L. A. "Muriel Spark: *The Go-Away Bird, Robinson, Memento Mori.*" *Etudes Anglaises,* 13 (1960), 486-487.

122. Legris, Maurice Roger. "Muriel Spark's Use of Non-Material: Prolegomena to A Theological Critique." Diss. Oregon, 1973. *Dissertation Abstracts,* 34A (1974), 7763-7764.

123. McConkey, James. Review of *The Ballad of Peckham Rye* and *The Go-Away Bird,* in *Epoch,* 10 (Fall 1960), 249-

124. McLeod, Patrick G. "Vision and the Moral Encounter: A Reading of Muriel Spark's Novels." Diss. Rice, 1973. *Dissertation Abstracts,* 34A (1973), 1286-1287.

125. Malin, Irving. "The Deceptions of Muriel Spark." *The Vision Obscured: Perceptions of Some Twentieth-Century Catholic Novelists.* Ed. Melvin J. Friedman. New York: Fordham University Press, 1970, pp. 95-107.

126. Malkoff, Karl. "Demonology and Dualism: The Supernatural in Isaac Singer and Muriel Spark." *Critical Views of Isaac Bashevis Singer.* Ed. Irving Malin. New York: New York University Press, 1969, pp. 149-168.

127. —. *Muriel Spark.* Essays on Modern Writers. New York and London: Columbia University Press, 1968.

128. Mansfield, Joseph Gerard. "Another World Than This: The Gothic and the Catholic in the Novels of Muriel Spark." Diss. Iowa, 1973. *Dissertation Abstracts,* 34A (1974), 5980.

129. Maurer, Robert. "Art Imitates Life Imitating Art." *Saturday Review,* 51 (5 October 1968), 31-32. Review of Spark's *Collected Stories* and *The Public Image.*

130. Meijer, Henk Romijn. "Het Satirische Talent van Muriel Spark." *Tirade,* 6 (March 1962), 157-169.

131. Mobley, Jonnie Patricia. "Toward Logres: The Operation of Efficacious Grace in Novels by C. S. Lewis, Charles Williams, Muriel Spark, and Gabriel Fielding." Diss. Southern California, 1973. *Dissertation Abstracts,* 34A (1974), 4274.

132. Müller, Norbert. "Muriel Spark." *Englische Literatur der Gegenwart in Einzeldarstellungen.* Ed. Horst W. Drescher. Stuttgart: Kröner, 1970, pp. 327-343.

133. Murphy, Carol. "A Spark of the Supernatural." *Approach*, 60 (Summer 1966), 26-30.

134. Niall, Brenda. "The Voice of Muriel Spark." *Twentieth Century*, 26 (Autumn 1972), 197-203.

135. Owen, Peter. "Peter Owen." *TLS* (26 March 1971), p. 353. Favorable response by Muriel Spark in *TLS* (9 April 1971), p. 423. Response by T. M. Rivers in *TLS* (16 April 1971), p. 449. On Muriel Spark's salary as first editor of the publishing company Peter Owen Ltd.

136. Pérez-Minick, Domingo. "De lo espeluznante a la alegoria." *Insula*, 27 (February 1972), 7.

137. Peters, W. J. "De Reputatie van Muriel Spark." *Streven*, 17, No. 1 (1964), 385-387.

138. Potter, Nancy. "Muriel Spark: Transformer of the Commonplace." *Renascence*, 17 (Spring 1965), 115-120.

139. Quigly, Isabel. "Like It or Lump It." *Tablet*, 221 (23/30 December 1967), 1344. On her *Collected Stories*, and *Collected Poems*.

140. Quinn, Joseph A. "A Study of the Satiric Element in the Novels of Muriel Spark." Diss. Purdue, 1969. *Dissertation Abstracts*, 30 (1970), 3954.

141. Reed, Douglas. "Taking Cocktails with Life." *Books and Bookmen*, 16 (August 1971), 10-14.

142. Reid, Alexander. "The Novels of Muriel Spark." *Scotland's Magazine*, 57 (April 1961), 55-56.

143. Richardson, Kenneth Ridley. "Spark, Muriel." *Twentieth Century Writing: A Reader's Guide to Contemporary Literature*. Ed. Kenneth R. Richardson. London: Newnes Books, 1969, pp. 577-578.

144. Richmond, Velma B. "The Darkening Vision of Muriel Spark." *Critique,* 15, No. 1 (1973), 71-85.

145. Ricks, Christopher. "Extreme Instances." *New York Review of Books,* 11 (19 December 1968), 31-32. Review of *The Public Image, Collected Stories,* and *Collected Poems.*

146. Rubin, Donald Stuart. "The Recusant Myth in Modern Fiction." Diss. Toronto, 1968. *Dissertation Abstracts,* 30A (1970), 4462. Includes a study of all of Spark's fictional work.

147. Schneider, Harold W. "A Woman in Her Prime: The Fiction of Muriel Spark." *Critique,* 5, No. 2 (Fall 1962), 28-45.

148. Shenker, Israel. "Portrait of a Woman Reading." *Book World,* 2 (29 September 1968), 2. An interview on the subject of Spark's reading.

149. Stanford, Derek. *Muriel Spark: A Biographical and Critical Study.* With a bibliography by Bernard Stone. Fontwell, Sussex: Centaur Press, 1963. Note: although the bibliography is terribly incomplete, it does contain some information on very early poems and editorials which are not listed here.

150. —. "The Early Days of Miss Muriel Spark." *Critic,* 20 (April-May 1962), 49-53.

151. —. "The Works of Muriel Spark: An Essay on Her Fictional Method." *Month,* 214 (August 1962), 92-99.

152. —. Untitled comments. *Contemporary Novelists.* Ed. James Vinson. London and Chicago: St. James Press, 1972, pp. 1160-1162.

153. Stubbs, Patricia. *Muriel Spark.* Writers and Their Work Series. Ed. Ian Scott-Kilvert. Harlow, Essex: Longman

Group, 1973.

154. Szöllösy, Klára. "Muriel Spark az olvasó szemével—a for-
dító szemével." *Nagyvilag,* 8 (May 1963), 760-765.

155. Toynbee, Philip. "Muriel Spark." *Observer* (7 November
1971), pp. 73-74. An interview.

156. Trevor, William. "A joke at the heart of the matter." *The*
(London) *Times* (25 November 1967), p. 22. Review of
her *Collected Stories 1,* and *Collected Poems 1.*

157. Vančura, Zdeněk. "Současné britské spisovatelky, 1:
Muriel Sparková." *Crosscurrents/Modern Fiction,* 52
(1970), 1-9.

158. Vormweg, Heinrich. "Muriel Spark's Welttheaterchen."
Merkur, 19 (1965), 793-795.

159. Waugh, Auberon. "The lost leader." *Spectator,* 219 (22
December 1967), 783. Review of her *Collected Stories,*
and *Collected Poems.*

160. —. "The Work of Muriel Spark: An Essay on Her Fictional
Method." *The Month,* 28 (July 1962), 92-99.

161. Weatherby, W. J. "My Conversion." *Twentieth Century,*
170 (Autumn 1961), 58-63. An interview.

162. Wildman, John Hazard. "Translated by Muriel Spark."
Nine Essays in Modern Literature. Ed. Donald E. Stanford. Baton Rouge: Louisiana State University Press,
1965, pp. 129-144, 188-190.

III. STUDIES AND REVIEWS OF
INDIVIDUAL WORKS

References to individual books by Spark also appear in the First Part of this bibliography. See the following numbers there: 70, 99, 149, 155, 166, 168, 172, 181, 190, 192, 193, 195, 207, 218, 222, 223, 227, 229, 237, 240, 245, 246, 248, 251, 255, 259, 261, 269, 272, 279, 280, 282, 286, 291, 294, 295, 301, 302, 311, 312, 315, 316, 329, 330, 333, 338, 339, 342, 343, 344, 346.

The Comforters

163. Anon. "New Fiction." *The* (London) *Times* (14 February 1957), p. 11.

164. —. "Questing Characters." *TLS* (22 February 1957), p. 256.

165. —. *"The Comforters."* *Booklist,* 54 (1 October 1957), 77.

166. Bacon, Martha. "Very Neat, This Tale—Engaging, Too." *New York Herald Tribune Book Review,* 34 (1 September 1957), 8.

167. Balliett, Whitney. "Moses in the Old Brit'n." *New Yorker,* 33 (18 January 1958), 99-101. P. 101.

168. Doyle, Paul A. *"The Comforters."* *Best Sellers,* 17 (1 September 1957), 173-174.

169. Hodgart, Patricia. "New Novels." *Manchester Guardian* (12 February 1957), p. 4.

170. Levin, Martin. "Spritely Tale." *Saturday Review,* 40 (31 August 1957), 25-26.

171. Pippett, Aileen. "Aunt Louisa's Secret." *New York Times Book Review* (1 September 1957), p. 16.

172. Reinhold, H. A. "Not So Harmless." *Commonweal,* 66 (23 August 1957), 526-527.

173. Rodger, Ian. "Drama: Comment, not Lament." *Listener,* 61 (15 January 1959), 143-144. P. 144. Review of Rayner Heppenstall's radio production of the novel.

174. Scrutton, Mary. "New Novels." *New Statesman and Nation,* 53 (23 February 1957), 253.

175. Waugh, Evelyn. "Something Fresh." *Spectator,* 198 (22 February 1957), 256.

Robinson

176. Anon. "Briefing: *Robinson.*" *Observer* (4 October 1964), p. 22.

177. —. "New Fiction." *The* (London) *Times* (10 July 1958), p. 13.

178. —. "Questions and Answers." *TLS* (27 June 1958), p. 357.

* 179. Boucher, Anthony. "Criminals at Large." *New York Times Book Review* (19 October 1958), p. 59.

180. Hughes, Riley. *"Robinson."* *Catholic World,* 189 (May 1959), 162.

181. Meyer, Helen T. "Robinson." *Best Sellers,* 18 (15 October 1958), 272-273.

182. New, William H. "The Island and the Madman: Recurrent

Imagery in the Major Novelists of the Fifties." *Arizona Quarterly*, 22 (Winter 1966), 328-337. P. 334.

183. Ohmann, Carol B. "Muriel Spark's *Robinson.*" *Critique*, 8, No. 1 (Fall 1965), 70-84.

184. Quigly, Isabel. "Novels." *Encounter*, 11 (September 1958), 82-84. P. 83.

185. Raven, Simon. "Somewhere in Europe." *Spectator*, 200 (27 June 1958), 848.

186. Richardson, Maurice. "New Novels." *New Statesman*, 56 (5 July 1958), 24-25. P. 25.

Memento Mori

187. Adams, Phoebe. Untitled book review. *Atlantic*, 204 (August 1959), 81.

188. Anon. "Crabbed Age and Youth." *TLS* (17 April 1959), p. 221.

189. —. "Danse Macabre." *Time*, 73 (15 June 1959), 97-98.

190. —. "*Memento Mori.*" *Kirkus*, 27 (15 March 1959), 232.

191. —. "*Memento Mori.*" *Reporter*, 20 (25 June 1959), 48.

192. —. "New Fiction." *The* (London) *Times* (26 March 1959), p. 15.

193. —. "Octogenarians Staged with Ingenuity. Nottingham Playhouse: *Memento Mori.*" *The* (London) *Times* (14 May 1964), p. 8.

194. Baisier, Leon. "*Memento Mori.*" *Best Sellers*, 19 (15 June 1959), 100.

195. Balliet, Whitney. "The Burning Bush." *New Yorker,* 35 (13 June 1959), 127-130. Pp. 127-129.

196. Bannon, Barbara A. *"Memento Mori." Publishers' Weekly,* 190 (24 October 1966), 52.

197. Bergonzi, Bernard. "The Novel No Longer Novel." *Listener,* 70 (19 September 1963), 415-416. P. 416.

* 198. Coleman, John. "Borderline." *Spectator,* 202 (27 March 1959), 447.

199. Engelborghs, M. "Een Ongewone Engelse Roman." *Kultuurleven,* 27 (February 1960), 140-142.

200. Finn, James. "Death and Old Age." *Commonweal,* 70 (18 September 1959), 524-526.

201. Fremantle, Anne. "The Wily Ways of the World." *Saturday Review,* 42 (27 June 1959), 15-16.

202. Gable, Sister Mariella. "Prose Satire and the Modern Christian Temper." *American Benedictine Review,* 11 (March-June 1960), 29-30, 33.

203. Hughes, Riley. *"Memento Mori." Catholic World,* 189 (July 1959), 323, 325.

204. Lucas, Barbara. *"Memento Mori." Twentieth Century,* 166 (September 1959), 213-215.

205. Maclaren-Ross, J. "New Fiction." *Punch,* 235 (8 April 1959), 496-497.

206. McCrindle, J. F. *"Memento Mori." Venture,* 3, No. 3 (1959), 77-78.

207. Naipaul, V. S. "Death on the Telephone." *New Statesman,* 57 (28 March 1959), 452.

208. Petersen, C. Review of *Memento Mori,* in *Books Today,* 3 (18 December 1966), 11.

209. Phelps, Robert. "In the Lengthening Shadow." *New York Times Book Review* (17 May 1959), p. 5.

210. Price, Martin. "The Difficulties of Commitment: Some Recent Novels." *Yale Review,* n.s. 48 (Summer 1959), 595-604. Pp. 597-598.

211. Quinton, Anthony. Untitled book review. *London Magazine,* 6 (September 1959), 84-88. Pp. 84-85.

212. Rees, Goronwy. "New Novels." *Listener,* 61 (2 April 1959), 607.

213. Rodger, Ian. "Drama: A Comdey of Age." *Listener,* 66 (24 August 1961), 291-292. Review of radio broadcast of book.

214. Scroggie, Jean. "Mementoes for Muriel Spark." *Daily Telegraph* (25 September 1970), p. 15.

215. Walbridge, Earle F. *"Memento Mori." Library Journal,* 84 (1 September 1959), 2523.

The Ballad of Peckham Rye

216. Anon. "A Devil Called Douglas." *Time,* 76 (15 August 1960), 82.

217. —. "Briefly Noted." *New Yorker,* 36 (27 August 1960), 102.

218. —. "Faith and Fancy." *TLS* (4 March 1960), p. 141.

219. —. "New Fiction." *The* (London) *Times* (3 March 1960), p. 15.

220. —. *"The Ballad of Peckham Rye."* Booklist, 57 (1 October 1960), 88.

221. —. *"The Ballad of Peckham Rye."* Kirkus, 28 (1 June 1960), 430.

222. Bryden, Ronald. "Childe Colin." *Spectator*, 204 (4 March 1960), 329.

223. Derrick, Christopher. "Human Research." *Tablet*, 214 (5 March 1960), 229-230.

224. Dierickx, J. "A Devil-figure in a Contemporary Setting: Muriel Spark's *The Ballad of Peckham Rye.*" *Revue des Langues Vivantes*, 33 (1967), 576-587.

225. Fraser, R. A. Review of *The Ballad of Peckham Rye*, in the *San Francisco Chronicle* (7 August 1960), p. 19.

226. Furbank, P. N. "New Novels." *Listener*, 63 (3 March 1960), 417.

227. Green, Lois Wagner. "Wiles of Wee Dougie." *Saturday Review*, 43 (30 July 1960), 18.

228. Hollander, John. "Plain and Fancy: Notes on Four Novels." *Yale Review*, n.s. 50 (Autumn 1960), 149-156. Pp. 153-154.

229. Hughes, Riley. *"The Ballad of Peckham Rye."* *Catholic World*, 192 (December 1960), 182-183.

230. Keon, Eric. "New Fiction." *Punch*, 238 (16 March 1960), 399.

231. Laws, Frederick. "Drama: Entertaining Picaroon." *Listener*, 64 (13 October 1960), 653-654. P. 653. Review of radio adaptation of the novel.

232. McLaughlin, Richard. *"Ballad of Peckham Rye."* *Spring-*

field Sunday Republican (11 September 1960), p. 5D.

233. Mott, Schuyler L. *"The Ballad of Peckham Rye." Library Journal,* 85 (July 1960), 2620.

234. Murray, John J. *"The Ballad of Peckham Rye." Best Sellers,* 20 (15 August 1960), 167.

235. Phelps, Robert. "With a Happy Touch of the Brimstone." *New York Herald Tribune Book Review,* 37 (7 August 1960), 3.

236. Pickrel, Paul. "Two From Abroad." *Harper's,* 221 (August 1960), 98-100. Pp. 99-100.

237. Poore, Charles. "Books of The Times." *New York Times,* 109 (30 July 1960), 15.

238. Quinton, Anthony. Untitled book review. *London Magazine,* 7 (May 1960), 78-81. P. 80.

239. Shrapnel, Norman. "An anatomy of violence." *Guardian* (4 March 1960), p. 8.

240. Shuttleworth, Martin. "Drama: Apotheosis." *Listener,* 67 (7 June 1962), 1005-1006. Review of radio broadcast of book.

* 241. —. "Plays of the Week: Satisfying." *Listener,* 67 (28 June 1962), 1131-1132. P. 1131.

242. Smith, William James. "Bizarre Vision of the Commonplace." *Commonweal,* 73 (28 October 1960), 130-131.

243. Sykes, Gerald. "The Bewitching Ways of Dougal Douglas." *New York Times Book Review* (28 August 1960), pp. 26-27.

244. West, Paul. "New Novels." *New Statesman,* 59 (5 March 1960), 341-342.

The Bachelors

245. Adams, Phoebe. "Potpourri." *Atlantic*, 207 (May 1961), 104.

246. Allen, Walter. "The Possessed." *New Statesman*, 60 (15 October 1960), 580-581.

247. Anon. "New Fiction." *The* (London) *Times* (13 October 1960), p. 17.

248. —. "Stag Party." *TLS* (14 October 1960), p. 657.

249. —. *"The Bachelors."* *Booklist*, 57 (15 April 1961), 520.

250. —. *"The Bachelors."* *Kirkus*, 29 (15 January 1961), 71.

251. —. *"The Bachelors."* *Time*, 77 (14 April 1961), 115.

* 252. Colimore, Vincent J. *"The Bachelors."* *Best Sellers*, 20 (1 March 1961), 453-454.

253. Denniston, Robin. Review of *The Bachelors*, in *Time and Tide* (29 October 1960), p. 1309.

254. Fay, Elizabeth. Review of *The Bachelors*, in the *Catholic Library World* (May-June 1961), p. 533.

255. Gilliatt, Penelope. "Black Laughs." *Spectator*, 205 (21 October 1960), 620-621.

256. Hughes, Catharine. *"The Bachelors."* *Catholic World*, 193 (August 1961), 332-333.

257. Hughes, Riley. "Happy Malice." *Renascence*, 14 (Autumn 1961), 49-51.

258. Hutchens, John K. Review of *The Bachelors*, in the *New York Herald Tribune* (1 March 1961), p. 21.

259. Keown, Eric. "New Fiction." *Punch,* 239 (2 November 1960), 647.

260. Lodge, David. "Various Vocations." *Tablet* (17 December 1960), pp. 1175-1176.

261. McConkey, James. Review of *The Bachelors,* in *Epoch,* 11 (Spring 1961), 124-125.

262. Phelps, Robert. "Muriel Spark's New One Sparkles." *New York Herald Tribune Book Review,* 37 (5 March 1961), 28.

263. Sheehan, E. *"The Bachelors."* America, 104 (18 March 1961), 796.

264. Shrapnel, Norman. "Living backwards." *Guardian* (21 October 1960), p. 9.

265. Smith, William James. *"The Bachelors."* Commonweal, 75 (8 December 1961), 294.

266. Weisberg, Edzia. "Fiction Chronicle." *Partisan Review,* 28 (June 1961), 716-722. Pp. 719-722.

The Prime of Miss Jean Brodie

267. Adams, Phoebe. "Potpourri." *Atlantic,* 209 (February 1962), 122.

268. Allen, Jay Presson. *The Prime of Miss Jean Brodie: A drama in three acts.* New York: Samuel French, 1969.

269. Anon. "Have done with you." *TLS* (16 April 1970), p. 401.

270. —. "Hidden Depths." *Newsweek,* 59 (22 January 1962), 81.

271. —. "Mistress of Style." *TLS* (3 November 1961), p. 785.

272. —. "New Fiction." *The* (London) *Times* (2 November 1961), p. 16.

273. —. "Novel becomes immaculate stage comedy. Wyndham Theatre: *The Prime of Miss Jean Brodie.*" *The* (London) *Times* (6 May 1966), p. 18.

274. —. "*The Prime of Miss Jean Brodie.*" *Booklist*, 58 (1 February 1962), 342.

275. —. "*The Prime of Miss Jean Brodie.*" *Kirkus*, 29 (1 December 1961), 1055.

276. —. "*The Prime of Miss Jean Brodie.*" *Time*, 79 (19 January 1962), 89.

277. —. "*The Prime of Miss Jean Brodie.*" *Virginia Quarterly Review*, 38 (Autumn 1962), cv-cvi.

* 278. —. Boegel, Joan P. "*The Prime of Miss Jean Brodie.*" *Library Journal*, 87 (1 January 1962), 114.

279. Diamond, Naomi. "*The Prime of Miss Jean Brodie.*" *Books Abroad*, 36 (Summer 1962), 323-324.

280. Dobie, Ann B. "*The Prime of Miss Jean Brodie:* Muriel Spark Bridges the Credibility Gap." *Arizona Quarterly*, 25 (Autumn 1969), 217-228.

281. Downer, Alan S. "Old, New, Borrowed, and (a Trifle) Blue: Notes on the New York Theatre, 1967-1968." *Quarterly Journal of Speech*, 54 (October 1968), 199-211. Includes comments on the stage production of *The Prime of Miss Jean Brodie*.

282. Doyle, Edward. Review of *The Prime of Miss Jean Brodie*, in the *Book-of-the-Month-Club News* (March 1962), p. 9.

283. Fitzgibbon, William C. "Books of The Times." *New York Times*, 111 (17 January 1962), 31.

284. Flint, R. W. "Prime Time in Edinburgh." *New Republic,* 146 (29 January 1962), 17, 20.

285. Gardiner, Harold C. *"The Prime of Miss Jean Brody."* *America,* 106 (27 January 1962), 564.

286. Hart, Francis Russell. "Region, Character, and Identity in Recent Scottish Fiction." *Virginia Quarterly Review,* 43 (Autumn 1967), 597-613. Pp. 601, 607-608, 609.

287. Hicks, Granville. "Treachery and the Teacher." *Saturday Review,* 45 (20 January 1962), 18.

* 288. Hogan, William. Review of *The Prime of Miss Jean Brodie,* in the *San Francisco Chronicle* (4 February 1962), p. 28.

289. Hughes, Catharine. *"The Prime of Miss Jean Brodie."* *Catholic World,* 194 (March 1962), 374, 376.

290. Hutchens, John K. Review of *The Prime of Miss Jean Brodie,* in the *New York Herald Tribune* (17 January 1962), p. 23.

291. Igoe, W. J. Review of *The Prime of Miss Jean Brodie,* in the *Chicago Sunday Tribune* (21 January 1962), p. 3.

292. King, Francis. Review of *The Prime of Miss Jean Brodie,* in *Time and Tide* (2 November 1961), p. 1845.

293. Kingston, Jeremy. "Theatre." *Punch,* 250 (11 May 1966), 701. Review of stage production of novel.

294. —. "Theatre." *Punch,* 251 (16 November 1966), 749. Review of the stage production of the novel.

295. Laffin, Gerry S. "Muriel Spark's Portrait of the Artist as a Young Girl." *Renascence,* 24 (Summer 1972), 213-223.

296. Lodge, David. "The uses and abuses of omniscience: Method and meaning in Muriel Spark's *The Prime of Miss*

Jean Brodie." *Critical Quarterly,* 12 (Autumn 1970), 235-257; reprinted in his *The Novelist at the Crossroads, and Other Essays on Fiction and Criticism* (see First Part No. 70), pp. 119-144.

297. Mallett, Richard. "At the Cinema." *Punch,* 256 (5 March 1969), 358. Review of the movie version of the novel.

298. Marks, Jason. "Book Trials: An Experiment in Learning." *CEA Forum,* 3 (October 1972), 4-5.

299. Miller, Karl. "Hard Falls." *New Statesman,* 62 (3 November 1961), 662-663.

300. Petersen, C. Review of *The Prime of Miss Jean Brodie,* in *Books Today,* 3 (27 February 1966), 13.

301. Phelps, Robert. "As Narrative or Parable, It Sparkles." *New York Herald Tribune Books,* 38 (21 January 1962), 5.

302. Pickrel, Paul. "Some Older Hands." *Harper's,* 224 (February 1962), 105-107. Pp. 105-106.

303. Price, Martin. "Splendid but Destructive Egotism." *New York Times Book Review* (21 January 1962), p. 5.

304. Quinn, J. J. *"The Prime of Miss Jean Brodie."* *Best Sellers,* 21 (1 February 1962), 427-428.

305. Shrapnel, Norman. "The Great Divide." *Guardian* (3 November 1961), p. 9.

306. Smith, Janet Adam. *"The Prime of Miss Jean Brodie."* *New Saltire,* 3 (Spring 1962), 92-93.

307. Tuohy, Frank. "Rewards and Bogies." *Spectator,* 207 (3 November 1961), 634.

308. Waugh, Evelyn. "Love, Loyalty, and Little Girls." *Cosmo-*

politan, 152 (February 1962), 38.

The Girls of Slender Means

309. Adler, Renata. "Muriel Spark." *The Village Voice* (September 1963); revised in *On Contemporary Literature*. Ed. Richard Kostelanetz (see First Part No. 62), pp. 591-596.

310. Anon. "Briefing: *Girls of Slender Means.*" *Observer* (31 July 1966), p. 18.

311. —. "Hell in the Royal Borough—." *TLS* (20 September 1963), p. 701; reprinted in *T.L.S. Essays and Reviews from The Times Literary Supplement 1963.* London: Oxford University Press, 1964, pp. 100-102.

312. —. "New Fiction." *The* (London) *Times* (19 September 1963), p. 15.

313. —. "Out of Eden." *Time*, 82 (13 September 1963), 114, 116.

314. —. "Profound Comedy." *Newsweek*, 62 (16 September 1963), 91-92.

315. —. *"The Girls of Slender Means."* *Virginia Quarterly Review*, 40 (Winter 1964), xiii.

316. Baro, Gene. "Ladies in waiting." *Book Week*, 1 (15 September 1963), 20.

317. Bishop, Bernardine. Review of *The Girls of Slender Means*, in the *Aylesford Review*, 6 (Winter 1963-64), 45-47.

318. Brooke, Jocelyn. "New Novels." *Listener*, 70 (26 September 1963), 481.

319. Brophy, Brigid. *"The Girls of Slender Means."* *London*

Magazine, n.s. 3 (December 1963), 76-80.

320. Butcher, Maryvonne.   "Remembrance of Things Past." *Tablet,* 217 (26 October 1963), 1150.

321. Casson, Allan. "Muriel Spark's *The Girls of Slender Means.*" *Critique*, 7, No. 3 (Spring-Summer 1965), 94-96.

322. Crane, Milton.   Review of *The Girls of Slender Means,* in the *Chicago Sunday Tribune* (15 September 1963), p. 5.

* 323. Daniel, John.   "The victims of passion." *Manchester Guardian Weekly*, 89 (26 September 1963), 11.

324. Gardiner, Harold C. *"The Girls of Slender Means."* *America* (26 October 1963), p. 488.

325. Grande, Luke M. *"The Girls of Slender Means."* *Best Sellers*, 23 (15 October 1963), 255-256.

326. Hicks, Granville. "Life Began in the Forties." *Saturday Review*, 46 (14 September 1963), 33-34.

327. Higginson, Jeannette. "Recent Novels." *Minnesota Review,* 4 (Spring 1964), 450-458. P. 457.

328. Hyman, Stanley Edgar. "The Girls of Slender Talents." *New Leader*, 46 (16 September 1963), 17-18. P. 18.

329. Jackson, Katherine Gauss. *"The Girls of Slender Means."* *Harper's*, 227 (November 1963), 137.

330. Johnson, Lucy. "Split Personality." *Progressive,* 28 (January 1964), 50-51.

331. Kelly, Mary E. *"The Girls of Slender Means."* *Library Journal*, 88 (1 October 1963), 3647.

332. Peterson, Virgilia. "Few Were More Delightful, Lovely or Savage." *New York Times Book Review* (15 September

1963), pp. 4, 44.

333. Prescott, Orville. "Immaculate Professional Polish." *New York Times,* 113 (20 September 1963), 31.

334. Price, R. G. G. "New Fiction." *Punch,* 245 (25 September 1963), 470.

335. Pryce-Jones, Alan. Review of *The Girls of Slender Means,* in the *New York Herald Tribune* (5 October 1963), p. 7.

336. Raven, Simon. "Heavens Below." *Spectator,* 211 (20 September 1963), 354.

337. Sale, Roger. "The Newness of the Novel." *Hudson Review,* 16 (Winter 1963-1964), 601-609. Pp. 605, 609.

338. Sears, Sallie. "Too Many Voices." *Partisan Review,* 31 (Summer 1964), 471, 473-475. Pp. 471, 473-474.

339. Smith, D. Review of *The Girls of Slender Means,* in the *Canadian Forum* (August 1964), p. 116.

340. Soule, George. "Must a Novelist be an Artist?" *Carleton Miscellany,* 5 (Spring 1964), 92-98. Pp. 92, 95-98.

341. Taylor, Ken. "The girls of the small screen." *Listener,* 93 (5 June 1975), 733, 735. On his turning the book into a three-part television serial for the BBC.

342. Updike, John. "Between a Wedding and a Funeral." *New Yorker,* 39 (14 September 1963), 192-194; reprinted in his *Assorted Prose.* London: Deutsch, 1965, pp. 210-214.

343. Vonalt, Larry P. "Five Novels." *Sewanee Review,* 73 (Spring 1965), 333-339. Pp. 335-337.

344. Wade, David. "Radio Drama: Fact and fiction." *Listener,* 76 (7 July 1966), 34. Review of radio play of book.

345. Walsh, George. *"The Girls of Slender Means."* *Cosmopolitan*, 155 (September 1963), 25.

346. Waugh, Auberon. "A Novel to (of all things) Enjoy." *National Review*, 15 (22 October 1963), 359-360.

347. Weeks, Edward. "The Beehive." *Atlantic*, 212 (October 1963), 148.

348. Wilkie, Brian. "Muriel Spark: From Comedy to Disaster and Grace." *Commonweal*, 79 (11 October 1963), 80-81.

349. Worthy, J. Review of *The Girls of Slender Means*, in *Books and Bookmen*, 11 (August 1966), 64.

The Mandelbaum Gate

350. Anon. "Fiction." *Saturday Review*, 50 (29 April 1967), 32.

351. —. "Paperbacks: *The Mandelbaum Gate.*" *The* (London) *Times* (4 November 1967), p. 22.

352. —. "Scrolls and Sideburns." *Newsweek*, 66 (18 October 1965), 130-131.

353. —. "Talking About Jerusalem." *TLS* (14 October 1965), p. 913; reprinted in *T.L.S. Essays and Reviews from The Times Literary Supplement.* London: Oxford University Press, 1965, pp. 34-36.

354. —. *"The Mandelbaum Gate."* *Booklist*, 62 (15 October 1965), 195.

355. —. *"The Mandelbaum Gate."* *Kirkus*, 33 (1 July 1965), 646.

356. —. *"The Mandelbaum Gate."* *Publishers' Weekly*, 191 (20

February 1967), 150.

357. —. *"The Mandelbaum Gate."* *Time,* 86 (5 November 1965), 128.

358. —. *"The Mandelbaum Gate."* *Virginia Quarterly Review,* 42 (Summer 1966), xc.

359. Bedford, Sybille. "Frontier Regions." *Spectator,* 215 (29 October 1965), 555-556.

360. Bradbury, Malcolm. "A Pilgrim's Progress." *New York Times Book Review* (31 October 1965), pp. 4, 52.

361. Bresler, Riva T. *"The Mandelbaum Gate."* *Library Journal,* 90 (1 October 1965), 4113.

362. Brooke, Jocelyn. "New Fiction." *Listener,* 74 (14 October 1965), 595.

363. Cohen, Gerda L. "Tilting The Balance." *Midstream,* 12 (January 1966), 68-70.

364. Cook, Roderick. *"The Mandelbaum Gate."* *Harper's,* 231 (November 1965), 128-129.

365. Dolbier, M. Review of *The Mandelbaum Gate,* in the *New York Herald Tribune,* 125 (18 October 1965), 25.

366. Enright, D. J. "Public Doctrine and Private Judging." *New Statesman,* 70 (15 October 1965), 563, 566; reprinted in his *Man Is An Onion.* London: Chatto and Windus, 1972, pp. 32-38.

367. Evans, Illtud. "Crossing-Point." *Tablet,* 219 (23 October 1965), 1184-1185.

368. Fremont-Smith, Eliot. "Between the Two Jerusalems." *New York Times,* 115 (18 October 1965), 33.

369. Fuller, Edmund. "Heterogeneous Heritage." *Wall Street Journal,* 166 (16 December 1965), 16.

370. Greeley, Andrew M. "Divine Spark." *Reporter,* 34 (24 March 1966), 56-58.

371. Gross, John. "Passionate Pilgrimage." *New York Review of Books,* 5 (28 October 1965), 12-15.

372. Grumbach, Doris. *"The Mandelbaum Gate."* America, 113 (23 October 1965), 474, 478.

373. Hebblethwaite, Peter. "How Catholic Is the Catholic Novel?" *TLS* (27 July 1967), pp. 678-679.

374. Hicks, Granville. "A Hard Journey to Jordan." *Saturday Review,* 48 (16 October 1965), 43-44.

375. Howard, Jane. "Muriel Spark: Mistress of Prim Skulduggery." *Life,* 59 (22 October 1965), 12, 15.

376. Janeway, Elizabeth. "A Changing Spark." *Holiday,* 38 (September 1965), 126, 128.

377. Johnson, Lucy. "Three Novels." *Progressive,* 29 (November 1965), 41-42. P. 41.

378. Kazin, Alfred. "Dispassionate pilgrimage." *Book Week,* 3 (17 October 1965), 2-3.

379. Kermode, Frank. "The Novel as Jerusalem: Muriel Spark's *Mandelbaum Gate." Atlantic,* 216 (October 1965), 92-94, 97-98; reprinted in his *Continuities* (see First Part No. 59), pp. 207-216.

380. Kriegel, Leonard. "Muriel Spark in Jerusalem." *Commonweal,* 83 (14 January 1966), 446, 448.

381. McDonnell, T. P. Review of *The Mandelbaum Gate,* in *Critic,* 24 (December 1965-January 1966), 79.

STUDIES AND REVIEWS OF INDIVIDUAL WORKS

382. McGuinness, Frank. Untitled book review. *London Magazine*, n.s. 5 (November 1965), 94-98. Pp. 97-98.

383. Maloof, Saul. Untitled book review. *Commonweal*, 83 (3 December 1965), 287-288. P. 287.

384. Mayne, Richard. "Fiery Particle." *Encounter*, 25 (December 1965), 61-62, 64, 66, 68.

385. Petersen, C. Review of *The Mandelbaum Gate*, in *Books Today*, 4 (16 April 1967), 9.

386. Proctor, Roy. "In the Front Rank." *North American Review*, n.s. 3 (January 1966), 35.

387. Ridley, C. A. Review of *The Mandelbaum Gate*, in the *National Observer*, 4 (29 November 1965), 25.

388. Schmidt, Sandra. "Memory's loss—novel's gain?" *Christian Science Monitor*, 57 (9 December 1965), 19.

389. Shrapnel, Norman. "Righteous readability." *Manchester Guardian Weekly*, 93 (21 October 1965), 11.

390. Shuttleworth, Martin. "New Novels." *Punch*, 249 (20 October 1965), 588.

391. Sullivan, Walter. "Updike, Spark and Others." *Sewanee Review*, 74 (Summer 1966), 709-716. Pp. 713-715.

392. Tracy, Honor. "The Richness of Muriel Spark." *New Republic*, 153 (9 October 1965), 28-29.

393. Tracy, Robert. *"The Mandelbaum Gate." Southern Review*, n.s. 3 (Spring 1967), 529-531.

394. Wilson, Angus. "Journey to Jerusalem." *Observer* (17 October 1965), p. 28.

395. Worthy, J. Review of *The Mandelbaum Gate*, in *Books*

and Bookmen, 11 (December 1965), 40.

396. Yglesias, Helen. "Going to Jerusalem." *Nation,* 201 (22 November 1965), 392-394.

The Public Image

397. Anon. "Fiction." *Saturday Review,* 52 (27 December 1969), 32-33. P. 32.

398. —. "More than Female Savagery." *Time,* 92 (1 November 1968), 102.

399. —. "Shallowness Everywhere." *TLS* (13 June 1968), p. 612; reprinted in *T.L.S. Essays and Reviews from The Times Literary Supplement 1968.* London: Oxford University Press, 1969, pp. 71-73.

400. —. *"The Public Image." Choice,* 6 (March 1969), 58.

401. —. *"The Public Image." Critic,* 27 (February-March 1969), 93.

402. —. *"The Public Image." Kirkus,* 36 (15 July 1968), 780.

403. —. *"The Public Image." Publishers' Weekly,* 194 (5 August 1968), 53.

404. Brendon, P. Review of *The Public Image,* in *Books and Bookmen,* 13 (July 1968), 32.

405. Byatt, A. S. "Empty Shell." *New Statesman,* 75 (14 June 1968), 807-808.

406. Clements, Robert J. "European Literary Scene." *Saturday Review,* 51 (3 August 1968), 19-20. P. 20.

407. Dawson, Helen. "Briefing: *The Public Image." Observer* (11 October 1970), p. 30.

408. Grumbach, Doris. *"The Public Image."* *America,* 119 (26 October 1968), 387-388.

409. Hill, William B. *"The Public Image."* *Best Sellers,* 28 (1 November 1968), 319.

410. Hoagland, Joan M. *"The Public Image."* *Library Journal,* 93 (August 1968), 2899.

411. Holmes, Richard. "Fiction: into a limbo of poise." *The* (London) *Times* (15 June 1968), p. 21.

412. Hope, Francis. "Mrs. Spark in Rome." *Observer* (16 June 1968), p. 24.

413. Jackson, Katherine Gauss. *"The Public Image."* *Harper's,* 237 (November 1968), 159-160.

414. Kermode, Frank. "Antimartyr." *Listener,* 79 (13 June 1968), 778-779.

415. Kiely, Robert. "A novel snaps the camera." *Christian Science Monitor,* 60 (14 November 1968), 15.

416. Maddocks, Melvin. "The Spark Flair for Well-bred Demonology." *Life,* 65 (11 October 1968), 10.

417. Maloff, Saul. "Lady-Tiger." *Newsweek,* 72 (21 October 1968), 108, 110.

418. Mount, Douglas. *"The Public Image."* *Publishers' Weekly,* 196 (6 October 1969), 52.

419. Ostermann, R. Review of *The Public Image,* in the *National Observer,* 7 (9 September 1968), B7.

420. Petersen, Clarence. "A nice idea." *Book World,* 3 (23 November 1969), 17.

421. Poore, Charles. "Wars Between Sexes." *New York Times,*

118 (24 October 1968), 45.

422. Price, R. G. G. "New Novels." *Punch*, 254 (12 June 1968), 864.

423. Pryce-Jones, David. Untitled book review. *London Magazine*, n.s. 8 (July 1968), 106, 108.

424. Sullivan, Richard. "The spark of recognition." *Book World*, 2 (29 September 1968), 3.

425. Trevor, William. "When images eat people." *Manchester Guardian Weekly*, 98 (20 June 1968), 11.

426. Waugh, Auberon. "Private answer." *Spectator*, 220 (7 June 1968), 778-779.

The Driver's Seat

427. Adams, Phoebe. *"The Driver's Seat."* *Atlantic*, 226 (October 1970), 150.

428. Anon. "Meal for a masochist." *TLS* (25 September 1970), p. 1074.

429. —. "Paperbacks." *Observer* (12 May 1974), p. 33.

430. —. *"The Driver's Seat."* *Antioch Review*, 30 (Fall/Winter 1970-1971), 458-459.

431. —. *"The Driver's Seat."* *British Book News* (December 1970), p. 984.

432. —. *"The Driver's Seat."* *Choice*, 8 (September 1971), 836.

433. —. *"The Driver's Seat."* *Kirkus*, 38 (15 July 1970), 767.

434. —. *"The Driver's Seat."* *Publishers' Weekly*, 198 (27 July 1970), 66.

435. Avant, John Alfred. *"The Driver's Seat."* *Library Journal*, 95 (July 1970), 2521.

436. Byatt, A. S. "A murder in hell." *The* (London) *Times* (24 September 1970), p. 14.

437. Davenport, Guy. "Hemingway as Walter Pater." *National Review*, 22 (17 November 1970), 1214-1216. Pp. 1215-1216.

438. Easton, Elizabeth. *"The Driver's Seat."* *Saturday Review*, 53 (10 October 1970), 34, 65.

439. Frakes, James R. "Her own murderer." *Book World*, 4 (18 October 1970), 2.

440. Hill, William B. *"The Driver's Seat."* *America*, 123 (28 November 1970), 464.

441. —. *"The Driver's Seat."* *Best Sellers*, 30 (1 November 1970), 325-326.

442. Jones, D. A. N. "Divided Selves." *New York Review of Books*, 15 (22 October 1970), 38-42. Pp. 39-40.

443. Kermode, Frank. "Sheerer Spark." *Listener*, 84 (24 September 1970), 425-426.

444. Kuehl, Linda. *"The Driver's Seat."* *Commonweal*, 93 (15 January 1971), 378-379.

445. Lodge, David. "Passing the Test." *Tablet*, 224 (10 October 1970), 978.

446. Maddocks, Melvin. *"The Driver's Seat."* *Life*, 69 (23 October 1970), 17.

447. Malpede, Karen. "A Two-Line Personal." *New Leader*, 53 (30 November 1970), 20-21.

448. Nye, Robert. "Study in suicide." *Guardian Weekly,* 103 (3 October 1970), 19.

449. Quigly, Isabel. "Reverse gear." *Financial Times* (1 October 1970), p. 24.

450. Review of *The Driver's Seat,* in the *Catholic Library World,* 42 (May 1971), 558.

451. Review of *The Driver's Seat,* in the *National Observer,* 9 (5 October 1970), 19.

452. Sheppard, R. Z. "A Whydunnit in Q-sharp Major." *Time,* 96 (26 October 1970), 119.

453. Sokolov, Raymond A. *"The Driver's Seat."* *Newsweek,* 76 (30 November 1970), 95.

454. Stade, George. "A whydunnit in q-sharp major." *New York Times Book Review* (27 September 1970), pp. 4-5, 54.

455. Thomas, Edward. Untitled book review. *London Magazine,* n.s. 10 (October 1970), 95-98. P. 96.

456. Tindall, Gillian. "Spark of Death." *New Statesman,* 80 (25 September 1970), 387-388.

457. Tomalin, Claire. "A slight case of murder." *Observer* (27 September 1970), p. 29.

458. Wolfe, Peter. "Choosing the Death." *New Republic,* 163 (3 October 1970), 27.

Not to Disturb

459. Adams, Phoebe. *"Not to Disturb."* *Atlantic,* 229 (April 1972), 128.

460. Allen, Bruce. "In a baronial Manor: revolution corrupted." *Library Journal*, 97 (15 March 1972), 1034.

461. Anon. "Grub Street Gothic." *TLS* (12 November 1971), p. 1409.

462. —. *"Not to Disturb."* *British Book News* (March 1972), p. 253.

463. —. *"Not to Disturb."* *Kirkus*, 40 (15 January 1972), 95.

464. —. *"Not to Disturb."* *Publishers' Weekly*, 201 (24 January 1972), 58.

465. —. *"Not to Disturb."* *Time*, 99 (17 April 1972), 92.

466. —. "Paperbacks." *Observer* (28 April 1974), p. 33.

467. Bell, Pearl K. "A Question of Credibility." *New Leader*, 55 (1 May 1972), 14-15.

468. Brown, F. J. Review of *Not to Disturb*, in *Books and Bookmen*, 17 (January 1972), 56-57.

469. Broyard, Anatole. "The Old Spark is Missing." *New York Times*, 121 (29 March 1972), 41.

470. Byatt, A. S. "Life, death and the media." *The* (London) *Times* (11 November 1971), p. 10.

471. Cuffe, Edwin D. *"Not to Disturb."* *America*, 126 (29 April 1972), 467.

472. Fielding, Gabriel. *"Not to Disturb."* *Critic*, 30 (July-August 1972), 67-68.

473. Frakes, J. R. "Mock-Mod-Gothic." *Book World*, 6 (16 April 1972), 4.

474. Frankel, Haskel. *"Not to Disturb."* *Saturday Review*, 55

(8 April 1972), 74.

475. Graver, Lawrence. "Attending the casseroles and a suicidal baron." *New York Times Book Review* (26 March 1972), pp. 6, 34-35.

476. Haney, Robert W. "The butler won't do it." *Christian Science Monitor*, 64 (20 April 1972), 13.

477. Hill, William B. *"Not to Disturb."* *America*, 126 (20 May 1972), 549.

478. —. *"Not to Disturb."* *Best Sellers*, 32 (15 April 1972), 42-43.

479. Kermode, Frank. "Foreseeing the Unforeseen." *Listener*, 86 (11 November 1971), 657-658.

480. Mano, D. Keith. "When They are Good..." *National Review*, 24 (9 June 1972), 646-647.

481. Nye, Robert. "Life-deploring." *Guardian*, 105 (20 November 1971), 19.

482. Page, Malcolm. *"Not to Disturb."* *West Coast Review*, 7 (April 1973), 11.

483. Quigly, Isabel. "Swiss-Gothick Sparks." *Financial Times* (11 November 1971), p. 24.

484. Raban, Jonathan. "Vague Scriptures." *New Statesman*, 82 (12 November 1971), 657-658.

485. Review of *Not to Disturb*, in the *National Observer*, 11 (8 April 1972), 23.

486. Tomalin, Claire. "The servants' revenge." *Observer* (14 November 1971), p. 33.

487. Waugh, Auberon. "Auberon Waugh on new novels."

Spectator, 227 (20 November 1971), 733-734. P. 733.

The Hothouse by the East River

488. Adams, Phoebe. *"The Hothouse by the East River."* *Atlantic,* 231 (May 1973), 122.

489. Anon. "Shadow boxing." *TLS* (2 March 1973), p. 229.

490. —. *"The Hothouse by the East River."* *British Book News* (May 1973), p. 342.

491. —. *"The Hothouse by the East River."* *Choice,* 10 (September 1973), 985.

492. —. *"The Hothouse by the East River."* *Publishers' Weekly,* 203 (5 March 1973), 73.

493. —. *"The Hothouse by the East River."* *Virginia Quarterly Review,* 49 (Autumn 1973), cxxxvii.

494. Brickner, Richard P. "Three novels: nightmares, conspirators, and maniacs." *New York Times Book Review* (29 April 1973), 24-27. Pp. 24-25.

495. Ellmann, Mary. "The Problem of Elsa." *New Statesman,* 85 (2 March 1973), 308.

496. Fallowell, Duncan. "Hothouse Madness." *Books and Bookmen,* 18 (April 1973), 101.

497. Foote, Timothy. "Ars Moriendi." *Time,* 101 (23 April 1973), 100.

498. Hill, William B. *"The Hothouse by the East River."* *America,* 129 (17 November 1973), 382.

499. Hope, Francis. "Like clockwork." *Observer* (4 March 1973), p. 37.

500. Howes, Victor. *"The Hothouse by the East River." Christian Science Monitor,* 65 (30 May 1973), 9.

501. Johnson, Diane. "Strange Fruit." *Book World,* 7 (29 April 1973), 4-5.

502. Kermode, Frank. "Books of the Year." *Observer* (16 December 1973), p. 33.

503. Loprete, Nicholas J., Jr. *"The Hothouse by the East River." Best Sellers,* 33 (1 September 1973), 246.

504. May, Derwent. "Holy Outrage." *Listener,* 89 (1 March 1973), 283-284.

505. Portis, Rowe. *"The Hothouse by the East River." Library Journal,* 98 (1 March 1973), 767-768.

506. Review of *The Hothouse by the East River,* in the *Antioch Review,* 32 (November 1973), 695.

507. Review of *The Hothouse by the East River,* in the *National Observer,* 12 (2 June 1973), 21.

508. Rome, Florence. Review of *The Hothouse by the East River,* in the *Chicago Tribune Book World* (29 April 1973), p. 3.

509. Seymour-Smith, Martin. "Raising the temperature." *Financial Times* (1 March 1973), p. 29.

510. Waugh, Auberon. "Spark plug." *Spectator,* 230 (17 March 1973), 331-332.

The Abbess of Crewe

511. Ackroyd, Peter. "Sending up." *Spectator,* 233 (16 November 1974), 634.

512. Adams, Phoebe. *"The Abbess of Crewe."* Atlantic, 234 (November 1974), 123-124.

513. Allen, Bruce. *"The Abbess of Crewe: a modern morality tale."* Library Journal, 99 (1 November 1974), 2873.

514. Annan, Gabriele. "Holy Watergate." *TLS* (15 November 1974), p. 1277.

515. Anon. "Bugs and Mybug." *Listener*, 92 (28 November 1974), 706.

516. —. *"The Abbess of Crewe; a modern morality tale."* Booklist, 71 (15 October 1974), 215.

517. —. *"The Abbess of Crewe."* British Book News (January 1975), p. 70.

518. —. *"The Abbess of Crewe."* Choice, 12 (March 1975), 78.

519. —. *"The Abbess of Crewe."* Kirkus, 42 (15 August 1974), 900.

520. —. *"The Abbess of Crewe."* Publishers' Weekly, 206 (19 August 1974), 74.

521. —. *"The Abbess of Crewe."* Time, 104 (11 November 1974), 112.

522. —. *"The Abbess of Crewe."* Virginia Quarterly Review, 51 (Spring 1975), liv.

523. Brockway, James. "Taking the holy water." *Books and Bookmen*, 20 (January 1975), 28-30.

524. Cooper, Susan. *"The Abbess of Crewe."* Christian Science Monitor, 66 (13 November 1974), 12.

525. Crain, Jane Larkin. *"The Abbess of Crewe."* Saturday Review/World, 2 (19 October 1974), 24, 28.

526. Cuffe, Edwin D. "Wimplegate? Watercloister?" *Book World* (17 November 1974), p. 1.

527. Hill, William B. *"The Abbess of Crewe."* *Best Sellers,* 34 (15 November 1974), 374.

528. Hutchinson, Tom. "Critics' choice." *The* (London) *Times* (28 November 1974), p. IV.

529. Kermode, Frank. "Books of the Year." *Observer* (15 December 1974), p. 19.

530. Malin, Irving. *"The Abbess of Crewe."* *New Republic,* 171 (12 October 1974), 29-30.

531. Murray, Isobel. "The bear truth." *Financial Times* (14 November 1974), p. 16.

532. Nye, Robert. "Sparkling Spark." *Guardian Weekly,* 111 (23 November 1974), 22.

533. Prescott, Peter S. "Spark: Shabby abbey." *Newsweek,* 84 (11 November 1974), 110.

534. Pritchard, William H. "Novel Sex and Violence." *Hudson Review,* 28 (Spring 1975), 147-160. P. 153.

535. Sage, Lorna. "Bugging the nunnery." *Observer* (10 November 1974), p. 33.

536. Tennant, Emma. "Holy Joke." *Listener,* 92 (14 November 1974), 649.

* 537. Wood, Michael. "Fiction in Extremis." *New York Review of Books,* 21 (28 November 1974), 29-31. P. 29.

The Takeover

538. Eaglen, Audrey B. *"The Takeover."* *Library Journal,* 101

(August 1976), 1660.

539. Fallowell, Duncan. "Campo dei fiori." *Spectator,* 236 (12 June 1976), 23.

540. Firth, Brian. "Batteries of alluring sense." *Tablet,* 230 (19 June 1976), 593.

* 541. Fox, Robin Lane. "Up at the Villas." *Financial Times* (10 June 1976), p. 25.

* 542. Kermode, Frank. "Diana of the Crossroads." *New Statesman,* 91 (4 June 1976), 746-747.

* 543. May, Derwent. "Maggie's Money." *Listener,* 95 (3 June 1976), 718.

* 544. Sage, Lorna. "Roman scandals." *Observer* (6 June 1976), p. 29.

The Go-Away Bird and Other Stories

545. Allen, Walter. "New Short Stories." *New Statesman,* 56 (20 December 1958), 888-890. P. 890.

546. Anon. "Briefly Noted." *New Yorker,* 36 (12 November 1960), 240.

547. —. "Confidence Trickster." *Time,* 76 (14 November 1960), 108, 110.

548. —. "New Fiction." *The* (London) *Times* (27 November 1958), p. 13.

549. —. "Sense and Sensitivity." *TLS* (19 December 1958), p. 733.

550. —. "*The Go-Away Bird.*" *Booklist,* 57 (1 December 1960), 211.

551. —. *"The Go-Away Bird."* Bookmark, 20 (December 1960), 67.

552. Bedford, Sybille. "Fantasy Without Whimsy." *Saturday Review*, 43 (19 November 1960), 28-29.

553. Birstein, Ann. "An Uncanny Aim." *Reporter*, 23 (10 November 1960), 55.

554. Burnette, Frances. *"The Go-Away Bird and Other Stories."* Library Journal, 85 (15 December 1960), 4488.

555. DeMott, Benjamin. "In and Out of Storytown." *Hudson Review*, 14 (Spring 1961), 133-141. Pp. 136-138.

556. Gransden, K. W. "The Light Touch." *Encounter*, 12 (February 1959), 74-76. P. 75.

557. Hughes, Riley. *"The Go-Away Bird."* Catholic World, 192 (February 1961), 310.

558. Kirgo, George. Review of *The Go-Away Bird*, in the *Chicago Sunday Tribune* (1 January 1961), p. 6.

559. Lonergan, Joan. Review of *The Go-Away Bird*, in the *Catholic Library World*, 109 (November 1960), p. 140.

560. Phelps, Robert. "The Devil's at Work Around the Clock." *New York Herald Tribune Book Review*, 37 (13 November 1960), 5.

561. Pippett, Aileen. "Salvation and Hocus Pocus are all Very Real." *New York Times Book Review* (30 October 1960), p. 4.

562. Price, R. G. G. *"The Go-Away Bird."* Punch, 236 (14 January 1959), 107.

563. Quinn, Miriam. *"The Go-Away Bird."* Best Sellers, 20 (15 November 1960), 318.

564. Quinton, Anthony. Untitled book review. *London Magazine,* 6 (June 1959), 68-72. Pp. 69-71.

565. Rogers, Thomas. "The Enchanted Void." *Commentary,* 31 (March 1961), 268-270.

566. Rogers, W. G. "Stories Worth Hearing Again." *New York Herald Tribune Books,* 38 (14 January 1962), 42.

567. Webb, W. L. "Autumn Harvest of Short Stories." *Manchester Guardian* (28 November 1958), p. 8.

Voices at Play

568. Anon. "Briefing: *Voices at Play." Observer* (2 October 1966), p. 22.

569. —. "Crossing the Barrier." *TLS* (17 February 1961), p. 110. Review of "The Danger Zone," included in *Voices at Play.*

570. —. "Ghouls and Ghosts." *TLS* (7 July 1961), p. 418.

571. —. "New Fiction." *The* (London) *Times* (29 June 1961), p. 15.

572. —. "Too Many Strands of Meaning: Miss Muriel Spark's New Radio Play." *The* (London) *Times* (16 February 1961), p. 16. Review of "The Danger Zone."

573. —. *"Voices at Play." Booklist,* 58 (15 June 1962), 719-720.

574. Burnette, Frances. *"Voices at Play." Library Journal,* 87 (July 1962), 2570.

575. Crozier, Mary. Review of *Voices at Play,* in *Guardian* (11 August 1961), p. 5.

576. Feld, Rose. *"Voices at Play." New York Herald Tribune Books,* 38 (6 May 1962), 6.

577. Frankel, Haskel. "The Ghostly Deus ex Machina." *Saturday Review,* 45 (2 June 1962), 35.

578. Hill, William B. *"Voices at Play." Best Sellers,* 22 (15 May 1962), 78.

579. Hodgart, Matthew. "Models of Mischief." *New Statesman,* 61 (30 June 1961), 1052-1054. P. 1053.

580. Hynes, Samuel. "A Minor Spark." *Commonweal,* 76 (8 June 1962), 285-286.

* 581. Jelliffe, R. A. Review of *Voices at Play,* in the *Chicago Sunday Tribune* (13 May 1962), p. 4.

582. Prescott, Orville. "Books of The Times." *New York Times,* 111 (7 May 1962), 29.

583. Simpson, N. F. Review of *Voices at Play,* in *Time and Tide* (29 June 1961), p. 1077.

584. Singer, Burns. "New Novels." *Listener,* 66 (13 July 1961), 69.

585. Waugh, Evelyn. "Threatened Genius: Difficult Saint." *Spectator,* 207 (7 July 1961), 28-29. P. 28.

586. Young, B. A. *"Voices at Play." Punch,* 241 (26 July 1961), 152.

Collected Stories I

587. Anon. "At Another Distance." *TLS* (30 November 1967), p. 1125.

588. —. *"Collected Stories 1." Booklist,* 65 (15 September

1968), 103.

589. —. *"Collected Stories: 1."* *Choice*, 6 (April 1969), 218.

590. —. *"Collected Stories: 1."* *Kirkus*, 36 (15 April 1968), 484.

591. —. *"Collected Stories: 1."* *Publishers' Weekly*, 193 (15 April 1968), 90.

592. Cushman, Jerome. "Collected Stories 1." *Library Journal*, 93 (1 June 1968), 2261.

593. Greene, George. "Compulsion to Love." *Kenyon Review*, 31 (Spring 1969), 267-272.

594. Johnson, R. A. Review of *Collected Stories: 1*, in *Studies in Short Fiction* (Summer 1972), p. 289.

595. Ostermann, R. Review of *Collected Stories: 1*, in the *National Observer*, 7 (9 September 1968), 87.

596. Price, R. G. G. *"Collected Stories 1."* *Punch*, 253 (29 November 1967), 831.

Doctors of Philosophy

597. Adams, Phoebe. "Potpourri." *Atlantic*, 217 (April 1966), 152.

598. Anon. "Idiom Exacts Revenge—Rash Choice in Farce. Arts Theatre: *Doctors of Philosophy.*" *The* (London) *Times* (3 October 1962), p. 12.

599. —. *"Doctors of Philosophy; a play."* *Booklist*, 62 (15 March 1966), 691-692.

600. —. *"Doctors of Philosophy; a play."* *Choice*, 4 (September 1967), 698.

601. —. *"Doctors of Philosophy."* TLS (19 July 1963), p. 530.

602. Gellert, Roger. "Pitiable Objects." *New Statesman,* 64 (12 October 1962), 501-502. P. 501.

603. Keown, Eric. "At the Play." *Punch,* 243 (10 October 1962), 537-538.

604. Mutalik-Desai, A. A. *"Doctors of Philosophy,* a Play by Muriel Spark." *Parashuramian* (March 1964), pp. 56-60.

605. Pepper, G. M. *"Doctors of Philosophy."* National Review, 18 (5 April 1966), 327.

606. Trewin, J. C. "Peak and Valley." *Illustrated London News,* 241 (13 October 1962), 572. A review of the play based upon the book.

The Fanfarlo and Other Verse

607. Anon. "Individual Voices." *TLS* (2 January 1953), p. 6.

* 608. Claudel, Alice Moser. *"The Fanfarlo and Other Verse."* Experiment, 7 (Winter 1957), 230-231.

609. Treece, Henry. *"The Fanfarlo and Other Verse."* Poetry Quarterly, 14, No. 3 (Autumn 1952), 92-93.

Collected Poems I

610. Anon. *"Collected Poems: 1."* Booklist, 65 (1 November 1968), 285.

611. —. *"Collected Poems: 1."* Choice, 6 (March 1969), 58.

612. —. *"Collected Poems: 1."* Kirkus, 36 (15 April 1968), 504.

613. —. *"Collected Poems: 1."* Publishers' Weekly, 193 (22 April 1968), 48.

614. —. "Verse and Versatility." *TLS* (15 February 1968), p. 155.

615. Blackburn, T. Review of *Collected Poems: 1,* in *Poetry Review* (Spring 1968), p. 57.

616. Cushman, Jerome. *"Collected Poems 1."* Library Journal, 93 (1 June 1968), 2246.

617. Press, John. "New Poetry." *Punch,* 254 (7 February 1968), 211.

Tribute to Wordsworth

618. Anon. "The Wordsworth Harvest." *TLS* (16 June 1950), p. 375.

619. Heppenstall, Rayner. "More About Wordsworth." *New Statesman and Nation,* 40 (1 July 1950), 17.

Child of Light:
A Reassessment of Mary Wollstonecraft Shelly

620. Anon. "Portrait of Mary Shelley." *TLS* (4 April 1952), p. 238.

621. Koszul, A. Review of *Child of Light,* in *Études Anglaises,* 5 (1952), 256-258.

622. Norman, Sylva. "Shelly Again." *Spectator,* 187 (23 November 1951), 716.

623. Treece, Henry. "What a Set!" *Poetry Quarterly,* 13, No. 4 (Winter 1951-1952), 188-189.

Emily Brontë: Her Life and Work

624. Anon. *"Emily Brontë: Her Life and Work."* *Kirkus,* 34 (1 September 1966), 929.

625. —. *"Emily Brontë: Her Life and Work."* *Library Journal,* 91 (15 October 1966), 5271-5272.

626. —. *"Emily Brontë: Her Life and Work."* *New Statesman and Nation,* 46 (19 December 1953), 804.

627. —. *"Emily Bronte."* *TLS* (20 November 1953), p. 739.

628. —. "Reader's Guide." *Yale Review,* n.s. 56 (Spring 1967), xxxvii-xxxviii.

629. Blondel, J. Review of *Emily Brontë: Her Life and Work,* in *Études Anglaises,* 8 (1954), 269-270.

630. Bloom, Edward A. "Emily Brontë Dissected." *Saturday Review,* 37 (13 November 1954), 34.

631. Burke, Herbert. *"Emily Brontë: Her Life and Work."* *Library Journal,* 85 (August 1960), 2792.

632. Cook, Roderick. *"Emily Brontë."* *Harper's,* 233 (September 1966), 114-115.

633. DeLissovoy, Susan. "Living Was Writing." *Reporter,* 36 (18 May 1967), 40, 42.

634. Kiely, Robert. "Brontë—double-teamed." *Christian Science Monitor,* 58 (13 October 1966), 4.

635. Robinson, J. K. Review of *Emily Brontë: Her Life and Work,* in *Books Today,* 3 (25 September 1966), 10.

636. Ward, Aileen. "The ways of the Brontës." *Book Week,* 4 (18 September 1966), 5, 19. P. 5.

637. Waring, W. *"Emily Brontë: Her Life and Work."* Library *Journal,* 91 (15 October 1966), 4956.

John Masefield

638. Anon. *"John Masefield."* New Statesman and Nation, 46 (21 November 1953), 651.

639. —. "The Earlier Mr. Masefield." *TLS* (11 September 1953), p. 578.

640. Farmer, A. J. Review of *John Masefield,* in *Études Anglaises,* 8 (1953), 270; and 9 (1954), 76.

641. Grigson, Geoffrey. "Gods, Graves and Gold." *New Statesman,* 63 (4 May 1962), 647-648. P. 648.

My Best Mary

642. Anon. "Shelley and Mary." *TLS* (17 April 1953), p. 248.

643. Bloom, Edward A. "The Shelleys: An Epistolatory Biography." *Saturday Review,* 37 (12 June 1954), 17.

644. Lewis, Naomi. "A Sea Coast in Bohemia." *New Statesman and Nation,* 45 (30 May 1953), 648, 650. P. 650.

645. Reeves, James. Review of *My Best Mary,* in *Observer* (26 April 1953), p. 9.

The Brontë Letters

646. Anon. *"The Brontë Letters."* TLS (25 June 1954), p. 414.

647. —. *"The Letters of the Brontës, a selection."* Booklist, 51 (1 October 1954), 61.

648. Bellasis, M. "Wild and Rainy." *Tablet,* 220 (19 November 1966), 1302-1303.

649. Bentley, Phillis. Review of *The Brontë Letters,* in the *Listener,* 51 (1954), 879.

650. Ferguson, DeLancey. "In Their Own Words." *New York Times Book Review* (12 September 1954), p. 29.

651. Quigly, Isabel. "Strong and Outspoken." *Spectator,* 218 (13 January 1967), 49.

Letters of John Henry Newman

652. Anon. "Reintroducing Newman." *TLS* (16 August 1957), p. 496.

653. O'Faolain, Sean. "A Liberal Tory?" *Spectator,* 199 (5 July 1957), 21.

654. Raymond, John. "More About John Henry." *New Statesman,* 54 (6 July 1957), 27-28.

655. Zeno, F. Review of *Letters of John Henry Newman,* in the *Dublin Review* (1957), pp. 369-373.

The Very Fine Clock

656. Anon. "Continuations and beginnings." *TLS* (4 December 1969), p. 1389.

657. —. *"The Very Fine Clock."* *Publishers' Weekly,* 194 (11 November 1968), 50.

658. Blake, Quentin. "Child's Eye View." *Punch,* 257 (17 December 1969), 1015.

659. Fuller, John. "Jacqueline and Co." *New Statesman,* 78 (31 October 1969), 626, 628.

660. Green, Candida Lycett. "Gorey hallelujah." *Spectator,* 223 (1 November 1969), 597.

661. Harmon, Elva. *"The Very Fine Clock."* *Library Journal,* 94 (15 June 1969), 2497-2498.

662. Jones, Olive. "Tick is a clock." *Books and Bookmen,* 15 (December 1969), 48-49. P. 48.

663. Maddocks, Melvin. "Country slickers." *Christian Science Monitor,* 60 (7 November 1968), B4.

664. Pippett, Aileen. *"The Very Fine Clock."* *New York Times Book Review* (29 December 1968), p. 20.

ANGUS [FRANK JOHNSTONE] WILSON
(Born in Bexhill, Sussex 1913)

I. PRIMARY WORKS: NOVELS

1. *Hemlock and After.* London: Secker and Warburg, 1952, 1960; New York: Viking Press, 1952; Harmondsworth: Penguin, 1956; as *Giftdryck.* Trans. Jane Lundblad. Stockholm: Norstedt, 1953; as *Skarn og Skarntyde.* Trans. Mogens Boisen. Copenhagen: Hagerup, 1953; as *Dolle Kervel.* Trans. Otto Nagtzaam. Amsterdam: De Arbeiderspers, 1954; as *La Ciguë et aprés.* Trans. Marie Tadié. Paris: R. Laffont, 1954; as *La cicuta e dopo.* Trans. Eugenio Montale. Milano: Garzanti, 1956; as *Después de la cicuta.* Trans. Ana Teresa Weyland. Buenos Aires: Comanía general Fabril editoria, 1961; as *Depois da cicuta.* Trans. Mário Henrique Leiria. Lisbon: Portugália, 1961.

2. *Anglo-Saxon Attitudes.* London: Secker and Warburg, 1956; Toronto: British Book Service, 1956; New York: Viking Press, 1956, 1960; Harmondsworth: Penguin, 1958, 1968; with a foreword by Frank Kermode. New York: New American Library, 1963; as *Prima che sia tardi.* Trans. Carlo Rossi Fantonetti. Milano: Garzanti, 1957; as *Epäjumala haudassa.* Trans. Mikko Kilpi. Helsinki: Werner Söderström, 1957; as *Attitudes anglosaxonnes.* Trans. Calude Elsen. Paris: Stock, 1957; as *Späte Entdeckungen.* Trans. Alexander Koval. Wiesbaden: Inselverl, 1957; also Reinbek and Hamburg: Rowohlt, 1961; as *Anglosaskie Pozy.* Trans. Adam Klimowïcz. Warsaw: Czytelnik, 1958; as *Britter Emellan.* Trans. Goran Salander. Stockholm, 1958; as *Anglo-*

saský Postoj. Trans. Jarmila Urbánkova. Prague: SNK-
LHU, 1960; as *Actitudes Anglosajonas.* Trans. Micaela
Mata and José M. Aroca. Barcelona: Seix y Barral,
1961; as *Anglosaksonski Maniri.* Trans. Hamo Džabic.
Beograd (Yugoslavia): Prosveta, 1961; as *Anglosaksi
Poosid.* Trans. Henno Rajandi. Tallin (Russia): Ëësti
raamat, 1970; as *Angolszász Furcsaságok.* Trans. Tibor
Szilágyi. Budapest: Magveto, 1972.

3. *The Middle Age of Mrs. Eliot.* London: Secker and War-
burg, 1958; Toronto: British Book Service, 1958; New
York: Viking Press, 1959; New York: Meridian Books,
1960; Harmondsworth: Penguin, 1961, 1969; as *Les
Quarante ans de Mrs. Eliot.* Trans. Claude Elsen. Paris:
Stock, 1959; as *Het Tweede leven van Meg Eliot.* Trans.
M. Mok. Amsterdam and Antwerp: Contact, 1960; as
Meg Eliot. Trans. Helmut Lindemann. Wiesbaden:
Insel-Verl, 1960; also Berlin: Aufbau-Verl, 1969; as *La
Madurez de la Señora Eliot.* Trans. Jorge Onfray and Wil-
fredo Reyes. Buenos Aires: Santiago de Chile, 1960; as
Una signora di mezza età. Trans. Ugo Tolomei. Milano:
Garzanti, 1961; as *Efter Sommaren.* Trans. Göran
Salander. Stockholm: Norstedt, 1961; as *Dojrzale Lata
Pani Eliot.* Trans. Adam Klimowicz. Warsaw: Czytelnik,
1963; as *Anglosaksonski Maniri.* Trans. Hamo Džabic.
Beograd (Yugoslavia): Prosveta, 1963.

4. *The Old Men at the Zoo.* London: Secker and Warburg,
1961, 1965; Toronto: British Book Service, 1961; New
York: Viking Press, 1961; Harmondsworth: Penguin,
1964; as *Die Alten Männer im Zoo.* Trans. Peter Stadel-
mayer. Frankfurt: Insel-Verl, 1962; as *Los Viejos Del
Zoo.* Trans. Jorge Ferrer Vidal. Barcelona: Plaza and
Janés, 1962; also Barcelona: Círculo de Lectores, 1969;
as *De Oude Mannen van de Dierentuin.* Trans. Maurits
Mok. Amsterdam: Contact, 1963, 1968; as *La Girafe et
les Vieillards.* Trans. Anne-Marie Soulac. Paris: Stock,
1963; as *Starci u Zoološkom Vrtu.* Trans. Živojin Simić.
Beograd (Yugoslavia): Prosveta, 1964; as *Vecchi allo
Zoo.* Trans. Franca Cancogi. Milano: Garzanti, 1966.

5. *Late Call.* London: Secker and Warburg, 1964; Don Mills, Ontario: Collins, 1964; New York: Viking Press, 1965; Harmondsworth: Penguin, 1968; as *L'Appel du Soir.* Trans. Marie-A. Revellat. Paris: Stock, 1965; as *Später Ruf.* Trans. Ursula von Zedlitz. Zürich and München: Droemer-Knaur, 1966, 1969; also Berlin: Deutsche Buch-Gemeinschaft, 1967; also Zürick: Neue Schweizer Bibliothek, 1969; as *Późne Wstawanie.* Trans. Cecylia Wojewoda. Warsaw: Czytelnik, 1967; as *Chemare Tîrzie.* Trans. Ady Florea and Nicolae Minei. Bucuresti (Romania): Editura pentru literatură universală, 1968; as *Que me Ilamen tarde.* Trans. Georgina Regás. Barcelona: Seix y Barral, 1968.

6. *No Laughing Matter.* London: Secker and Warburg, 1967; Don Mills, Ontario: Collins, 1967; New York: Viking, 1967; Harmondsworth: Penguin, 1969; as *En jouant le jeu.* Trans. Jean Autret. Paris: Stock, 1969; as *Per Gioco Ma Sul Serio.* Trans. Paola Ojetti. Milano: Feltrinelli, 1969; also Milano: Club degli editori, 1971; as *Kein Grund zum Lachen.* Trans. Maria Dessauer. Zürick and München: Droemer Knaur, 1969, 1973; also Gütersloh: Bertelsmann, 1971; also Stuttgart: Europ. Buch, 1971.

7. *As If By Magic.* London: Secker and Warburg, 1973; New York: Viking Press, 1973; as *Wie durch Magie.* Trans. Werner Peterich. München and Zürich: Droemer-Knaur, 1975.

PRIMARY WORKS: SHORT STORIES

8. "Sugared Almonds." *Nation and Athenaeum,* 35 (26 July 1924), 535-537. (Authenticity not established).

9. "Life and Letters." *Partisan Review,* 16 (October 1949), 982-994.

10. *The Wrong Set and Other Stories.* London: Secker and

Warburg, 1949, 1961, 1969; New York: Morrow, 1950; Harmondsworth: Penguin, 1959, 1960, as *Dåligt sällskap, og andra noveller.* Trans. Aida Tornell. Stockholm: Norstedt, 1956; as *Halb Seltskond.* Trans. E. Roks. Tallin (Russia): Gaz.-žurn. izd., 1959; as *La Parte Sbagliata.* Trans. Argia Michettoni. Milano: Garzanti, 1962; as *La Mala Gente.* Trans. Mary Rowe. Barcelona: G. P., 1964; as *Warui Nakama.* Trans. Kudo Akio and Suzuki Yasushi. Tokyo: Hakusuisha, 1968; selections from *The Wrong Set* with selections from *Such Darling Dodos,* as *Frisk Luft og andre Noveller.* Trans. Eivind Hauge. Oslo: Cappelen, 1957; with *Heart of Elm* as *Warui Nakama: Nire-no-ki.* Trans. Kazuo Sakamoto and Shôzo Kizumi. Tokyo: Nan'un-dô, 1960.

Contents: "Fresh Air Fiend"—"Union Reunion"—"Saturnalia"—"Realpolitik"—"A Story of Historical Interest" —"The Wrong Set"—"Crazy Crowd"—"A Visit in Bad Taste"—"Raspberry Jam"—"Significant Experience"— "Mother's Sense of Fun"—"Et Dona Ferentes."

11. "The Old, Old Message." *New Statesman and Nation,* 40 (23 December 1950), 648, 650.

12. *Such Darling Dodos and Other Stories.* London: Secker and Warburg, 1950, 1959; Toronto: S. J. R. Saunders, 1951; New York: Morrow, 1951; Harmondsworth: Penguin, 1960, 1968; as *Was für Reizende Vögel.* Trans. Wolfgang von Einsiedel and Hilde Speil. München: Taschenbuch Verl, 1963; as *Aquellos Adorables Tipos Raros.* Trans. Jorge Ferrer Vidal. Barcelona: Plaza Janés, 1965; "Mother's Sense of Fun," from *Such Darling Dodos,* as "Mutters Sinn für Humor," in *England Erzählt.* Trans. Hilde Spiel. Frankfurt: Fischer-Bucherei, 1960.

Contents: "Rex Imperator"—"A Little Companion"— "Learning's Little Tribute"—"Sister Superior"—"Such Darling Dodos"—"Necessity's Child"—"Christmas Day in the Workhouse"—"Mummy to the Rescue"—"Heart of

Elm"—"What Do Hippos Eat?"

13. *A Bit Off the Map and Other Stories.* London: Secker and Warburg, 1957; Toronto: British Book Service, 1957; New York: Viking Press, 1957; Harmondsworth: Penguin, 1968; "More Friend Than Lodger," from *A Bit Off the Map,* as *Mehr Freund als Untermieter.* Trans. Hilde Spiel. Frankfurt: Insel-Verlag, 1961.

   Contents: "A Bit Off the Map"—"A Flat Country Christmas"—"More Friend Than Lodger"—"Once a Lady"—"After the Show"—"Higher Standards"—"A Sad Fall"—"Ten Minutes to Twelve."

14. *Death Dance: Twenty-Five Stories.* New York: Viking, 1969, 1970. Contains all but six stories from his previous three collections: "Fresh Air Fiend," "Significant Experience" (from *The Wrong Set...*); "Rex Imperator," "Sister Superior," "Heart of Elm" (from *Such Darling Dodos...*), and "Ten Minutes to Twelve" (from *A Bitt Off the Map...*). No new stories are included.

PRIMARY WORKS: PLAYS

15. *The Mulberry Bush: A Play in Three Acts* (produced in London, 1956). London: Secker and Warburg, 1956; London: Evans Brothers, 1957; in *Novelists Theatre: Three Plays.* Harmondsworth: Penguin, 1966.

16. "After the Show" (an unpublished 1959 television play which is an adaptation of his "A Bit Off the Map").

17. "The Stranger" (an unpublished 1960 television play).

18. "Skeletons and Assegais: Family Reminiscences" (a radio play—produced for the B.B.C. Third Programme, 1962); in *Transatlantic Review,* 9 (Spring 1962), 19-43.

19. "The Invasion" (an unpublished 1963 television play).

20. "The Foundation of Modern Japan." *Spectator,* 167 (12 December 1941), 550-551. Wilson discusses the influence of China upon Japan, and the latter's parallel to Hitler's Germany.

21. "New Novels." *New Statesman and Nation,* 38 (27 August 1949), 226-227. Review of Max Van Der Meersch's *The Poor Girl,* Jean Orieux's *Fontagre,* Anthony Rhodes's *The Uniform,* and Erik De Mauny's *The Huntsman in His Career.*

22. "New Novels." *New Statesman and Nation,* 38 (24 September 1949), 336, 338. Review of Arthur Miller's *Focus,* and Ernest Frost's *The Dark Peninsula.*

23. "Short Stories." *New Statesman and Nation,* 38 (15 October 1949), 435-436. Review of Frances Towers's *Tea With Mr. Rochester,* Christopher Sykes's *Character and Situation,* and *The Pick of To-day's Short Stories,* ed. by John Pudney.

24. "Short Stories." *New Statesman and Nation,* 38 (3 December 1949), 656, 658. Review of Elizabeth Bowen's *Encounters,* Jean-Paul Sartre's *Intimacy,* Delmore Schwartz's *The World is a Wedding,* Rhys Davies's *Boy With a Trumpet,* and Nigel Kneale's *Tomato Cain.*

25. "Proust as a Set Book." *New Statesman and Nation,* 38 (24 December 1949), 760. Review of F. C. Green's *The Mind of Proust.*

26. "Letters from Proust." *New Statesman and Nation,* 39 (18 March 1950), 312. Review of Proust's *Letters to a Friend,* trans. by A. and E. Henderson.

27. "Dickens and the Divided Conscience." *Month,* 189 (May 1950), 349-360.

28. "Proust Alone." *New Statesman and Nation,* 40 (11 November 1950), 434, 436. Review of *Letters of Marcel*

Proust, ed. and trans. by Mina Curtiss.

29. "The Day Before Yesterday." *New Statesman and Nation*, 41 (24 February 1951), 222, 224. Review of *English Stories from New Writing*, ed. by John Lehmann.

30. "Broken Promise." *Listener* (12 April 1951), pp. 575-576.

31. "A Letter from London." *American Mercury*, 72 (May 1951), 571-577. On the quality of life in the English Welfare State. On English eccentricity.

32. "Revolution in British Reading." *American Mercury*, 73 (December 1951), 47-54.

33. "The Novels of William Godwin." *World Review*, 28 (June 1951), 37-40.

* 34. "The Prince of Middlebrows." *New Statesman and Nation*, 43 (15 March 1952), 312, 314. Review of Rupert Hart-Davis's *Hugh Walpole*.

* 35. "New Short Stories." *New Statesman and Nation*, 43 (21 June 1952), 738. Review of Robert Penn Warren's *The Circus in the Attic*, Wallace Stegner's *The Woman on the Wall*, Irwin Shaw's *Mixed Company*, Kay Boyle's *The Smoking Mountain*, and Frances Bellerby's *A Breathless Child*.

36. "A Tattered Idyll." *New Statesman and Nation*, 44 (4 October 1952), 382, 384. Review of Ralph M. Wardle's *Mary Wollstonecraft*.

* 37. "Mr. Huxley's Split Mind." *New Statesman and Nation*, 44 (1 November 1952), 516, 518. Review of Aldous Huxley's *The Devils of Loudun*.

* 38. *Emile Zola: An Introductory Study of His Novels*. London: Secker and Warburg, 1952, 1964; rev. ed., 1965; New York: Morrow, 1952, 1961; Gloucester, Massa-

chusetts: Paul Smith, 1962; rev. ed., London: Mercury
Books, 1965; rev. ed., Don Mills, Ontario: Collins, 1965.

39. "The Diffident Hero." *New Statesman and Nation,* 45 (21
March 1953), 347. Review of George Seaver's biography,
Francis Younghusband.

* 40. "Parties: Being a Host." *Punch,* 224 (22 April 1953), 482.
A witty "Study" of cocktail parties.

* 41. "On Parties: Being a Guest." *Punch,* 224 (20 May 1953),
602. A witty account of a party given by one Lucy
Ellesmere-Scrant.

* 42. "Throughout the Country." *New Statesman and Nation,*
45 (13 June 1953), 696, 698. On his celebration of
Coronation festivities in Essex.

43. "So Completely Unspoiled." *Punch,* 224 (6 July 1953),
14. A witty account of an unnamed, "unspoilt" English
resort.

44. "New Short Stories." *New Statesman and Nation,* 46 (15
August 1953), 187. Review of J. D. Salinger's *For
Esmé—with Love and Squalor,* Gwyn Jones's *Shepherd's
Hey,* and J. B. Priestley's *The Other Place.*

* 45. " 'Zola and His Characters.' " *TLS* (30 October 1953), p.
693. A letter to the editor, in defense of F. W. J. Hem-
mings' *Emile Zola.*

* 46. *For Whom the Cloche Tolls: A Scrapbook of the Twenties,*
with Philippe Jullian. London: Methuen, 1953; London:
Secker and Warburg, 1973; New York: Viking Press,
1973; New York: Curtis Books, 1973.

47. "The New and Old Isherwood." *Encounter,* 3 (August
1954), 62-68. Review of Isherwood's *The World in the
Evening.*

48. "The Short Story Changes." *Spectator,* 193 (1 October 1954), 401-402. Review of five books by M. Lane, J. Stafford, C. S. Forester, A. White, and L. Auchincloss.

* 49. "Arnold Bennett's Novels." *London Magazine,* 1 (October 1954), 59-67.

50. "Dishonourable Pleasure." *Spectator,* 193 (3 December 1954), 726, 728. Review of Jack Loudan's *O Rare Amanda!*

51. Editor. *British Science Fiction Library.* London: Sidgwick and Jackson, 1954.

52. "The Higher S. F." *Spectator,* 194 (11 February 1955), 160, 162. Review of *Best S. F.: Science Fiction Stories,* ed. by Edmund Crispin.

53. "Oscar Wilde." *London Magazine,* 2 (February 1955), 71-78. On Wilde's life and writings.

* 54. "Great Catherine." *Spectator,* 194 (4 March 1955), 261-262. Review of *The Memoirs of Catherine the Great,* ed. by D. Maroger.

* 55. "Ladies of Devonshire House." *Spectator,* 194 (1 April 1955), 410, 412. Review of D. M. Stuart's *Dearest Bess,* and *Three Howard Sisters,* ed. by Maud, Lady Leconfield.

56. "The Fires of Violence." *Encounter,* 4 (May 1955), 75-78. Review of Robert Penn Warren's *Night Rider.*

57. "Clarity of Vision." *Spectator,* 194 (3 June 1955), 711. Review of Rebecca West's *A Train of Powder.*

* 58. "Italian Short Stories." *Spectator,* 194 (10 June 1955), 748. Review of *Modern Italian Short Stories,* ed. by W. J. Strachan.

59. "Flight to Nowhere." *Encounter,* 4 (June 1955), 73-74, 76.

Review of Richard Gerber's *Utopian Fantasy*.

* 60. "Science Fiction." *Spectator*, 195 (8 July 1955), 64-65. Review of six novels.

61. "Hogarth." *Spectator*, 195 (22 July 1955), 129-130. Review of Peter Quennell's *Hogarth's Progress*.

62. "Ivy Compton-Burnett." *London Magazine*, 2 (July 1955), 64-70.

* 63. "The Naïve Emancipator." *Encounter*, 5 (July 1955), 73-76. Review of Aldous Huxley's *The Genius and the Goddess*.

64. " 'One of Us.' " *Spectator*, 195 (26 August 1955), 284-285. Review of Anthony Glyn's *Elinor Glyn*.

65. "The House Party Novels." *London Magazine*, 2 (August 1955), 53-56. Review of Aldous Huxley's *Crome Yellow*, and *Those Barren Leaves*.

* 66. " 'To Know and Yet Not to Fear Reality.' " *Encounter*, 5 (August 1955), 79-82. Review of Trilling's *The Opposing Self*.

67. "Jazzman." *Spectator*, 195 (9 September 1955), 342. Review of Artie Shaw's *The Trouble with Cinderella*.

68. "This Gentl'd Isle." *Encounter*, 5 (September 1955), 84-87. Review of Geoffrey Gorer's *Exploring British Character*.

* 69. "World's Greatest Museum." *Holiday*, 18 (September 1955), 48, 50-52, 54-55, 93. Then assistant superintendent of the British Museum, Wilson takes readers on a tour and history of the Museum. His accout is witty, and sometimes autobiographical.

70. "The Capel Letters." *Spectator*, 195 (18 November 1955),

679-680. Review of *The Capel Letters,* ed. by the Marquess of Anglesey.

71. "New Short Stories." *New Statesman and Nation,* 50 (19 November 1955), 679-680. Review of Walter De La Mare's *A Beginning,* Eudora Welty's *The Bride of the Innisfallen,* and H. E. Bates's *The Daffodil Sky.*

* 72. "Two Ladies." *Spectator,* 195 (2 December 1955), 772-773. Review of Averil Stewart's *Alicella.*

73. "At the Heart of Lawrence." *Encounter,* 5 (December 1955), 81-83. Review of F. R. Leavis' *D. H. Lawrence.*

74. "Introduction," to *Observer Prize Stories: A. D. 2500.* London: Heinemann, 1955.

75. Untitled autobiographical comments. *Twentieth Century Authors: First Supplement.* Ed. Stanley J. Kunitz. New York: H. W. Wilson, 1955, pp. 1093-1094.

76. "Exorcising the Past." *Encounter,* 6 (January 1956), 86-88. Review of A. L. Rowse's *The Expansion of Elizabethan England.*

* 77. "The Anglo-Saxon World." *New Statesman and Nation,* 51 (11 February 1956), 158-159. Review of Peter Hunter Blair's *An Introduction to Anglo-Saxon England.*

78. *"Beaverbrook." Encounter,* 6 (February 1956), 88-90. Review of Tom Driberg's *Beaverbrook.*

* 79. "Galsworthy's *Forsyte Saga." New Statesman and Nation,* 51 (3 March 1956), 187.

* 80. "The Scholar in the Pantry." *Encounter,* 6 (March 1956), 76-78. Review of J. Jean Hecht's *The Domestic Servant Class in Eighteenth Century England.*

* 81. "Too Wide a Net." *New Statesman and Nation,* 51 (21

April 1956), 426-427. Review of Mario Praz's *The Hero in Eclipse in Victorian Fiction.*

* 82. "Novels and High Brows." *Encounter,* 6 (April 1956), 75-77. Review of George H. Ford's *Dickens and His Readers.*

83. Untitled book review. *London Magazine,* 3 (May 1956), 69-71. Review of Thomas Mann's *Confessions of Felix Krull.*

* 84. "When Europe Trembled." *Encounter,* 6 (June 1956), 91-93. Review of T. D. Kendrick's *The Lisbon Earthquake.*

* 85. "New Novels." *Encounter,* 7 (August 1956), 83-86. A review of five novels.

* 86. "A. D. 1956." *Encounter,* 7 (October 1956), 80-83. Review of Toynbee's *An Historian's Approach to Religion.*

87. "Bernard Shaw." *London Magazine,* 3 (December 1956), 53-58. A centenary estimation of Shaw's ideas and plays. Reply by T. F. Evans, in *London Magazine,* 4 (February 1957), 60-61.

88. "Suicides in London." *Encounter,* 7 (December 1956), 82, 84-85. Review of Peter Sainsbury's *Suicide in London.*

* 89. Introduction to *Marcel Proust and Deliverance From Time,* by Germaine Brée. London: Chatto and Windus, 1956.

* 90. "An Oddity Off Stage." *New Statesman and Nation,* 53 (26 January 1957), 109-110. Review of Douglas Grant's biography, *Margaret the First.*

91. "A Church of Compromise." *Encounter,* 8 (February 1957), 81-83. Review of G. K. Balleine's *Past Finding Out.*

* 92. "Toil and Trouble." *New Statesman and Nation*, 53 (2 March 1957), 282. Review of Christina Hole's *A Mirror of Witchcraft.*

93. "Pickings." *New Statesman and Nation*, 53 (13 April 1957), 491-492. Review of John Montgomery's *The Twenties.*

* 94. "A Century of Japanese Writing." *Encounter*, 8 (April 1957), 83-85. Review of *Modern Japanese Literature*, ed. by Donald Keene.

* 95. With C. P. Snow and others. "Hungarian Writers on Trial." *The* (London) *Times* (29 October 1957), p. 11. A letter to the Editor. A protest.

96. "The Revolt of Samuel Butler." *Atlantic*, 200 (November 1957), 190, 192, 194, 196, 198. On the Anti-Victorian attitudes of his parents' generation; on Butler's life and work in relation to Anti-Victorianism.

* 97. "A Conversation with E. M. Forster." *Encounter*, 9 (November 1957), 52-57.

* 98. "Some Japanese Observations." *Encounter*, 9 (December 1957), 51-55. Discussion of his favorable impressions of the Japanese people.

* 99. With others. "Homosexual Acts: Call to Reform Law." *The* (London) *Times* (7 March 1958), p. 11. A letter to the Editor.

100. "Mood of the Month—III." *London Magazine*, 5 (April 1958), 40-44. On "the status of the writer, the writer in a status society and the function of the novel in a status society." Several of the novelists included in this bibliography are discussed in passing.

* 101. "Bexhill and After." *Spectator*, 200 (9 May 1958), 583-584. On his schooldays at Bexhill, Seaford, and West-

minster.

102. "Diversity and Depth." *TLS* (15 August 1958), p. viii. On the need for depth with breath in the contemporary novel. Reference is made to George Eliot and Dostoevsky as "adult," serious novelists, who possess diversity and depth. Woolf and the other "Bloomsbury" novelists lack social seriousness. The contemporary English novel has a lack of active characterization. Reference is made to Lessing, Lehmann, Powell, and Snow.

* 103. "The Jolliest Resort in the World." *Holiday,* 24 (August 1958), 46, 48-49, 116-117, 119. A witty, satirical account of a middle class resort town: Brighton, on England's southern coast.

* 104. With Rosamond Lehmann, Iris Murdoch, and others. " 'Lolita.' " *The* (London) *Times* (23 January 1959), p. 11. A letter to the Editor. A plea against the possible banning of Nabokov's novel.

* 105. "The Literary View." *Observer* (8 February 1959), p. 19. Review of William Cooper's *Prince Genji.*

* 106. "Nabokov's Basement." *Spectator,* 202 (20 March 1959), 412. Review of Nabokov's *Dozen.*

* 107. "Realist or Romantic?" *Observer* (26 April 1959), p. 23. Review of H. J. Hunt's *Balzac's Comedie Humaine.*

* 108. "Man of Letters." *Spectator,* 202 (12 June 1959), 861. Review of Christopher Hassall's *Edward Marsh.*

* 109. "The Intellectual on the Aisle." *Encounter,* 12 (June 1959), 68-70. Review of Mary McCarthy's *Sights and Spectacles.*

110. "Fulfillment in Time." *Observer* (20 September 1959), p. 22. Review of G. D. Painter's *Marcel Proust: A Biography.*

111. "Room at the Top-ism." *Spectator,* 203 (2 October 1959), 435. An attack on "corrupting pseudo-realism" in English politics, especially as employed by the Tory campaign.

* 112. "Harrod and Hero-Worship." *Spectator,* 203 (9 October 1959), 479-480. Review of R. F. Harrod's *The Prof.*

113. "New Playwrights." *Partisan Review,* 26 (Fall 1959), 631-634. Review of new plays by four writers, including Doris Lessing.

* 114. "The Flaubert-James line." *Manchester Guardian Weekly,* 81 (3 December 1959), 11. Review of Miriam Alliott's *Novelists on the Novel.*

* 115. "Layabout." *Spectator,* 204 (8 January 1960), 46. Review of Frank Norman's *Stand on Me.*

* 116. "Rescuing the Workers." *Spectator,* 204 (29 January 1960), 140-141. Review of Clancy Sigall's *Weekend in Dinlock.*

117. "Waugh's Knox." *Encounter,* 14 (January 1960), 78-80. Review of Evelyn Waugh's *Ronald Knox.*

118. "Albert Camus: Humanist." *Spectator,* 204 (26 February 1960), 293. Rejoinder by Donat O'Donnell follows immediately after, pp. 293-294. Wilson praises Camus' affirmation of life, but feels that Camus' style weakened his ability to create characters of fictional value. O'Donnell deals with Wilson's belief that Camus had wrongly imposed a rigorous stylisation upon himself; therefore damaging his art.

119. With Rosamond Lehmann, C. P. Snow, and others. "Spanish Prisoners." *The* (London) *Times* (1 March 1960), p. 11. A protest letter against the Spanish government's arrest of author Luis Goytisolo, and others.

120. "Good Companion." *Listener,* 63 (3 March 1960), 405-406. Review of J. B. Priestley's *Literature and Western Man.*

* 121. "Going to Ground." *Observer* (13 March 1960), p. 20. Review of Raleigh Trevelyan's *A Hermit Disclosed.*

122. "For Gentiles." *Spectator,* 204 (22 April 1960), 586-587. Review of Norman Bentwich's *The Jews in Our Time.*

123. Untitled book review. *London Magazine,* 7 (April 1960), 71-73. Review of R. W. B. Lewis's *The Picaresque Saint,* and Germaine Brée's *Camus.*

124. "New Woman." *Spectator,* 204 (6 May 1960), 668-669. Review of Maurice Collis' *Nancy Astor.*

* 125. "Anti-Bourgeois Legend." *Encounter,* 14 (May 1960), 74-75. Review of Ellen Moers' *The Dandy.*

* 126. "No One There." *Spectator,* 205 (22 July 1960), 138. Review of Goronwy Rees' *A Bundle of Sensations.*

* 127. "Pictures of Health." *Observer* (14 August 1960), p. 20. Review of Richard Rees's *For Love of Money.*

128. "Paleskin's Redface." *Encounter,* 15 (August 1960), 82-83. Review of Edmund Wilson's *Apologies to the Iroquois.*

129. "Charles Dickens: A Haunting." *Critical Quarterly,* 2 (Summer 1960), 101-108; reprinted in *The Dickens Critics.* Ed. George H. Ford and Lauriat Lane, Jr. Ithaca: Cornell University Press; also London: Oxford University Press, 1962; reprinted in *Dickens: Modern Judgements.* Ed. A. E. Dyson. New York: Macmillan, 1968.

130. "Vision, Vision! Mr. Woodcock!" *New Statesman,* 60 (3 September 1960), 298, 300. On how the trade unions

could help the arts in Britain. Wilson discusses three ways.

131. "New Catalogue for British Museum." *Canadian Library*, 17 (January 1961), 182-183.

* 132. "The Status of S. F." *Observer* (12 March 1961), p. 28. Review of Amis's *New Maps of Hell.*

* 133. "Novelist's Choice." *The* (London) *Times* (15 June 1961), p. 17. On what he has read, and his reading habits. Response by J. Burnaby in *The Times* (22 June 1961), p. 13.

* 134. "If It's New and Modish is It Good?" *New York Times Book Review* (2 July 1961), pp. 1, 12.

135. "The Heroes and Heroines of Dickens." *Review of English Literature*, 2 (July 1961), 9-18.

136. "Ideology and the novel." *Manchester Guardian Weekly*, 85 (3 August 1961), 10. Review of Irving Howe's *Politics and the Novel.*

137. "The Last Amateurs." *Listener*, 66 (3 August 1961), 181. Review of Carolyn Heilbrun's *The Garnett Family.*

138. "Outsider on Olympus." *Observer* (22 August 1961), p. 18. Review of A. O. J. Cockshut's *The Imagination of Charles Dickens.*

* 139. "Champagne with Rose." *New Statesman*, 62 (15 September 1961), 351. Review of *Saying Life: the Memoirs of Sir Francis Rose.*

* 140. With Doris Lessing, Iris Murdoch, and others. "Dr. Agostinho Neto." *The* (London) *Times* (2 October 1961), p. 13. A letter to the Editor. A plea that the Portuguese government release the distinguished Angolan writer from prison.

141. *"The Last Hours of Sandra Lee."* London Magazine, n.s. 1 (December 1961), 89, 91-92. Review of William Sansom's novel.

142. "A Plea Against Fashion in Writing." *Moderna Sprak,* 55 (1961), 345-350.

143. "The Whites in South Africa." *Partisan Review,* 28, No. 5-6 (1961), 612-632. On Apartheid.

144. "The Novelist and the Narrator." *English Studies Today, Second Series: Lectures and Papers Read at the Fourth Conference of the International Association of University Professors of English Held at Lausanne and Berne, August 1959.* Ed. G. A. Bonnard. Bern: Francke, 1961, pp. 43-50.

145. "South African Exiles." *Observer* (21 January 1962), p. 31. Review of Rensburg's *Guilty Land,* and Blumberg's *White Madam.*

146. "Fourteen Points." *Encounter,* 18 (January 1962), 10-12. A discussion of fourteen things that make him angry.

* 147. " 'Mythology' in John Cowper Powy's Novels." *Review of English Literature,* 4 (January 1962), 10-12.

* 148. "Talk of America." *The* (London) *Times* (12 February 1962), p. 11. A letter to the Editor. A protest against anti-American innuendoes in English newspaper reports.

149. "Beaverbrook's England." *New Statesman,* 63 (16 March 1962), 374. Review of Lord Beaverbrook's Memoir of Sir James Dunn, *Courage.*

* 150. "Who Cares?" *Guardian* (8 June 1962), p. 6. Review of Murdoch's *An Unofficial Rose.*

151. With others. "Pressure Against South Africa." *The* (London) *Times* (22 June 1962), p. 13. A letter to the

Editor. A call for peaceful pressures to be placed on the South African Government.

* 152. "Mary, Quite Contrary." *Encounter*, 18 (June 1962), 71-72. Review of Mary McCarthy's *On the Contrary*.

153. "Not for Banning." *New Statesman*, 64 (13 July 1962), 50-51. Review of *To Deprave and Corrupt*, ed. by John Chandos.

* 154. "Social Reform and Mr. Scrooge." *Observer* (5 August 1962), p. 14. Review of Philip Collins's *Dickens and Crime*.

155. "The Theatre of Three or Four." *Listener*, 68 (30 August 1962), 327. Review of John Bowen's book of three television plays, *The Essay Prize*.

* 156. "The Tragic View of Life." *Observer* (16 September 1962), p. 22. Review of John Wain's *Sprightly Running*.

* 157. "John Cowper Powys." *New Statesman*, 64 (26 October 1962), 588.

158. "Evil in the English Novel." Articles first appearing in various issues of *The Listener:* 1. "Richardson and Jane Austen." 68 (27 December 1962), 1079-1080; 2. "George Eliot to Virginia Woolf." 69 (3 January 1963), 15-16; 3. "Outside the central tradition." 69 (10 January 1963), 63-65; 4. "Evil and the Novelist today." 69 (17 January 1963), 115-117; entire series reprinted in *Kenyon Review*, 29 (March 1967), 167-194.

Responses to Wilson's series of essays appeared in volume 69 of *Listener* as follows: Ben Vincent (3 January 1963), p. 31; William L. Fryer, Lila M. Gough, Nigel Ronald, and E. Michael Merry (10 January 1963), pp. 74-75; Bonamy Dobrée, Emrys Jones, and H. H. Hanney (17 January 1963), p. 127; William L. Fryer responds to H. H. Hanney (24 January 1963), p. 169. Wilson replies to his critics in *Listener,* 69 (24 January 1963), 169.

* 159. "Envy," in *The Seven Deadly Sins.* London: *Sunday Times Publications,* 1962; New York: Morrow, 1962, pp. 2-11; Freeport, New York: Books for Libraries Press, 1970; as *Los Siete Pecados Capitale.* Trans. Marta I. Guastavino. Buenos Aires: Compañia general fabril editora, 1964.

* 160. "A Moment of Crystal." *Spectator,* 211 (5 July 1963), 22-23. On Japanese literature.

* 161. "State of Grace." *New Statesman,* 66 (11 October 1963), 492-493. Review of Diana Athill's *Instead of a Letter.*

162. *The Wild Garden; or, Speaking of Writing.* London: Secker and Warburg, 1963; Berkeley, California: University of California Press, 1963, 1965.

163. "Mr. Angus Heriot." *The* (London) *Times* (10 February 1964), p. 14. A letter to the editor. A eulogy.

164. "The challenge of Kipling." *Observer* (29 March 1964), p. 23. Review of *Kipling's Mind and Art,* ed. by A. Rutherford.

165. "Visionary among the rationalists." *Observer* (10 May 1964), p. 26. Review of Leonard Woolf's *Beginning Again.*

166. "Modern man's burden?" *Observer* (31 May 1964), p. 27. Review of Jacques Barzun's *Science: The Glorious Entertainment.*

167. "Merrie England." *Commentary,* 37 (June 1964), 74-75. Review of John Wain's *Sprightly Running.*

168. "Party of One—Confessions of a Zoo-lover." *Holiday,* 35 (June 1964), 12, 16-18, 20, 22. On his life-long love of zoos.

169. "Gardens of Eden?" *Observer* (5 July 1964), p. 26. Review of Edward Hyams's *The English Garden.*

170. "Passionate Mockery." *Observer* (19 July 1964), p. 23. Review of Henry de Montherlant's novel, *Chaos and Night.*

171. "The Delights of Abroad." *Observer* (27 September 1964), p. 24. Review of William Sansom's *Away to it All.*

172. "Waiting for the real Sade." *Observer* (13 December 1964), p. 27. Review of the Marquis de Sade's *Justine.*

173. "Books of the Year." *Observer* (20 December 1964), p. 7. Wilson picks his three top selections.

174. *Tempo: The Impact of Television on the Arts.* London: Studio Vista, 1964; London: Headway Publications, 1964; Chester Springs, Pennsylvania: Dufour, 1966.

175. With William Golding. "The Condition of the Novel." *New Left Review,* No. 29 (January-February 1965), 19-40.

176. "Dickens's private voice." *Observer* (14 February 1965), p. 27. Review of Steven Marcus's *Dickens From Pickwick to Dombey,* and *The Letters of Charles Dickens: Vol. 1. 1820-1839.* ed. by Madeline House and Graham Storey.

177. With others. "Mihajlo Mihajlov." *The* (London) *Times* (23 March 1965), p. 13. A letter to the Editor. A plea for the release of the author-professor who was arrested by his government in Yugoslavia.

178. "Mrs. Thirkell in exile." *Observer* (18 April 1965), p. 26. Review of Graham McInnes's *The Road to Gundagai.*

179. "The horror game." *Observer* (20 May 1965), p. 27. Review of James Purdy's *Cabot Wright Begins.*

180. "Sense and sensitivity." *Observer* (27 June 1965), p. 22. Review of Elizabeth Bowen's *A Day in the Dark,* and Elizabeth Taylor's *A Dedicated Man.*

181. "Travelling companions." *Observer* (8 August 1965), p. 20. Review of Hugh Honour's *The Companion Guide to Venice,* and Georgina Masson's *The Companion Guide to Rome.*

182. "Intellectuals on tape." *Observer* (29 August 1965), p. 21. Review of A. Alvarez's *Under Pressure.*

183. "Labour's First Year: A Review of the Government's Record." *New Statesman,* 70 (15 October 1965), 557. Wilson expresses his hope for a more positive socialistic government.

184. "Journey to Jerusalem." *Observer* (17 October 1965), p. 28. Review of Muriel Spark's *Mandelbaum Gate.*

185. "Blood-brothers and scarecrows." *Observer* (7 November 1965), p. 27. Review of Günter Grass's *Dog Years,* and Max Frisch's *A Wilderness of Mirrors.*

186. "Class-Room Distinctions." *Observer* (5 December 1965), p. 27. Review of Christopher Dilke's *Dr. Moberly's Mint-Mark,* John Carleton's *Westminster School,* and *The Manchester Grammar School* ed. by J. A. Graham and B. A. Phythian.

187. "Tearooms and Cottages." *New Statesman,* 70 (10 December 1965), 936-937. Review of Mark Gertler's *Selected Letters.*

188. "Books of the Year." *Observer* (19 December 1965), p. 22. Wilson picks his three top selections.

189. "Preface" to *No Room for Tourists,* a novel by Margaret Black, 1965.

190. "Tragi-comedy from Africa." *Observer* (30 January 1966), p. 27. Review of Chinua Achebe's *A Man of the People,* and *African English Literature: An Anthology,* ed. by Anne Tibble.

191. "Tropical Greene." *Manchester Guardian Weekly,* 94 (3 February 1966), 10. Review of Graham Greene's novel, *The Comedians.*

192. "Insights into Isherwood." *Observer* (20 March 1966), p. 26. Review of Christopher Isherwood's *Exhumations.*

193. "Making with the metaphysics." *Observer* (1 May 1966), p. 27. Review of John Fowles's *The Magus.*

194. "Mosaic of Italian life." *Observer* (15 May 1966), p. 27. Review of Carlo Emilio Gadda's *That Awful Mess on Via Merulana.*

195. "Speaking Out: Only Fools Laugh at Their Woes." *Saturday Evening Post,* 239 (21 May 1966), 12, 16. On the falseness of the English sense of humor.

196. "Symphony of a thousand pages." *Observer* (12 June 1966), p. 26. Review of Marguerite Young's *Miss Macintosh, My Darling.*

197. With Kingsley Amis, Iris Murdoch and others. "Rights Denied to Soviet Jews." *The* (London) *Times* (27 June 1966), p. 11. A letter to the Editor.

198. "Florence-worship." *Observer* (17 July 1966), p. 23. Review of Eve Borsook's *The Companion Guide to Florence.*

199. "The universal novelist." *Observer* (6 November 1966), p. 27. Review of John Bayley's *Tolstoy and the Novel.*

200. "Books of the Year." *Observer* (18 December 1966), p. 23. Wilson picks his three top selections.

PRIMARY WORKS: OTHER

201. "The Artist as Your Enemy is Your Only Friend." *Southern Review*, 2 (1966), 101-114.

202. Editor. *A Maugham Twelve*, by Somerset Maugham. London: Heinemann, 1966; Don Mills, Ontario: Collins, 1966; as *Cakes and Ale, and Twelve Short Stories*. Garden City, New York: Doubleday, 1967.

203. "George." *Adam International Review*, No. 310-312 (1966), pp. 120-122.

204. "Introduction," to *Oliver Twist*. Ed. Peter Fairclough. Harmondsworth: Penguin, 1966.

205. "Cosmopolitan paperbacks." *Observer* (5 February 1967), p. 26. Review of *The New Writing in the U.S.A.*, ed. by Donald Allen and Robert Creeley; *German Writing Today*, ed. by Christopher Middleton; *Italian Writing Today*, ed. by Raleigh Trevelyan; and *African Writing Today*, ed. by Ezekiel Mphahlele.

206. "Cherry or bilberry pie?" *Observer* (26 February 1967), p. 27. Review of Brian Murphy's *The Computer in Society; Class*, ed. by Richard Mabey; *The Left*, ed. by Gerald Kaufmann; and *Confrontations with Judaism*, ed. by Philip Longworth.

207. "Feminine in-fighter." *Observer* (2 April 1967), p. 27. Review of Dorothy M. Richardson's *Pilgrimage*.

208. "Cassic of the rural past." *Observer* (9 April 1967), p. 27. Review of Sybil Marshall's *Fenland Chronicle*.

209. "Between two islands." *Observer* (30 April 1967), p. 27. Review of V. S. Naipaul's *The Mimic Men*.

210. "Lower depths of literature." *Observer* (21 May 1967), p. 27. Review of George Gissing's *New Grub Street*.

211. "Restrictions in South Africa." *The* (London) *Times* (12

July 1967), p. 9. A letter to the Editor. A protest against South Africa's interference with the livelihood of playwright Athol Fugard.

212. "Eros denied in the British Museum." *Observer* (16 October 1966), p. 26. Review of Peter Fryer's *Private Case-Public Scandal.*

213. "The Dilemma of the Contemporary Novelists." *Approaches to the Novel.* Ed. John Colmer. London: Oliver and Boyd, 1967, pp. 115-132.

214. "Not all pure Marat-Sade." *Observer* (3 March 1968), p. 29. Reviw of T. R. Fyvel's *Intellectuals Today.*

215. "Bursaries." *TLS* (21 March 1968), p. 293. A letter to the editor. In defence of the Arts Council's methods of giving bursaries.

216. "Expatriate extravaganza." *Observer* (7 April 1968), p. 24. Review of Lawrence Durrell's novel *Tunc.*

217. "In the Jane Austen tradition." *Observer* (28 April 1968), p. 28. Review of Elizabeth Taylor's *The Wedding Group.*

218. "The two faces of Bloomsbury." *Observer* (2 June 1968), p. 27. Review of Quentin Bell's *Bloomsbury.*

219. "Obscene Publications." *TLS* (27 June 1968), p. 679. A letter to the editor. In defence of the guest-list for a Conference convened by the Arts Council.

220. "The historical approach." *Observer* (21 July 1968), p. 22. Review of Raymond Chapman's *The Victorian Debate.*

221. "Bury St. Edmunds Abbey." *The* (London) *Times* (10 August 1968), p. 9. An open letter by Wilson and others who oppose the proposal to demolish houses in the ruins of Bury St. Edmunds Abbey.

222. "Involvement: Writer's Reply." *London Magazine,* n.s. 8 (August 1968), 15-16. Wilson answers a question put to him by the editor of *London Magazine.*

223. "Autopsy on a lonely heart." *Observer* (22 September 1968), p. 30. Review of J. R. Ackerley's *My Father and Myself.*

224. "Sexual Revolution." *Listener,* 80 (10 October 1968), 457-460. On women writers and women in literature. Wilson concentrates on Richardson's *Clarissa,* Jane Austen, George Eliot, and Virginia Woolf. He comments, too, on the work of Rhys and Drabble.

225. "The pursuit of evil." *Observer* (27 October 1968), p. 29. Review of L. P. Hartley's *Poor Clare,* and *L. P. Hartley: the collected short stories.*

226. "Books of the Year." *Observer* (22 December 1968), p. 17. Wilson chooses his top three selections.

227. "Poor big rich girl." *Observer* (26 January 1969), p. 27. Review of Elizabeth Bowen's *Eva Trout.*

228. "How the other half lived." *Observer* (16 February 1969), p. 29. Review of *Charles Booth's London* ed. by Albert Fried and Richard M. Elman.

229. "Gentlemen and players." *Observer* (18 May 1969), p. 30. Review of John Gross's *The Rise and Fall of the Man of Letters.*

230. "East Anglian attitudes." *Observer* (1 June 1969), p. 27. Review of Ronald Blythe's *Akenfield.*

231. "Ivy Compton-Burnett." *Observer* (31 August 1969), p. 20. A eulogy.

232. "A novelist for all seasons." *Observer* (23 November 1969), p. 31. Review of *Charles Dickens: A Centenary Volume,*

ed. by E. W. F. Tomlin, *The Uncollected Writings of Charles Dickens*, ed. by Harry Stone, and *The Letters of Charles Dickens: Volume 2 1840-41*, ed. by Madeleine House and Graham Storey.

233. "A novelist's progress." *Observer* (14 December 1969), p. 30. Review of Malcolm Foster's *Joyce Cary.*

234. "Books of the Year." *Observer* (21 December 1969), p. 17. Wilson chooses his three top selections which includes Bowen's *Eva Trout.*

235. "The Neighbourhood of Tombuctoo: Conflicts in Jane Austen's Novels." *Critical Essays on Jane Austen.* Ed. B. C. Southam. London: Routledge and Kegan Paul, 1969.

236. "Culture and classlessness." *Observer* (1 March 1970), p. 33. Review of Richard Hoggart's three volumes of essays: *Speaking To Each Other; About Society;* and *About Literature.*

237. "Peking to Fiesole." *Observer* (19 April 1970), p. 30. Review of Harold Acton's *More Memoirs of an Aesthete.*

238. "Charles Dickens: A Failed Middle-Class Marriage." *Observer* (24 May 1970), p. 374.

239. "Light and Dark in Dickens." *Listener,* 83 (28 May 1970), 701-703. On devils, murderers and death in Dickens's work; on Dickens as a young story-teller; on Dickens's renunciation of Victorian society.

240. "Courage and cunning." *Observer* (31 May 1970), p. 31. Review of Isaac Babel's *You Must Know Everything.*

241. "First of the moderns?" *Observer* (21 June 1970), p. 31. Review of *The Letters of George Meredith,* and V. S. Pritchett's *George Meredith and English Comedy.*

242. "Molars and incisors." *Observer* (19 July 1970), p. 24. Review of Günter Grass's *Local Anaesthetic.*

243. "Sex in never never land." *Observer* (20 September 1970), p. 27. Review of Janet Dunbar's *J. M. Barrie,* and Cecil Roberts's *The Bright Twenties.*

244. "In the great tradition." *Observer* (18 October 1970), p. 34. Review of F. R. and Q. D. Leavis's *Dickens the Novelist.*

245. "Right about turn." *Observer* (22 November 1970), p. 30. Review of Kingsley Amis's *What Became of Jane Austen?*

246. "Books of the Year." *Observer* (20 December 1970), p. 17. Wilson picks his four top selections.

247. "Dickens and Dostoevsky." *Dickens Memorial Lectures 1970.* London: The Dickens Fellowship, 1970, pp. 41-61.

248. "Dickens on Children and Childhood." *Dickens 1970: Centenary Essays.* Ed. Michael Slater. London: Chapman and Hall, 1970, pp. 195-227.

249. *The World of Charles Dickens.* London: Studio Vista, 1970; London: Secker and Warburg, 1970; New York: Viking Press, 1970; Harmondsworth: Penguin, 1972; as *Le Monde de Charles Dickens.* Trans. Suzanne Nétillard. Paris: Gallimard, 1972.

250. "In darkest East Anglia." *Observer* (10 January 1971), p. 27. Review of George Ewart Evans's *Where Beards Wag All.*

251. "The first and the last." *Observer* (7 February 1971), p. 26. Review of Ivy Compton-Burnett's *Dolores,* and *The Last and the First.*

252. "Aesthete with a sword." *Observer* (14 March 1971), p. 36.

Review of Yukio Mishima's *Sun and Steel.*

253. "LM and KM." *Observer* (4 July 1971), p. 28. Review of *Katherine Mansfield: The Memories of L.M.*

254. "One man band." *Observer* (10 October 1971), p. 32. Review of *The World of George Orwell,* ed. by Miriam Gross.

255. "Issyvoo and his parents." *Observer* (24 October 1971), p. 36. Review of Christopher Isherwood's *Kathleen and Frank.*

256. "Books of the Year." *Observer* (19 December 1971), p. 17. Wilson picks his two top selections.

257. "Little Nell and 'Derby Day'." *Dickens Studies Newsletter,* 2 (1971), 88-89.

258. "Charles Dickens Today." *Adam International Review,* No. 346-348 (1971), 11-14.

259. "Introduction," to *England,* by Edwin Smith. London: Thames and Hudson, 1971; New York: Viking Press, 1971.

260. "Respectable Americans." *Observer* (11 June 1972), p. 29. Review of Anthony Bailey's *In the Village.*

261. "Virginia among the wolves." *Observer* (18 June 1972), p. 32. Review of Quentin Bell's *Virginia Woolf: A Biography.*

262. "Books versus biceps." *Observer* (8 October 1972), p. 39. Review of E. M. Forster's *The Life to Come and Other Stories.*

263. "Radical parallels." *Observer* (3 December 1972), p. 37. Review of Lytton Stachey's *The Really Interesting Question and other papers.*

264. "Books of the Year." *Observer* (17 December 1972), p. 25. Wilson picks his two top selections which includes Drabble's *The Needle's Eye*.

265. Untitled comments. *Contemporary Novelists.* Ed. James Vinson. London and Chicago: St. James Press, 1972, pp. 1374-1375. Defence of his work.

266. Untitled comments in the *Iowa Review,* 3, No. 4 (1972), 106-108.

267. *Dickens,* with A. E. Dyson. Santa Monica, California: BFA Educational Media, 1972.

268. "English influence on literature in Western Europe has reached a low ebb." *The* (London) *Times* (2 January 1973), pp, VIII, XI.

269. "The glory that was Greece." *Observer* (7 January 1973), p. 34. Review of J. Mordaunt Crook's *The Greek Revival.*

270. "Local colour." *Observer* (21 January 1973), p. 34. Review of Norman Scarfe's *The Suffolk Landscape,* Neville Blackburne's *The Restless Ocean,* and *Aldeburgh Anthology,* ed. by Ronald Blythe.

271. "Romantic materialist." *Observer* (11 March 1973), p. 36. Review of Carola Oman's *The Wizard of the North.*

272. "Homage to Firbank." *Observer* (1 April 1973), p. 37. Review of Brigid Brophy's *Prancing Novelist.*

273. "A self-made heroine." *Observer* (20 May 1973), p. 36. Review of John Rosenberg's *Dorothy Richardson: The Genius They Forgot.*

274. "Putting us in the picture." *Observer* (29 July 1973), p. 32. Review of Benedict Nicolson's *Courbet: The Studio of the Painter,* and Donald Posner's *Watteau: A Lady At*

Her Toilet.

275. "For the nation." *Observer* (5 August 1973), p. 27. Review of *The National Trust Guide*, ed. by R. Fedden and R. Joekes.

276. "A gift for words and humbug." *New York Times Book Review* (19 August 1973), pp. 3-4. Review of Dudley Barker's *G. K. Chesterton.* Response by John R. Aherne in *New York Times Book Review* (14 October 1973), p. 50.

277. "Cities of dreadful night?" *Observer* (2 September 1973), p. 35. Review of *The Victorian City: Images and Realities*, ed. by H. J. Dyos and Michael Wolff.

278. "Morality under the Microscope." *New Statesman,* 86 (26 October 1973), 602-603. Review of Mark Kinkead-Weekes's *Samuel Richardson: Dramatic Novelist.*

279. "Beaton's jungle book." *Books and Bookmen,* 19 (October 1973), 30-31. Review of Cecil Beaton's *The Strenuous Years: Diaries 1945-55.*

280. "A high talent flogging an old genre." *New York Times Book Review* (11 November 1973), p. 6. Review of Amis's *The Riverside Villas Murder.*

281. "The druid of Wessex." *Observer* (2 December 1973), p. 34. Review of John Cowper Powys's *Weymouth Sands,* and *Rodmoor;* Glen Cavaliero's *John Cowper Powys,* and John A. Brebner's *The Demon Within.*

282. "Books of the Year." *Observer* (16 December 1973), p. 33. Wilson picks his top three selections.

283. "Political Metaphors: 1. The Politics of the Family—introduced by Frank Kermode." *Listener,* 91 (10 January 1974), 41-42. On his *No Laughing Matter;* on the family relationship and the emancipation of individuals.

284. "Graves of academe." *Spectator,* 232 (12 January 1974), 45. Review of Anne Mulkeen's *Wild Thyme, Winter Lightning.*

285. "Art and the Establishment." *Listener,* 91 (17 January 1974), 78. Wilson discusses his values of art.

286. "The lower depths." *Observer* (3 February 1974), p. 30. Review of Gillian Tindall's *The Born Exile.*

287. "Battle for the B.M." *Observer* (24 February 1974), p. 32. Review of Edward Miller's *That Noble Cabinet.*

288. "International children's book day messages." *Horn Book,* 50 (April 1974), 229-230. On the books he read as a child, and on his childhood in general.

289. "Curious peach." *Guardian,* 110 (4 May 1974), 22. Review of Jan Morris's *Conundrum.*

290. "Progress down the middle." *Observer* (12 May 1974), p. 37. Review of Günter Grass's *From the Diary of a Snail.*

291. "Montherlant's Worlds." *New Statesman,* 87 (17 May 1974), 697-698. Review of Montherlant's *The Boys.*

292. "Fauntleroy's creator." *Observer* (2 June 1974), p. 33. Review of Ann Thwaite's *Waiting for the Party: The Life of Frances Hodgson Burnett 1849-1924.*

293. "A man from the Midlands." *TLS* (12 July 1974), pp. 737-738. Review of Margaret Drabble's *Arnold Bennett.*

294. "Dickens in America." *Observer* (25 August 1974), p. 23. Review of *The Letters of Charles Dickens,Vol. III, 1842-1843,* ed. by Madeline House, et. al.

295. "A lady and her lions." *Observer* (1 September 1974), p. 26. Review of *Ottoline at Garsington: Memoirs of Lady Ottoline Morrell,* ed. by Robert Gathorne-Hardy.

296. "The mystical years." *Observer* (15 September 1974), p. 28. Review of Sybille Bedford's *Aldous Huxley, Volume II, 1939-1963.*

297. "Victorian morality." *Observer* (17 November 1974), p. 33. Review of Nirad C. Chaudhuri's *Scholar Extraordinary.*

298. "The Great Cham." *Observer* (24 November 1974), p. 33. Review of John Wain's *Samuel Johnson.*

299. "Dostoevsky reinstated." *Observer* (26 January 1975), p. 29. Review of Leonid Grossman's *Dostoevsky.*

300. "Love in a cold climate." *Observer* (2 February 1975), p. 29. Review of *The Letters of J. R. Ackerley,* ed. by Neville Braybrooke.

301. "Anatomy of a village." *Observer* (16 February 1975), p. 30. Review of Rowland Parker's *The Common Stream.*

302. Untitled comment. *New Statesman,* 89 (30 May 1975), 719. Reasons are stated in favor of Britain's remaining inside the Common Market.

303. "The Kipling daemon." *Observer* (15 June 1975), p. 30. Review of Philip Mason's *Kipling: the Glass, the Shadow and the Fire.*

304. "From Zululand to Bloomsbury." *Observer* (14 September 1975), p. 25. Review of *The Autobiography of William Plomer.*

305. "The young Virginia." *Observer* (21 September 1975), p. 23. Review of John Lehmann's *Virginia Woolf and Her World,* and *The Flight of the Mind: The Letters of Virginia Woolf 1888-1912* ed. by Nigel Nicolson.

306. "Tour de force." *Observer* (19 October 1975), p. 27. Review of Paul Theroux's *The Great Railway Bazaar.*

307. "Dreamers of dreams." *Observer* (23 November 1975), p. 31. Review of Penelope Fitzgerald's *Edward Burne-Jones,* Jack Lindsay's *William Morris,* and *Edwardian Architecture* ed. by Alastair Service.

308. "Books of the Year." *Observer* (14 December 1975), p. 19. Wilson picks his four top selections.

309. "Which Miss Austen?" *Observer* (14 December 1975), p. 24. Review of Marilyn Butler's *Jane Austen and the War of Ideas,* and Barbara Hardy's *A Reading of Jane Austen.*

310. *"Clarissa."* *Horizon,* 17 (Winter 1975), 103-107. On Samuel Richardson's famous novel.

311. Editor. *An Anthology, Green River Review, 1968-1973.* University Center, Michigan: Green River Press, 1975.

312. "Introduction," to *The Return of Sherlock Holmes,* by Authur Conan Doyle. London: Cape, 1975.

313. "An area of prejudice." *Observer* (25 January 1976), p. 30. Review of Valentine Cunningham's *Everywhere Spoken Against.*

314. "Mary Ann into George." *Observer* (7 March 1976), p. 27. Review of Ruby V. Redinger's *George Eliot: The Emergent Self.*

315. An interview with Angus Wilson appears in *Gay News,* No. 92 (8-21 April 1976). Source supplied by Wilson.

316. "Remembrance of things past." *New York Times Book Review* (11 April 1976), pp. 6-7. Review of Céleste Albaret's *Monsieur Proust.*

317. "Animal magnetism." *Observer* (2 May 1976), p. 31. Review of Wilfred Blunt's *The Ark in the Park,* and Gwynne Vevers's *London's Zoo: An Anthology.*

318. "Bloomsbury's best." *Observer* (6 June 1976), p. 29. Review of *Moments of Being: Unpublished Autobiographical Writings of Virginia Woolf.*

319. "High living and halitosis." *Observer* (13 June 1976), p. 27. Review of Sandra Jobson Darroch's *Ottoline.*

* 320. *"Kipling: The Glass, the Shadow and the Fire."* *Critic*, 34 (Spring 1976), 88-90. Review of Philip Mason's book.

II. GENERAL SECONDARY STUDIES, INTERVIEWS, BIOGRAPHICAL SKETCHES, AND MISCELLANEOUS ITEMS

General references to Wilson's work also appear in the First Part of this bibliography. See the following numbers there: 1, 6, 7, 8, 9, 10, 11, 12, 16, 17, 18, 19, 26, 27, 28, 29, 30, 31, 32, 34, 35, 36, 37, 38, 40, 44, 45, 48, 51, 52, 55, 56, 58, 60, 64, 66, 70, 71, 73, 75, 78, 79, 80, 85, 89, 90, 91, 94, 95, 96, 98, 100, 101, 103, 104, 107, 110, 111, 112, 115, 118, 123, 124, 125, 127, 129, 130, 131, 133, 136, 143, 144, 145, 154, 158, 159, 165, 188, 191, 194, 204, 205, 206, 213, 225, 226, 228, 231, 236, 238, 241, 250, 276, 285, 293, 308, 313, 314, 320, 322, 334.

321. Allen, Walter. *The Modern Novel in Britain and the United States* (see First Part No. 6), pp. 270-274.

322. Anon. "J. T. Black Book Prizes." *The* (London) *Times* (2 March 1959), p. 6. A notice of Wilson's receiving the prize for his *The Middle Age of Mrs. Eliot.*

323. —. "New Members of Arts Council." *The* (London) *Times* (25 January 1967), p. 12. A notice of Wilson's appointment.

324. —. "New Year Honours." *The* (London) *Times* (1 January 1968), p. 6, col. 3. Notice of Wilson's receiving a C.B.E. Honor.

325. —. "Plays of Moment." *TLS* (25 December 1959), p. 752. Report on Wilson's comments on contemporary English drama.

326. —. Untitled book review. *Choice*, 11 (April 1974), 263. Comments on *As If By Magic,* and *For Whom the Cloche Tolls.*

327. —. "Wilson, Angus." *Contemporary Authors: A Bio-Bibliographical Guide to Current Authors and Their Works.* First rev., vols. 5-8. Ed. Barbara Harte and Carolyn Riley. Detroit, Michigan: Gale Research, 1969, pp. 1260-1262.

328. —. "Wilson, Angus." *Current Biography Yearbook, 1959.* Ed. Charles Moritz. New York: H. W. Wilson, 1959, pp. 487-488.

329. —. "Writers' Conference Draws an Audience of 2,000." *The* (London) *Times* (21 August 1962), p. 4. Includes an account of Wilson's ideas on the state of the English novel.

330. Bergonzi, Bernard. *The Situation of the Novel* (see First Part No. 12), pp. 151-161.

331. —. Untitled comments. *Contemporary Novelists.* Ed. James Vinson. London and Chicago: St. James Press, 1972, pp. 1376-1377.

332. Biles, Jack I. "An Interview in London with Angus Wilson." *Studies in the Novel,* 2, No. 1 (Spring 1970), 76-87. Interview of December 24 and 28, 1964. Includes comments on Golding and Greene.

333. Bradbury, Malcolm. "The Short Stories of Angus Wilson." *Studies in Short Fiction,* 3 (Winter 1966), 117-125.

334. —. "The Fiction of Pastiche: the Comic Mode of Angus Wilson," in his *Possibilities* (see First Part No. 16), pp. 211-230.

335. Cockshut, A. O. J. "Favored Sons: The Moral World of

Angus Wilson." *Essays in Criticism,* 9 (January 1959), 50-60.

336. Coleman, Terry. "Angus Wilson's attitudes." *Guardian* (29 August 1967), p. 4. A biographical sketch.

337. Cox, C. B. "Angus Wilson: Studies in Depression," in his *The Free Spirit* (see First Part No. 27), pp. 117-157.

338. "Cred în tulburătorul azi." *Cronica,* 7 (March 1972), 13, 16. An interview.

339. Davy, Richard. "Group to plead for detained Czechs." *The* (London) *Times* (10 March 1972), p. 7. An appeal by international committee of writers and intellectuals for release of political prisoners in Czechoslovakia.

340. Delpech, Jeanine. "Les masques d'Angus Wilson." *Nouvelles Littéraires* (10 Avril 1969), p. 3.

341. Den Haan, Jacques. *Een Leven Als Een Oordeel.* Amsterdam: Meulenhoff/De Bezige Bij, 1968. Contains chapters on Durrell, Wain, and Wilson.

342. Devlin, Tim. "Angus Wilson and the art of the unexpected." *The* (London) *Times* (30 May 1973), p. 18. An interview.

343. Dick, Kay. "Portrait: Angus Wilson's Countryside." *Ramparts,* 3 (November 1964), 5-8.

344. Drescher, Horst W. "Angus Wilson: An Interview." *Die Neueren Sprachen,* 17 (July 1968), 351-356.

345. Durston, J. H. "Abroad with some not-so-innocents." *House and Garden,* 110 (November 1956), 36-37.

346. Edelstein, Arthur. "Angus Wilson: the Territory Behind." *Contemporary British Novelists.* Ed. Charles Shapiro (see First Part No. 107), pp. 144-161.

347. Engelborghs, Maurits. "Kroniek: Engelse letteren: Werk van Angus Wilson." *Dietsche Warande en Belfort,* 3 (1957), 181-189.

348. Fraser, G. S. *The Modern Writer and His World* (see First Part No. 40), pp. 152-155.

349. Gindin, James. "Angus Wilson," in his *Harvest of a Quiet Eye* (see First Part No. 44), pp. 277-304.

350. —. "Angus Wilson's Qualified Nationalism," in his *Postwar British Fiction* (see First Part No. 45), pp. 145-164.

351. —. "The Fable Begins to Break Down." *Wisconsin Studies in Contemporary Literature,* 8 (Winter 1967), 1-18. Pp. 8-10.

352. Gransden, K. W. *Angus Wilson.* Writers and Their Work, no. 208. Ed. Ian Scott-Kilvert. Harlow, Essex: Longmans, Green, 1969.

353. Halio, Jay. *Angus Wilson.* Writers and Critics Series. Ed. A. Norman Jeffares. Edinburgh and London: Oliver and Boyd, 1964.

354. —. "The Novels of Angus Wilson." *Modern Fiction Studies,* 8 (Summer 1962), 171-181; reprinted in his *Angus Wilson.* Writers and Critics Series. Ed. A. Norman Jeffares. Edinburgh and London: Oliver and London, 1964.

355. Harris, Marilyn Riley. "Self-Awareness and Family Influence in the Works of Angus Wilson." Diss. Georgia State, 1974. *Dissertation Abstracts,* 35A (1975), 4523-4524.

356. Hazard, Eloise Perry. "Angus Wilson." *Saturday Review of Literature,* 34 (17 February 1951), 9. A biographical sketch.

357. Howard, Phillip. "Fond salute to little Lord Fauntleroy." *The* (London) *Times* (25 May 1974), p. 3. On Wilson's

opening of the private preview of the exhibit.

358. Jacque, Valentina. "English Short Stories in Russia." *Soviet Literature*, 1 (1963), 153-157. Includes comments on Wilson's work.

359. Jenkins, Alan. "Hemlock—and Before." *Spectator*, 193 (17 September 1954), 331. An analysis of a privately owned notebook of Wilson's, which contains the first drafts of three short stories.

360. Karl, Frederick R. "A Question of Morality: Angus Wilson," in his *A Reader's Guide to the Contemporary English Novel* (see First Part No. 55), pp. 244-249.

361. Katona, Anna. "Angus Wilson's Fiction and its Relation to the English Tradition." *Acta Literaria Academiae Scientiarum Hungariae*, 10 (1968), 1-2, 111-127.

362. Kermode, Frank. "House of Fiction: Interviews with Seven English Novelists." *Partisan Review*, 30 (Spring 1963), 61-82. Pp. 68-70.

363. McDowell, Frederick P. W. "An Interview with Angus Wilson." *Iowa Review*, 3, No. 4 (Fall 1972), 77-105.

364. —, and Sharon Graves. *The Angus Wilson Manuscripts in the University of Iowa Libraries: A Catalogue.* Iowa City: Friends of the University of Iowa Library, 1969. Contains McDowell's "The Angus Wilson Manuscripts," pp. 1-5; and McDowell and Graves' "Catalogue of the Angus Wilson Manuscripts," pp. 6-16.

365. Mandel, Siegfried. "The Author." *Saturday Review*, 39 (6 October 1956), 22. A biographical sketch.

366. Millgate, Michael. "Angus Wilson." *Paris Review*, No. 17 (Autumn/Winter 1958), 88-105; reprinted in *Writers at Work: The Paris Review Interviews*, 1st series. Ed. Malcolm Cowley. New York: Viking Press, 1958, pp. 251-

266.

367. Moorcock, Michael. An interview with Angus Wilson, in *Books and Bookmen* (May 1973).

368. Narita, Seiju. "A Reformer, not a Revolutionary." *Eigo Seinen*, 115 (1969), 752-759. An interview.

369. Oakland, John. "Angus Wilson and Evil in the English Novel." *Renascence*, 26 (Autumn 1973), 24-36.

370. Oka, Teruo. *Angus Wilson*. Tokyo: Kenkyusha, 1970. (In Japanese).

371. Poston, Lawrence, III. "A Conversation with Angus Wilson." *Books Abroad*, 40 (Winter 1966), 29-31.

372. Pritchett, V. S. "London Literary Letter: A Report on Writers and Writing." *New York Times Book Review* (11 May 1958), p. 18. On Wilson's view of the status of the English writer.

373. Raban, Jonathan. "Angus Wilson." *New Review*, 1 (April 1974), 16-19, 21-24. On Wilson's life, interests, and work. Much of the essay includes comments by Wilson.

374. Rabinovitz, Rubin. "Angus Wilson," in his *The Reaction Against Experiment in the English Novel, 1950-1960* (see First Part No. 96), pp. 64-96.

375. Richardson, Kenneth Ridley. "Wilson, Angus." *Twentieth Century Writing: A Reader's Guide to Contemporary Literature*. Ed. Kenneth Richardson. London: Newnes Books, 1969, pp. 654-657.

376. Riddell, Edwin. "The Humanist Character in Angus Wilson." *English*, 21 (Summer 1972), 45-53.

377. Robinson, Robert. "Wilson stories." *Listener*, 95 (4 March 1976), 283. An interview.

378. Rosselli, John. "Miss Schlegel, Meet Mr. Angus Wilson." *New Statesman and Nation*, 45 (14 March 1953), 290, 292. A parody of Wilson's writing.

379. Scheer-Schäzler, Brigitte. "Angus Wilson." *Englische Literatur der Gegenwart in Einzeldarstellungen.* Ed. Horst W. Drescher. Stuttgart: Kröner, 1970, pp. 104-132.

380. Schlüter, Kurt. "Angus Wilson." *Englische Dichter der Moderne. Ihr Leben und Werk. Unter Mitarbeit Zahlreicher Fachgelehrter.* Eds. Rudolf Sühnel and Dieter Riesner. Berlin: Erich Schmidt, 1971, pp. 536-545.

381. —. *Kuriose Welt im Modernen Englischen Roman. Dargestellt an Ausgewählten Werken von Evelyn Waugh und Angus Wilson.* Berlin: Erich Schmidt Verlag, 1969. See pp. 126-233.

382. Schultze, Bruno. "Das Bild der Wirklichkeit in der Romanen Angus Wilson." *Die Neueren Sprachen,* 22 (1973), 210-220.

383. Scott-Kilvert, Ian. "Angus Wilson." *A Review of English Literature,* 1 (April 1960), 42-53.

384. Sewell, Michael Walker. "Parent and Child in the Garden: The Early Novels of Angus Wilson." Diss. Iowa, 1974. *Dissertation Abstracts,* 35A (1975), 4556-4557.

385. Shaw, Valerie A. *"The Middle Age of Mrs. Eliot* and *Late Call:* Angus Wilson's Traditionalism." *Critical Quarterly,* 12 (Spring 1970), 9-27.

386. Smith, William J. "Angus Wilson's England: The Novelist as Social Historian." *Commonweal,* 82 (26 March 1965), 18-21.

387. Spiel, Hilde. *Welt im Widerschein.* München: Beck, 1960, pp. 75-81.

388. Stokes, Henry Scott. "British drive for trade in Tokyo." *The* (London) *Times* (26 September 1969), p. 7. Notice of Wilson's participation as a lecturer.

389. Vallette, Jacques. "Lettres Anglo-Saxonne: Angus Wilson un peu par lui-même." *Mercure de France,* 332, No. 1142 (October 1958), 313-316.

390. Wilson, Edmund. "Emergence of Angus Wilson," in his *The Bit Between My Teeth: A Literary Chronicle 1950-1965.* New York: Farrar, Straus, and Giroux, 1965, pp. 270-273.

391. Zanderer, Leo. "Wilson, Angus." *Encyclopedia of World Literature in the 20th Century.* Vol. 3. New York: Ungar, 1971, pp. 532-533.

392. Zimmerman, Muriel. "The Fiction of Angus Wilson." Diss. Temple, 1967. *Dissertation Abstracts,* 28A (1968), 4195-4196.

III. STUDIES AND REVIEWS OF INDIVIDUAL WORKS

References to individual books by Wilson also appear in the First Part of this bibliography. See the following numbers there: 5, 83, 94, 99, 134, 164, 173, 174, 183, 186, 193, 196, 201, 233, 252, 253, 277, 281, 292, 302, 307, 324, 325, 327, 328, 338, 340, 341, 345, 347.

Hemlock and After

393. Anon. "Corruption Rife." *TLS* (8 August 1952), p. 516.

394. —. *"Hemlock and After."* *Kirkus*, 20 (15 July 1952), 429.

395. —. "The Lower Depths." *Time*, 60 (29 September 1952), 97-98.

396. Cox, C. B. "The Humanism of Angus Wilson: A Study of *Hemlock and After.*" *Critical Quarterly*, 3 (Autumn 1961), 227-237.

397. Hilton, James. "A Scintillating Novel of a Seamy London Wasteland." *New York Herald Tribune Book Review*, 29 (5 October 1952), 3.

398. Hush, Thea. "The Choice of Books in Public Libraries." *TLS* (30 January 1953), p. 73; responses by P. Hepburn Reid, and Gilbert Benthall, in *TLS* (6 February 1953), p. 89; by W. E. Simnett, and John O'Leary in *TLS* (13 February 1953), p. 105.

399. Jenkins, Elizabeth. "New Fiction." *Manchester Guardian* (18 July 1952), p. 4.

400. Jones, Ernest. "Contemporary Fable." *Nation,* 175 (11 October 1952), 331.

401. Kerr, Walter. "A Cold Eye on the Best People." *Commonweal,* 57 (24 October 1952), 72-73.

* 402. Meewis, Wim. *"Hemlock and After."* *Nieuw Vlaams Tijdschrift* (Antwerp), 12, No. 8 (1958), 888-891. (In Flemish).

403. Peden, William. "The Traitorous Leader." *Saturday Review,* 35 (4 October 1952), 35.

404. Pickrel, Paul. *"Hemlock and After."* *Yale Review,* n.s. 42 (Winter 1953), xiv.

405. Rolo, Charles J. *"Hemlock and After."* *Atlantic,* 190 (November 1952), 110.

406. Schwartz, Delmore. "Long After Eden." *Partisan Review,* 19 (November-December 1952), 701-706. Pp. 704-706.

407. Scott, J. D. "New Novels." *New Statesman and Nation,* 44 (2 August 1952), 142.

408. Strong, L. A. G. "Fiction." *Spectator,* 189 (18 July 1952), 110.

409. Wagenknecht, Edward. Review of *Hemlock and After,* in the *Chicago Sunday Tribune* (12 October 1952), p. 7.

410. Walbridge, Earle F. *"Hemlock and After."* *Library Journal,* 77 (15 September 1952), 1507.

411. Weaver, William Fense. "Bernard's Dilemma." *New York Times Book Review* (28 September 1952), p. 4.

412. West, Anthony. "Decline and Fall." *New Yorker,* 28 (27 September 1952), 99-101.

413. Wogatzky, Karin. *Angus Wilson: 'Hemlock and After.' A Study in Ambiguity.* Schweizer Anglistische Arbeiten, 62. Bern: Francke, 1971.

Anglo-Saxon Attitudes

414. Amis, Kingsley. "Dodos Less Darling." *Spectator,* 196 (1 June 1956), 764-765; reprinted in *New Republic,* 135 (15 October 1956), 27-28.

415. Anon. "A Carnival of Humbug." *Time,* 68 (29 October 1956), 108.

416. —. *"Anglo-Saxon Attitudes, a novel."* *Booklist,* 53 (15 September 1956), 36.

417. —. *"Anglo-Saxon Attitudes."* *Bookmark,* 16 (November 1956), 37.

418. —. *"Anglo-Saxon Attitudes."* *Kirkus,* 24 (15 August 1956), 591.

419. —. *"Anglo-Saxon Attitudes."* *Tamarack Review,* 1 (Autumn 1956), 94.

420. —. "Mourning Becomes Elvira." *TLS* (18 May 1956), p. 296.

421. —. "New Fiction." *The* (London) *Times* (17 May 1956), p. 13.

422. Bittner, William. "Hemlock and Piltdown." *Nation,* 183 (13 October 1956), 311-312.

423. Corke, Hilary. "Lack of Confidence." *Encounter,* 7 (July 1956), 75-78. Pp. 77-78.

424. Cosman, Max. Review of *Anglo-Saxon Attitudes,* in the *New Mexico Quarterly,* 27 (April 1957), pp. 131-133.

425. Cournos, John. *"Anglo-Saxon Attitudes." Commonweal,* 65 (7 December 1956), 257.

426. Cranston, Maurice. "Mr. Wilson's Comic Saga." *Manchester Guardian* (15 May 1956), p. 4.

* 427. Daiches, David. "Human Relations." *New York Times Book Review* (7 October 1956), p. 5.

428. Fiedler, Leslie. "British Fiction." *Commentary,* 23 (March 1957), 294, 296-298. Pp. 296-298.

429. Fuller, Edmund. Review of *Anglo-Saxon Attitudes,* in the *Chicago Sunday Tribune* (21 October 1956), p. 4.

430. Gill, Brendan. "New Old Ways." *New Yorker,* 32 (6 October 1956), 176, 178.

431. Gray, James. *"Anglo-Saxon Attitudes." Saturday Review,* 39 (6 October 1956), 22.

432. Hobson, Harold. "English View of 'Attitudes'." *Christian Science Monitor,* 48 (5 July 1956), 13.

433. Holzhauer, Jean. "Through the Foggy Social Sounds of England Today." *Commonweal,* 65 (19 October 1956), 76-77.

434. Hughes, Riley. *"Anglo-Saxon Attitudes." Catholic World,* 184 (January 1957), 311.

435. J. V. Review of *Anglo-Saxon Attitudes,* in the *San Francisco Chronicle* (25 November 1956), p. 16.

436. McLaughlin, Richard. Review of *Anglo-Saxon Attitudes,* in the *Springfield Republican* (18 November 1956), p. 10C.

437. O'Rourke, Elizabeth. *"Anglo-Saxon Attitudes."* Best Sellers, 16 (1 December 1956), 306-307.

438. Price, R. G. G. "Hemlock and After and After." *Punch,* 230 (27 June 1956), 775-776.

439. Pritchett, V. S. Review of *Anglo-Saxon Attitudes* in the *Griffin* (October 1956), pp. 18-19.

440. —. "The World of Angus Wilson." *New Statesman and Nation,* 51 (12 May 1956), 533-534.

441. Rolo, Charles J. "Scandal in a coffin." *Atlantic,* 198 (October 1956), 105-106.

442. Stallings, Sylvia. "Angus Wilson's Finely Plotted, Absorbing Novel of English Life." *New York Herald Tribune Book Review,* 33 (7 October 1956), 1, 8.

443. Van Ghent, Dorothy. "Recent Fiction: The Race, The Moment, and The Milieu." *Yale Review,* n.s. 46 (Winter 1956), 274-288. Pp. 285-286.

444. Willis, Katherine Tappert. *"Anglo-Saxon Attitudes."* Library Journal, 81 (1 October 1956), 2255.

445. Wyndham, Francis. Untitled book review. *London Magazine,* 3 (July 1956), 81-83.

The Middle Age of Mrs. Eliot

446. Anon. *"The Middle Age of Mrs. Eliot."* Booklist, 55 (1 February 1959), 277.

447. —. *"The Middle Age of Mrs. Eliot."* Bookmark, 18 (April 1959), 175.

448. —. *"The Middle Age of Mrs. Eliot."* Kirkus, 27 (15 January 1959), 59.

449. —. "The Widow Britannia." *Time,* 73 (30 March 1959), 91-92.

450. —. "Vitality of Angus Wilson." *The* (London) *Times* (20 November 1958), p. 15.

451. Curran, Charles. "Room at the Bottom." *New Republic,* 140 (1 June 1959), 18-19.

452. Engle, Paul. Review of *The Middle Age of Mrs. Eliot,* in the *Chicago Sunday Tribune* (29 March 1959), p. 4.

453. Fletcher, John. "Women in Crises: Louise and Mrs. Eliot." *Critical Quarterly,* 15 (Summer 1973), 157-170. A detailed study of Wilson's *The Middle Age of Mrs. Eliot* and Calude Simon's *The Grass.*

454. Fremantle, Anne. "Prism of Relations." *Commonweal,* 70 (8 May 1959), 160-161.

455. Hicks, Granville. "The Importance of People." *Saturday Review,* 42 (21 March 1959), 22.

456. Hogan, William. Review of *The Middle Age of Mrs. Eliot,* in the *San Francisco Chronicle* (16 April 1959), p. 43.

457. Hoggart, Richard. "Explorations of Loneliness." *Manchester Guardian Weekly,* 79 (4 December 1958), 10.

458. —. "Some Kinds of Isolation." *Manchester Guardian* (28 November 1958), p. 6.

459. Hughes, Riley. *"The Middle Age of Mrs. Eliot." Catholic World,* 189 (July 1959), 322.

460. Johnson, Pamela Hansford. "Three-Legged Race." *New Statesman,* 56 (22 November 1958), 732.

461. Kaufmann, R. J. "Uses of the Past: Angus Wilson." *Nation,* 188 (23 May 1959), 478-480.

462. Kermode, Frank. "Mr. Wilson's People." *Spectator* (21 November 1958), 705-706; reprinted in his *Puzzles and Epiphanies* (see First Part No. 60), pp. 193-197.

463. Lucas, Barabara. *"The Middle Age of Mrs. Eliot."* *Twentieth Century,* 165 (January 1959), 96-98.

464. Moore, Harry T. "Warm Friends Grew Cold." *New York Times Book Review* (22 March 1959), pp. 5, 30.

465. Nyren, Karl. *"The Middle Age of Mrs. Eliot."* *Library Journal,* 84 (1 April 1959), 1154.

466. Peterson, Virgilia. "Angus Wilson's Novel of a Woman's Violent Awakening to Reality." *New York Herald Tribune Book Review,* 35 (22 March 1959), 1.

* 467. Price, R. G. G. *"The Middle Age of Mrs. Eliot."* *Punch,* 235 (3 December 1958), 738.

468. Raymond, John. "Meg Eliot Surprised." *TLS* (21 November 1958), p. 672; reprinted in his *The Doge of Dover and Other Essays.* London: Macgibbon and Kee, 1960, pp. 170-178.

469. Rees, Goronwy. "New Novels." *Listener,* 60 (27 November 1958), 892.

470. Rolo, Charles. "Portrait of a Woman." *Atlantic,* 203 (April 1959), 138-139.

471. Schlüter, Kurt. "Angus Wilson: *The Middle Age of Mrs. Eliot."* *Der Moderne Englische Roman Interpretationen.* Ed. Horst Oppel (see First Part No. 83), pp. 359-375.

472. Wain, John. "Books: Comment on Widowhood." *New Yorker,* 35 (11 April 1959), 164-166.

473. Wyndham, Francis. Untitled book review. *London Magazine,* 6 (February 1959), 64-66. Pp. 64-65.

The Old Men at the Zoo

474. Adams, Phoebe. "War in Fantasy." *Atlantic*, 208 (November 1961), 191.

475. Anon. "Animal Crackers." *Time*, 78 (3 November 1961), 86.

476. —. "Beyond the Fringe." *TLS* (29 September 1961), p. 641.

477. —. "Briefing: *The Old Men at the Zoo.*" *Observer* (21 June 1964), p. 22.

478. —. "Caged." *Newsweek*, 58 (6 November 1961), 104.

479. —. "New Fiction." *The* (London) *Times* (28 September 1961), p. 15.

480. —. *"The Old Men at the Zoo."* *Booklist*, 58 (1 February 1962), 342-343.

481. —. *"The Old Men at the Zoo."* *Bookmark*, 21 (November 1961), 39.

482. —. *"The Old Men at the Zoo."* *Kirkus*, 29 (15 August 1961), 747.

483. Bowen, John. "Wish Fulfilment." *Punch*, 241 (4 October 1961), 515.

484. Bowen, Robert O. "Variations on a Palling Theme." *National Review*, 12 (16 January 1962), 29-30.

485. Cox, C. B. *"The Old Men at the Zoo."* *Critical Quarterly*, 3 (Winter 1961), 369-370.

486. Davis, Robert Gorham. "The Caged and Uncaged." *New York Times Book Review* (29 October 1961), pp. 4-5, 34.

487. Derrick, Christopher. "Uphill." *Tablet,* 215 (7 October 1961), 954.

488. Engle, Paul. Review of *The Old Men at the Zoo,* in the *Chicago Sunday Tribune* (5 November 1961), p. 6.

489. Fadiman, Clifton. Review of *The Old Men at the Zoo,* in the *Book-of-the-Month-Club News* (November 1961), p. 7.

490. Furbank, P. N. "Moments of Awful Truth." *John O'London's,* 5 (28 September 1961), 359.

491. Griffin, Lloyd W. *"The Old Men at the Zoo."* *Library Journal,* 86 (15 October 1961), 3494.

492. Gross, John. "Elephants and Blind Men." *Commentary,* 33 (March 1962), 265-267.

493. Halio, Jay L. "Response vs. Responsibility." *Critique,* 5 (Spring-Summer 1962), 77-82; reprinted in *Angus Wilson.* Writers and Critics Series, Ed. A. Norman Jeffares. Edinburgh and London: Oliver and Boyd, 1964, pp. 84-92.

494. Hicks, Granville. "Politics on an Animal Farm." *Saturday Review,* 44 (21 October 1961), 22.

495. Hope, Francis. "Novels." *Encounter,* 17 (November 1961), 77, 79, 81. Pp. 77, 79.

496. Johnson, Lucy. "High Polish." *Progressive,* 26 (January 1962), 49-50.

497. Lid, Richard W. Review of *The Old Men at the Zoo,* in the *San Francisco Chronicle* (5 November 1961), p. 29.

498. Lindberg, Margaret. "Angus Wilson: *The Old Men at the Zoo* as Allegory." *Iowa English Yearbook,* 14 (Fall 1969), 44-48.

499. MacGillivray, Arthur. *"The Old Men at the Zoo."* *Best Sellers*, 21 (1 December 1961), 361.

500. McLaughlin, Richard. *"The Old Men at the Zoo."* *Springfield Sunday Republican* (31 December 1961), p. 4D.

501. Mitgang, Herbert. "Books of the Times." *New York Times*, 111 (2 December 1961), 21.

502. Mortimer, John. "A Fatal Giraffe." *Spectator*, 207 (29 September 1961), 431.

503. Pickrel, Paul. "The Other Wilson." *Harper's*, 223 (November 1961), 110, 114.

504. Pritchett, V. S. "Bad-Hearted Britain." *New Statesman and Nation*, 62 (29 September 1961), 429-430.

505. Pugh, Griffith T. "From the Recent Books." *English Journal*, 51 (May 1962), 374-377. P. 375.

506. Raphael, Frederic. Review of *The Old Men at the Zoo*, in *Time and Tide* (26 October 1961), p. 1804.

507. Rubin, Louis D., Jr. "Six Novels and S. Levin." *Sewanee Review*, 70 (Summer 1962), 504-514. Pp. 506-508.

508. Spector, Robert Donald. "The Way it Was in 1970-1973." *New York Herald Tribune Books*, 38 (29 October 1961), 4.

* 509. Symons, Julian. "Politics and the Novel." (see First Part No. 322), pp. 151-153.

510. Waugh, Evelyn. *"Old Men at the Zoo."* *Spectator*, 207 (13 October 1961), 501.

511. Williams, Raymond. "The End of a Mimic." *Guardian* (29 September 1961), p. 7.

512. Wylder, D. E. Review of *The Old Men at the Zoo,* in the *New Mexico Quarterly,* 33 (Autumn 1963), 357-359.

Late Call

513. Anon. "Among the Aspidistras." *Newsweek,* 65 (11 January 1965), 80-81.

514. —. "Anglo-Saxon Platitudes." *Time,* 85 (22 January 1965), 79-80.

515. —. "Friefly Noted." *New Yorker,* 40 (16 January 1965), 128.

516. —. *"Late Call." Booklist,* 61 (15 January 1965), 473.

517. —. *"Late Call." Choice,* 2 (June 1965), 230.

518. —. "New Fiction." *The* (London) *Times* (12 November 1964), p. 18.

519. —. "Not Painted—But Made Up." *TLS* (12 November 1964), p. 1013; reprinted in *T.L.S. Essays and Reviews from The Times Literary Supplement, 1964.* London: Oxford University Press, 1965, pp. 103-105.

520. —. "Paperbacks: *Late Call." Observer* (28 April 1968), p. 26.

521. —. "Paperbacks: *Late Call." The* (London) *Times* (27 April 1968), p. 21.

522. Barrett, William. "Reader's choice." *Atlantic,* 215 (March 1965), 190-191.

523. Baumbach, Jonathan. "In Time to Save Her Soul" *Saturday Review,* 48 (16 January 1965), 29.

524. Bergonzi, Bernard. "A New Angus Wilson." *New York*

Review of Books, 4 (25 February 1965), 21-23.

525. Bowen, John. "What is Sylvia?" *New York Times Book Review* (10 January 1965), p. 5.

526. Bradbury, Malcolm. "New Novels." *Punch,* 248 (6 January 1965), 32.

527. Cook, Roderick. *"Late Call."* *Harper's* 230 (February 1965), 127-128.

528. Cummings, Elizabeth W. *"Late Call."* *Library Journal,* 90 (1 February 1965), 669-670.

529. Curley, Daniel. "The Virtues of Service." *New Leader,* 48 (15 February 1965), 21-22. P. 22.

530. Daniel, John. "Two versions of modern Britain." *Manchester Guardian Weekly,* 91 (19 November 1964), 10.

531. Elliott, Margaret. "Sylvia Finds Out Who She is the Hard Way." *Life,* 58 (19 February 1965), 12.

532. Evans, Illtud. "Our World and Welcome to It." *Tablet,* 218 (21 November 1964), 1317.

533. Green, Howard. "The Countess' Hat." *Hudson Review,* 18 (Summer 1965), 278-289. Pp. 278-279.

534. Gross, John. "Blessed are the pure in heart." *Observer* (8 November 1964), p. 27.

535. —. "Sylvia is a love, that's who." *Book Week,* 2 (10 January 1965), 5.

536. Hamilton, Alex. Review of *Late Call,* in *Books and Bookmen,* 10 (January 1965), p. 28.

537. Hill, William B. *"Late Call."* *Best Sellers,* 24 (15 February 1965), 446.

538. Hope, Francis. "Grace and Favour." *New Statesman,* 68 (27 November 1964), 834, 836.

539. Johnson, B. S. "Getting On." *Spectator,* 213 (13 November 1964), 644.

540. Johnson, Lucy. "Two Witty Novels." *Progressive,* 29 (March 1965), 40-42.

541. Maddocks, Melvin. "Encore to Cleverness." *Christian Science Monitor,* 57 (14 January 1965), 7.

542. Millgate, Jane. "Who is Sylvia?" *Tamarack Review,* 34 (Winter 1965), 111-114.

543. Pryce-Jones, Alan. Review of *Late Call,* in the *New York Herald Tribune,* 124 (14 January 1965), 19.

544. Smith, P. D. Review of *Late Call,* in *Saturday Night,* 80 (August 1965), p. 28.

545. Spender, Stephen. "Must There Always be a Red Brick England?" *Encyclopaedia Britannica. Great Ideas Today, 1965.* New York: Atheneum, 1965, pp. 177-180.

546. Tracy, Honor. "O Brave New Hell." *New Republic,* 152 (6 February 1965), 23-24, 26.

547. Wall, Stephen. "New novels." *Listener,* 72 (19 November 1964), 806.

No Laughing Matter

548. Anon. "Briefing: *No Laughing Matter.*" *Observer* (8 June 1969), p. 32.

549. —. *"No Laughing Matter."* *Booklist,* 64 (1 November 1967), 319-320.

550. —. *"No Laughing Matter."* Choice, 5 (September 1968), 780.

551. —. *"No Laughing Matter."* Kirkus, 35 (15 September 1967), 1165.

552. —. *"No Laughing Matter."* Publishers' Weekly, 192 (11 September 1967), 67-68.

553. —. "Playing the Game." *TLS* (5 October 1967), p. 933; reprinted in *T.L.S. Essays and Reviews from The Times Literary Supplement 1967.* London: Oxford University Press, 1968, pp. 201-204.

554. —. "The Hindsight Saga." *Time,* 90 (1 December 1967), 121-122.

555. Bergonzi, Bernard. *"No Laughing Matter* by Angus Wilson." *London Magazine,* 7 (November 1967), 89-91; reprinted in his *The Situation of the Novel* (see First Part No. 12), pp. 159-161.

556. Boston, Richard. "Family Troubles." *New York Times Book Review* (26 November 1967), pp. 4, 74.

557. Brendon, P. Review of *No Laughing Matter,* in *Books and Bookmen,* 13 (November 1967), 42.

558. Carroll, John M. *"No Laughing Matter."* Library Journal, 92 (1 October 1967), 3449.

559. Derwent, May. "Chronorama." *Listener,* 78 (5 October 1967), 444.

560. Dienstag, Eleanor. *"No Laughing Matter."* Commonweal, 87 (8 March 1968), 695-696.

561. Gardner, Marilyn. "Family novel on the level of history." *Christian Science Monitor,* 59 (7 December 1967), 23.

562. Gardner, Paul. "an english generation." *Catholic World,* 206 (February 1968), 236.

563. Gillie, Christopher. "The Shape of Modern Fiction: Angus Wilson's *No Laughing Matter.*" *Delta,* No. 43 (June 1968), pp. 18-23.

564. Hicks, Granville. "They lived in Three Worlds." *Saturday Review,* 50 (18 November 1967), 27-28.

565. Halio, Jay L. "Angus Wilson's *No Laughing Matter.*" *Massachusetts Review,* 10 (Spring 1969), 394-397.

566. Kums, Guido. "Reality in Fiction: *No Laughing Matter.*" *English Studies,* 53 (December 1972), 523-531.

567. Lask, Thomas. "Ancient Warfare." *New York Times,* 117 (23 November 1967), 31.

568. Lenihan, Liam. *"No Laughing Matter."* *Nation,* 206 (15 April 1968), 512.

569. Loprete, Nicholas J. *"No Laughing Matter."* *Best Sellers,* 27 (1 January 1968), 390.

570. Mayne, Richard. "A British Museum." *Reporter,* 38 (8 February 1968), 44, 46-47.

571. Montagnes, Anne. "Anglo-Saxon Attitudes." *Saturday Night,* 83 (May 1968), 44.

572. Nemoianu, Virgil. "Un nou roman al lui Angus Wilson." *Calmul Valorilor.* Cluj: Dacia, 1971, pp. 188-191.

573. Parrinder, Patrick. "Pastiche and After." *Cambridge Review,* 89A (4 November 1967), 66-67.

574. Price, R. G. G. "New Novels." *Punch,* 253 (4 October 1967), 524.

575. Pritchett, V. S. "Ventriloquists." *New York Review of Books,* 10 (18 January 1968), 10, 12, 14.

576. Raphael, F. "Book Bazaar." *Harper's Bazaar,* 101 (February 1968), 106.

577. Ratcliffe, Michael. "The Death of Privacy." *The* (London) *Times* (5 October 1967), p. 8.

578. Raven, Simon. "Angus Agonistes." *Spectator,* 219 (6 October 1967), 396-397.

579. Servotte, Herman. "A Note on the Formal Characteristics of Angus Wilson's *No Laughing Matter." English Studies,* 50 (February 1969), 58-64.

580. —. "Experiment en traditie: Angus Wilson's *No Laughing Matter." Dietsche Warande en Belfort,* 113 (1968), 324-335.

581. Share, Bernard. Review of *No Laughing Matter,* in *Dublin Magazine,* 7 (Autumn/Winter 1968), 103-104.

582. Sokolov, Raymond A. "Six Characters in Search." *Newsweek,* 70 (20 November 1967), 114B, 114D, 115.

583. Steiner, George. "Good Night, Ladies." *New Statesman,* 74 (6 October 1967), 436-437.

584. Sudrann, Jean. "The Lion and the Unicorn: Angus Wilson's Triumphant Tragedy." *Studies in the Novel,* 3, No. 4 (Winter 1971), 390-400.

585. Tuoby, Frank. "The master of mimicry." *Manchester Guardian Weekly,* 97 (12 October 1967), 11.

As If By Magic

586. Adams, Phoebe. *"As If By Magic." Atlantic,* 232 (No-

venber 1973), 128.

587. Amis, Martin. "Kith of Death." *New Statesman*, 85 (1 June 1973), 811-812.

588. Anon. *"As If By Magic."* *British Book News* (August 1973), p. 558.

589. —. *"As If By Magic."* *Kirkus*, 41 (1 August 1973), 837.

590. —. *"As If By Magic."* *Publishers' Weekly*, 204 (10 September 1973), 41.

591. —. *"As If By Magic."* *Virginia Quarterly Review*, 40 (Summer 1974), lxxxii.

592. —. "The green and brown revolution." *TLS* (1 June 1973), p. 605; reprinted in *T.L.S. Twelve: Essays and Reviews from The Times Literary Supplement 1973*. London: Oxford University Press, 1974, pp. 60-64.

593. —. "Third-World Follies." *Newsweek*, 82 (26 November 1973), 108.

594. Bayley, John. "The trends that fail." *Guardian*, 108 (9 June 1973), 24.

595. Bridges, Linda. *"As If By Magic."* *National Review*, 26 (13 September 1974), 1055.

596. Drabble, Margaret. "Books I love." *Mademoiselle*, 81 (August 1975), 94ff.

597. —. "Books of the Year." *Observer* (16 December 1973), p. 33.

598. Evans, William R. *"As If By Magic."* *Best Sellers*, 33 (15 January 1974), 470-471.

599. Hope, Francis. "Busting out all over." *Observer* (27 May

1973), p. 36.

600. Jones, D. A. N. "Magic and Trickery." *Listener*, 89 (31 May 1973), 726.

601. McSweeney, Kerry. "The Editor's Column." *Queen's Quarterly*, 81 (Spring 1974), 165-168.

602. Maddocks, Melvin. "Vile Bodies Revisited." *Time*, 102 (3 December 1973), 107-108.

603. Moorcock, Michael. "Angus Wilson's Magic." *Books and Bookmen*, 18 (July 1973), 32-35.

604. Palmer, Tony. "The wayward Wilson." *Spectator*, 230 (2 June 1973), 685-686.

605. Price, Martin. "The Stuff of Fiction: Some Recent Novels." *Yale Review*, n.s. 63 (Summer 1974), 554-566. Pp. 563-566.

606. Raban, Jonathan. "Global Charades." *Encounter*, 41 (July 1973), 78-83.

607. Ratcliffe, Michael. "The natural noise of the world." *The* (London) *Times* (31 May 1973), p. 10.

608. Review of *As If By Magic,* in the *National Observer*, 12 (10 November 1973), 23.

609. Scholes, Marthe. *"As If By Magic."* *Library Journal*, 98 (August 1973), 2339.

610. Symons, Julian. Review of *As If By Magic,* in *Book World*, 7 (11 November 1973), 13.

611. White, Edmund. *"As If By Magic."* *New York Times Book Review* (14 October 1973), p. 7.

The Wrong Set and Other Stories

612. Anon. "Surprise Around the Corner." *Time,* 55 (10 April 1950), 96, 98-99.

613. —. *"The Wrong Set." Kirkus,* 18 (15 January 1950), 33.

614. —. Untitled book review. *TLS* (26 March 1949), p. 197.

615. Barry, Iris. " 'With All the Awful Reality of Life.' " *New York Herald Tribune Book Review,* 26 (19 March 1950), 4.

616. Benét, Rosemary Carr. "On the Way Up or Down." *Saturday Review of Literature,* 33 (18 March 1950), 15.

617. Davis, Robert Gorham. "Fiction Chronicle." *Partisan Review,* 17 (May-June 1950), 519-523. P. 523.

618. Engle, Paul. Review of *The Wrong Set,* in the *Chicago Sunday Tribune* (19 March 1950), p. 6.

619. Jones, Ernest. "From the Head." *Nation,* 170 (1 April 1950), 302-303.

620. Miles, George. *"The Wrong Set." Commonweal,* 51 (31 March 1950), 659-660.

621. Pickrel, Paul. "Outstanding Novels." *Yale Review,* n.s. 39 (Summer 1950), 765-768. Pp. 767-768.

622. Review of *The Wrong Set,* in the *Wisconsin Library Bulletin,* 46 (April 1950), p. 19.

623. Rofe, L. G. "Etched in Acid." *New York Times Book Review* (21 May 1950), p. 26.

624. Scott, J. D. "Short Stories." *New Statesman and Nation,* 37 (30 April 1949), 452.

625. W. R. W. Review of *The Wrong Set*, in the *San Francisco Chronicle* (30 April 1950), p. 28.

626. Willis, Katherine Tappert. *"The Wrong Set." Library Journal*, 75 (15 March 1950), 492-493.

627. Wilson, Edmund. "Bankrupt Britons and Voyaging Romantics." *New Yorker*, 26 (15 April 1950), 128-130. Pp. 128-129.

Such Darling Dodos and Other Stories

628. Anon. "Briefly Noted." *New Yorker*, 26 (6 January 1951), 85-86.

629. —. "North Oxford to China." *TLS* (28 July 1950), p. 465.

630. —. *"Such Darling Dodos." Atlantic*, 187 (March 1951), 86.

631. —. *"Such Darling Dodos, and Other Stories." Booklist*, 47 (15 February 1951), 220.

632. —. *"Such Darling Dodos." Kirkus*, 18 (1 November 1950), 661.

633. Boyle, Frances Alter. *"Such Darling Dodos." Library Journal*, 76 (1 January 1951), 41.

634. Kupferberg, Hubert. "Names Writ in Vitriol." *New York Herald Tribune Book Review*, 27 (14 January 1951), 8.

635. Laski, Marghanita. "Fiction." *Spectator*, 184 (28 July 1950), 126, 128. P. 128.

636. Mallet, Isabelle. "Genteelness and Humbug." *New York Times Book Review* (14 January 1951), p. 5.

637. Peden, William. "Extreme Personalities." *New Republic*, 124 (26 March 1951), 20.

638. Pickrel, Paul. "Outstanding Novels." *Yale Review,* n.s. 40 (Spring 1951), 573-576. P. 576.

639. Poster, William S. "Antipodal Fiction." *Partisan Review,* 18 (May-June 1951), 353-357. Pp. 356-357.

640. Richardson, John. "New Short Stories." *New Statesman and Nation,* 40 (12 August 1950), 181-182.

641. West, Ray B., Jr. "Two-Way Irony." *Saturday Review of Literature,* 34 (20 January 1951), 11-12.

A Bit Off the Map and Other Stories

642. Amis, Kingsley. "Dodos on the Wing." *Spectator,* 199 (18 October 1957), 521.

643. Arnold, James W. *"A Bit Off the Map."* *Best Sellers,* 17 (1 February 1958), 368.

644. Anon. *"A Bit Off the Map, and Other Stories."* *Booklist,* 54 (1 December 1957), 202.

645. —. *"A Bit Off the Map."* *Kirkus,* 25 (1 August 1957), 554.

646. —. "Brilliant Gossip." *Time,* 70 (25 November 1957), 126, 129.

647. —. "Human Frailty." *TLS* (18 October 1957), p. 621.

648. —. *"Paperbacks: A Bit Off the Map."* *Observer* (28 April 1968), p. 27.

649. —. "Teddy Boy's Anthropologist." *The* (London) *Times* (17 October 1957), p. 13.

650. Bacon, Martha. "More Than a Dash of Bitters." *New York Herald Tribune Book Review,* 34 (17 November 1957), 6.

651. Clay, George R. "The Case Against Boredom." *Reporter,* 17 (26 December 1957), 38-40. Pp. 38, 39.

* 652. Corke, Hilary. "New Novels." *Listener,* 58 (24 October 1957), 667.

653. Fuller, Edmund. Review of *A Bit Off the Map,* in the *Chicago Sunday Tribune* (22 December 1957), p. 3.

654. Fuller, Roy. Untitled book review. *London Magazine,* 4 (December 1957), 60-62, 65. Pp. 60-61.

655. Green, Martin. "Artist Astray." *Chicago Review,* 12 (Autumn 1958), 76-79.

656. Harley, John. *"A Bit Off the Map and Other Stories."* *Library Journal* (15 September 1957), p. 2144.

657. Maclaren-Ross, J. "Up to the Moment." *Punch,* 233 (6 November 1957), 550-551.

658. Millgate, Michael. "Angus Wilson's Guide to Modern England." *New Republic,* 137 (25 November 1957), 17-18.

659. Moore, Harry T. "Teddy Boys and Genteel Madmen." *New York Times Book Review* (17 November 1957), p. 4.

660. Peden, William. "London 'Crowd'." *Saturday Review,* 40 (30 November 1957), 16.

661. Raymond, John. "Mid-Century Blues." *New Statesman,* 54 (12 October 1957), 464, 466.

662. Wakefield, Dan. "Post-Post-Kipling." *Commonweal,* 67 (13 December 1957), 293-294.

663. Weightman, J. G. "The Month: A Personal Diary." *Twentieth Century,* 163 (January 1958), 70-77. P. 73.

Death Dance: Twenty-Five Stories

664. Anon. *"Death Dance."* Publishers' Weekly, 195 (10 March 1969), 70.

665. Baldeshwiler, Eileen. *"Death Dance: Twenty-Five Stories."* Studies in Short Fiction, 8 (Summer 1971), 477-478.

666. Carroll, John M. *"Death Dance: Twenty-Five Stories."* Library Journal, 94 (1 June 1969), 2252.

667. Cassill, R. V. "Tales of an old world and a new one." *Book World*, 3 (25 May 1969), 4.

668. Oates, Joyce Carol. *"Death Dance: Twenty-Five Stories."* Saturday Review, 52 (5 July 1969), 33-34.

The Mulberry Bush

669. Anon. "After the Show." *The* (London) *Times* (21 September 1959), p. 5.

670. —. "Dramatic Themes." *TLS* (10 February 1956), p. 82.

671. —. "Theatre Royal Bristol: 'The Mulberry Bush'." *The* (London) *Times* (28 September 1955), p. 3. Review of the stage play.

672. E. O. D. K. Untitled book review. *Punch*, 230 (2 May 1956), 533.

673. Granger, Derek. "Themes for New Voices." *London Magazine*, 3 (December 1956), 41-47. Pp. 41, 44, 47.

674. Hope-Wallace, Phillip. Review of *The Mulberry Bush*, in *Time and Tide* (7 April 1956), p. 387.

675. Inglis, Brian. *"The Mulberry Bush."* Spectator, 195 (7 October 1955), 450.

676. —. *"The Mulberry Bush."* *Spectator,* 196 (23 March 1956), 386.

677. Worsley, T. C. "A New Voice." *New Statesman,* 50 (1 October 1955), 395.

The Stranger

678. Anon. "Mr. Angus Wilson's *The Stranger." The* (London) *Times* (21 November 1960), p. 16.

The Invasion

679. Anon. "Shrewd Playing of Double Game." *The* (London) *Times* (1 April 1963), p. 14.

Emile Zola: An Introductory Study of His Novels

680. Anon. "Critic of Society." *TLS* (16 May 1952), p. 330.

681. —. *"Emile Zola."* *Booklist,* 48 (15 June 1952), 338.

682. —. *"Emile Zola."* *New Yorker,* 28 (23 August 1952), 86.

683. —. "Popular Pessimist." *Time,* 59 (30 June 1952), 84, 86.

684. Charques, R. D. "Zola Reconsidered." *New Statesman and Nation,* 188 (29 February 1952), 268, 270.

685. Davis, Joe Lee. *"Emile Zola." New Republic,* 127 (21 July 1952), 22-23.

686. Korg, Jacob. "An Englishman on Zola." *Nation,* 174 (21 June 1952), 607.

687. LeSage, L. *"Emile Zola." Saturday Review,* 35 (2 August 1952), 34.

688. Peyre, Henri. "Zola's Obsessions." *New York Times Book Review* (18 May 1952), p. 5.

* 689. Pritchett, V. S. "Zola." *New Statesman and Nation*, 43 (29 March 1952), 377-378.

690. Walbridge, Earle F. *"Emile Zola."* *Library Journal*, 77 (15 May 1952), 893.

For Whom the Cloche Tolls

691. Adams, Phoebe. *"For Whom the Cloche Tolls."* *Atlantic*, 233 (February 1964), 96.

692. Anon. *"For Whom the Cloche Tolls."* *Publishers' Weekly*, 202 (11 December 1972), 37.

* 693. —. *"For Whom the Cloche Tolls."* *Queen's Quarterly*, 81 (Summer 1974), 323.

* 694. Blakeston, Oswell. *"For Whom the Cloche Tolls."* *Books and Bookmen*, 19 (October 1973), 105.

695. Davenport, Guy. "Maisie Markham dreamed her life like a lucky Emma Bovary." *New York Times Book Review* (15 April 1973), p. 5.

696. Hill, William B. *"For Whom the Cloche Tolls."* *Best Sellers*, 34 (1 April 1974), 9.

697. McLellan, Joseph. "Briefly Noted." *Book World* (17 February 1974), p. 4.

698. Palmer, Tony. "All in favour." *Spectator*, 231 (4 August 1973), 157-158. P. 158.

699. Stonier, G. W. "What They Saw in Maisie." *New Statesman and Nation*, 45 (20 June 1953), 752-753.

The Seven Deadly Sins

700. Anon. "Pride and Pasta." *Newsweek,* 60 (3 December 1962), 106-107.

701. —. *"The Seven Deadly Sins."* New Yorker, 38 (29 December 1962), 78.

702. —. *"The Seven Deadly Sins."* Publishers' Weekly, 191 (6 February 1967), 77.

703. —. "Those Fine Old Deadly Sins." *Time,* 80 (23 November 1962), 65-66.

704. De Mott, Benjamin. "Too Much In-Touch." *Harper's,* 226 (January 1963), 91-93. Pp. 92-93.

705. Dolbier, Maurice. "Tenderly Treating the Sins of Old." *New York Herald Tribune Books,* 39 (25 November 1962), 3.

706. Elmen, P. Review of *The Seven Deadly Sins,* in the *Christian Scholar* (Spring 1964), p. 81.

707. Mayhew, Leonard F. X. "Genial Hosts to Pride and Company." *Commonweal,* 77 (28 December 1962), 369.

708. Willis, Katherine Tappert. *"Seven Deadly Sins."* Library Journal, 87 (1 December 1962), 441.

The Wild Garden

709. Anon. "Getting Stockport Right." *New Statesman,* 66 (15 November 1963), 706.

710. —. "Getting Themselves Taped." *TLS* (21 November 1963), p. 948; reply by Wilson in *TLS* (November 1963), p. 993.

711. —. "The Three-Legged Race." *TLS* (21 November 1963), p. 947.

712. Bowen, John. "A Quartet of Self-Examinations." *Punch*, 245 (11 December 1963), 866.

713. Bradbury, Malcolm. *"The Wild Garden."* *Listener*, 70 (28 November 1963), 892, 895.

714. Davis, Robert Gorham. "The Roots of the Story." *New York Times Book Review* (16 February 1964), pp. 22, 26.

715. Ghose, Zulfikar. "Artists and Entertainers." *Spectator*, 211 (13 December 1963), 798.

716. Hicks, Granville. "Talks Along the Thames." *Saturday Review*, 46 (14 December 1963), 39-40.

717. Ohmann, Richard. "The Private Corridor of Angus Wilson's Mind." *Commonweal*, 79 (21 February 1964), 638-640.

* 718. Pryce-Jones, Alan. "On explaining the unexplainable." *Book Week*, 1 (9 February 1964), 2, 19.

719. Willis, Katherine Tappert. *"The Wild Garden."* *Library Journal*, 88 (1 December 1963), 4646.

Tempo: The Impact of Television on the Arts

720. Anon. *"Tempo; the Impact of Television on the Arts."* *Choice*, 4 (March 1967), 53.

721. —. *"The Impact of Televison on the Arts."* *TLS* (4 February 1965), p. 93.

722. Gross, John. "That's Show Business." *New Statesman*, 68 (25 December 1964), 994-995. P. 995.

A Maugham Twelve

723. Dickinson, Peter. *"A Maugham Twelve."* *Punch*, 251 (23 November 1966), 791.

724. Taubman, Robert. "Military Idiot." *New Statesman*, 72 (21 October 1966), 595-596. P. 596.

The World of Charles Dickens

725. Anon. "Briefly Noted." *New Yorker*, 46 (19 September 1970), 137.

726. —. "Dickens: 1812-1870." *TLS* (4 June 1970), pp. 597-598.

727. —. "1970 books—a spot review." *Christian Science Monitor*, 63 (27 November 1970), B4.

728. —. "Sight and Smell: *The World of Charles Dickens."* *Economist*, 235 (20 June 1970), 54.

729. —. *"The World of Charles Dickens."* *Best Sellers*, 30 (15 September 1970), 236.

730. —. *"The World of Charles Dickens."* *British Book News* (July 1970), p. 560.

731. —. *"The World of Charles Dickens."* *Choice*, 7 (December 1970), 1378.

732. —. *"The World of Charles Dickens."* *Publishers' Weekly*, 197 (22 June 1970), 59.

733. Bayley, John. "Irresistible Dickens." *New York Review of Books*, 15 (8 October 1970), 8, 10, 12. P. 8.

734. Bell, Pearl K. "A Curious Grudgery." *New Leader*, 54 (25 January 1971), 15-16.

735. Bowen, Elizabeth. "Dickens and the demon toy box." *Spectator*, 224 (30 May 1970), 713.

736. Carey, John. "When Dickens starts laughing." *Listener*, 83 (28 May 1970), 724-725. P. 724.

737. Cosgrave, Mary Silva. *"The World of Charles Dickens."* *Horn Book Magazine*, 47 (February 1971), 73-74.

738. Dawson, Helen. "Briefing: *The World of Charles Dickens."* *Observer* (8 October 1972), p. 35.

739. Donoghue, Denis. Review of *The World of Charles Dickens*, in *Nineteenth-Century Fiction*, 27 (September 1972), 216-218.

740. Fernandez, Diane, and Patrick Reumaux. "Angus Wilson parle de Dickens." *Quinzaine Litteraine*, 155 (January 1-15, 1973), 5-6. In French.

741. Fido, M. A. Untitled book review. *Victorian Studies*, 15 (September 1971), 101-102.

742. Fielding, K. J. Review of *The World of Charles Dickens*, in the *Dickensian*, 66 (September 1970), 248.

743. —. "The novelist as sun, the novels as planets revolving around him." *New York Times Book Review* (13 September 1970), p. 7.

744. Ford, George H. "Dickens and Fame: Dickens in the 1960's." *Dickensian*, 66 (May 1970), 163-182. Includes comments on *The World of Charles Dickens*.

745. Fowles, John. "Guide to a man-made planet." *Life*, 69 (4 September 1970), 8-9.

746. Galvin, Thomas J. *"The World of Charles Dickens."* *Library Journal*, 95 (15 September 1970), 2920.

747. Gross, John. "Tale of two Dickenses." *Observer* (24 May 1970), p. 30.

748. Hibbert, Christopher. "A failure to judge women." *Book World*, 4 (13 September 1970), 5.

749. Holloway, John. "Dickens' Word-World." *Encounter*, 34 (June 1970), 63-68. P. 63.

750. Hutchens, John K. "One Thing and Another." *Saturday Review*, 53 (19 December 1970), 30.

751. Katona, Anna. Review of *The World of Charles Dickens*, in *Helikon*, 17 (1971), 503-504.

752. Kirstein, Lincoln. *"The World of Charles Dickens."* *Nation*, 211 (21 December 1970), 666. Very brief comment.

753. Lalley, J. M. "The Topography of Genius." *Modern Age*, 15 (Spring 1971), 185-190.

754. Lane, Lauriat, Jr. "Satire, Society, and Symbol in Recent Dickens Criticism." *Studies in the Novel*, 5 (Spring 1973), 125-138. Includes comments on *The World of Charles Dickens.*

755. Lloyd, Eric. "Mr. Dickens: Some Great Expectations Fulfilled." *Wall Street Journal*, 176 (21 August 1970), 6.

756. Millar, Neil. "The Inimitable Boz." *Christian Science Monitor*, 62 (1 October 1970), 11.

757. Monod, Sylvère. Review of *The World of Charles Dickens*, in the *Dickens Studies Newsletter*, 2 (1971), 217-236.

758. O'Connor, John J. "Suggestions for Christmas Book Giving: *The World of Charles Dickens."* *Wall Street Journal*, 176 (8 December 1970), 22.

759. Porterfield, Christopher. Review of *The World of Charles*

Dickens, in *Time,* 96 (28 December 1970), 59-60.

760. Price, Martin. "Taking Dickens Seriously." *Yale Review,* n.s. 61 (Winter 1972), 271-279. Pp. 278-279.

761. Pritchett, V. S. "A Visionary Society." *New Statesman,* 79 (5 June 1970), 807-808.

762. Snow, C. P. "Books to give." *Financial Times* (26 November 1970), p. 33.

763. —. "Salute to Dickens." *Financial Times* (4 June 1970), p. 12.

764. Wall, Stephen. Review of *The World of Charles Dickens,* in *Essays in Criticism* (July 1971), p. 261.

765. Williams, Raymond. "The Dickens celebration." *Guardian Weekly,* 102 (6 June 1970), 18.

766. Wing, George. "Some recent Dickens criticism and scholarship." *Ariel,* 1 (October 1970), 56-66. Pp. 59-60.

767. Wolff, Geoffrey. "Man Mountain." *Newsweek,* 76 (31 August 1970), 73-74.

768. Yglesias, Helen. "Monsters, Bores, Clowns, Idiots." *Nation,* 211 (23 November 1970), 540-541.

England

769. Anon. *"England." New Yorker,* 47 (15 May 1971), 148.

770. —. *"England." Publishers' Weekly,* 199 (8 February 1971), 72.

771. —. "Quick guide." *The* (London) *Times* (8 April 1971), p. 11.

* 772. R. F. G. *"England."* *Best Sellers*, 31 (15 April 1971), 45.

ADDENDUM

Note: An asterisk has been placed in front of an entry within the text to indicate that one or more entries are to follow immediately. All such additional entries are of course found here.

BY KINGSLEY AMIS

95a. "Finding Out About Jazz." *Observer* (15 April 1956), p. 13. An introduction to what he will cover in future articles on jazz.

98a. "The World of Jazz: 'Yeah, Tell Me More.' " *Observer* (13 May 1956), p. 10. On the music of Fats Waller.

100a. "The World of Jazz: 'It Can't Be Any Good.' " *Observer* (17 June 1956), p. 8. On several British Musicians.

102a. "University Jazz." *Observer* (15 July 1956), p. 10.

103a. "Jazz and the Egghead." *Observer* (12 August 1956), p. 3. A review of André Hodeir's *Jazz: Its Evolution and Essence.*

104a. "Jazz on Record." *Observer* (16 September 1956), p. 13. On *Introduction to Jazz, by the Rev. A. L. Kershaw.*

106a. "The World of Jazz: Rhythm and Blues." *Observer* (21 October 1956), p. 13. On the music of Earl Bostic.

107a. "Guides to Noise." *Observer* (2 December 1956), p. 13. Review of Leonard Feather's *The Encyclopaedia of Jazz,* and H. Panassié and M. Gautier's *Dictionary of Jazz.*

107b. "For Jazz Lovers." *Observer* (16 December 1956), p. 8. Review of several records.

108a. "World of Jazz: The New Sound." *Observer* (30 December 1956), p. 11. On the different styles of jazz.

109a. "Make Mine Chicago Style." *Observer* (27 January 1957), p. 10. Review of the music of jazz musician Eddie Condon.

110a. "Not Really the Blues." *Observer* (10 February 1957), p. 10. Review of concert at Royal Festival Hall which featured Eddie Condon and his All Stars.

110b. "Singing the Blues." *Observer* (17 February 1957), p. 10. Review of Negro folk music and jazz.

111a. "From the Golden Gate." *Observer* (17 March 1957), p. 12. On white revivalist bands and jazz.

112a. "Jazz Turntable." *Observer* (5 May 1957), p. 14. Review of four jazz L. P. recordings.

112b. "The Noise Makers." *Observer* (2 June 1957), p. 17. Review of Raymond Horrick's *Count Basie and His Orchestra,* and *Jazzmen* edited by Frederick Ramsey, Jr. and Charles Edward Smith.

114a. "Jazz Turntable." *Observer* (30 June 1957), p. 10. Review of five jazz recordings.

120a. "Pater and Old Chap." *Observer* (13 October 1957), p. 15. Review of Warwick Deeping's *Sorrell and Son.*

126a. "Performer's Music." *Observer* (8 December 1957),

p. 19. Review of three books on jazz.

126b. "Mainly Modern." *Observer* (29 December 1957), p. 9. Review of seven jazz recordings.

128a. "Jazz Turntable: Dixieland Blues." *Observer* (9 February 1958), p. 12. Review of several LP records.

129a. "Jazz Turntable: All Sorts of Blues." *Observer* (16 March 1958), p. 15. Review of several LP records.

130a. "Jazz Turntable: Ladies First." *Observer* (13 April 1958), p. 14. Review of several records by women.

131a. "Jazz Turntable: Weary Blues." *Observer* (11 May 1958), p. 14. On Josh White, and Louis Armstrong. Amis also attacks the jazz recording companies.

131b. "Jazz Turntable: Charlie's Art." *Observer* (15 June 1958), p. 14. On Charlie Parker, Artie Shaw, and others.

132a. "Jazz in Hard Covers." *Observer* (20 July 1958), p. 14. Review of five jazz recordings.

132b. "A Good Modernist." *Observer* (17 August 1958), p. 12. Review of the jazz music of Gerry Mulligan.

132c. "Farewell Blues." *Observer* (21 September 1958), p. 16. Review of two recordings.

137a. "The Case for Science Fiction: Where Novelists Fear to Tread." *Observer* (29 November 1959), p. 8. A defence of science fiction.

137b. "Science Fiction." *Observer* (13 December 1959), p. 23. Review of five science fiction books.

139a. "New Prey for the Monster." *Observer* (20 March 1960), p. 21. Review of seven science fiction books.

139b. "Science Fiction." *Observer* (10 April 1960), p. 21. Review of five science fiction books.

139c. "Possible Worlds." *Observer* (15 May 1960), p. 25. Review of four science fiction books.

139d. "More or Less Familiar." *Observer* (5 June 1960), p. 18. Review of Vladimir Nabokov's *Invitation to a Beheading*, Dan Jacobson's *The Evidence of Love*, Edna O'Brien's *The Country Girls*, and Lillian Smith's *One Hour*.

139e. "The Powell Country." *Observer* (19 June 1960), p. 26. Review of Anthony Powell's *Casanova's Chinese Restaurant*.

140a. "Hunting the Symbol." *Observer* (3 July 1960), p. 27. Review of Peter Coleridge's *The Running Footsteps*, R. Prawer Jhabvala's *The Householder*, Ira Morris's *The Paper Wall*, and Friedrich Dürrenmatt's *A Dangerous Game*.

140b. "The Cancelled Horoscope." *Observer* (17 July 1960), p. 28. Review of E. Litvinoff's *The Lost Europeans*, A. Salkey's *Escape to an Autumn Pavement*, L. Levine's *The Great Alphonse*, C. Blackstock's *The Briar Patch*, and H. E. Bates's *When the Green Woods Laugh*.

140c. "Directed Anger." *Observer* (31 July 1960), p. 20. Review of D. Lytton's *The Goddam White Man*, J. Tucker's *Equal Partners*, D. J. Enright's *Insufficient Poppy*, T. Chamales's *Go Naked in the World*, and P. H. Bonner's *The Art of Llewellyn Jones*.

141a. "The Insolent Chariots." *Observer* (14 August 1960), p. 21. Review of H. Livingston's *The Detroiters*, P. G. Wodehouse's *Jeeves in the Offing*, D. Lodge's *The Picturegoers*, P. Vansittart's *A Sort of Forgetting*, and B. Grimault's *Berthe in Paradise*.

141b. "James Bond in 2009." *Observer* (21 August 1960), p. 26. Review of five books of science fiction.

141c. "O God! Oh Montreal!" *Observer* (28 August 1960), p. 26. Review of Brian Moore's *The Luck of Ginger Coffey*, A. Goodman's *The Golden Youth of Lee Prince*, H. Tracy's *A Number of Things*, and C. Clift's *Walk to the Paradise Gardens*.

141d. "Assassin's Progress." *Observer* (11 September 1960), p. 26. Review of R. Condon's *The Manchurian Candidate*, J. Stroud's *The Shorn Lamb*, P. Frankau's *Road Through the Woods*, A. Sinclair's *The Project*, and Flannery O'Connor's *The Violent Bear It Away*.

142a. "Dublin Flashbacks." *Observer* (25 September 1960), p. 23. Review of G. Fielding's *Through Streets Broad and Narrow*, S. Stein's *What the World Owes Me*, J. Masters's *The Venus of Konpara*, and J. R. Ackerley's *We Think the World of You*.

142b. "Mainly Milk and Water." *Observer* (9 October 1960), p. 23. Review of John Rae's *The Custard Boys*.

142c. "The Time of Your Life." *Observer* (16 October 1960), p. 22. Review of several books of science fiction.

145a. "Junior Spaceman." *Observer* (4 December 1960), p. 28. Review of several science fiction books for children.

147a. "Across the Frontier." *Observer* (15 January 1961), p. 29. Review of four science fiction books.

147b. "What Marriage Did for Our Joe." *Observer* (29 January 1961), p. 29. Review of William Cooper's *Scenes from Provincial Life*, and *Scenes from Married Life*.

148a. "Star material." *Observer* (9 April 1961), p. 30. Review of five science fiction books.

149a. "The quickest way out of Westchester." *Observer* (11 June 1961), p. 27. Review of Peter DeVries's *Through the Fields of Clover.*

151a. "Interplanetary flipthrough." *Observer* (3 September 1961), p. 24. Review of six science fiction books.

151b. "Time and Space." *Observer* (1 October 1961), p. 31. Review of five science fiction books.

151c. "Investigation at the Drones Club." *Observer* (15 October 1961), p. 28. Review of P. G. Wodehouse's *Ice in the Bedroom,* and Richard Usborne's *Wodehouse at Work.*

157a. "Out of Your Depth." *Observer* (13 May 1962), p. 29. Review of Edna O'Brien's *The Lonely Girl,* and Anthony Burgess's *A Clockwork Orange.*

157b. "The Vegetables Take Over." *Observer* (20 May 1962), p. 25. Review of seven science fiction books.

159a. "A mixed-grill of futures." *Observer* (9 September 1962), p. 24. Review of four science fiction books.

159b. "Cracks in the crystal ball." *Observer* (7 October 1962), p. 24. Review of Anthony Burgess's *The Wanting Seed,* and several science fiction books.

159c. "Have ray-gun, will travel." *Observer* (18 November 1962), p. 25. Review of four science fiction books.

160a. "What's Left for Patriotism." *Observer* (20 January 1963), p. 21. On his definition of patriotism.

161a. "Inner Space." *Observer* (27 January 1963), p. 22. Review of J. G. Ballard's *The Drowned World.*

161b. "The words are wild." *Observer* (24 February 1963), p. 24. Review of seven science fiction books, including

Ray Bradbury's *Something Wicked This Way Comes.*

162a. "Where Good and Bad Meet." *Observer* (17 March 1963), p. 24. On British and American science fiction magazines.

162b. "Inner Space and Elsewhere." *Observer* (7 July 1963), p. 22. Review of several books of science fiction.

162c. "Spectacular Manifestation at Trieste." *Observer* (11 August 1963), p. 17. On an international science fiction film festival which was viewed by Amis.

163a. "Science Fiction." *Observer* (8 December 1963), p. 24. Review of seven books of science fiction, including Kurt Vonnegut's *Cat's Cradle*, and Isaac Asimov's *Nine Tomorrows.*

267a. "Words and Meanings." *New Statesman*, 92 (20 August 1976), 237. On a variety of words.

267b. "London Diary." *New Statesman*, 92 (3 September 1976), 305.

ON KINGSLEY AMIS

292a. Green, Martin. "The Gentlemen of England." *Observer* (16 October 1960), p. 17. Includes comments on Amis.

321a. Toynbee, Philip. "The Face of the Fifties: Dragons and Dragon-killers." *Observer* (20 December 1959), p. 16. Includes comments on Amis.

340a. O'Faolain, Sean. "New Novels." *Observer* (24 January 1954), p. 9. Review of *Lucky Jim.*

344a. Toynbee, Philip. "The Politics of *Lucky Jim." Observer* (13 January 1957), p. 11.

366a. Toynbee, Philip. "Class Comedy." *Observer* (21 August 1955), p. 9. Review of *That Uncertain Feeling.*

409a. Miller, Karl. "Girl, with Tigers." *Observer* (18 September 1960), p. 26. Review of *Take a Girl Like You.*

442a. Weightman, John. "Mr. Amis goes metaphysical." *Observer* (17 November 1963), p. 24. Review of *One Fat Englishman.*

654a. Anon. "Out of the frying pan." *Economist*, 261 (16 October 1976), 143. Review of *The Alteration.*

654b. Carey, John. "If." *New Statesman*, 92 (8 October 1976), 483. Review of *The Alteration.*

654c. Johnson, Pamela Hansford. "In Father Bond's day." *Listener*, 97 (7 October 1976), 453. Review of *The Alteration.*

654d. Murray, Isobel. "Chorister's sad plight." *Financial Times* (7 October 1976), p. 25. Review of *The Alteration.*

654e. Totton, Nick. "Diminuendo." *Spectator*, 237 (9 October 1976), 22-23. P. 23. Review of *The Alteration.*

671a. Wyndham, Francis. "Towards a Stiff Upper Lip." *Observer* (23 September 1962), p. 25. Review of *My Enemy's Enemy.*

677a. Alvarez, A. "A Joke's a Joke." *Observer* (18 November 1956), p. 11. Review of *A Case of Samples.*

BY ELIZABETH BOWEN

111a. "Exploring Ireland." *Observer* (4 May 1952), p. 7. Review of Rachel Knappett's *Wait Now!*

111b. "A City Growing." *Observer* (18 May 1952), p. 7. Review of Maurice Craig's *Dublin: 1660-1860.*

111c. "Ascendancy." *Observer* (16 November 1952), p. 8. Review of Brian Fitzgerald's *The Anglo-Irish.*

116a. "The Informer." *Observer* (19 July 1953), p. 9. Review of Whittaker Chambers's *Witness.*

ON ELIZABETH BOWEN

271a. Smith, Stevie. "Miss Bowen and Mr. Graves." *Observer* (6 March 1955), p. 8. Review of *A World of Love.*

381a. Nicolson, Harold. "A Celt Exposed to Sunlight." *Observer* (3 July 1960), p. 27. Review of *A Time in Rome.*

BY MARGARET DRABBLE

120a. "A tale of gloom." *Listener,* 96 (2 September 1976), 283-284. Review of *The Diaries of Evelyn Waugh* edited by Michael Davie.

120b. "Very heaven." *Spectator,* 237 (11 September 1976), 22. Review of *The Autobiography of Arthur Ransome.*

120c. "Chanel Number One." *Listener,* 96 (30 September 1976), 401. Review of Edmonde Charles-Roux's *Chanel.*

120d. "Muriel Spark: a glittering, knowing novel about the decline of the West." *New York Times Book Review* (3 October 1976), pp. 1-2. Review of Spark's *The Takeover.*

ON MARGARET DRABBLE

153a. Raven, Simon. "Brisk despair of young middle-age." *Observer* (31 March 1963), p. 25. Review of *A Summer Bird-Cage.*

346a. Mellors, John. "Council Writers." *Listener,* 96 (5 August 1976), 158-159. P. 158. Review of *New Stories I.*

BY WILLIAM GOLDING

20a. "Rich and Strange." *Observer* (10 April 1960), p. 20. Review of *Captain Cousteau's Underwater Treasury*, edited by Jacques-Yves Cousteau and James Dugan.

21a. "The Way It Was." *Observer* (22 May 1960), p. 21. Review of Ray Parkin's *Out of the Smoke.*

28a. "Almost for Adults." *Observer* (4 December 1960), p. 28. Review of several books for children.

ON WILLIAM GOLDING

306a. Prawer, Siegbert S. "William Golding: *Lord of the Flies.*" *Zeitgenössische Englische Dichtung. Einführung in die Englische Literaturbetrachtung Mit Interpretationen, II: Prosa.* Ed. Werner Hüllen. Frankfurt: Hirschgraben, 1966, pp. 115-122.

315a. Smith, Stevie. "New Novels." *Observer* (19 September 1954), p. 13. Review of *Lord of the Flies.*

350a. Davenport, John. "The Twilight of the Cave-men." *Observer* (18 September 1955), p. 11. Review of *The Inheritors.*

383a. —. "New Novels." *Observer* (28 October 1956), p. 17. Review of *Pincher Martin.*

435a. Toynbee, Philip. "Down to Earth." *Observer* (25 October 1959), p. 22. Review of *Free Fall.*

ON L. P. HARTLEY

802a. Paul, David. "Life With Grannie." *Observer* (7 December 1952), p. 9. Review of *Simonetta Perkins.*

844a. Toynbee, Philip. "Misgivings About Mr. Hartley." *Observer* (11 May 1958), p. 16. Review of *Eustace and Hilda: A Trilogy.*

875a. Cecil, Lord David. "Imagination." *Observer* (11 October 1953), p. 10. Review of *The Go-Between.*

908a. Davenport, John. "Mr. Hartley and Others." *Observer* (2 October 1955), p. 10. Review of *A Perfect Woman.*

929a. —. "Mr. Hartley and Others." *Observer* (7 July 1957), p. 15. Review of *The Hireling.*

954a. —. "Beatification." *Observer* (15 May 1960), p. 25. Review of *Facial Justice.*

1030a. Wilson, Angus. "New Novels." *Observer* (29 August 1954), p. 7. Review of *The White Wand.*

1035a. Vansittart, Peter. "The snaffle and the curb." *Observer* (21 May 1961), p. 24. Review of *Two for the River.*

BY RICHARD HUGHES

65a. "The Monster." *Observer* (1 June 1952), p. 7. Review of Gavin Maxwell's *Harpoon at a Venture.*

ON RICHARD HUGHES

194a. Davenport, John. "Richard Hughes Returns to the Novel." *Observer* (8 October 1961), p. 29. Review of *The Fox in the Attic.*

BY ROSAMOND LEHMANN

6a. *A Sea-Grape Tree.* London: Collins, 1976. (Her most recent novel).

ON ROSAMOND LEHMANN

200a. Laski, Marghanita. "Modern Love." *Observer* (5 April 1953), p. 7. Review of *The Echoing Grove.*

211a. Johnson, Marigold. "Adonis anadyomene." *TLS* (12 November 1976), p. 1437. Review of *A Sea-Grape Tree.*

211b. Quigly, Isabel. "Among Misfits and others." *Financial Times* (28 October 1976), p. 12. Review of *A Sea-Grape Tree.*

BY DORIS LESSING

47a. "Freud Among the Tea-Cups." *Observer* (9 November 1958), p. 19. Review of three theatre productions.

48a. "The Living Past." *Observer* (16 November 1958), p. 19. Review of two theatre productions.

48b. "Two Brands of Corn." *Observer* (23 November 1958), p. 17. Review of the theatre production of *Hook, Line and Sinker.*

48c. "The Düsseldorf Monster." *Observer* (30 November 1958), p. 17. Review of four theater productions including Bertolt Brecht's *Mother Courage.*

48d. "A Time for Rebellion." *Observer* (7 December 1958), p. 15. Review of three theatre productions.

ON DORIS LESSING

158a. Krouse, Agate Nesaule. "Doris Lessing's Feminist Plays." *World Literature Written in English,* 15 (November 1976), 305-322.

241a. Laski, Marghanita. "All Too Clear." *Observer* (19 October 1952), p. 9. Review of *Martha Quest.*

243a. Paul, David. "New Novels." *Observer* (28 June 1953), p. 10. Review of *Five: Short Novels.*

259a. Wain, John. "Possible Worlds." *Observer* (12 October 1958), p. 20. Review of *A Ripple from the Storm.*

ADDENDUM: DORIS LESSING

460a. McDowell, Judith H. *"The Memoirs of a Survivor."* *World Literature Written in English,* 15 (November 1976), 323, 325-326.

504a. Spark, Muriel. "New Short Stories." *Observer* (15 December 1957), p. 12. Review of *The Habit of Loving.*

570a. Mills, John. *"The Story of a Non-Marrying Man."* *West Coast Review,* 9 (January 1975), 53-55.

ON BRIAN MOORE

86a. Studing, Richard. "A Brian Moore Bibliography." *Éire-Ireland*, 10 (Autumn 1975), 89-105.

124a. Wilson, Angus. "Jungle World." *Observer* (9 February 1958), p. 15. Review of *The Feast of Lupercal.*

124b. Amis, Kingsley. "O God! Oh Montreal!" *Observer* (28 August 1960), p. 26. Review of *The Luck of Ginger Coffey.*

176a. Raven, Simon. "Brisk despair of young middle-age." *Observer* (31 March 1963), p. 25. Review of *An Answer from Limbo.*

329a. Porter, Raymond J. "Mystery, Miracle, and Faith in Brian Moore's *Catholics.*" *Éire-Ireland*, 10 (Autumn 1975), 79-88.

359a. Adams, Phoebe-Lou. *"The Doctor's Wife."* *Atlantic*, 238 (November 1976), 118.

359b. Amiel, Barbara. "More lonely passions." *Macleans*, 89 (4 October 1976), 84. Review of *The Doctor's Wife.*

359c. Brookner, Anita. "The pleasure principle." *TLS* (19 November 1976), p. 1445. Review of *The Doctor's Wife.*

359d. Clemons, Walter. "Falling in Love Again." *Newsweek* (20 September 1976), p. 88. Review of *The Doctor's Wife.*

ADDENDUM: BRIAN MOORE

359e. Feld, Ross. *"The Doctor's Wife."* *Saturday Review* (18 September 1976), p. 30.

359f. Gray, Paul. "Rx for Guilt." *Time* (6 September 1976), p. 73. Review of *The Doctor's Wife.*

359g. Moynahan, Julian. *"The Doctor's Wife."* *New York Times Book Review* (26 September 1976), p. 7.

359h. Quigly, Isabel. "Poles apart." *Financial Times* (18 November 1976), p. 41. Review of *The Doctor's Wife.*

BY IRIS MURDOCH

38a. "Mr. Gellner's Game." *Observer* (29 November 1959), p. 5. Review of Ernest Gellner's *Words and Things.*

ON IRIS MURDOCH

62a. Anon. "In the Picture." *Observer* (25 June 1961), p. 24. A biographical sketch of Iris Murdoch.

72a. Blow, Simon. "An interview with Iris Murdoch." *Spectator,* 237 (25 September 1976), 24-25.

169a. Wilson, Angus. "New Novels." *Observer* (6 June 1954), p. 7. Review of *Under the Net.*

174a. Davenport, John. "New Novels." *Observer* (1 April 1956), p. 9. Review of *The Flight from the Enchanter.*

186a. Hopkinson, Tom. "A Natural Novelist." *Observer* (5 May 1957), p. 17. Review of *The Sandcastle.*

196a. Davenport, John. "Symbols and Sentiments." *Observer* (2 November 1958), p. 22. Review of *The Bell.*

230a. Seddon, George. "Lost among the bedclothes." *Observer* (30 June 1963), p. 22. Review of the stage production of *A Severed Head.*

232a. Toynbee, Philip. "Too Fruity to be True." *Observer* (18 June 1961), p. 28. Review of *A Severed Head.*

250a. Davenport, John. "Where only guilt is real." *Observer*

ADDENDUM: IRIS MURDOCH

(8 September 1963), p. 24. Review of *The Unicorn*.

479a. Anon. "Out of the frying pan." *Economist*, 261 (16 October 1976), 143. Review of *Henry and Cato*.

479b. Caute, David. "To the Life." *New Statesman*, 92 (24 September 1976), 419-420. P. 420. Review of *Henry and Cato*.

479c. Tennant, Emma. "The strong and the weak." *Listener*, 96 (23 September 1976), 379. Review of *Henry and Cato*.

479d. Totton, Nick. "The new learning." *Spectator*, 237 (25 September 1976), 19-20. P. 19. Review of *Henry and Cato*.

BY V. S. NAIPAUL

123a. "India: Synthesis and Mimicry." *New York Review of Books*, 23 (16 September 1976), 14-19.

123b. "India: Paradise Lost." *New York Review of Books*, 23 (28 October 1976), 10, 12, 14-16.

ON V. S. NAIPAUL

136a. Boxill, Anthony. "The Physical and Historical Environment of V. S. Naipaul's *The Mystic Masseur* and *The Suffrage of Elvira.*" *Journal of Canadian Fiction*, 3 (1975), 52-55.

197a. Davenport, John. "Earl's Court and Elsewhere." *Observer* (20 April 1958), p. 17. Review of *The Suffrage of Elvira*.

206a. —. "New England Schooldays." *Observer* (19 April 1959), p. 22. Review of *Miguel Street*.

238a. Macinnes, Colin. "Caribbean Masterpiece." *Observer* (1 October 1961), p. 31. Review of *A House for Mr. Biswas*.

292a. Boxill, Anthony. "The Paradox of Freedom: V. S. Naipaul's *In a Free State.*" *Critique*, 18, No. 1 (1976), 81-91.

358a. Pope-Hennessy, James. "Return to the Caribbean." *Observer* (29 July 1962), p. 18. Review of *The Middle Passage*.

BY ANTHONY POWELL

440a. *To Keep the Ball Rolling: The Memoirs of Anthony Powell. Volume One, Infants of the Spring.* London: Heinemann, 1976.

ON ANTHONY POWELL

452a. Anon. "Who's Who." *Observer* (19 June 1960), p. 28. A biographical sketch of Anthony Powell.

465a. Breslin, John B. *"A Dance to the Music of Time." America,* 135 (30 October 1976), 281-282.

481a. Gutierrez, Donald. "The Discrimination of Elegance: Anthony Powell's *A Dance to the Music of Time." The Malahat Review,* 34 (April 1974), 126-141.

545a. Tucker, James. *The Novels of Anthony Powell.* London: Macmillan, 1976.

646a. Toynbee, Philip. "Comic Intentions." *Observer* (22 June 1952), p. 7. Review of *A Buyer's Market.*

656a. Davenport, John. "New Novels." *Observer* (15 May 1955), p. 17. Review of *The Acceptance World.*

678a. —. "New Novels." *Observer* (27 October 1957), p. 18. Review of *At Lady Molly's.*

696a. Amis, Kingsley. "The Powell Country." *Observer* (19 June 1960), p. 26. Review of *Casanova's Chinese Restaurant.*

741a. Toynbee, Philip. "Facing the Music of Time." *Observer* (24 June 1962), p. 24. Review of *The Kindly Ones.*

925a. Reedy, Gerard C. *"Hearing Secret Harmonies."* *America,* 135 (13 November 1976), 331.

951a. Anon. "Choreography." *Economist,* 261 (16 October 1976), 142, 144. Review of *To Keep the Ball Rolling.*

951b. Bayley, John. "Background Music." *Listener,* 97 (7 October 1976), 451-452. Review of *To Keep the Ball Rolling.*

951c. Curtis, Anthony. "Slow time." *Financial Times* (7 October 1976), p. 25. Review of *To Keep the Ball Rolling.*

951d. Raban, Jonathan. "First Person Plural." *New Statesman,* 92 (1 October 1976), 450-451. P. 450. Review of *To Keep the Ball Rolling.*

951e. Raven, Simon. "On the margin." *Spectator,* 237 (9 October 1976), 19. Review of *To Keep the Ball Rolling.*

BY JEAN RHYS

12a. *Sleep It Off, Lady.* London: Deutsch, 1976; New York: Harper and Row, 1976. (A book of short stories).

ON JEAN RHYS

39a. Porter, Dennis. "Of Heroines and Victims: Jean Rhys and *Jane Eyre.*" *Massachusetts Review,* 17 (Autumn 1976), 540-552.

158a. Bailey, Paul. "True romance." *TLS* (22 October 1976), p. 1321. Review of *Sleep It Off, Lady.*

158b. Macauley, Robie. "Things unsaid and said too often." *New York Times Book Review* (21 November 1976), pp. 7, 50. Review of *Sleep It Off, Lady.*

158c. Murray, Isobel. "Uncomfortable honesty." *Financial Times* (4 November 1976), p. 27. Review of *Sleep It Off, Lady.*

158d. Pollitt, Katha. *"Sleep It Off, Lady." Saturday Review* (13 November 1976), pp. 40-41.

158e. Wood, Michael. "Endangered Species." *New York Review of Books,* 23 (11 November 1976), 30-32. Pp. 30-31. Review of *Sleep It Off, Lady.*

ON ALAN SILLITOE

104a. Wain, John. "Possible Worlds." *Observer* (12 October 1958), p. 20. Review of *Saturday Night and Sunday Morning.*

126a. Wyndham, Francis. "War: Abstract and Actual." *Observer* (22 May 1960), p. 19. Review of *The General.*

136a. Davenport, John. "Leaden Days of Youth." *Observer* (15 October 1961), p. 29. Review of *Key to the Door.*

226a. Seymour-Smith, Martin. "Miner in Khaki." *Financial Times* (9 December 1976), p. 12. Review of *The Widower's Son.*

246a. Spark, Muriel. "Borstal Boy." *Observer* (11 October 1959), p. 21. Review of *The Loneliness of the Long-Distance Runner.*

264a. Wardle, Irving. "Return of the prodigal." *Observer* (13 October 1963), p. 24. Review of *The Ragman's Daughter.*

BY C. P. SNOW

111a. "The Universe of Modern Man." *Observer* (22 January 1961), p. 28. Review of Stephen Toulmin and June Goodfield's *The Fabric of the Heavens.*

484a. "When bombs fell." *Financial Times* (5 August 1976), p. 12. Review of Tom Harrisson's *Living Through the Blitz.*

484b. "Strange bedfellows." *Financial Times* (12 August 1976), p. 10. Review of R. W. Thompson's *Churchill and Morton.*

484c. "Lord Dalliance." *Financial Times* (26 August 1976), p. 10. Review of Philip Ziegler's *Melbourne.*

484d. "Temporary captain." *Financial Times* (2 September 1976), p. 23. Review of *The Diaries of Evelyn Waugh,* edited by Michael Davie.

484e. "Men of letters." *Financial Times* (9 September 1976), p. 34. Review of Reginald Pound's *A. P. Herbert,* and *The Autobiography of Arthur Ransome,* edited by Rupert Hart-Davis.

484f. "The greatest?" *Financial Times* (16 September 1976), p. 15. Review of Geoffrey Thurley's *The Dickens Myth: Its Genesis and Structure,* and Wolf Mankowitz's *Dickens of London.*

484g. "Second sex." *Financial Times* (23 September 1976), p. 13. Review of Patricia Meyer Spacks's *The Female Imagination,* Elizabeth Taylor's *Blaming,* and Derek

Barton's *An Englishman's Breakfast.*

484h. "Vanishing I." *Financial Times* (30 September 1976), p. 14. Review of Peter Quennell's *The Marble Foot.*

484i. "Straight bat." *Financial Times* (7 October 1976), p. 25. Review of Lord Home's *The Way the Wind Blows.*

484j. "Master printer." *Financial Times* (15 October 1976), p. 20. Review of George D. Painter's *William Caxton: A Quincentenary Biography.*

484k. "High office hindsight." *Financial Times* (4 November 1976), p. 27. Review of Harold Wilson's *The Governance of Britain,* and Selwyn Lloyd's *Mr. Speaker, Sir.*

484l. "Adolf's admirer." *Financial Times* (11 November 1976), p. 14. Review of David Pryce-Jones's *Unity Mitford: A Quest.*

484m. "Cheerful soul." *Financial Times* (18 November 1976), p. 41. Review of John Colville's *Footprints in Time.*

484n. "One-sided dialogue." *Financial Times* (2 December 1976), p. 31. Review of Philip Mason's *The Dove in Harness.*

484o. "Hard-hearted hedonist." *Financial Times* (9 December 1976), p. 12. Review of Mark Holloway's *Norman Douglas.*

484p. "Into the melting pot." *Financial Times* (16 December 1976), p. 35. Review of Irving Howe's *The Immigrant Jews of New York: 1881 to the Present.*

484q. "Celtic Arnold." *Financial Times* (23 December 1976), p. 10. Review of A. L. Rowse's *Matthew Arnold: Poet and Prophet.*

484r. "Strategic Slim." *Financial Times* (30 December 1976), p. 8. Review of Ronald Lewin's *Slim: the Standard Bearer.*

ON C. P. SNOW

653a. Jaki, Stanley L. "A Hundred Years of Two Cultures." *The University of Windsor Review,* 11 (Fall-Winter 1975), 55-79.

856a. Smith, Stevie. "New Novels." *Observer* (2 May 1954), p. 9. Review of *The New Men.*

883a. Wain, John. "New Novels." *Observer* (9 September 1956), p. 12. Review of *Homecomings.*

892a. Davenport, John. "Seen from the Inside." *Observer* (30 March 1958), p. 17. Review of *The Conscience of the Rich.*

1187a. Wain, John. "Fiction from Moscow." *Observer* (10 December 1961), p. 27. Review of *Winter's Tales 7.*

BY MURIEL SPARK

66a. "An Exile's Path." *Observer* (30 November 1952), p. 8. Review of Sean O'Faolain's *Newman's Way.*

67a. "Eyes and Noses." *Observer* (18 January 1953), p. 6. On both facial features, especially noses.

67b. "Ballads." *Observer* (25 January 1953), p. 8. Review of *British Popular Ballads* edited by John E. Housman.

67c. "Wilde Lives." *Observer* (26 April 1953), p. 8. Review of Patrick Byrne's *The Wildes of Merrion Square.*

67d. "Awkward Saint." *Observer* (20 September 1953), p. 10. Review of J. B. Perrin and G. Thibon's *Simone Weil as We Knew Her.*

70a. "Knight and Saint." *Observer* (24 January 1954), p. 9. Review of Leslie Paul's *Sir Thomas More*, and E. E. Reynolds's *St. Thomas More.*

70b. "Byzantine." *Observer* (28 February 1954), p. 9. Review of H. Lamb's *Theodora and the Emperor.*

70c. "Displaced Persons." *Observer* (23 May 1954), p. 8. Review of Kathryn Hulme's *The Wild Place.*

70d. "Psychic Searchlight." *Observer* (1 August 1954), p. 7. Review of Dr. D. J. West's *Psychical Research Today.*

70e. "Charts of the Mind." *Observer* (12 September 1954), p. 11. Review of Lawrence Hyde's *I Who Am: A Study of the Self.*

70f. "Underground." *Observer* (23 October 1955), p. 12. Review of *William Weston: the Autobiography of an Elizabethan.*

71a. "Short Stories." *Observer* (4 December 1955), p. 11. Review of four books of short stories.

71b. "Ghosts." *Observer* (1 January 1956), p. 7. Review of *Shane Leslie's Ghost Book,* and *The Third Ghost Book* edited by Cynthia Asquith.

71c. "Involution." *Observer* (22 January 1956), p. 9. Review of Jocelyn Brooke's *The Dog at Clambercrown.*

71d. "Snobisme." *Observer* (5 February 1956), p. 11. Review of Princess Marthe Bibesco's *Marcel Proust at the Ball.*

71e. "Domestic Front." *Observer* (12 February 1956), p. 11. Review of Verily Anderson's *Spam To-morrow.*

71f. "More Stories." *Observer* (11 March 1956), p. 17. Review of Vernon Lee's *Pope Jacynth,* Mary Lavin's *The Patriot Son,* Shirley Ann Grau's *The Black Prince,* and Villy Sorensen's *Strange Stories.*

71g. "Shorter Notices." *Observer* (1 April 1956), p. 9. Review of L. A. G. Strong's *Flying Angel.*

71h. "More Stories." *Observer* (29 April 1956), p. 13. Review of Mika Waltari's *Moonscape,* Willa Cather's *The Old Beauty,* and Louis Golding's *Mario on the Beach.*

71i. "Kierkegaard." *Observer* (29 July 1956), p. 9. Review of *Meditations from Kierkegaard* edited by T. H. Croxall.

71j. "Elegance." *Observer* (21 October 1956), p. 17. Review of Frederick Gorst's *Of Carriages and Kings.*

71k. "Nurse and Patriot." *Observer* (28 October 1956), p. 17.

Review of Kathryn Hulme's *The Nun's Story.*

71l. "Short Stories." *Observer* (2 December 1956), p. 12. Review of *Modern English Short Stories*, and *Pick of To-day's Short Stories.*

71m. "Short Stories." *Observer* (16 December 1956), p. 11. Review of Alberto Moravia's *Roman Tales.*

71n. "Northern Muse." *Observer* (17 February 1957), p. 14. Review of Rowena Farre's *Seal Morning.*

71o. "Short Stories." *Observer* (21 April 1957), p. 11. Review of four books of short stories.

71p. "Priest of the Plague." *Observer* (12 May 1957), p. 16. Review of Philip Caraman's *Henry Morse: Priest of the Plague.*

71q. "Three Storytellers." *Observer* (2 June 1957), p. 17. Review of V. Meynell's *Collected Stories*, V. Sneider's *A Long Way from Home*, and M. Stirling's *Journeys We Shall Never Make.*

71r. "Among the Natives." *Observer* (25 August 1957), p. 12. Review of Syd Kyle-Little's *Whispering Wind*, Wilbur Chaseling's *Yulengor*, Gustaf Bolinder's *Indians on Horseback*, and Archie Carr's *The Windward Road.*

71s. "Romantic." *Observer* (29 September 1957), p. 14. Review of Arthur Helps and Elizabeth Jane Howard's *Bettina: A Portrait.*

71t. "Short Stories." *Observer* (6 October 1957), p. 14. Review of three books of short stories.

71u. "Amphibian Man." *Observer* (20 October 1957), p. 19. Review of Rufus Noel-Buxton's *Westminster Wader.*

71v. "Melancholy Humour." *Observer* (3 November 1957),

p. 16. Review of Stevie Smith's book of poems *Not Waving But Drowning.*

71w. "New Short Stories." *Observer* (15 December 1957), p. 12. Review of four books of short stories: *Winter's Tales 3*, Doris Lessing's *The Habit of Loving*, William Saroyan's *The Whole Voyald*, and Sarah G. Millin's *Two Bucks Without Hair.*

72a. "Beerbohm." *Observer* (12 January 1958), p. 14. Review of Max Beerbohm's *Mainly on the Air.*

72b. "Best-Sellers of the Century—9: Daughter of the Soil." *Observer* (12 January 1958), p. 15. On Margaret Mitchell's *Gone With the Wind.*

72c. "More Minou." *Observer* (19 January 1958), p. 16. Review of Minou Drouet's *Then There Was Fire.*

72d. "A Striking Autobiography." *Observer* (26 January 1958), p. 16. Review of Ved Mehta's *Face to Face.*

72e. "Short Stories." *Observer* (16 March 1958), p. 16. Review of Martha Gellhorn's *Two By Two*, Joseph Whitehill's *Able Baker and Others*, and John Prebble's *My Great-Aunt Appearing Day.*

72f. "Short Stories." *Observer* (20 April 1958), p. 17. Review of *The Stories of Sean O'Faolain*, and Tom Hopkinson's *The Lady and the Cut-Throat.*

72g. "Decorative Art." *Observer* (4 May 1958), p. 16. Review of George Burchett's *Memoirs of a Tattooist.*

72h. "Off Centre." *Observer* (25 May 1958), p. 16. Review of Anna Kavan's *A Bright Green Field.*

72i. "The Little Flower." *Observer* (25 May 1958), p. 17. Review of *Autobiography of a Saint*, trans. by Ronald Knox.

72j. "Short Stories." *Observer* (8 June 1958), p. 17. Review of Joan Donovan's *Dangerous Worlds.*

72k. "Short Stories." *Observer* (29 June 1958), p. 17. Review of P. H. Newby's *Ten Miles from Anywhere.*

72l. "Ritual and Recipe." *Observer* (27 July 1958), p. 14. Review of Garry Hogg's *Cannibalism and Human Sacrifice.*

72m. "Short Stories." *Observer* (7 September 1958), p. 17. Review of six books of short stories.

72n. "Crazy Mixed-up Abbot." *Observer* (14 September 1958), p. 16. Review of Peter F. Anson's *Abbot Extraordinary: A Memoir of Aelred Carlyle.*

72o. "Short Stories." *Observer* (19 October 1958), p. 20. Review of five books of short stories.

72p. "Vienna to Kent." *Observer* (11 January 1959), p. 18. Review of Robert Neumann's *The Plague House Papers.*

72q. "Short Stories." *Observer* (15 February 1959), p. 21. Review of John Cheever's *The Housebreaker of Shady Hill,* H. E. Bates's *The Watercress Girl,* H. Kubly's *Varieties of Love,* and N. Lofts's *Heaven in Your Hand.*

72r. "Anne Frank." *Observer* (8 March 1959), p. 22. Review of Ernst Schnabel's *The Footsteps of Anne Frank.*

72s. "Adventures of the Mind." *Observer* (8 March 1959), p. 23. Review of E. M. Butler's *Paper Boats.*

72t. "Into the Interior." *Observer* (26 April 1959), p. 22. Review of A. Vinci's *Red Cloth and Green Forest,* L. Clark's *Yucatan Adventure,* and H. Sick's *Tukani.*

72u.   "Dons and Noble Savages." *Observer* (10 May 1959), p. 24. Review of R. Longrigg's *Wrong Number*, J. Hawkes's *Providence Island*, J. Duncan's *My Friends the Miss Boyds*, and D. Raymond's *The Five Days*.

72v.   "Youth, Flutes and Zuleikas." *Observer* (24 May 1959), p. 21. Review of A. Piper's *Sweet and Plenty*, J. Playfair's *Andiamo!*, R. McLaughlin's *The Notion of Sin*, R. White's *Elephant Hill*, and Bryher's *Gate to the Sea*.

72w.   "An Irishman Comes to London." *Observer* (7 June 1959), p. 25. Review of M. Campbell's *Oh, Mary, This London*, A. A. Murray's *Anybody's Spring*, M. Browne's *Whom the Gods Love*, and E. Keeley's *The Libation*.

72x.   "Breaking the Novelist's Rules." *Observer* (21 June 1959), p. 18. Review of J. Rosenberg's *A Company of Strangers*, A. Curvers's *Tempo Di Roma*, J. O'Donovan's *The Visited*, and R. Foreman's *Long Pig*.

72y.   "New Novels." *Observer* (5 July 1959), p. 11. Review of Y. Dayan's *New Face in the Mirror*, E. Mavor's *Summer in the Greenhouse*, and R. Jenkins's *Love is a Fervent Fire*.

72z.   "New Novels." *Observer* (19 July 1959), p. 11. Review of M. Duras's *The Square*, J. R. Ullman's *The Day On Fire*, J. Ross's *Boy in a Grey Overcoat*, and O. Blakeston's *Hop Thief*.

$72z_1$.   "New Fiction." *Observer* (2 August 1959), p. 8. Review of G. Johnston's *The Darkness Outside*, R. Robinson's *Black-Feller, White-Feller*, N. Coulehan's *Quadrantus Rex*, and O. Malet's *The Horses of the Sun*.

$72z_2$.   "Borstal Boy." *Observer* (11 October 1959), p. 21. Review of Alan Sillitoe's *The Loneliness of the Long-Distance Runner*.

72z₃. "Top Cats on Show." *Observer* (29 November 1959), p. 4. A review of several books on cats.

72z₄. "Home and Away." *Observer* (20 December 1959), p. 17. Review of M. Shadbolt's *The New Zealanders*, F. King's *So Hurt and Humiliated*, P. Ustinov's *Add a Dash of Pity*, and two anthologies of short stories: *Winter's Tales 5*, and *Pick of To-day's Short Stories*.

73a. "From All Angles." *Observer* (13 March 1960), p. 19. Review of Joyce Cary's *Spring Song and Other Stories*.

73b. "American Life-Patterns." *Observer* (8 May 1960), p. 19. Review of Alfred Grossman's *Acrobat Admits*, James Purdy's *Malcolm*, and Kenneth Martin's *A Matter of Time*.

73c. "A Classic of the Deep South." *Observer* (19 June 1960), p. 28. Review of Allen Tate's *The Fathers*.

73d. "New Short Stories." *Observer* (2 October 1960), p. 26. Review of A. C. West's *River's End and Other Stories*, P. Mortimer's *Saturday Lunch with the Brownings*, E. Enright's *The Riddle of the Fly*, and K. Cicellis's *The Way to Colonos*.

73e. "Worlds Apart." *Observer* (13 November 1960), p. 27. Review of John Wain's *Nuncle and Other Stories*, and Tennessee Williams's *Three Players of a Summer Game*.

74a. "A Foretaste of Eternity." *Observer* (18 December 1960), p. 21. Review of Pierre Teilhard de Chardin's *Le Milieu Divin*.

74b. "Minor Victorian." *Observer* (19 February 1961), p. 29. Review of Ronald Chapman's *Father Faber*.

74c. "A Monument to Newman." *Observer* (4 March 1962), p. 30. Review of Meriol Trevor's *Newman: The*

ADDENDUM: MURIEL SPARK

Pillar of the Cloud.

ON MURIEL SPARK

86a. Anon. "In the Picture." *Observer* (16 October 1960), p. 24. A biographical sketch.

108a. Hope, Francis. "Joking in earnest." *Observer* (28 April 1963), p. 26. An interview.

118a. Keyser, Barbara. "Muriel Spark's Gargoyles." *Descant,* 20 (Fall 1975), 32-39.

179a. Davenport, John. "Courage and Cowardice." *Observer* (29 June 1958), p. 17. Review of *Robinson.*

198a. —. "O Death, Where is Thy Sting?" *Observer* (22 March 1959), p. 25. Review of *Memento Mori.*

241a. Smith, Stevie. "A Gothic Comedy." *Observer* (6 March 1960), p. 19. Review of *The Ballad of Peckham Rye.*

252a. Davenport, John. "Voice of the Sixties?" *Observer* (16 October 1960), p. 22. Review of *The Bachelors.*

278a. —. "Treachery in the Classroom." *Observer* (29 October 1961), p. 30. Review of *The Prime of Miss Jean Brodie.*

288a. Holloway, John. "Narrative Structure and Text Structure: Isherwood's *A Meeting by the River,* and Muriel Spark's *The Prime of Miss Jean Brodie.*" *Critical Inquiry,* 1 (March 1975), 581-604.

323a. Davenport, John. "Mrs. Spark's roses." *Observer* (22 September 1963), p. 25. Review of *The Girls of Slender Means.*

537a. Adams, Phoebe-Lou. *"The Takeover."* *Atlantic,* 238

1108

(November 1976), 116.

537b. Clemons, Walter. "Funny Money." *Newsweek* (18 October 1976), p. 105. Review of *The Takeover.*

537c. Drabble, Margaret. "Muriel Spark: a glittering, knowing novel about the decline of the West." *New York Times Book Review* (3 October 1976), pp. 1-2. Review of *The Takeover.*

541a. Gray, Paul. "Decline and Fall?" *Time* (18 October 1976), pp. 109-110. Review of *The Takeover.*

542a. Kuehl, Linda. *"The Takeover." Saturday Review* (18 September 1976), p. 32.

543a. Price, James. "Money and Sex and So On." *Encounter,* 47 (September 1976), 76-81. Pp. 76-78. Review of *The Takeover.*

544a. Wood, Michael. "Endangered Species." *New York Review of Books,* 23 (11 November 1976), 30-32. P. 30. Review of *The Takeover.*

581a. Mortimer, John. "Nightmare in broad daylight." *Observer* (2 July 1961), p. 26. Review of *Voices at Play.*

608a. Massingham, Hugh. "New Poems." *Observer* (22 June 1952), p. 7. Review of *The Fanfarlo and Other Verse.*

BY ANGUS WILSON

34a. "A Critic's Failure." *Observer* (16 March 1952), p. 7. Review of Edmund Wilson's *I Thought of Daisy.*

34b. "A Personal Odyssey." *Observer* (11 May 1952), p. 7. Review of Nancy Mitford's *Pigeon Pie.*

35a. "World of Dreams." *Observer* (29 June 1952), p. 7. Review of Ray Bradbury's *The Illustrated Man.*

35b. "Science Fiction: Fantasy Free." *Observer* (28 September 1952), p. 8. Review of several science fiction books.

37a. "Prizewinners." *Observer* (7 December 1952), p. 9. Review of *The Observer Prize Stories.*

38a. "Gothic Tales." *Observer* (22 February 1953), p. 8. Review of Bertrand Russell's *Satan in the Suburbs.*

40a. "Victorian Lioness." *Observer* (26 April 1953), p. 8. Review of Eileen Bigland's *Marie Corelli.*

40b. "Fun and Games." *Observer* (17 May 1953), p. 13. Review of J. Coates's *Patience*, R. P. Lister's *Rebecca Redfern*, A. Rhodes's *A Ball in Venice*, and F. Singleton's *A Change of Sky.*

41a. "A Brazilian Classic." *Observer* (31 May 1953), p. 15. Review of Machado de Assis's *Epitaph of a Small Winner*, H. A. Manhood's *A Long View of Nothing*, and Tom Clarkson's *The Wounded.*

42a. "The Undefeated." *Observer* (21 June 1953), p. 11. Review of Philip Hamburger's *J. P. Marquand, Esquire: a Portrait in the form of a novel.*

45a. "Virginia Woolf." *Observer* (1 November 1953), p. 9. Review of Virginia Woolf's *A Writer's Diary.*

45b. "Truculent Hero." *Observer* (22 November 1953), p. 8. Review of Gilbert Harding's *Along My Line.*

46a. "Orwell and the Intellectuals." *Observer* (24 January 1954), p. 8. Review of George Orwell's *England, Your England and Other Essays.*

46b. "New Novels." *Observer* (28 February 1954), p. 9. Review of G. Smith's *The Flaw in the Crystal,* S. Asch's *A Passage in the Night,* and Prudencio de Pereda's *Fiesta.*

46c. "New Novels." *Observer* (14 March 1954), p. 9. Review of M. Cost's *Invitation from Minerva,* P. H. Johnson's *An Impossible Marriage,* and R. Braddon's *Those in Peril.*

46d. "New Novels." *Observer* (28 March 1954), p. 9. Review of Ray Bradbury's *Fahrenheit 451,* J. D. Scott's *The End of an Old Song,* and S. Groussard's *The Woman with No Past.*

46e. "New Novels." *Observer* (11 April 1954), p. 11. Review of E. Juenger's *African Diversions,* R. Llewellyn's *A Flame for Doubting Thomas,* and L. Steni's *Soldier Adrift.*

46f. "Out of the Ordinary." *Observer* (9 May 1954), p. 9. Review of Saul Bellow's *The Adventures of Augie March,* I. Silone's *A Handful of Blackberries,* and D. Karp's *One.*

46g. "New Novels." *Observer* (23 May 1954), p. 9. Review

of J. Masters's *Bhowani Junction*, R. J. Sender's *The Affable Hangman*, M. L. Settle's *The Love Eaters*, and H. Tracy's *The Deserters.*

46h.   "New Novels." *Observer* (6 June 1954), p. 7. Review of Iris Murdoch's *Under the Net*, P. Skelton's *The Charm of Hours*, N. Macmillan's *The Other Side of the Square*, P. Mortimer's *A Villa in Summer*, and L. Louth's *Old Men Have Grey Beards.*

46i.   "Other New Novels." *Observer* (20 June 1954), p. 9. Review of S. B. Hough's *The Primitives*, J. Common's *The Ampersand*, D. Grubb's *The Night of the Hunter*, and J. Henry's *Yield to the Night.*

46j.   "New Fiction." *Observer* (1 August 1954), p. 7. Review of R. Trickett's *The Course of Love*, C. H. B. Kitchin's *Jumping Joan*, L. Walmsley's *The Golden Waterwheel*, and John Lodwick's *The Butterfly Net.*

46k.   "New Novels." *Observer* (15 August 1954), p. 7. Review of E. Wilson's *Swamp Angel*, D. Abse's *Ash on a Young Man's Sleeve*, H. Mason's *Photo Finish*, and J. C. Badcock's *Waybent.*

46l.   "New Novels." *Observer* (29 August 1954), p. 7. Review of L. P. Hartley's *The White Wand*, J. Brooks's *A Pride of Lions*, E. Crankshaw's *The Creedy Case*, and D. Marr-Johnson's *Bella North.*

49a.   "New Light on George Eliot." *Observer* (21 November 1954), p. 8. Review of *The George Eliot Letters: Vols. I-III.* Edited by Gordon S. Haight.

54a.   "The Cockney and the Jew." *Observer* (20 March 1955), p. 8. Review of James H. Robb's *Working-Class Anti-Semite: A Psychological Study in a London Borough.*

55a.   "The Ladder of Class." *Observer* (24 April 1955), p. 15. Review of T. H. Pear's *English Social Differences.*

55b. "Full-blooded Hero." *Observer* (15 May 1955), p. 17. Review of André Maurois's *Alexandre Dumas.*

55c. "Humanist." *Observer* (22 May 1955), p. 16. Review of H. Idris Bell's *The Crisis of Our Time.*

58a. "Giant and Mystic." *Observer* (26 June 1955), p. 21. Review of John Cowper Powys's *A Glastonbury Romance.*

60a. "The Soviet Style." *Observer* (17 July 1955), p. 8. Review of Ilya Ehrenburg's *The Ninth Wave.*

63a. "Labour in Vain." *Observer* (7 August 1955), p. 8. Review of Robert Baldick's *The Life of J. K. Huysmans.*

66a. "Studies in Civility." *Observer* (4 September 1955), p. 11. Review of Harold Nicolson's *Good Behaviour.*

69a. "Experimental." *Observer* (23 October 1955), p. 13. Review of Leon Edel's *The Psychological Novel.*

69b. "King of Beasts." *Observer* (6 November 1955), p. 10. Review of Armand Lanoux's *Zola.*

69c. "A Reticent Biography." *Observer* (13 November 1955), p. 10. Review of Charles Carrington's *Rudyard Kipling.*

72a. "Scholar-Critic." *Observer* (18 December 1955), p. 10. Review of Humphry House's *All in Due Time.*

77a. "The Other Browning." *Observer* (12 February 1956), p. 11. Review of H. E. Wortham's *Victorian Eton and Cambridge.*

77b. "Suffering." *Observer* (26 February 1956), p. 11. Review of Christine Arnothy's *I Am Fifteen and I Do Not Want to Die.*

79a. "The Novelist and the Theatre." *Observer* (18 March 1956), p. 16. On the "divorce between English novelists and the English theatre."

80a. "A Pastoral Poet." *Observer* (8 April 1956), p. 13. Review of John and Anne Tibble's *John Clare: His Life and Poetry.*

81a. "Mr. Priestley as Essayist." *Observer* (22 April 1956), p. 12. Review of J. B. Priestley's *All About Ourselves.*

82a. "Sound Man's Scrapbook." *Observer* (27 May 1956), p. 13. Review of Charles Furth's *Life Since 1900.*

84a. "A Generation of Poujadists?" *Observer* (1 July 1956), p. 11. Review of George Scott's *Time and Place.*

84b. "Success Story." *Observer* (15 July 1956), p. 9. Review of *The George Eliot Letters. Vols. IV-VII,* edited by Gordon S. Haight.

84c. "Facetiae." *Observer* (12 August 1956), p. 9. Review of J. Maclaren-Ross's *The Funny Bone.*

84d. "Where Do We Go From Here?" *Observer* (26 August 1956), p. 9. Review of *The New Outline of Modern Knowledge,* edited by Alan Pryce-Jones.

85a. "Buried Treasure." *Observer* (30 September 1956), p. 12. Review of *Recent Archaeological Excavations in Britain* edited by R. L. S. Bruce-Mitford.

85b. "Her Excellency." *Observer* (14 October 1956), p. 17. Review of Alden Hatch's *Clare Boothe Luce: Ambassadore Extraordinary.*

86a. "Off the Rails." *Observer* (25 November 1956), p. 12. Review of Robert Halsband's *Lady Mary Wortley Montagu.*

86b. "Light on Lawrence." *Observer* (16 December 1956), p. 10. Review of Graham Hough's *The Dark Sun.*

89a. "Foreword" to John Petty's *Five Fags a Day.* London: Secker and Warburg, 1956.

90a. "Passion & Irony." *Observer* (27 January 1957), p. 13. Review of *The Collected Stories of Isaac Babel.*

90b. "A Medieval Materialist." *Observer* (10 February 1957), p. 12. Review of Iris Origo's *The Merchant of Prato.*

92a. "Private Passions." *Observer* (3 March 1957), p. 14. Review of Zola's *The Abbé Mouret's Sin, A Love Affair, The Beast in Man,* and *Doctor Pascal.*

92b. "Sketch of a Superman." *Observer* (7 April 1957), p. 16. Review of Herbert J. Hunt's *Honore De Balzac.*

94a. "Scholar and King." *Observer* (12 May 1957), p. 17. Review of Eleanor Duckett's *Alfred the Great and His England.*

94b. "The Insect Hunter." *Observer* (26 May 1957), p. 16. Review of Evelyn Cheesman's *Things Worth While.*

94c. "Cigars & Brandy." *Observer* (9 June 1957), p. 12. Review of Robert Standish's *The Prince of Storytellers.*

94d. "Unknown Dickens." *Observer* (21 July 1957), p. 13. Review of John Butt and Kathleen Tillotson's *Dickens at Work.*

94e. "Medieval Tapestry." *Observer* (1 September 1957), p. 12. Review of Alfred Duggan's *The Devil's Brood.*

94f. "Sex and Snobbery." *Observer* (6 October 1957), p. 13. Review of Michael Arlen's *The Green Hat.*

94g. "Protest Meeting." *Observer* (13 October 1957), p. 18.

Review of *Declaration* edited by Tom Maschler.

95a.   "Dumas: Father and Son."   *Observer* (3 November 1957), p. 17.   Review of André Maurois's *Three Musketeers: A Study of the Dumas Family*.

95b.   "Sound and Fury."   *Observer* (24 November 1957), p. 18.   Review of Paul Murray Kendall's *Warwick the Kingmaker*.

97a.   "Critical Angles."   *Observer* (8 December 1957), p. 17. Review of Thomas Moser's *Joseph Conrad*, and Richard Curle's *Joseph Conrad and His Characters*.

98a.   "New Novels."   *Observer* (26 January 1958), p. 16. Review of B. Linn's *A Letter to Elizabeth*, F. King's *The Man on the Rock*, D. Karp's *Leave Me Alone*, and M. Jones's *On the Last Day*.

98b.   "Jungle World." *Observer* (9 February 1958), p. 15. Review of Brian Moore's *The Feast of Lupercal*, Anthony Burgess's *The Enemy in the Blanket*, Alfred Hayes's *My Face for the World*, and Edith Pargeter's *The Assize of the Dying*.

98c.   "Death in Life."   *Observer* (23 February 1958), p. 17. Review of Ernst Pawel's *The Dark Tower*, Bernard Wolfe's *In Deep*, Jean Cocteau's *The Miscreant*, and Ercole Patti's *A Love Affair in Rome*.

99a.   "New Novels." *Observer* (9 March 1958), p. 16. Review of S. Ashton-Warner's *Spinster*, H. Slater's *The Malefactor*, P. Vansittart's *Orders of Chivalry*, and B. Breuer's *The Actress*.

99b.   "Egoist-Idealist."   *Observer* (23 March 1958), p. 16. Review of Robin Jenkins's *The Changeling*, May Sarton's *The Birth of a Grandfather*, and Denise Robins's *The Untrodden Snow*.

99c. "A Jew Among Gentiles." *Observer* (6 April 1958), p. 14. Review of A. Van der Veen's *The Intruder*, W. J. White's *The Hard Man*, E. Ryman's *Teddy Boy*, and Jean-Paul Clébert's *The Blockhouse.*

99d. "Back to Galsworthy." *Observer* (13 April 1958), p. 17. Review of James Gould Cozzens's *By Love Possessed.*

99e. "Jane Austen in Japan." *Observer* (27 April 1958), p. 17. Review of Junichiro Tanizaki's *The Makioka Sisters*, Osamu Dazai's *The Setting Sun*, and Francis Stuart's *Victors and Vanquished.*

101a. "Two Kinds of Witch-Hunt." *Observer* (11 May 1958), p. 17. Review of Herbert Steinhouse's *Ten Years After*, and Alan Thomas's *The Director.*

101b. "A School for Scandal." *Observer* (25 May 1958), p. 16. Review of William Saroyan's *Papa, You're Crazy*, R. Peyrefitte's *Special Friendships*, V. Hull's *The Monkey Puzzle*, and H. Suyin's *The Mountain is Young.*

101c. "The Apprentice Emperor." *Observer* (8 June 1958), p. 17. Review of Chinua Achebe's *Things Fall Apart*, Res Warner's *The Young Caesar*, N. Devas's *Bonfire*, and B. Van Orden's *Water Music.*

101d. "Through Childhood's Eyes." *Observer* (22 June 1958), p. 17. Review of M. Crawford's *No Bedtime Story*, J. Hanley's *An End and a Beginning*, M. McMinnies's *The Visitors*, and A. Thirkell's *Close Quarters.*

101e. "Moravia: Heir to Zola." *Observer* (6 July 1958), p. 17. Review of Alberto Moravia's *Two Women*, H. Laxness's *The Happy Warriors*, S. O'Hanlon's *Gather No Moss*, and M. Wharton's *Sheldrake.*

101f. "Ancient & Modern." *Observer* (20 July 1958), p. 15. Review of H. F. M. Prescott's *Son of Dust*, A. Andersch's *Flight to Afar,* S. Mitchel's *Clerks in Lowly Orders,* R. H. Ward's *The Wilderness,* and J. P. Marquand's *Life at Happy Knoll.*

101g. "New Novels." *Observer* (3 August 1958), p. 10. Review of R. Vailland's *The Law,* P. DeVries's *Mackerel Plaza,* A. Karmel's *Mary Ann,* W. Brebner's *Two Lakes,* and S. W. Baron's *Matters of Concern.*

103a. "A Total View of Culture." *Observer* (19 October 1958), p. 21. Review of Raymond Williams's *Culture and Society.*

103b. "The English Church." *Observer* (23 November 1958), p. 15. Review of *Collin's Guide to English Parish Churches,* edited by John Betjeman.

103c. "Playboys of the Western World." *Observer* (14 December 1958), p. 15. Review of two theatre productions: *West Side Story* and *The Bright One.*

103d. "Panto Pleasures." *Observer* (21 December 1958), p. 11. Review of three theatre productions.

103e. "Children's Hours." *Observer* (28 December 1958), p. 7. Review of three theatre productions.

103f. "At the Theatre: Beating the Boom." *Observer* (4 January 1959), p. 13. Review of several plays.

103g. "At the Theatre: Reluctant Killers." *Observer* (11 January 1959), p. 17. Review of Willis Hall's *The Long and the Short and the Tall,* and Clemence Dane's *Eighty in the Shade.*

104a. "Middle-Class Morality." *Observer* (25 January 1959), p. 17. Review of the play, *The Woman on the Stair.*

104b. "At the Theatre: Charades and Revolution." *Observer* (1 February 1959), p. 17. Review of four plays.

105a. "At the Theatre: From Lancashire to the West End." *Observer* (15 February 1959), p. 19. Review of four plays.

106a. "Strindberg in a Comic Vein." *Observer* (22 March 1959), p. 25. Review of Strindberg's *The People of Hemso.*

107a. "Freedom of Thought." *Observer* (31 May 1959), p. 25. Review of *The Broken Mirror*, edited by Pawel Mayewski.

108a. "The Two Faces of Japan." *Observer* (28 June 1959), p. 21. Review of Osamu Dazai's *No Longer Human*, and Yasunari Kawabata's *Thousand Cranes.*

109a. "The Man Behind the Mask." *Observer* (9 August 1959), p. 10. Review of Yoti Lane's *The Psychology of the Actor*, and Peter Bull's *I Know the Face But...*

112a. "Merely a Novelist." *Observer* (25 October 1959), p. 23. Review of Richard H. Barker's *Marcel Proust.*

112b. "The Ternan Affair." *Observer* (29 November 1959), pp. 1-2. Review of Felix Aylmer's *Dickens Incognito.*

114a. "Aesthete in Japan." *Observer* (3 January 1960), p. 16. Review of Sacheverell Sitwell's *Bridge of the Brocade Sash.*

115a. "Bovary in Italy." *Observer* (17 January 1960), p. 21. Review of Alberto Moravia's *The Wayward Wife.*

116a. "Horror Below the Quarterdeck." *Observer* (31 January 1960), p. 20. Review of Jocelyn Baines's *Joseph Conrad.*

121a. "Divine Idiot." *Observer* (10 April 1960), p. 21. Review of Saverio Montalto's *A Voice from the Cell.*

125a. "Man in the Mirror." *Observer* (5 June 1960), p. 19. Review of Paul Léautaud's *Journal of a Man of Letters.*

125b. "Falling Between Two Stools." *Observer* (12 June 1960), p. 27. Review of Colin MacInnes's *Mr. Love and Justice.*

125c. "The Pulpit and the Column." *Observer* (3 July 1960), p. 26. Review of Adam Fox's *Dean Inge.*

126a. "Before the Crack-Up." *Observer* (31 July 1960), p. 21. Review of Siegfried Sassoon's *Memoirs of a Fox-Hunting Man.*

127a. "Chorus of Love-Hate." *Observer* (28 August 1960), p. 26. Review of George Lamming's *The Pleasures of Exile,* and *Alienation* edited by Timothy O'Keeffe.

132a. "County companions." *Observer* (23 April 1961), p. 31. Review of Norman Scarfe's *Suffolk: A Shell Guide,* and Nikolaus Pevsner's *Suffolk.*

133a. "A Critic in Utopia." *Observer* (25 June 1961), p. 25. Review of Kathleen Nott's *A Clean, Well-Lighted Place.*

134a. "The Brother's Story." *Observer* (23 July 1961), p. 20. Review of Winifred Gérin's *Branwell Bronte.*

139a. "Richness in a narrow place." *Observer* (17 September 1961), p. 30. Review of Ivy Compton-Burnett's *The Mighty and Their Fall.*

140a. "The lives of the saints of Sarsaparilla." *Observer* (29 October 1961), p. 30. Review of Patrick White's *Riders in the Chariot.*

140b. "Victorians at school." *Observer* (3 December 1961), p. 29. Review of David Newsome's *Godliness and Good Learning: Four Studies on a Victorian Ideal.*

147a. "Academic crossfire on the novel." *Observer* (4 February 1962), p. 31. Review of Ian Gregor and Brian Nicholas's *The Moral and the Story.*

148a. "Views of the Damned." *Observer* (4 March 1962), p. 30. Review of Christopher Isherwood's *Down There on a Visit.*

150a. "A positive answer to Communism." *Observer* (17 June 1962), p. 25. Review of John Strachey's *The Strangled Cry.*

152a. "Genius from the lower depths." *Observer* (8 July 1962), p. 24. Review of two books by Jack London: *The People of the Abyss,* and *A Daughter of the Snows.*

154a. "Riches of the Sphinx." *Observer* (19 August 1962), p. 17. Review of Ada Leverson's *The Little Ottleys.*

156a. "Priestley looks back." *Observer* (23 September 1962), p. 28. Review of J. B. Priestley's *Margin Released.*

157a. "The middle-class passenger." *Observer* (28 October 1962), p. 27. Review of Katherine Anne Porter's *Ship of Fools.*

157b. "Inside Young England." *Observer* (11 November 1962), p. 25. Review of Ray Gosling's *Sum Total.*

157c. "Judgments on genius." *Observer* (25 November 1962), p. 29. Review of David Magarshack's *Dostoevsky: A Life,* Ronald Hingley's *The Undiscovered Dostoevsky,* and Jessie Coulson's *Dostoevsky: A Self-Portrait.*

159a. "Looking Back in Pleasure." *Observer* (20 January 1963), p. 23. Review of Compton Mackenzie's *My Life and Times.*

159b. "Friends, foes and fidgets." *Observer* (26 May 1963),

p. 27. Review of V. Wyndham's *The Sphinx and Her Circle: A memoir of Ada Leverson,* R. Croft-Cooke's *Bosie: The Story of Lord Alfred Douglas,* and H. M. Hyde's *Oscar Wilde: The Aftermath.*

159c. "The world of J. C. Powys." *Observer* (23 June 1963), p. 23. A eulogy.

160a. "The Knowing Child." *Observer* (7 July 1963), p. 22. Review of *Selected Writings of Truman Capote.*

160b. "Myth-lover and life-lover." *Observer* (11 August 1963), p. 17. Review of Leslie Fiedler's *No! In Thunder,* and Martin Green's *Re-Appraisals.*

160c. "Rebirth and revival." *Observer* (25 August 1963), p. 18. Review of Günter Grass's *Cat and Mouse,* and Yukio Mishima's *After the Banquet.*

160d. "From Welfare to Affluence." *Observer* (22 September 1963), p. 24. Review of Harry Hopkins's *The New Look.*

161a. "Other People's Lives: A Nineties boyhood." *Observer* (13 October 1963), p. 25. Review of Compton Mackenzie's *My Life and Times: Octave Two 1891-1900.*

161b. "Reconstructing our yesterdays." *Observer* (17 November 1963), p. 24. Review of Ronald Blythe's *The Age of Illusion: England in the Twenties and Thirties.*

161c. "Squeers and Co." *Observer* (22 December 1963), p. 16. Review of Phillip Collins's *Dickens and Education.*

320a. *The Naughty Nineties.* London: Eyre Methuen, 1976.

ON ANGUS WILSON

402a. Muir, Edwin. "The Damned." *Observer* (13 July 1952),

p. 7. Review of *Hemlock and After.*

427a. Davenport, John. "New Novels." *Observer* (13 May 1956), p. 12. Review of *Anglo-Saxon Attitudes.*

467a. Quinton, Anthony. "Away from the Dodos." *Observer* (16 November 1958), p. 21. Review of *The Middle Age of Mrs. Eliot.*

509a. Wain, John. "Angus Wilson takes off into the future." *Observer* (24 September 1961), p. 30. Review of *The Old Men at the Zoo.*

652a. Davenport, John. "Micro-Master." *Observer* (13 October 1957), p. 19. Review of *A Bit Off the Map.*

689a. Stonier, G. W. "Zolaesque." *Observer* (2 March 1952), p. 7. Review of *Emile Zola.*

693a. Beaton, Cecil. "Bright Old Things." *Observer* (28 June 1953), p. 10. Review of *For Whom the Cloche Tolls.*

694a. Conrad, Peter. "In search of an author." *Spectator,* 237 (11 September 1976), 23-24. Review of *For Whom the Cloche Tolls.*

718a. Raven, Simon. "Inside Story." *Observer* (10 November 1963), p. 25. Review of *The Wild Garden.*

772a. Jones, D. A. N. "Art workers." *Listener,* 96 (29 July 1976), 126. Review of *The Naughty Nineties.*

772b. Keating, Peter. "Opulence and its illusions." *TLS* (5 November 1976), p. 1392. Review of *The Naughty Nineties.*

772c. Tindall, Gillian. "Such Darling Dodos." *New Statesman,* 92 (13 August 1976), 213. Review of *The Naughty Nineties.*